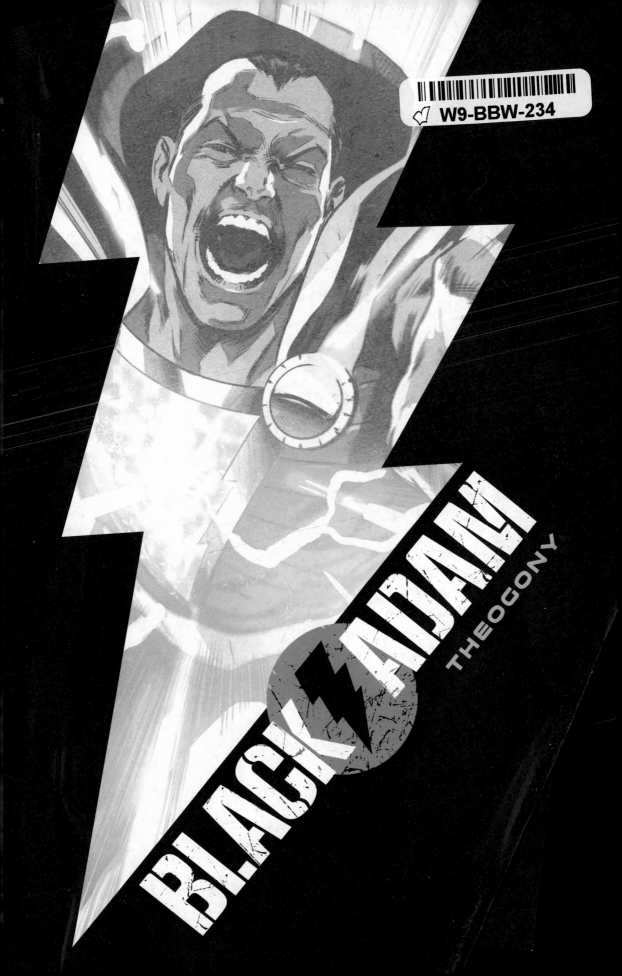

BLACK ADAM

THEOGONY

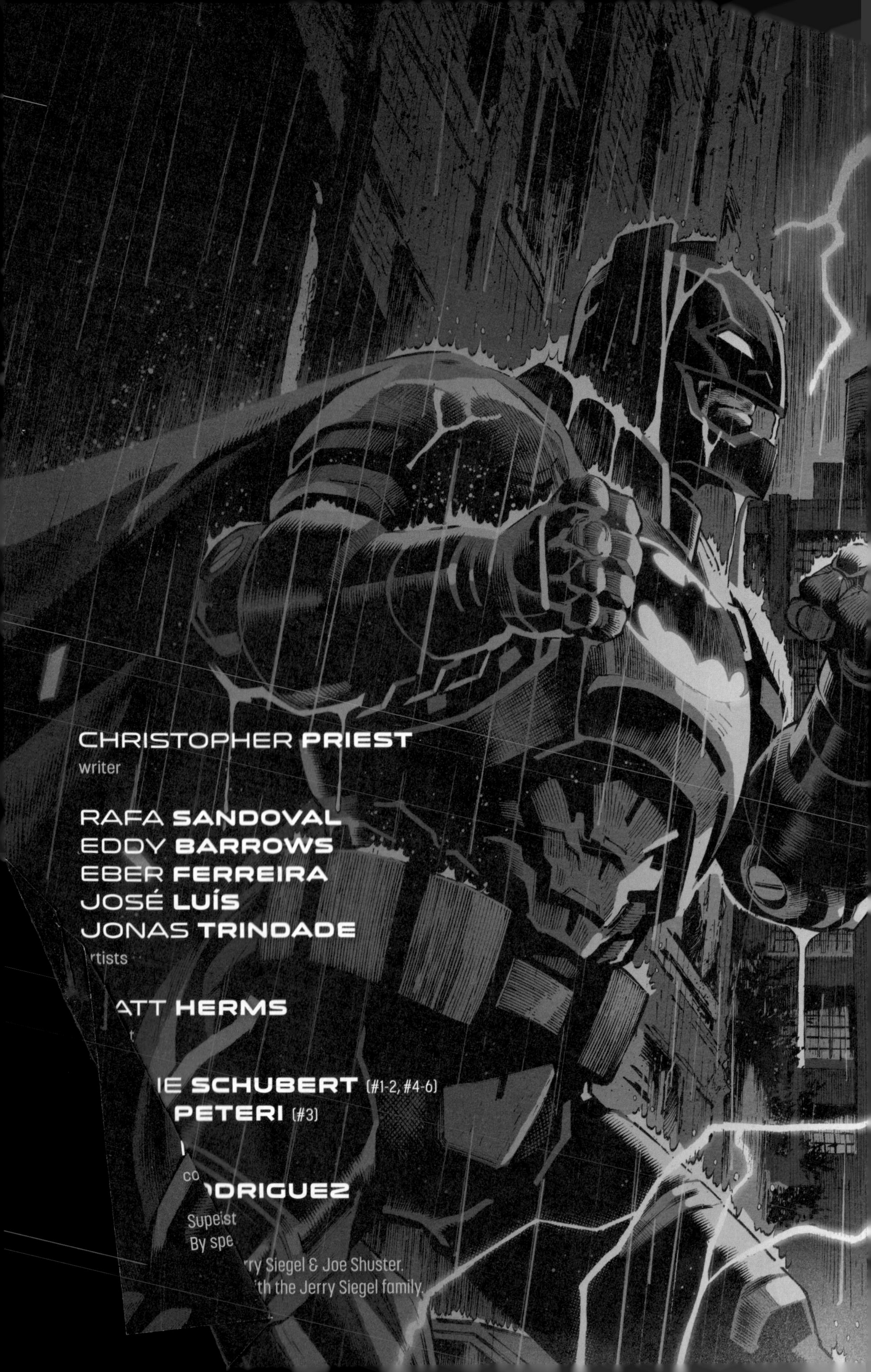

CHRISTOPHER **PRIEST**
writer

RAFA **SANDOVAL**
EDDY **BARROWS**
EBER **FERREIRA**
JOSÉ **LUÍS**
JONAS **TRINDADE**
rtists

ATT **HERMS**

IE **SCHUBERT** (#1-2, #4-6)
PETERI (#3)

co
DRIGUEZ

Supe ist
By spe
ry Siegel & Joe Shuster.
th the Jerry Siegel family.

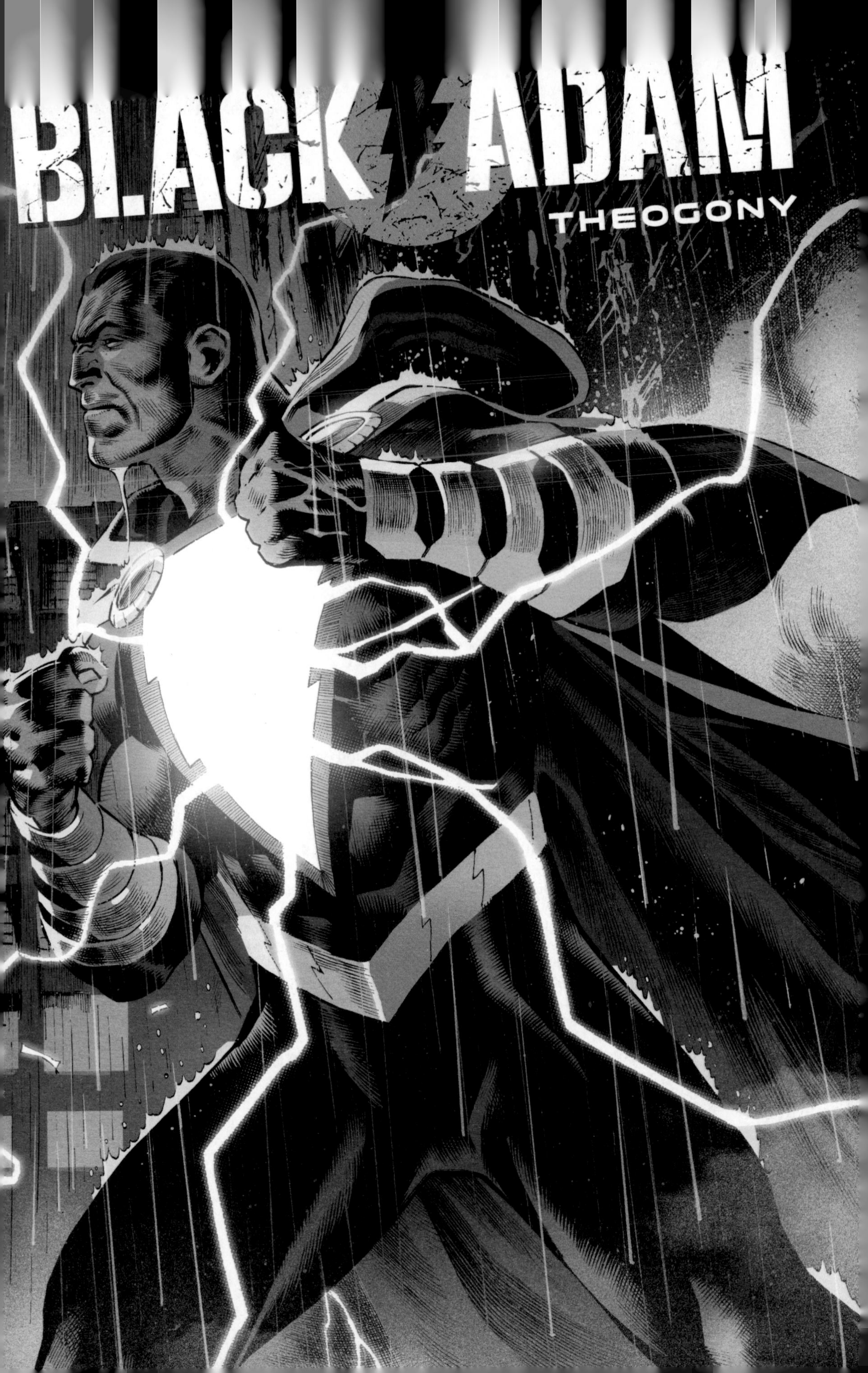
BLACK ADAM
THEOGONY

PAUL KAMINSKI
Editor - Original Series & Collected Edition

CHRIS ROSA
Associate Editor - Original Series

IVAN COHEN
Associate Editor - Collected Edition

STEVE COOK
Design Director - Books

MEGEN BELLERSEN
Publication Design

ERIN VANOVER
Publication Production

MARIE JAVINS
Editor-in-Chief, DC Comics

ANNE DePIES
Senior VP - General Manager

JIM LEE
Publisher & Chief Creative Officer

DON FALLETTI
VP - Manufacturing Operations
& Workflow Management

LAWRENCE GANEM
VP - Talent Services

ALISON GILL
Senior VP - Manufacturing & Operations

JEFFREY KAUFMAN
VP - Editorial Strategy & Programming

NICK J. NAPOLITANO
VP - Manufacturing Administration & Design

NANCY SPEARS
VP - Revenue

BLACK ADAM VOL. 1: THEOGONY

DC Comics, 4000 Warner Blvd., Bldg. 700, 2nd Floor, Burbank, CA 91522
Printed by Solisco Printers, Scott, QC, Canada. 3/31/23. First Printing.
ISBN: 978-1-77952-009-8

Library of Congress Cataloging-in-Publication Data is available.

PEFC Certified

This product is from
sustainably managed
forests and controlled
sources

PEFC
PEFC/26-31-02   www.pefc.org

***Black Adam* #1** cover by Irvin Rodriguez

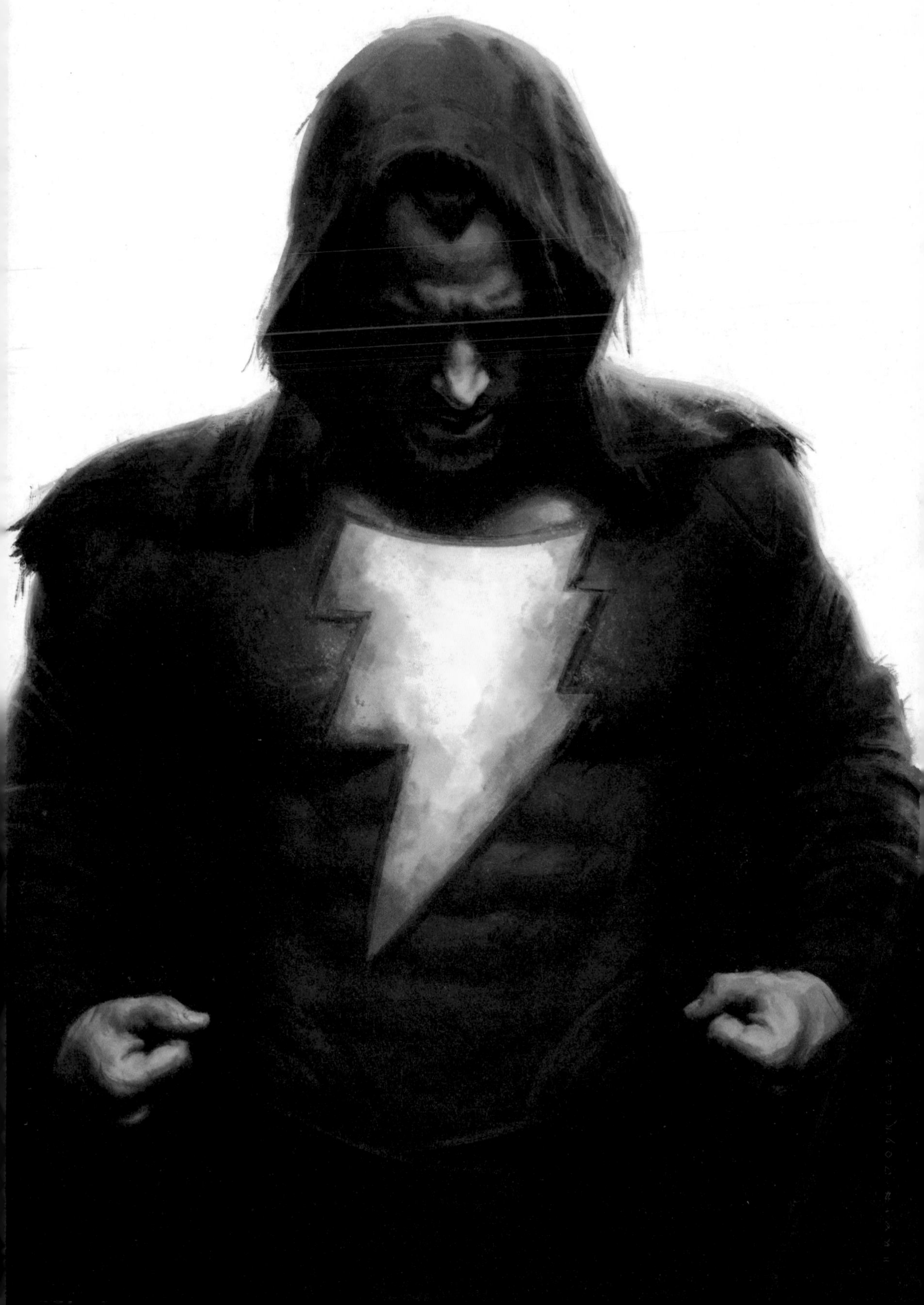

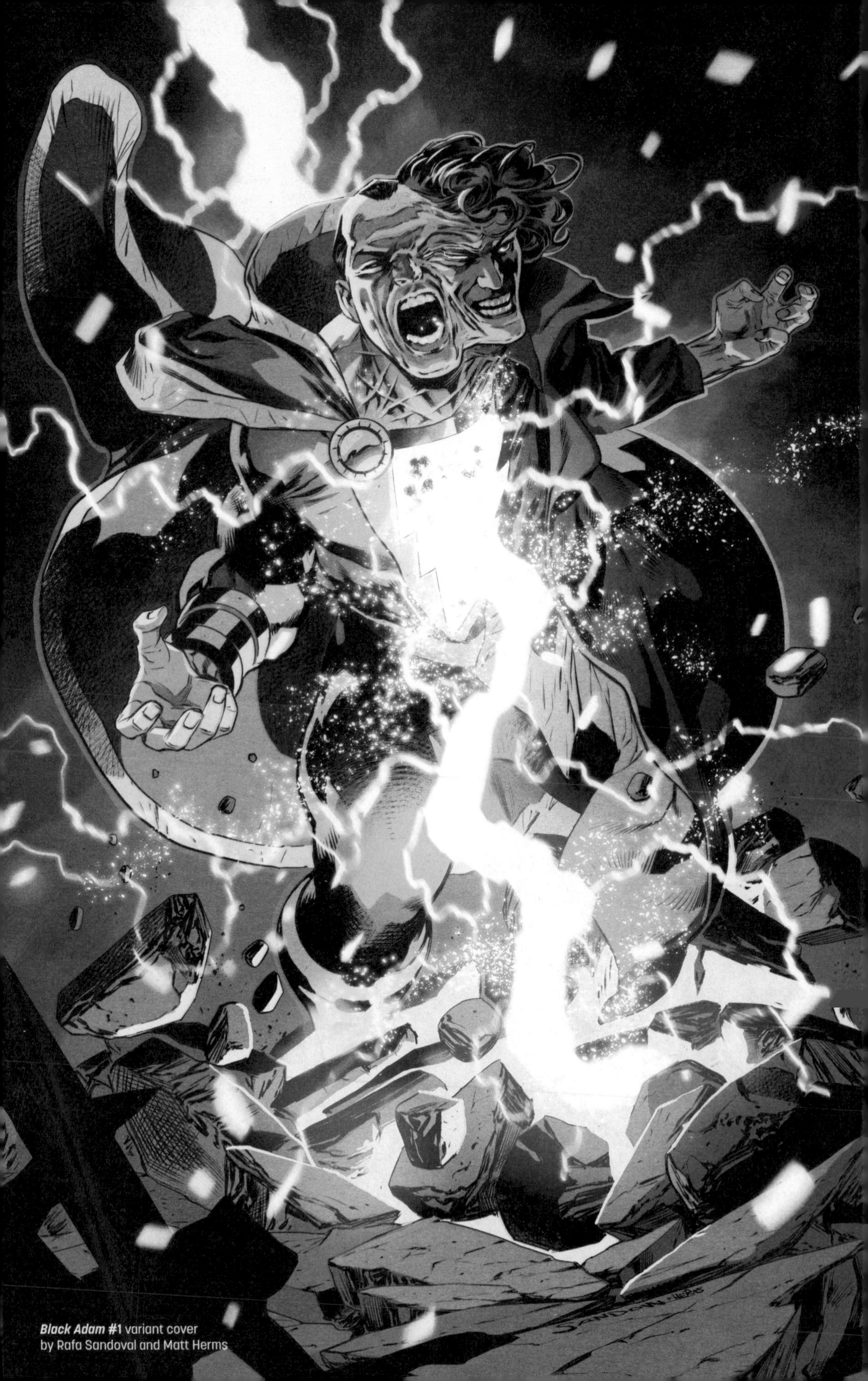

Black Adam #1 variant cover
by Rafa Sandoval and Matt Herms

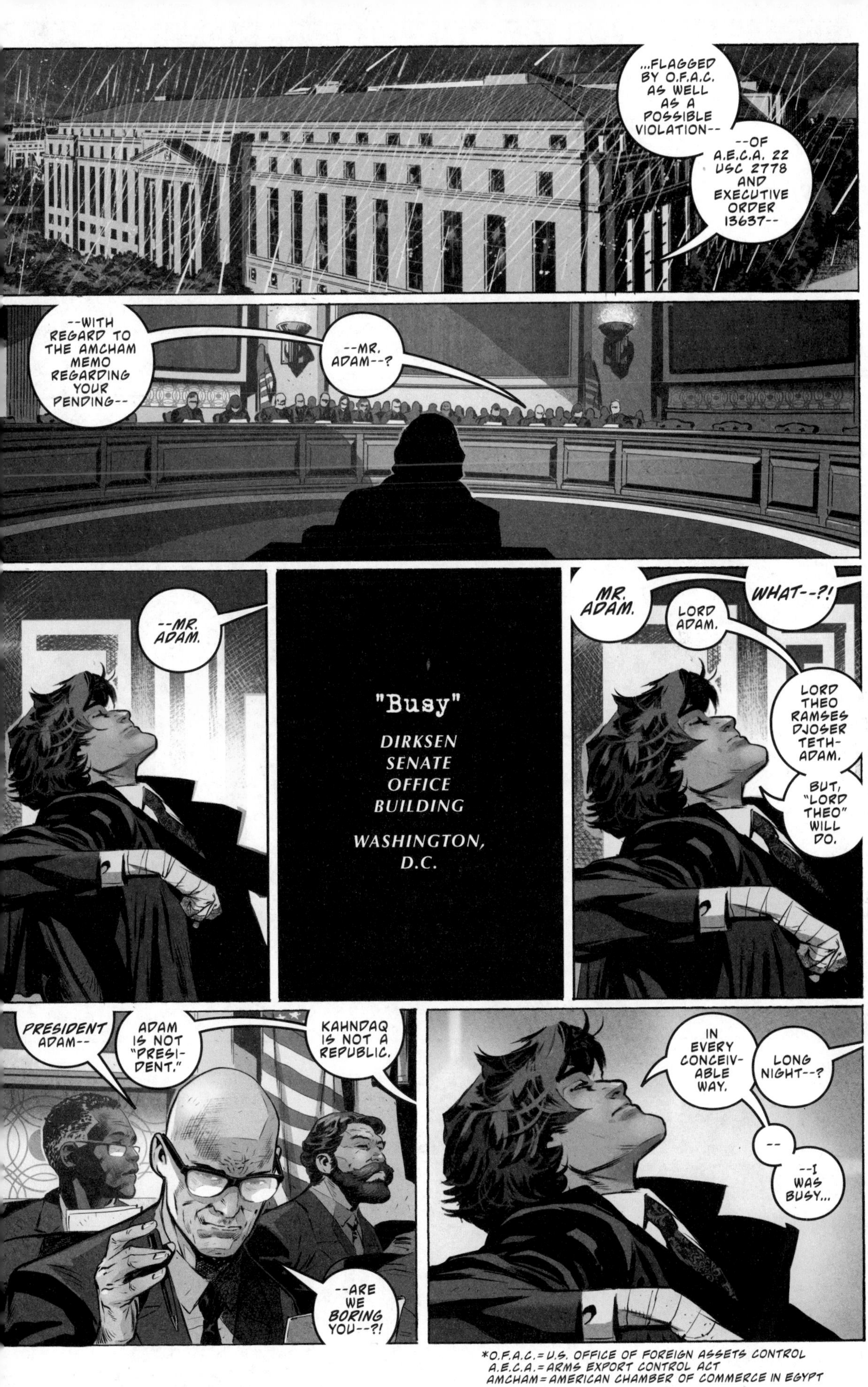
...FLAGGED BY O.F.A.C. AS WELL AS A POSSIBLE VIOLATION--
--OF A.E.C.A. 22 USC 2778 AND EXECUTIVE ORDER 13637--
--WITH REGARD TO THE AMCHAM MEMO REGARDING YOUR PENDING--
--MR. ADAM--?
--MR. ADAM.
"Busy"
DIRKSEN SENATE OFFICE BUILDING
WASHINGTON, D.C.
MR. ADAM.
WHAT--?!
LORD ADAM.
LORD THEO RAMSES DJOSER TETH-ADAM.
BUT, "LORD THEO" WILL DO.
PRESIDENT ADAM--
ADAM IS NOT "PRESI-DENT."
KAHNDAQ IS NOT A REPUBLIC.
--ARE WE BORING YOU--?!
IN EVERY CONCEIV-ABLE WAY.
LONG NIGHT--?
--
--I WAS BUSY...

*O.F.A.C. = U.S. OFFICE OF FOREIGN ASSETS CONTROL
A.E.C.A. = ARMS EXPORT CONTROL ACT
AMCHAM = AMERICAN CHAMBER OF COMMERCE IN EGYPT

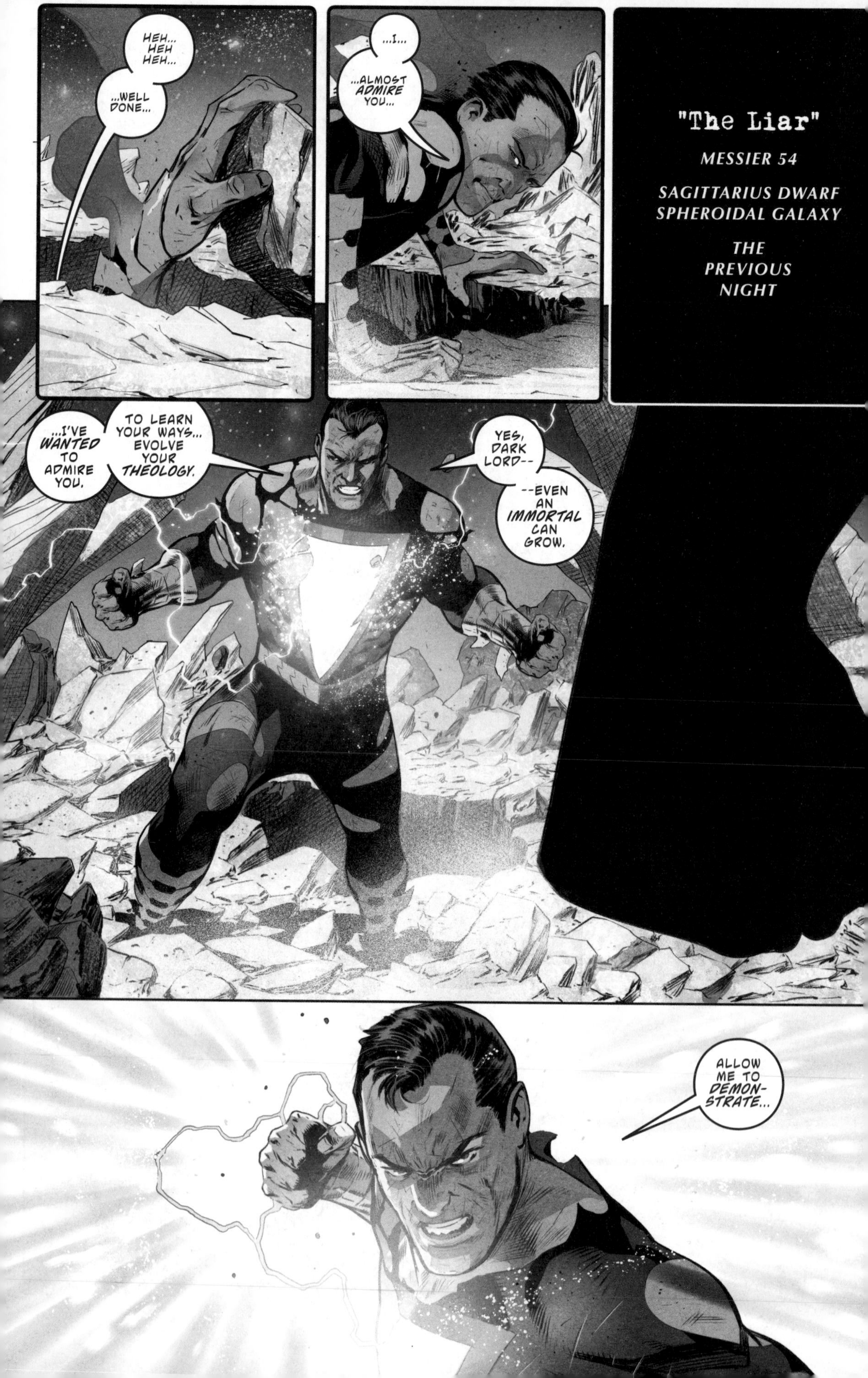
HEH... HEH HEH...
...WELL DONE...
...I...
...ALMOST ADMIRE YOU...
"The Liar"
MESSIER 54
SAGITTARIUS DWARF SPHEROIDAL GALAXY
THE PREVIOUS NIGHT
...I'VE WANTED TO ADMIRE YOU.
TO LEARN YOUR WAYS... EVOLVE YOUR THEOLOGY.
YES, DARK LORD--
--EVEN AN IMMORTAL CAN GROW.
ALLOW ME TO DEMON-STRATE...

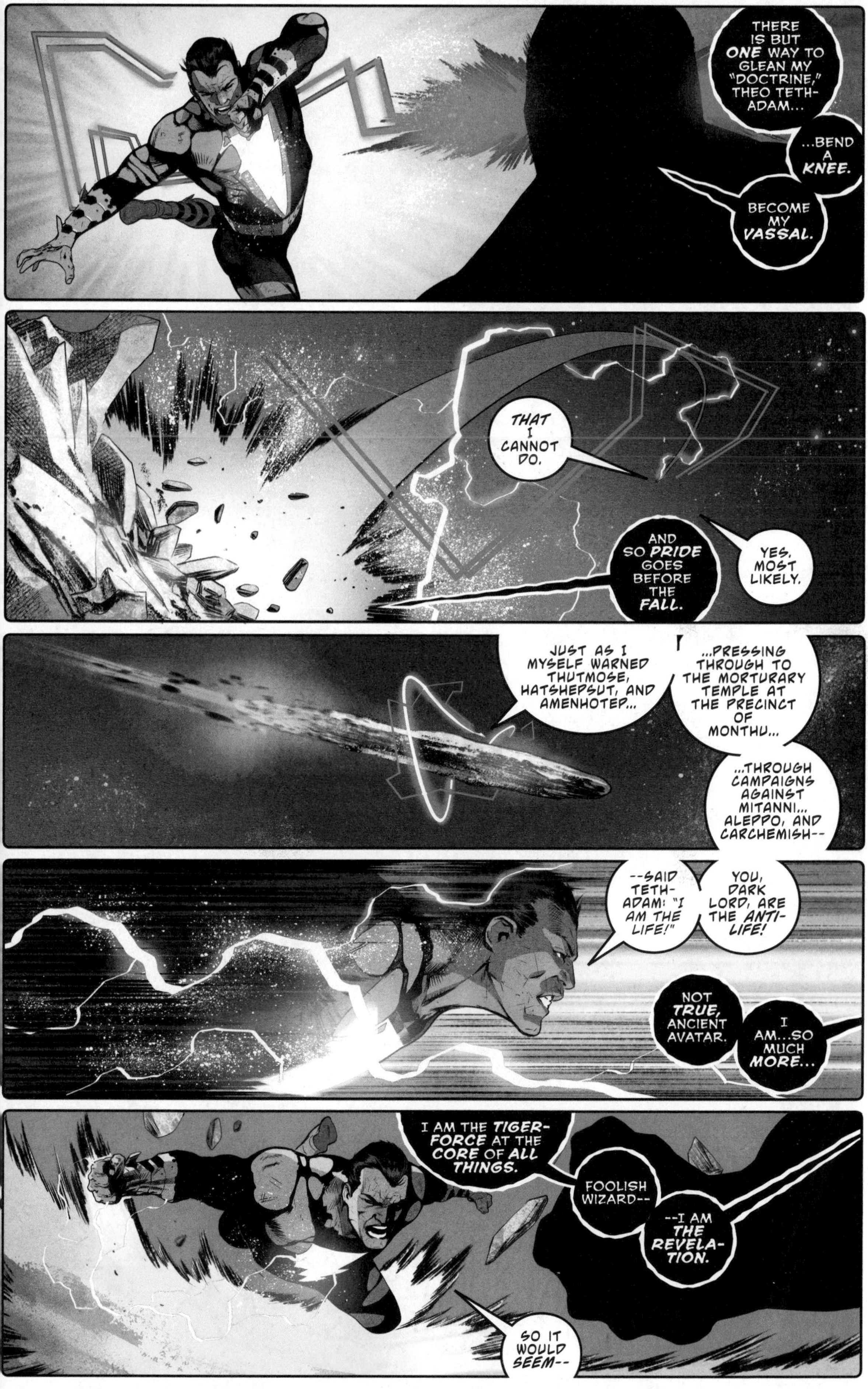
THERE IS BUT ONE WAY TO GLEAN MY "DOCTRINE," THEO TETH-ADAM...
...BEND A KNEE.
BECOME MY VASSAL.
THAT I CANNOT DO.
YES. MOST LIKELY.
AND SO PRIDE GOES BEFORE THE FALL.
JUST AS I MYSELF WARNED THUTMOSE, HATSHEPSUT, AND AMENHOTEP...
...PRESSING THROUGH TO THE MORTURARY TEMPLE AT THE PRECINCT OF MONTHU...
...THROUGH CAMPAIGNS AGAINST MITANNI... ALEPPO, AND CARCHEMISH--
--SAID TETH-ADAM: "I AM THE LIFE!"
YOU, DARK LORD, ARE THE ANTI-LIFE!
NOT TRUE, ANCIENT AVATAR.
I AM...SO MUCH MORE...
I AM THE TIGER-FORCE AT THE CORE OF ALL THINGS.
FOOLISH WIZARD--
--I AM THE REVELATION.
SO IT WOULD SEEM--

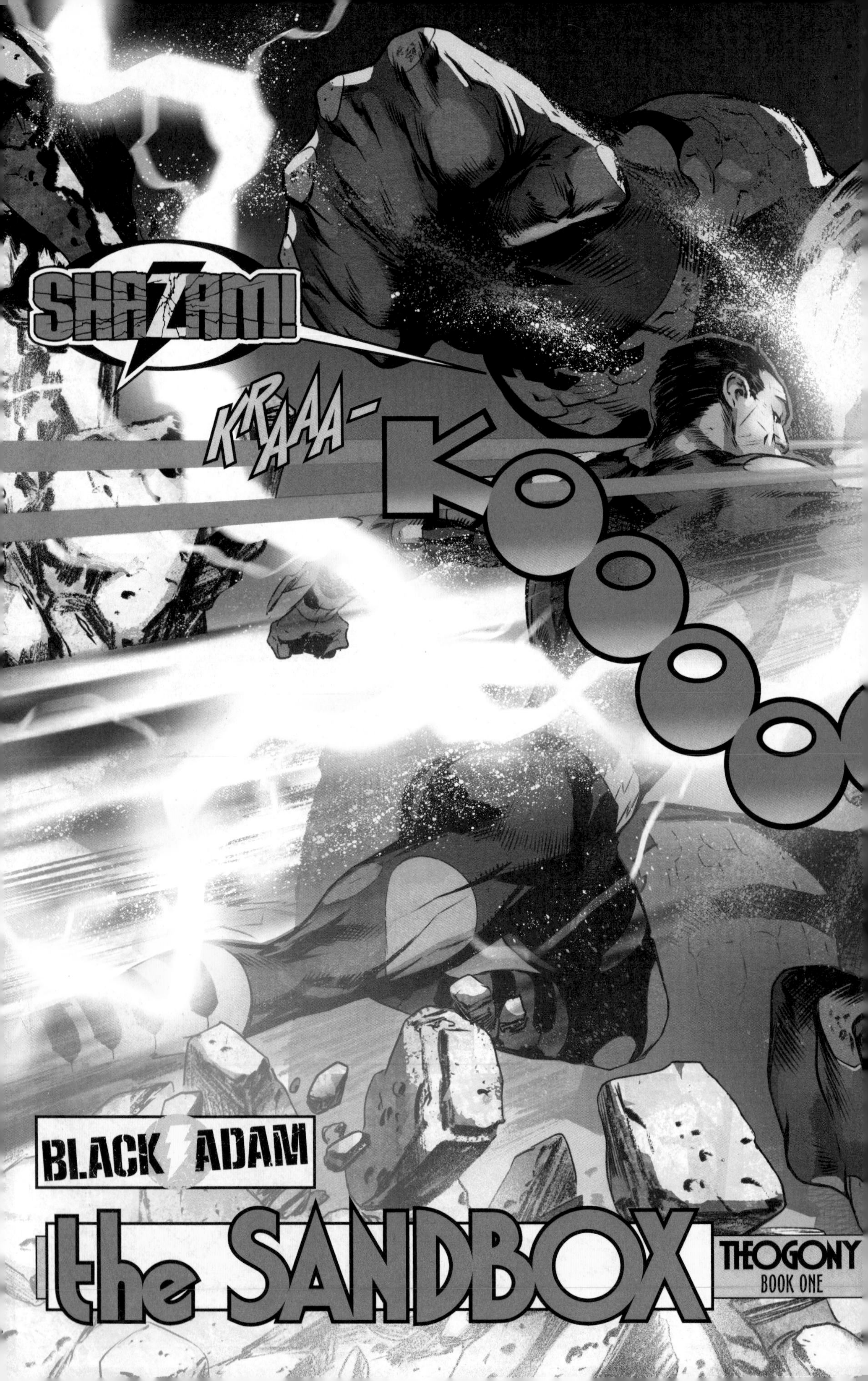
SHAZAM!
KRAAA-KOOOOO
BLACK ADAM
the SANDBOX
THEOGONY
BOOK ONE

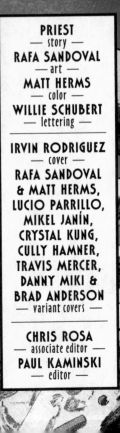

PRIEST
— story —
RAFA SANDOVAL
— art —
MATT HERMS
— color —
WILLIE SCHUBERT
— lettering —

IRVIN RODRIGUEZ
— cover —
**RAFA SANDOVAL
& MATT HERMS,
LUCIO PARRILLO,
MIKEL JANÍN,
CRYSTAL KUNG,
CULLY HAMNER,
TRAVIS MERCER,
DANNY MIKI &
BRAD ANDERSON**
— variant covers —

CHRIS ROSA
— associate editor —
PAUL KAMINSKI
— editor —

EDITOR'S NOTE: BLACK ADAM #1
TAKES PLACE BEFORE THE DEATH
OF THE JUSTICE LEAGUE --PK

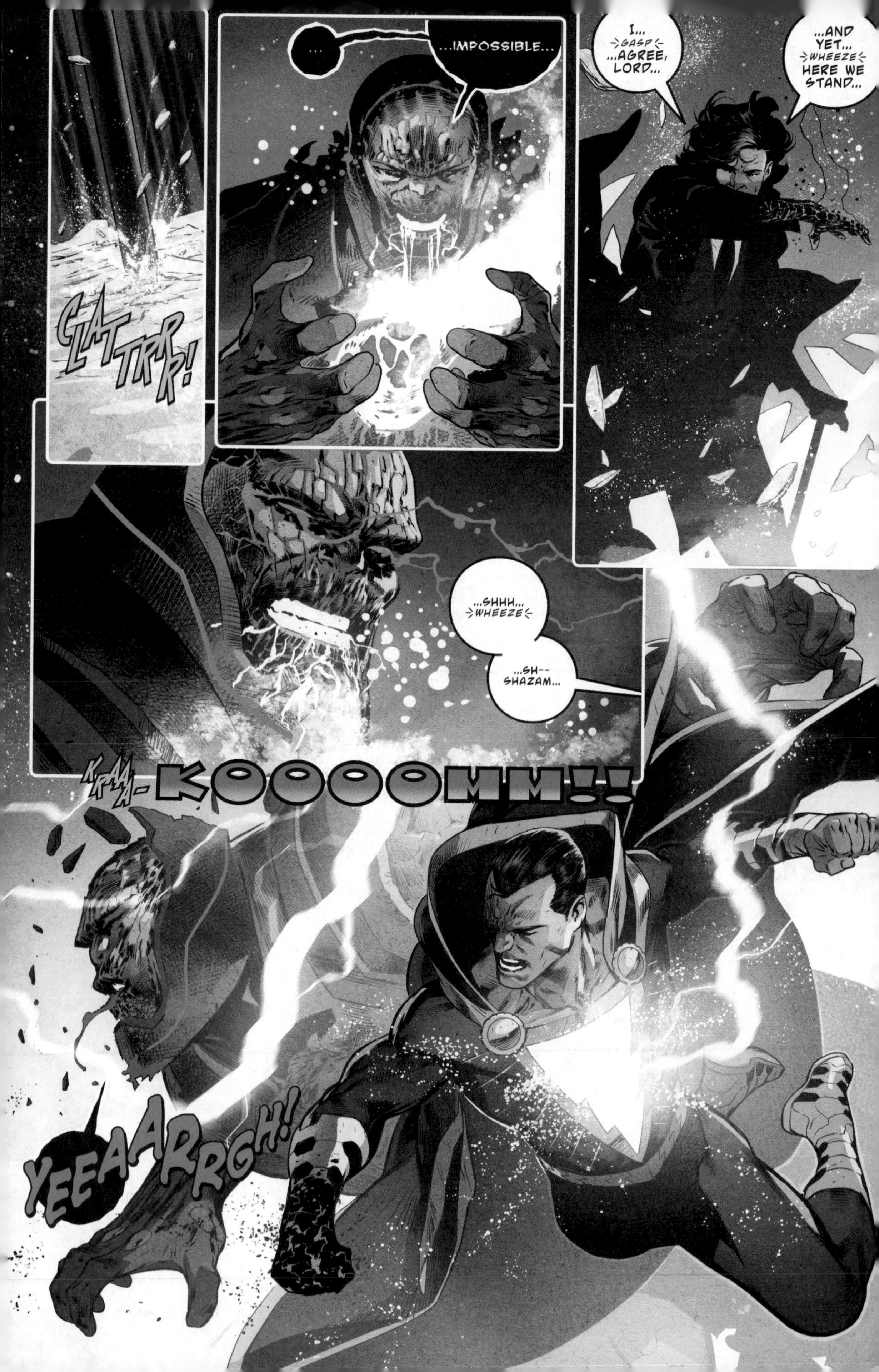

CLATTRRR!
...
...IMPOSSIBLE...
I... GASP ...AGREE, LORD...
...AND YET... WHEEZE HERE WE STAND...
...SHHH... WHEEZE
...SH-- SHAZAM...
KRAAA-KOOOOOMM!!
YEEAARRGH!

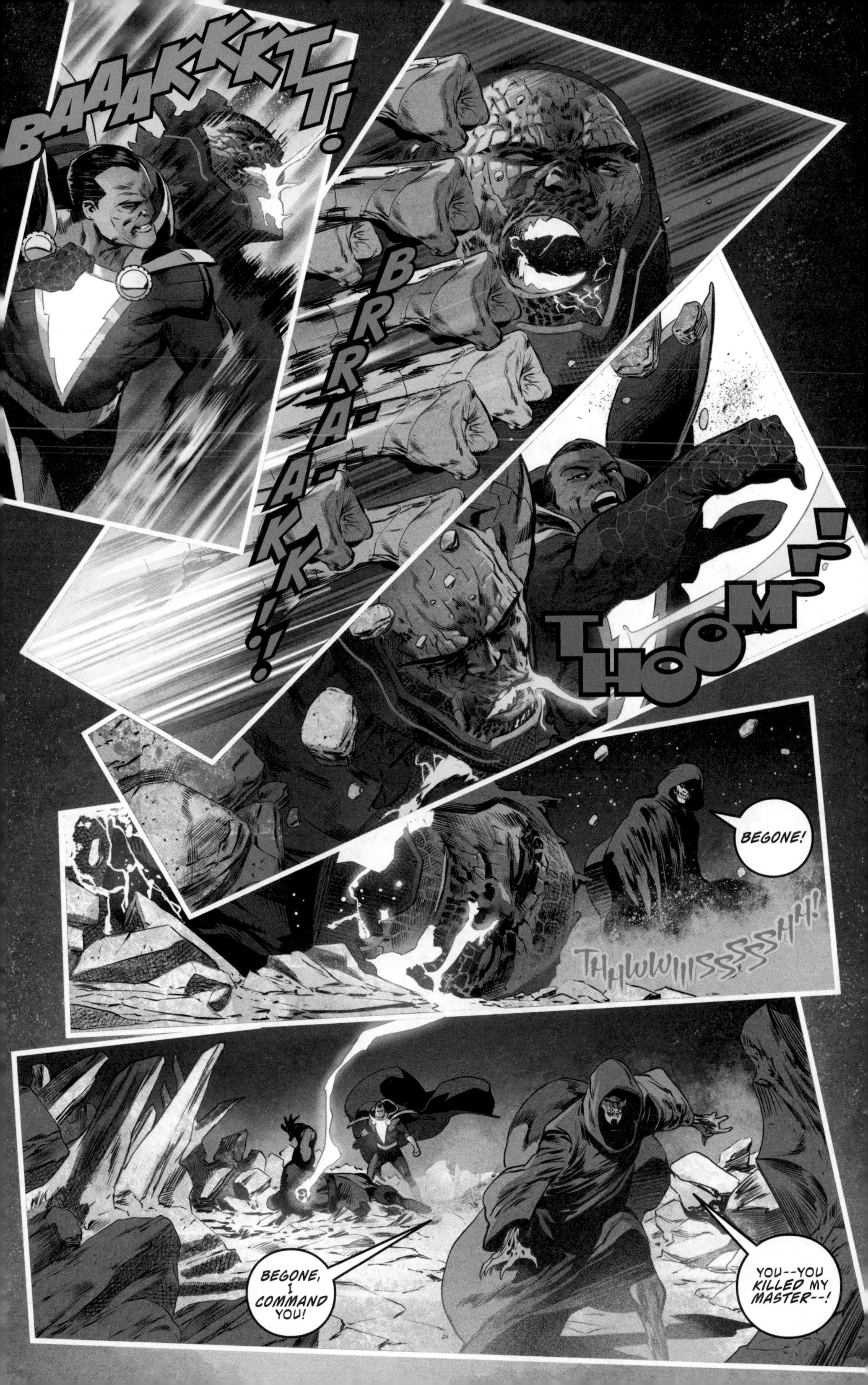
BAAAKKKTT!
BRRA-AKKK!!
THOOOM!
BEGONE!
THHWWIIISSSSHH!
BEGONE, I COMMAND YOU!
YOU--YOU KILLED MY MASTER--!

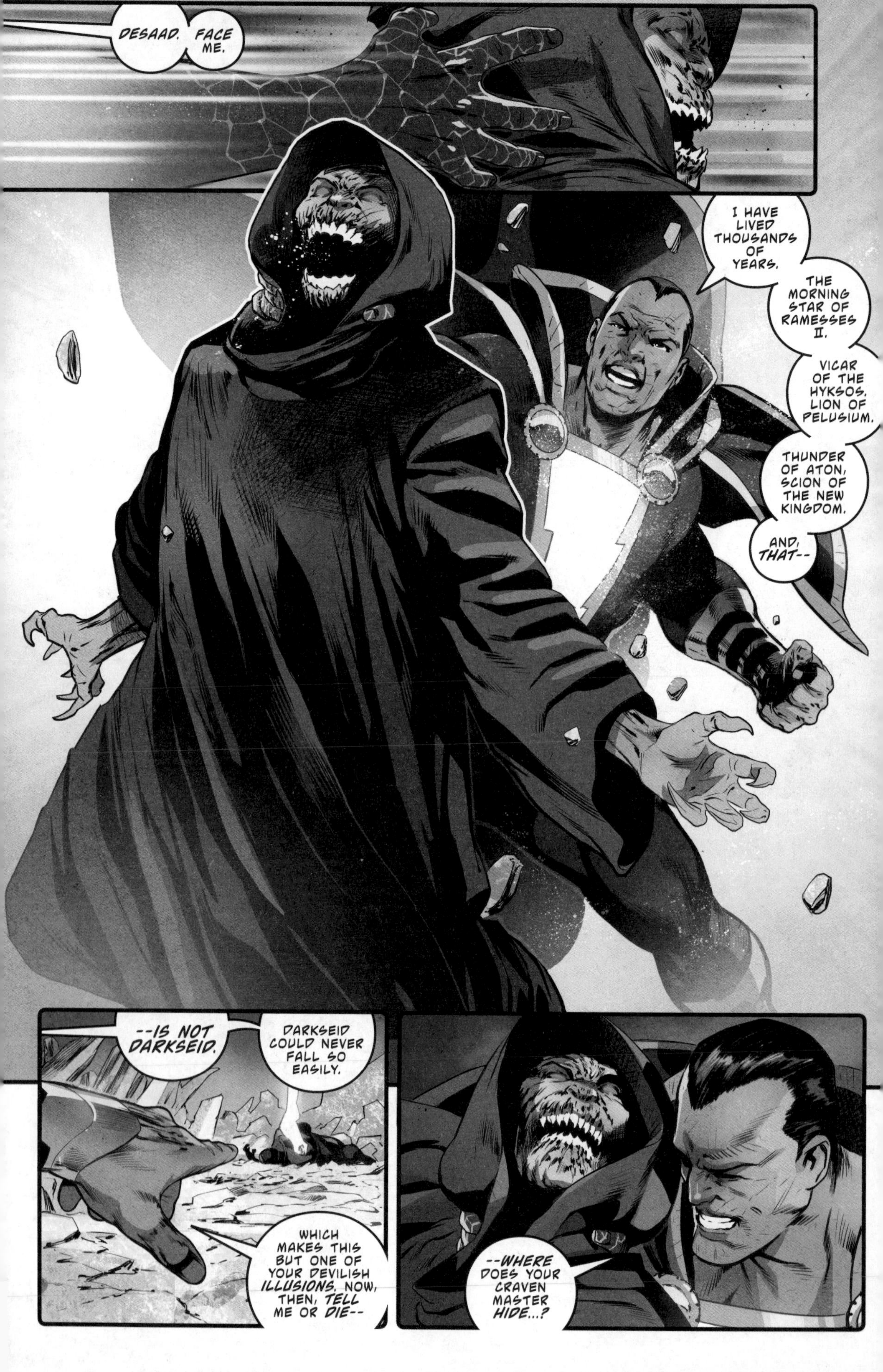
DESAAD.
FACE ME.
I HAVE LIVED THOUSANDS OF YEARS.
THE MORNING STAR OF RAMESSES II.
VICAR OF THE HYKSOS. LION OF PELUSIUM.
THUNDER OF ATON, SCION OF THE NEW KINGDOM.
AND, THAT--
--IS NOT DARKSEID.
DARKSEID COULD NEVER FALL SO EASILY.
WHICH MAKES THIS BUT ONE OF YOUR DEVILISH ILLUSIONS. NOW, THEN, TELL ME OR DIE--
--WHERE DOES YOUR CRAVEN MASTER HIDE...?

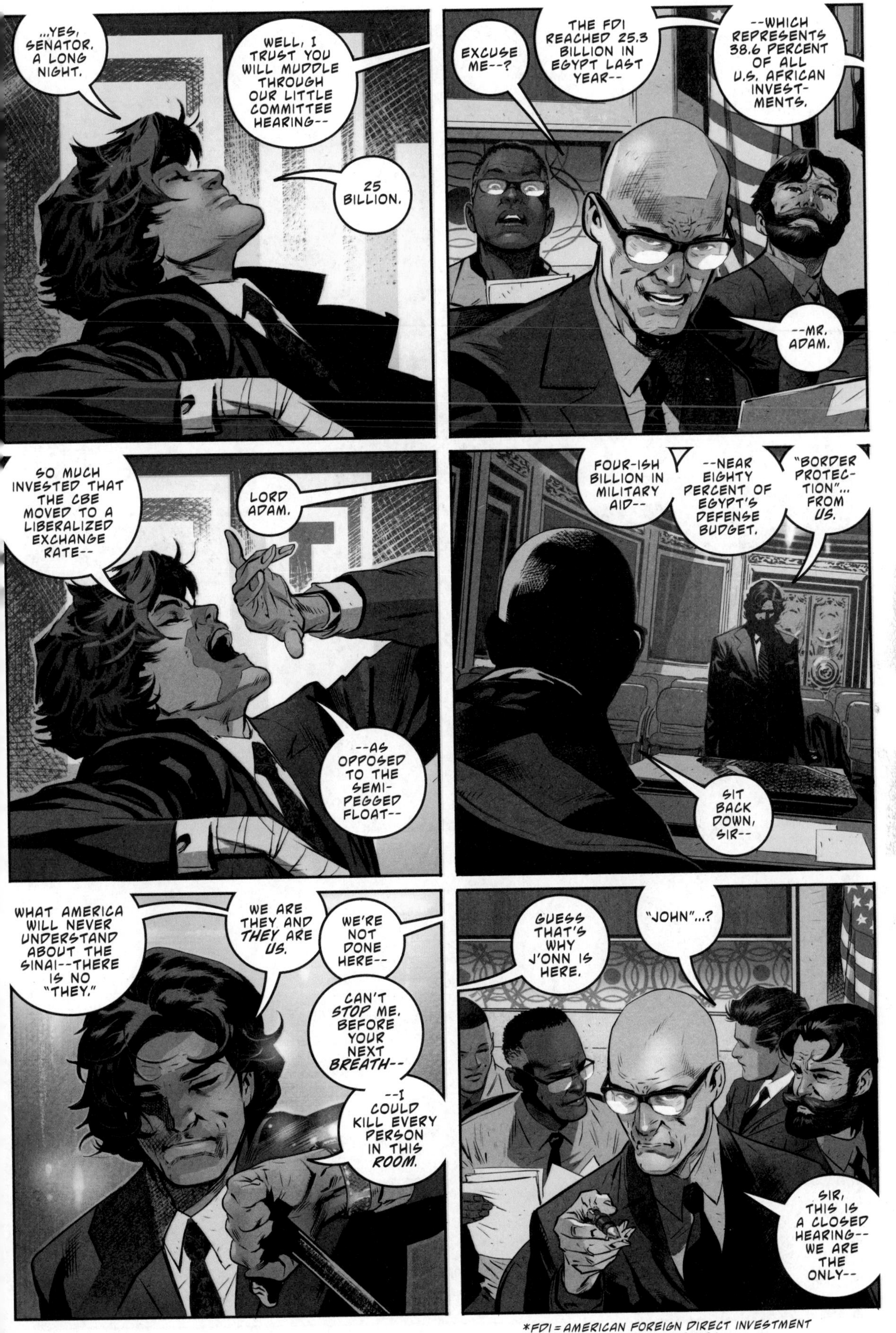
...YES, SENATOR. A LONG NIGHT.
WELL, I TRUST YOU WILL MUDDLE THROUGH OUR LITTLE COMMITTEE HEARING--
25 BILLION.
EXCUSE ME--?
THE FDI REACHED 25.3 BILLION IN EGYPT LAST YEAR--
--WHICH REPRESENTS 38.6 PERCENT OF ALL U.S. AFRICAN INVESTMENTS.
--MR. ADAM.
SO MUCH INVESTED THAT THE CBE MOVED TO A LIBERALIZED EXCHANGE RATE--
LORD ADAM.
--AS OPPOSED TO THE SEMI-PEGGED FLOAT--
FOUR-ISH BILLION IN MILITARY AID--
--NEAR EIGHTY PERCENT OF EGYPT'S DEFENSE BUDGET.
"BORDER PROTECTION"... FROM US.
SIT BACK DOWN, SIR--
WHAT AMERICA WILL NEVER UNDERSTAND ABOUT THE SINAI--THERE IS NO "THEY."
WE ARE THEY AND THEY ARE US.
WE'RE NOT DONE HERE--
CAN'T STOP ME. BEFORE YOUR NEXT BREATH--
--I COULD KILL EVERY PERSON IN THIS ROOM.
GUESS THAT'S WHY J'ONN IS HERE.
"JOHN"...?
SIR, THIS IS A CLOSED HEARING--WE ARE THE ONLY--

*FDI = AMERICAN FOREIGN DIRECT INVESTMENT
CBE = CENTRAL BANK OF EGYPT

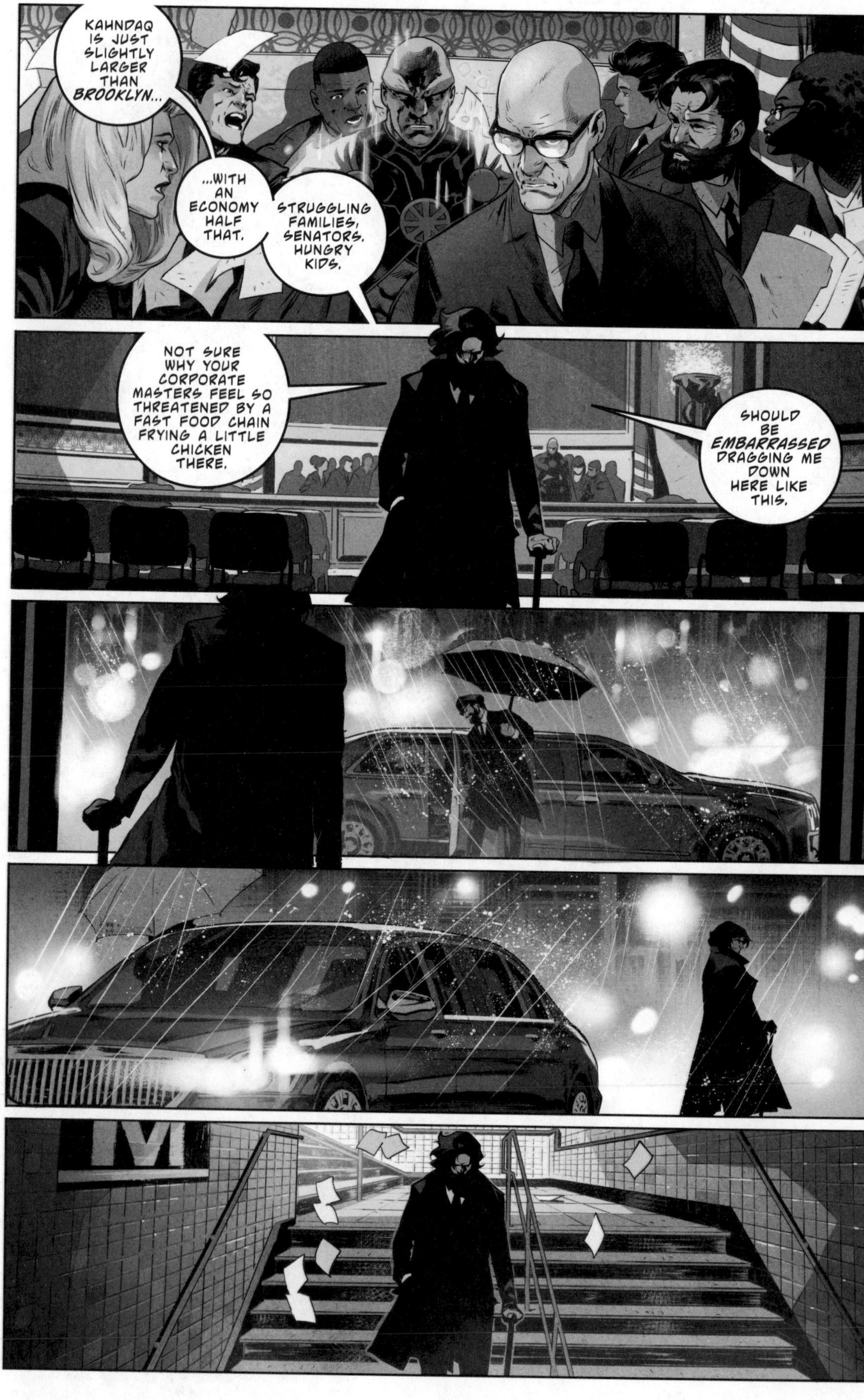

KAHNDAQ IS JUST SLIGHTLY LARGER THAN BROOKLYN...
...WITH AN ECONOMY HALF THAT.
STRUGGLING FAMILIES, SENATORS. HUNGRY KIDS.
NOT SURE WHY YOUR CORPORATE MASTERS FEEL SO THREATENED BY A FAST FOOD CHAIN FRYING A LITTLE CHICKEN THERE.
SHOULD BE EMBARRASSED DRAGGING ME DOWN HERE LIKE THIS.
M

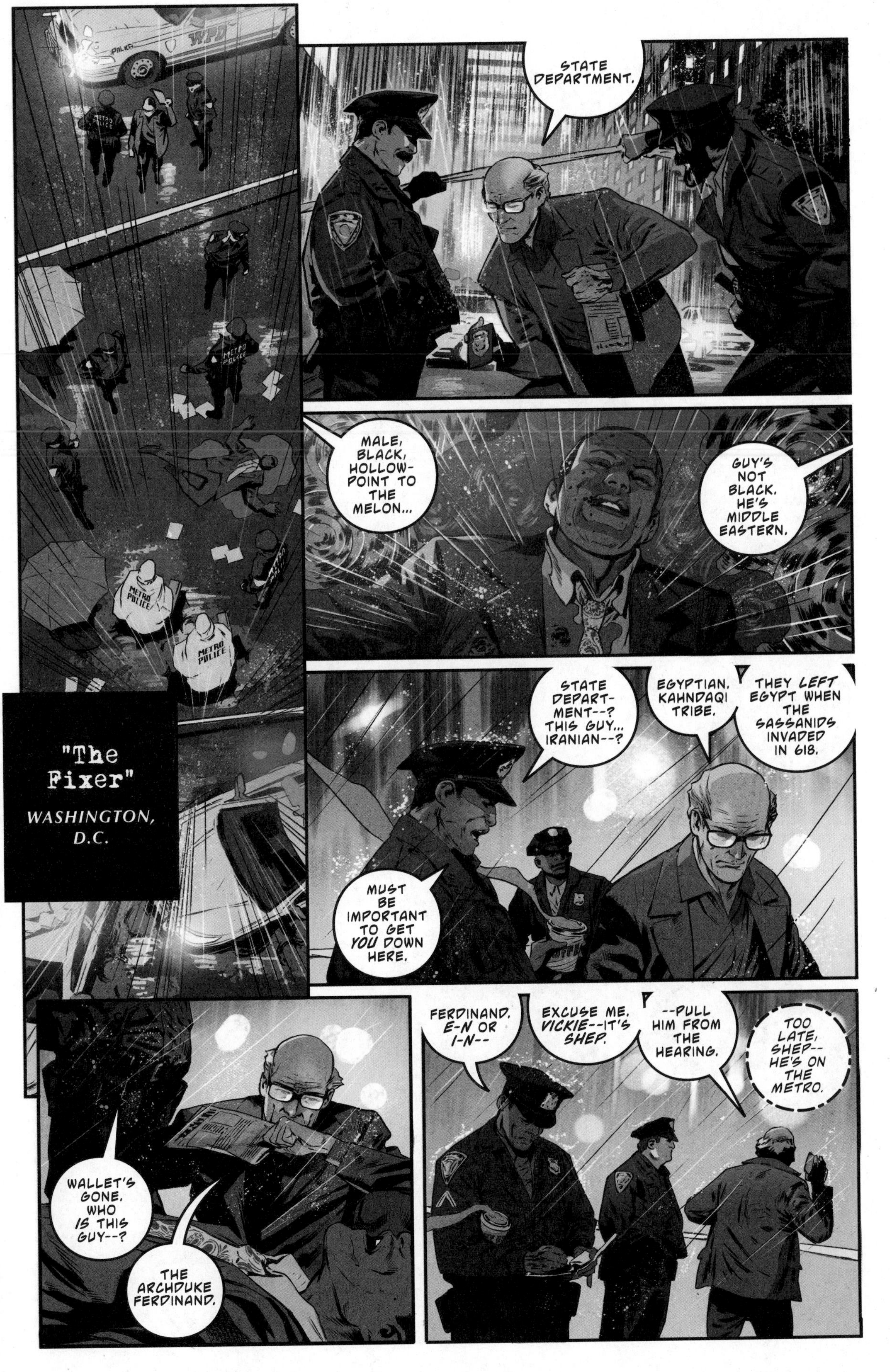
STATE DEPARTMENT.
MALE, BLACK, HOLLOW-POINT TO THE MELON...
GUY'S NOT BLACK. HE'S MIDDLE EASTERN.
"The Fixer"
WASHINGTON, D.C.
STATE DEPART-MENT--? THIS GUY... IRANIAN--?
EGYPTIAN. KAHNDAQI TRIBE.
THEY LEFT EGYPT WHEN THE SASSANIDS INVADED IN 618.
MUST BE IMPORTANT TO GET YOU DOWN HERE.
WALLET'S GONE. WHO IS THIS GUY--?
THE ARCHDUKE FERDINAND.
FERDINAND. E-N OR I-N--
EXCUSE ME. VICKIE--IT'S SHEP.
--PULL HIM FROM THE HEARING.
TOO LATE, SHEP--HE'S ON THE METRO.

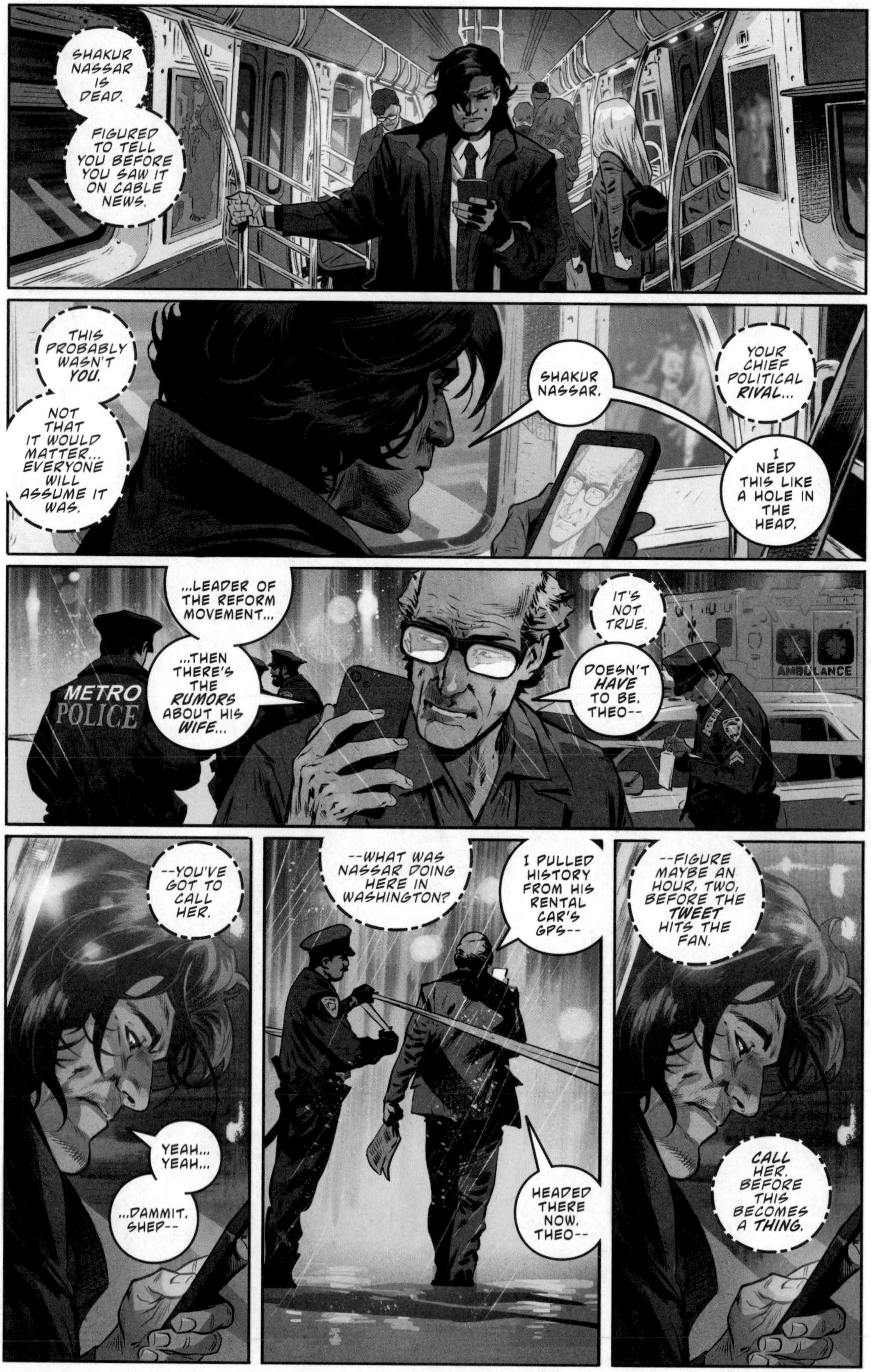

SHAKUR NASSAR IS DEAD.
FIGURED TO TELL YOU BEFORE YOU SAW IT ON CABLE NEWS.
THIS PROBABLY WASN'T YOU.
NOT THAT IT WOULD MATTER... EVERYONE WILL ASSUME IT WAS.
SHAKUR NASSAR.
YOUR CHIEF POLITICAL RIVAL...
I NEED THIS LIKE A HOLE IN THE HEAD.
...LEADER OF THE REFORM MOVEMENT...
...THEN THERE'S THE RUMORS ABOUT HIS WIFE...
METRO POLICE
IT'S NOT TRUE.
DOESN'T HAVE TO BE. THEO--
AMBULANCE
--YOU'VE GOT TO CALL HER.
YEAH... YEAH...
...DAMMIT, SHEP--
--WHAT WAS NASSAR DOING HERE IN WASHINGTON?
I PULLED HISTORY FROM HIS RENTAL CAR'S GPS--
HEADED THERE NOW. THEO--
--FIGURE MAYBE AN HOUR, TWO, BEFORE THE TWEET HITS THE FAN.
CALL HER. BEFORE THIS BECOMES A THING.

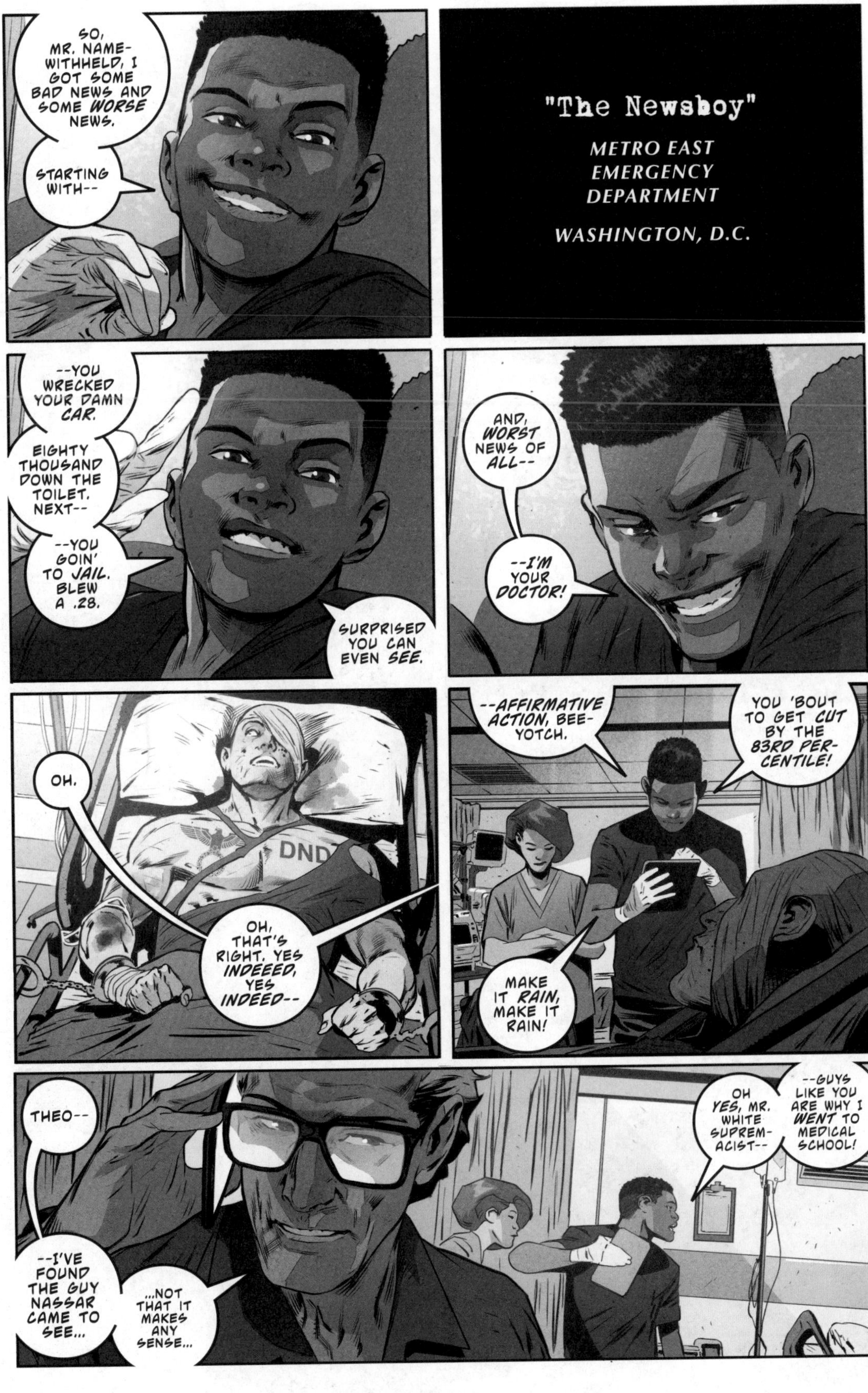
SO, MR. NAME-WITHHELD, I GOT SOME BAD NEWS AND SOME WORSE NEWS.
STARTING WITH--
"The Newsboy"
METRO EAST EMERGENCY DEPARTMENT
WASHINGTON, D.C.
--YOU WRECKED YOUR DAMN CAR.
EIGHTY THOUSAND DOWN THE TOILET. NEXT--
--YOU GOIN' TO JAIL. BLEW A .28.
SURPRISED YOU CAN EVEN SEE.
AND, WORST NEWS OF ALL--
--I'M YOUR DOCTOR!
OH.
DND
OH, THAT'S RIGHT. YES INDEEED, YES INDEED--
--AFFIRMATIVE ACTION, BEE-YOTCH.
YOU 'BOUT TO GET CUT BY THE 83RD PER-CENTILE!
MAKE IT RAIN, MAKE IT RAIN!
THEO--
--I'VE FOUND THE GUY NASSAR CAME TO SEE...
...NOT THAT IT MAKES ANY SENSE...
OH YES, MR. WHITE SUPREM-ACIST--
--GUYS LIKE YOU ARE WHY I WENT TO MEDICAL SCHOOL!

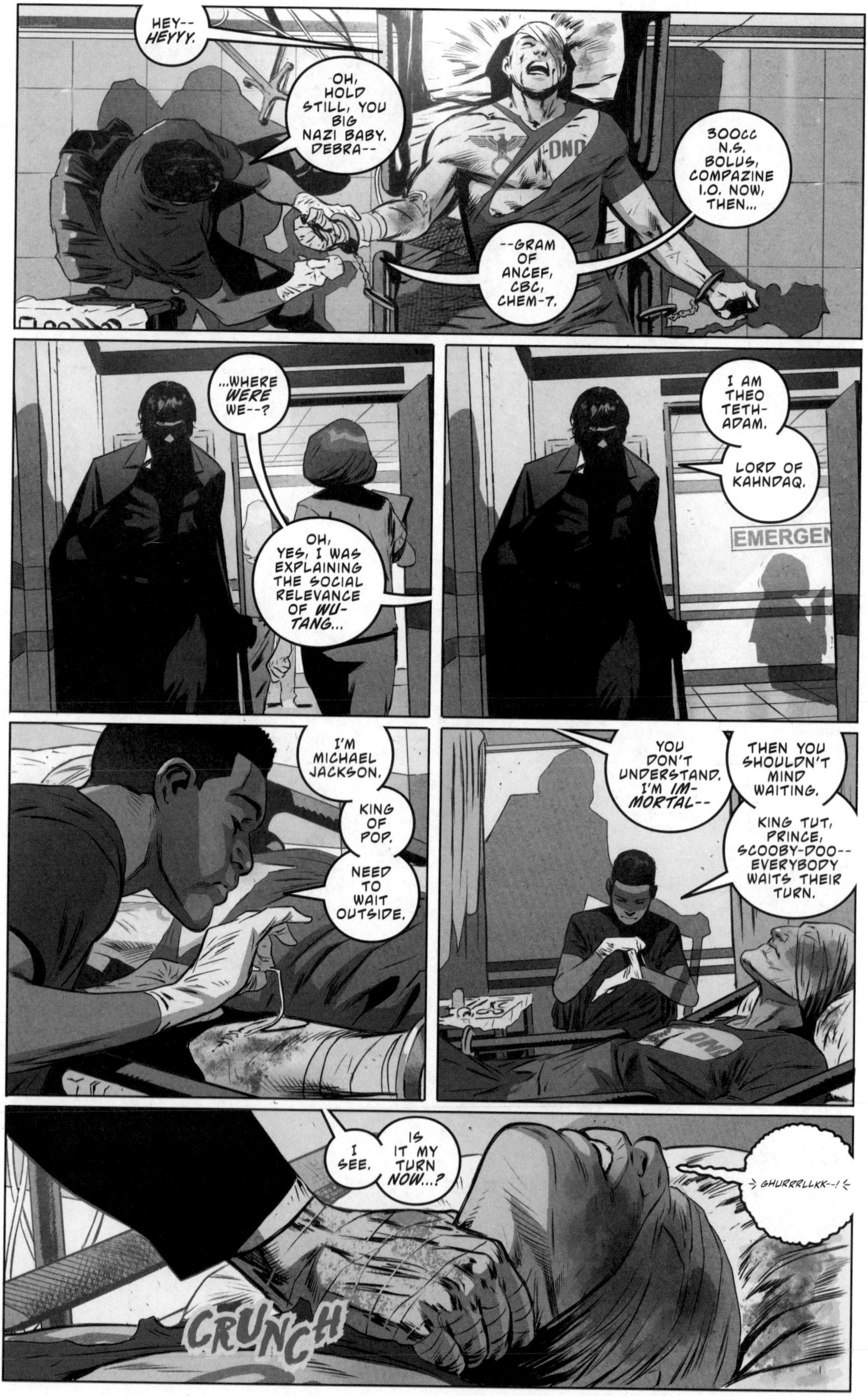
HEY--
HEYYY.
OH, HOLD STILL, YOU BIG NAZI BABY. DEBRA--
300cc N.S. BOLUS, COMPAZINE I.O. NOW, THEN...
--GRAM OF ANCEF, CBC, CHEM-7.
...WHERE WERE WE--?
OH, YES, I WAS EXPLAINING THE SOCIAL RELEVANCE OF WU-TANG...
I AM THEO TETH-ADAM.
LORD OF KAHNDAQ.
EMERGEN
I'M MICHAEL JACKSON.
KING OF POP.
NEED TO WAIT OUTSIDE.
YOU DON'T UNDERSTAND. I'M IM-MORTAL--
THEN YOU SHOULDN'T MIND WAITING.
KING TUT, PRINCE, SCOOBY-DOO--EVERYBODY WAITS THEIR TURN.
I SEE.
IS IT MY TURN NOW...?
GHURRRLLKK--!
CRUNCH

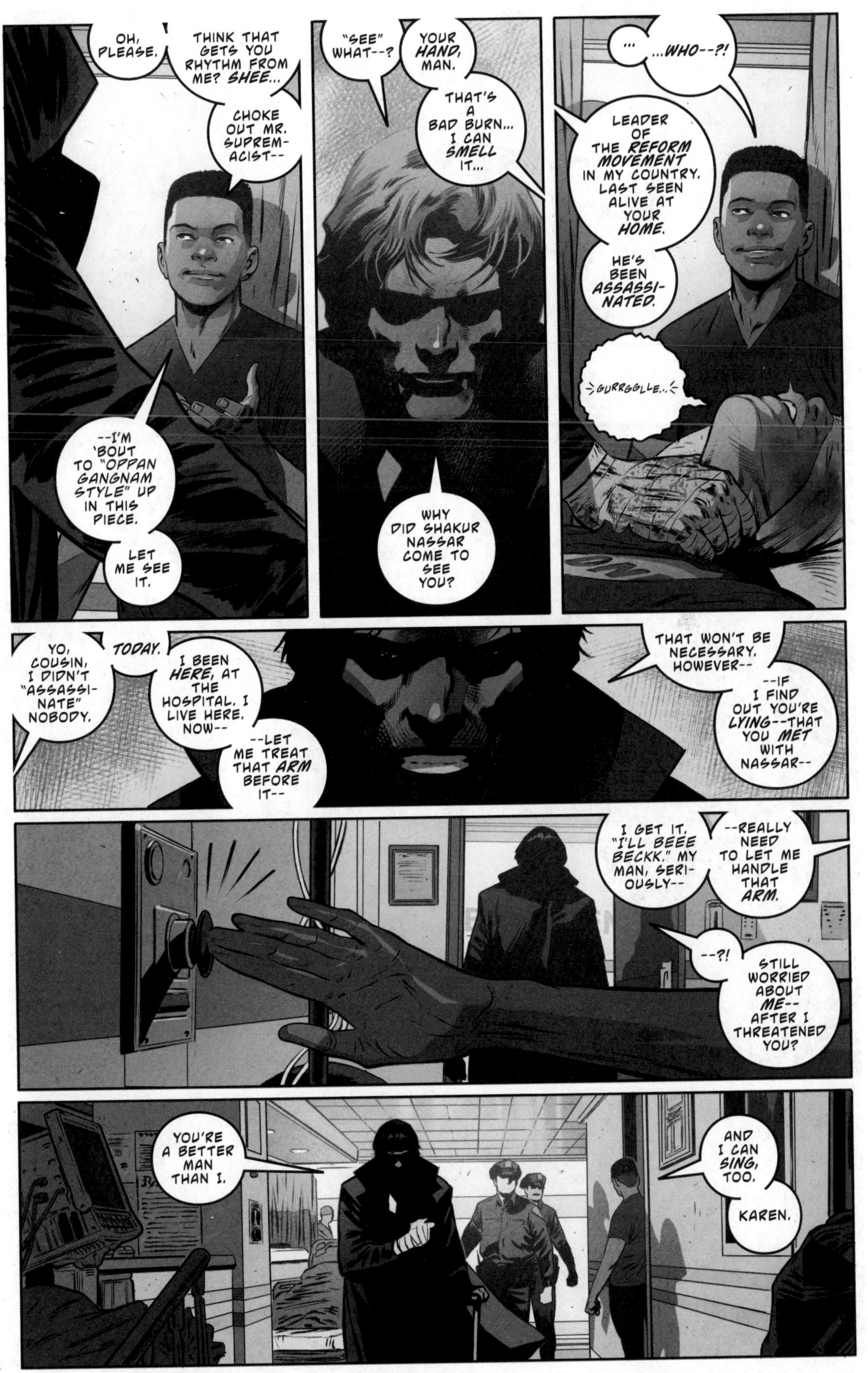
OH, PLEASE.
THINK THAT GETS YOU RHYTHM FROM ME? SHEE...
CHOKE OUT MR. SUPREMACIST--
--I'M 'BOUT TO "OPPAN GANGNAM STYLE" UP IN THIS PIECE.
LET ME SEE IT.
"SEE" WHAT--?
YOUR HAND, MAN.
THAT'S A BAD BURN... I CAN SMELL IT...
WHY DID SHAKUR NASSAR COME TO SEE YOU?
...
...WHO--?!
LEADER OF THE REFORM MOVEMENT IN MY COUNTRY. LAST SEEN ALIVE AT YOUR HOME.
HE'S BEEN ASSASSINATED.
GURRGGLLE...
YO, COUSIN, I DIDN'T "ASSASSINATE" NOBODY.
TODAY.
I BEEN HERE, AT THE HOSPITAL. I LIVE HERE. NOW--
--LET ME TREAT THAT ARM BEFORE IT--
THAT WON'T BE NECESSARY. HOWEVER--
--IF I FIND OUT YOU'RE LYING--THAT YOU MET WITH NASSAR--
I GET IT. "I'LL BEEE BECKK." MY MAN, SERIOUSLY--
--REALLY NEED TO LET ME HANDLE THAT ARM.
--?!
STILL WORRIED ABOUT ME--AFTER I THREATENED YOU?
YOU'RE A BETTER MAN THAN I.
AND I CAN SING, TOO.
KAREN.

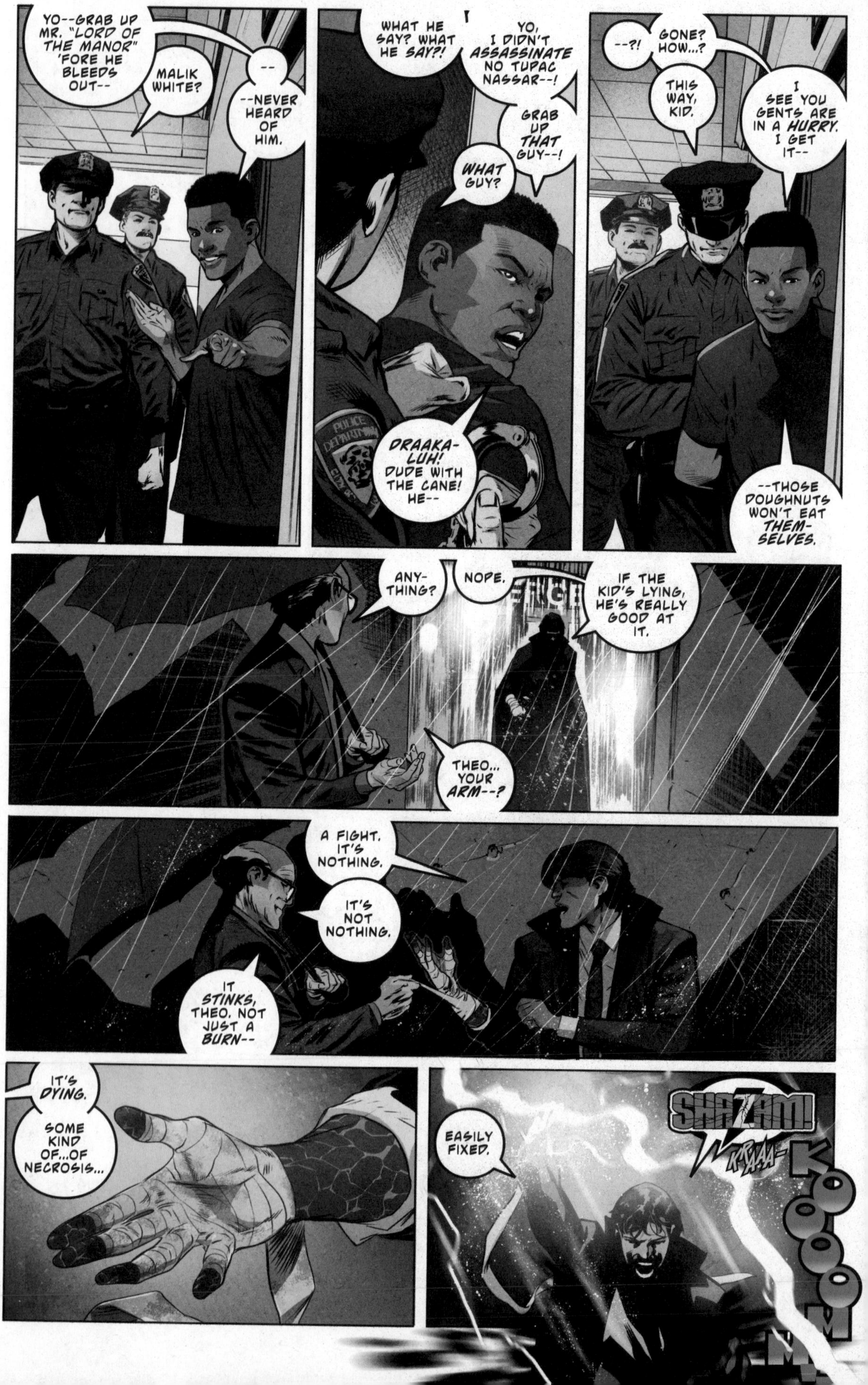
YO--GRAB UP MR. "LORD OF THE MANOR" 'FORE HE BLEEDS OUT--
MALIK WHITE?
--
--NEVER HEARD OF HIM.
WHAT HE SAY? WHAT HE SAY?!
YO, I DIDN'T ASSASSINATE NO TUPAC NASSAR--!
GRAB UP THAT GUY--!
WHAT GUY?
DRAAKA-LUH! DUDE WITH THE CANE! HE--
--?!
GONE? HOW...?
THIS WAY, KID.
I SEE YOU GENTS ARE IN A HURRY. I GET IT--
--THOSE DOUGHNUTS WON'T EAT THEM-SELVES.
ANY-THING?
NOPE.
IF THE KID'S LYING, HE'S REALLY GOOD AT IT.
THEO... YOUR ARM--?
A FIGHT. IT'S NOTHING.
IT'S NOT NOTHING.
IT STINKS, THEO. NOT JUST A BURN--
IT'S DYING.
SOME KIND OF...OF NECROSIS...
EASILY FIXED.
SHAZAM!
KRAAA-KOOOOOM

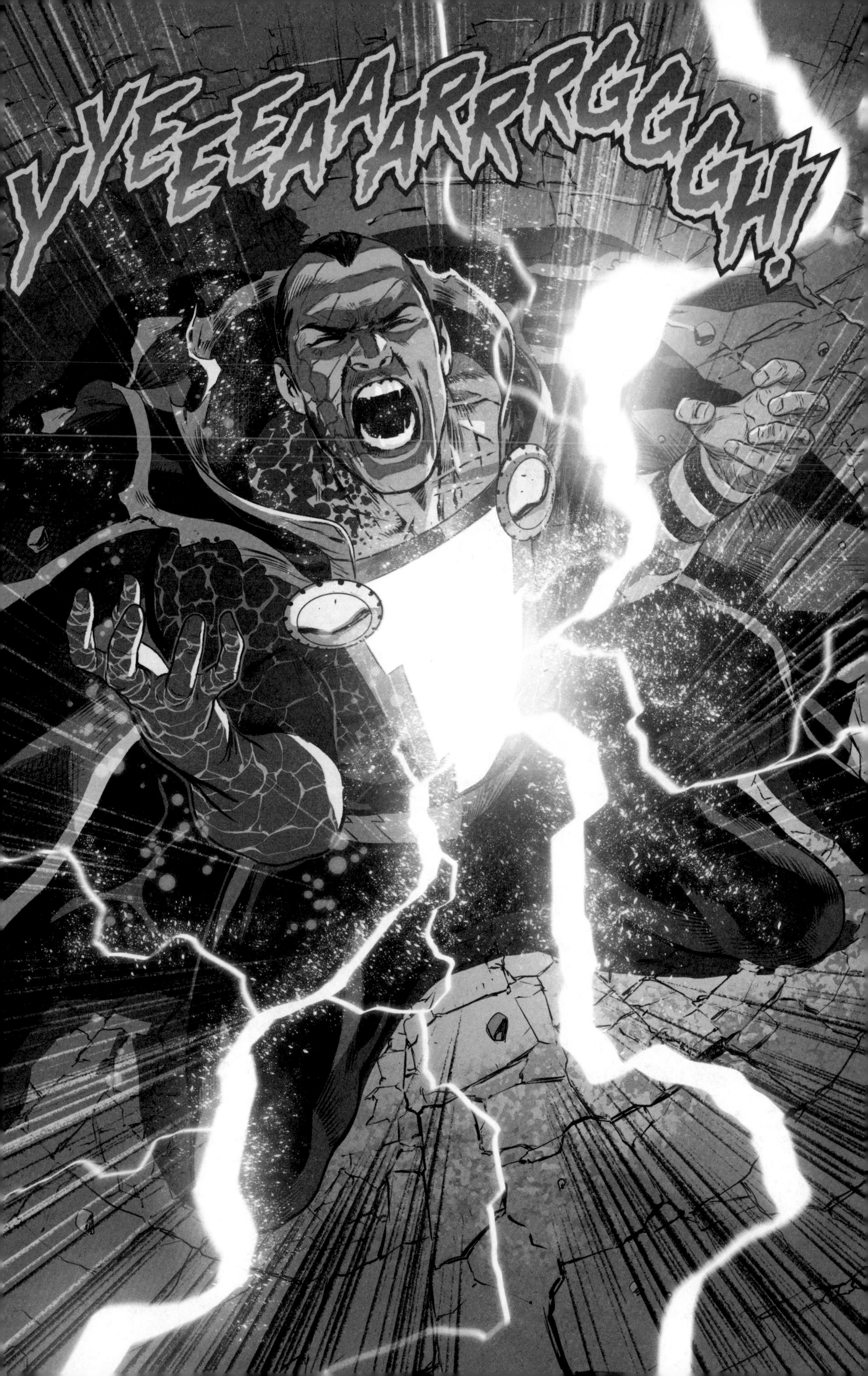
YYEEEAAARRRGGGH!

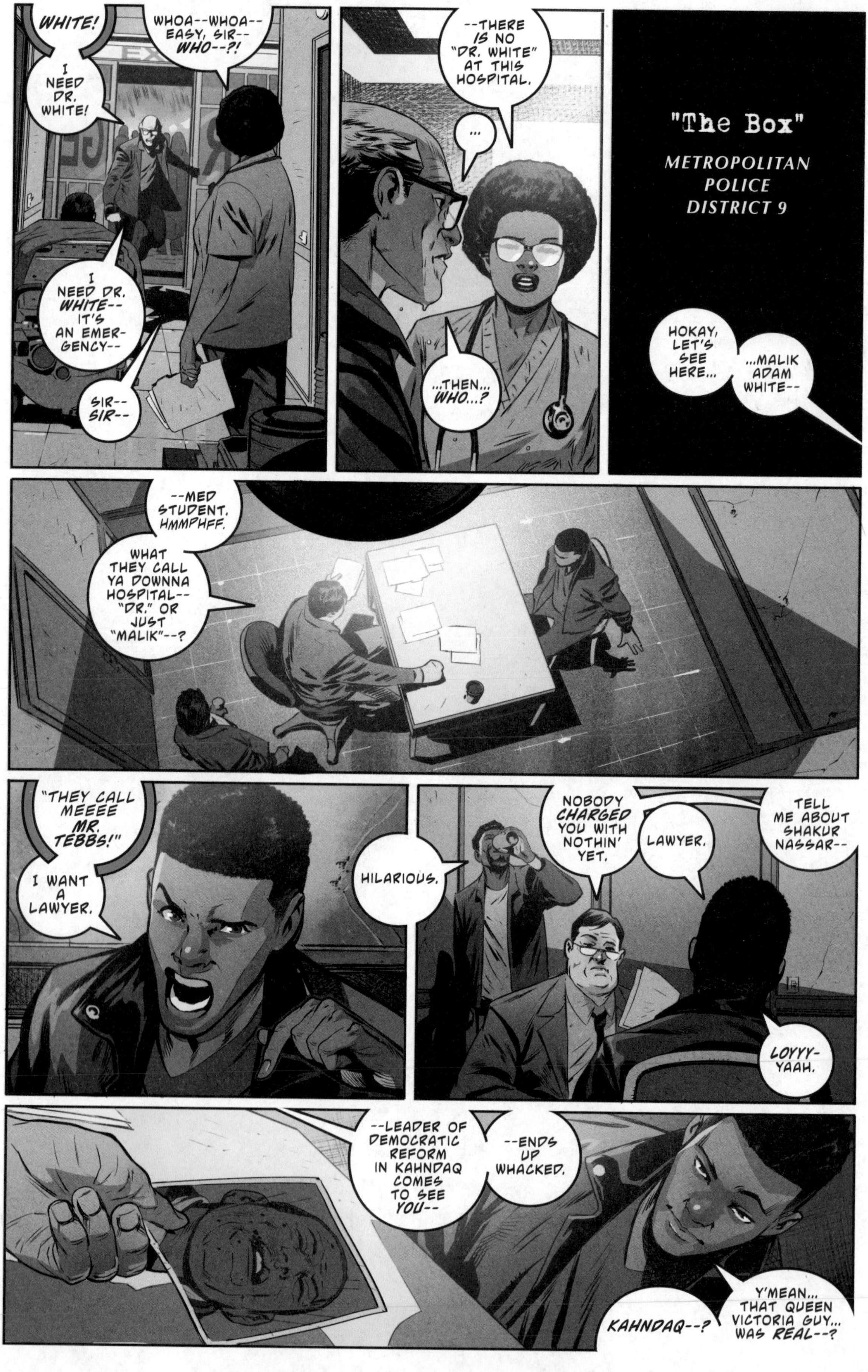
WHITE!
I NEED DR. WHITE!
WHOA--WHOA-- EASY, SIR-- WHO--?!
I NEED DR. WHITE-- IT'S AN EMERGENCY--
SIR-- SIR--
--THERE IS NO "DR. WHITE" AT THIS HOSPITAL.
...
...THEN... WHO...?
"The Box"
METROPOLITAN POLICE DISTRICT 9
HOKAY, LET'S SEE HERE...
...MALIK ADAM WHITE--
--MED STUDENT. HMMPHFF.
WHAT THEY CALL YA DOWNNA HOSPITAL-- "DR." OR JUST "MALIK"--?
"THEY CALL MEEEE MR. TEBBS!"
I WANT A LAWYER.
HILARIOUS.
NOBODY CHARGED YOU WITH NOTHIN' YET.
LAWYER.
TELL ME ABOUT SHAKUR NASSAR--
LOYYY-YAAH.
--LEADER OF DEMOCRATIC REFORM IN KAHNDAQ COMES TO SEE YOU--
--ENDS UP WHACKED.
KAHNDAQ--?
Y'MEAN... THAT QUEEN VICTORIA GUY... WAS REAL--?

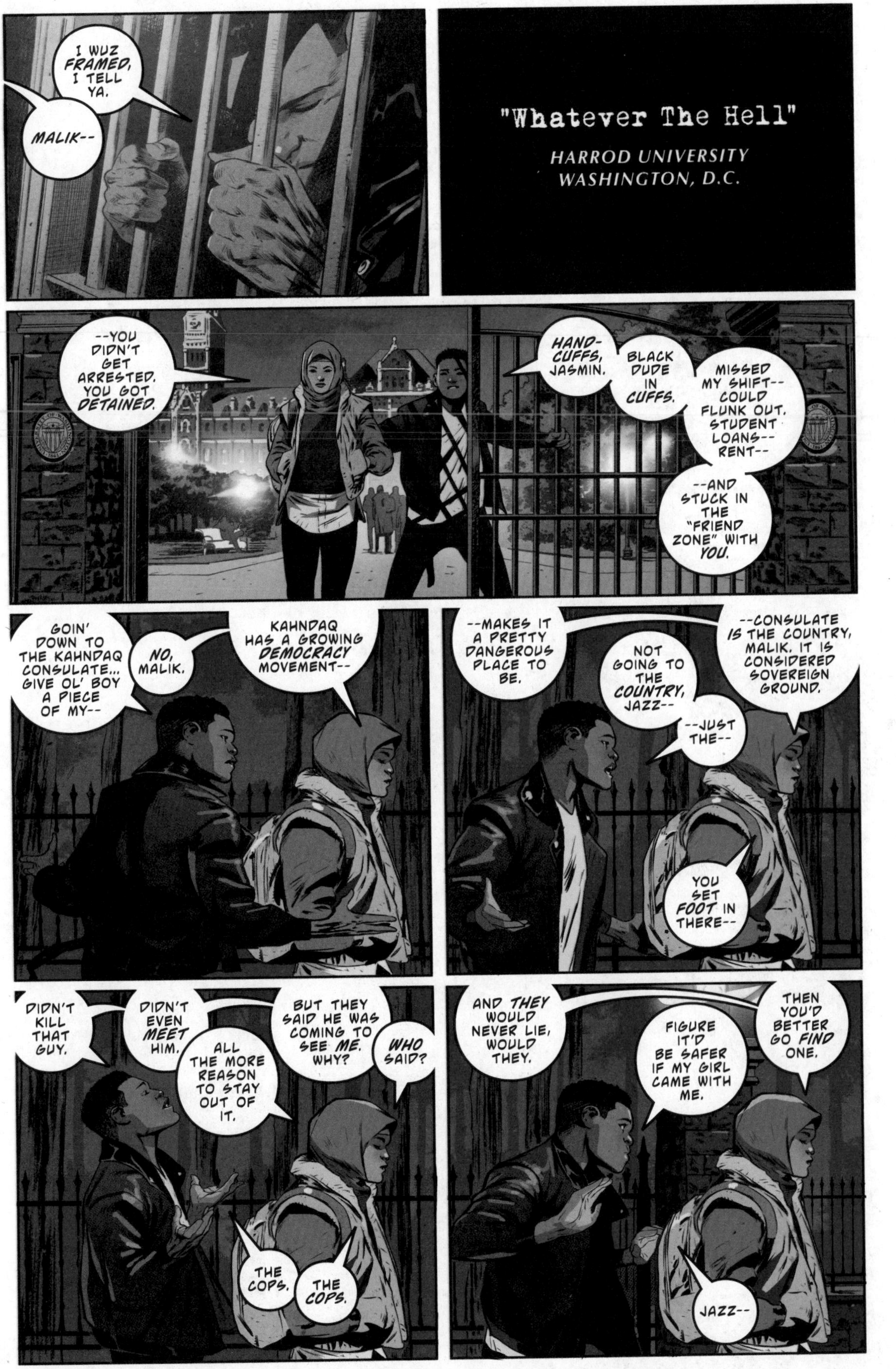
I WUZ FRAMED, I TELL YA.
MALIK--
"Whatever The Hell"
HARROD UNIVERSITY
WASHINGTON, D.C.
--YOU DIDN'T GET ARRESTED. YOU GOT DETAINED.
HAND-CUFFS, JASMIN.
BLACK DUDE IN CUFFS.
MISSED MY SHIFT--COULD FLUNK OUT. STUDENT LOANS--RENT--
--AND STUCK IN THE "FRIEND ZONE" WITH YOU.
GOIN' DOWN TO THE KAHNDAQ CONSULATE... GIVE OL' BOY A PIECE OF MY--
NO, MALIK.
KAHNDAQ HAS A GROWING DEMOCRACY MOVEMENT--
--MAKES IT A PRETTY DANGEROUS PLACE TO BE.
NOT GOING TO THE COUNTRY, JAZZ--
--JUST THE--
--CONSULATE IS THE COUNTRY, MALIK. IT IS CONSIDERED SOVEREIGN GROUND.
YOU SET FOOT IN THERE--
DIDN'T KILL THAT GUY.
DIDN'T EVEN MEET HIM.
ALL THE MORE REASON TO STAY OUT OF IT.
BUT THEY SAID HE WAS COMING TO SEE ME. WHY?
WHO SAID?
THE COPS.
THE COPS.
AND THEY WOULD NEVER LIE, WOULD THEY.
FIGURE IT'D BE SAFER IF MY GIRL CAME WITH ME.
THEN YOU'D BETTER GO FIND ONE.
JAZZ--

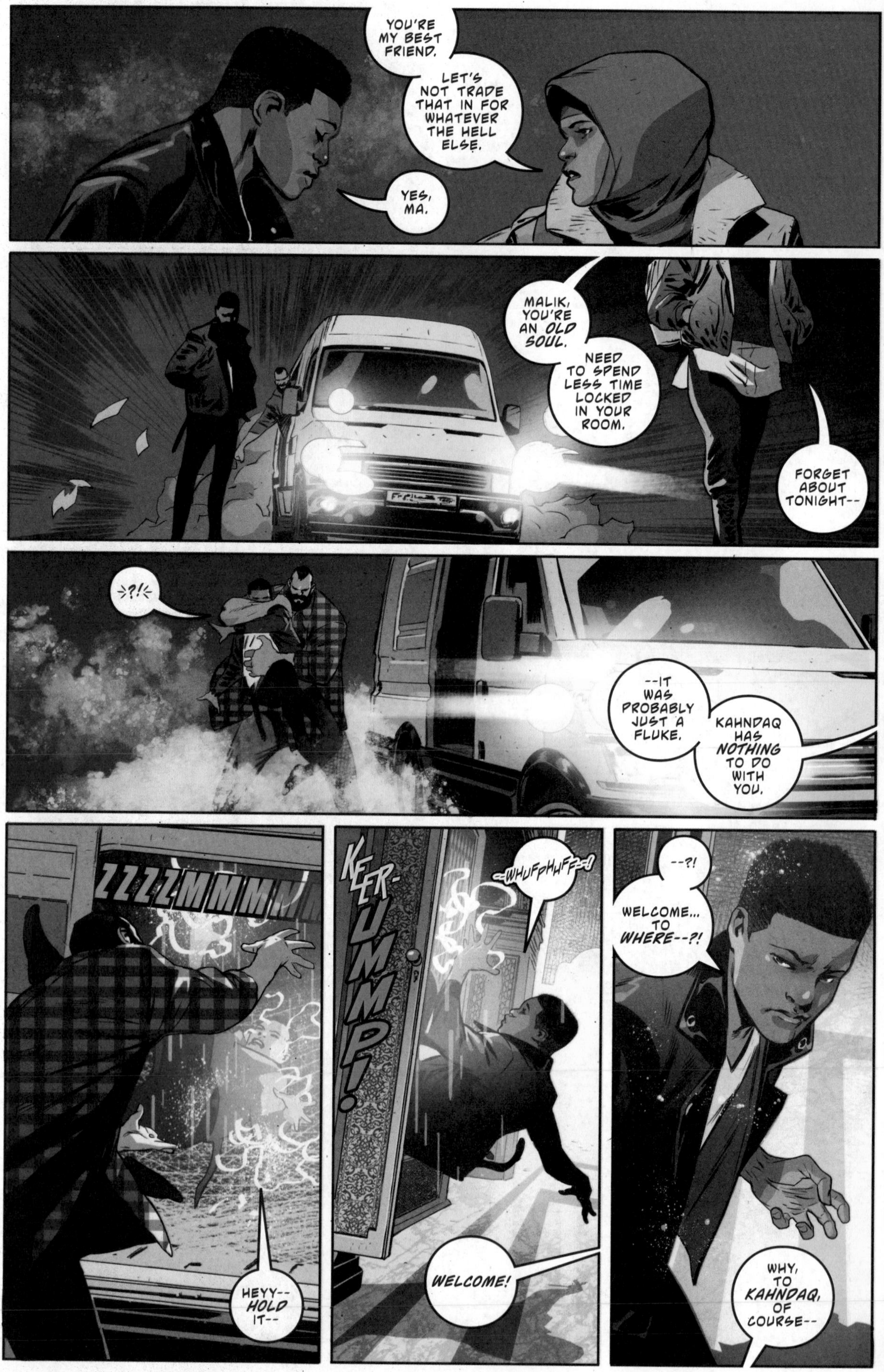
YOU'RE MY BEST FRIEND.
LET'S NOT TRADE THAT IN FOR WHATEVER THE HELL ELSE.
YES, MA.
MALIK, YOU'RE AN OLD SOUL.
NEED TO SPEND LESS TIME LOCKED IN YOUR ROOM.
FORGET ABOUT TONIGHT--
--?!--
--IT WAS PROBABLY JUST A FLUKE.
KAHNDAQ HAS NOTHING TO DO WITH YOU.
ZZZZMMMMM
HEYY-- HOLD IT--
KEER-UMMMP!
--WHUFPHUFF--!
WELCOME!
--?!
WELCOME... TO WHERE--?!
WHY, TO KAHNDAQ, OF COURSE--

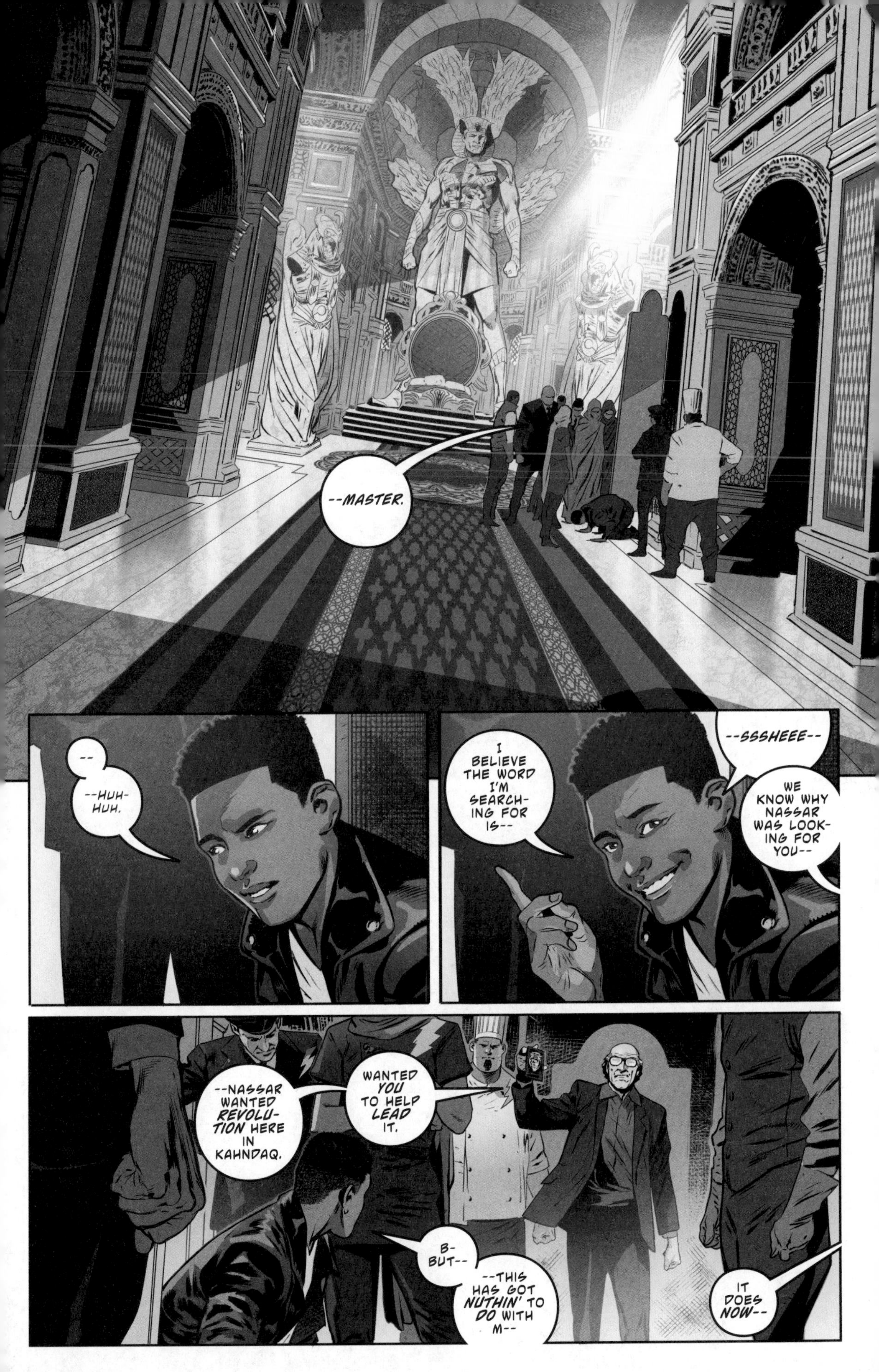
--MASTER.
--
--HUH-HUH.
I BELIEVE THE WORD I'M SEARCHING FOR IS--
--SSSHEEE--
WE KNOW WHY NASSAR WAS LOOKING FOR YOU--
--NASSAR WANTED REVOLUTION HERE IN KAHNDAQ.
WANTED YOU TO HELP LEAD IT.
B-BUT--
--THIS HAS GOT NUTHIN' TO DO WITH M--
IT DOES NOW--

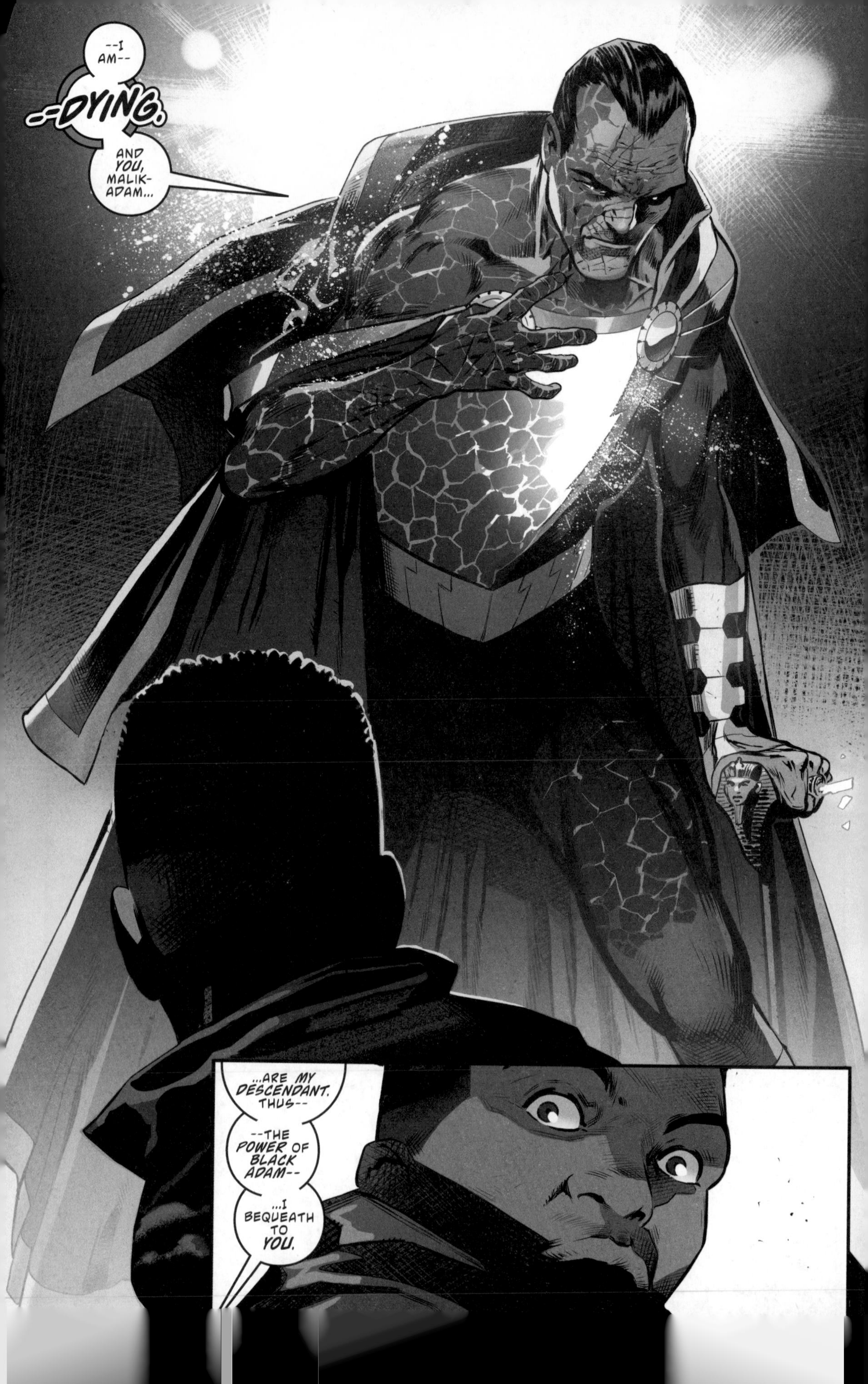
--I AM--
--DYING.
AND YOU, MALIK-ADAM...
...ARE MY DESCENDANT. THUS--
--THE POWER OF BLACK ADAM--
...I BEQUEATH TO YOU.

***Black Adam* #2** cover by Irvin Rodriguez

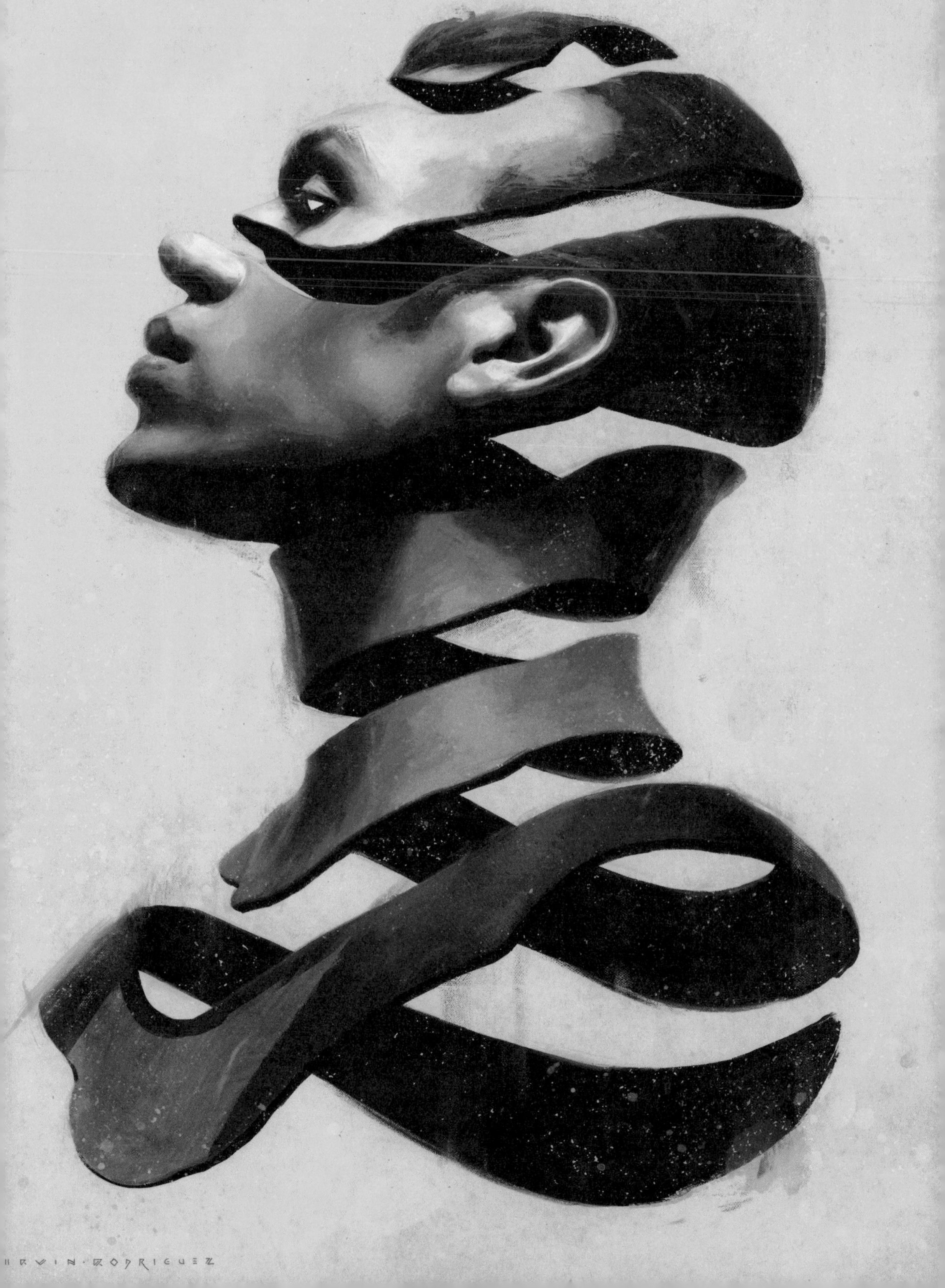
IRVIN·RODRIGUEZ

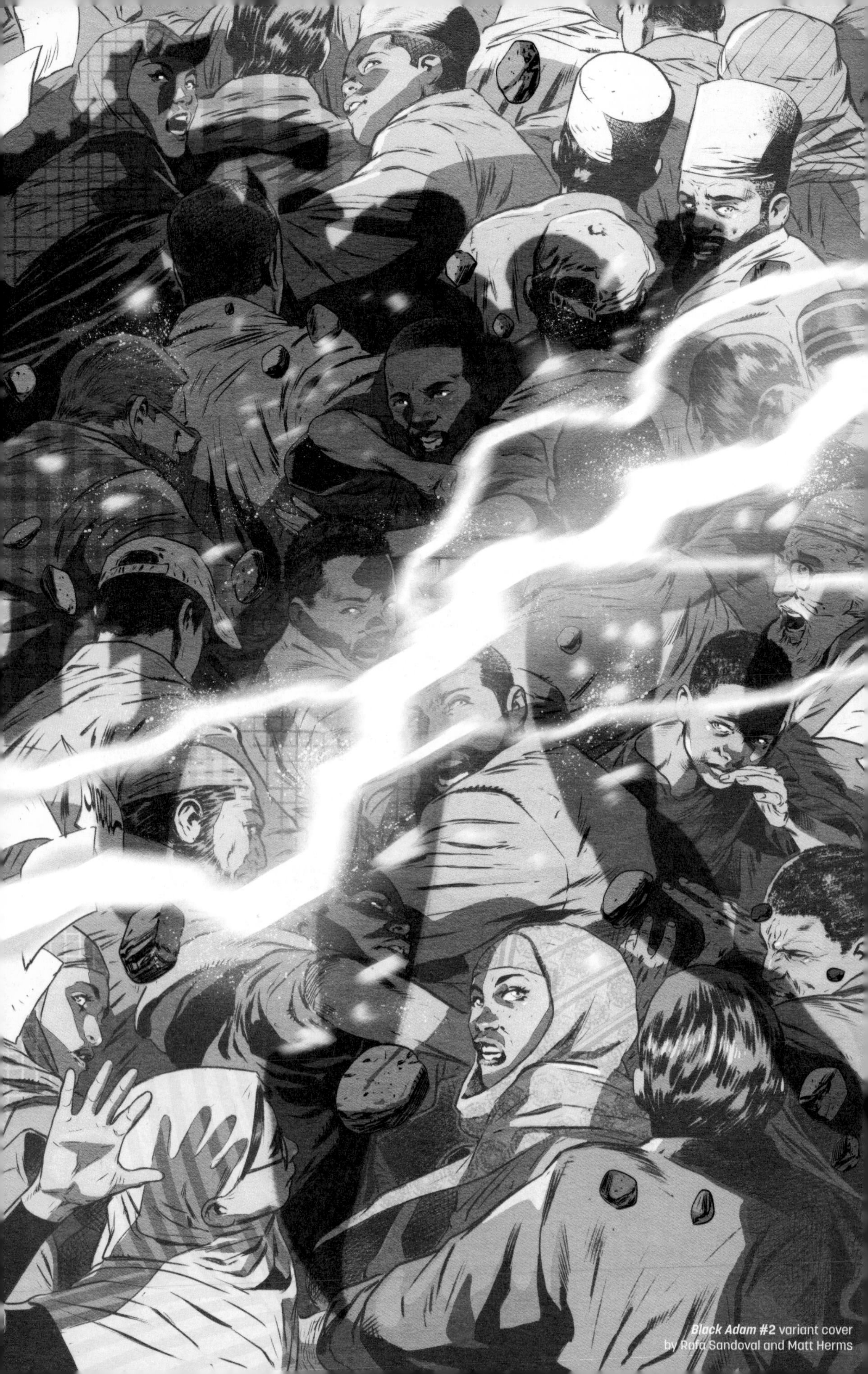

Black Adam #2 variant cover
by Rafa Sandoval and Matt Herms

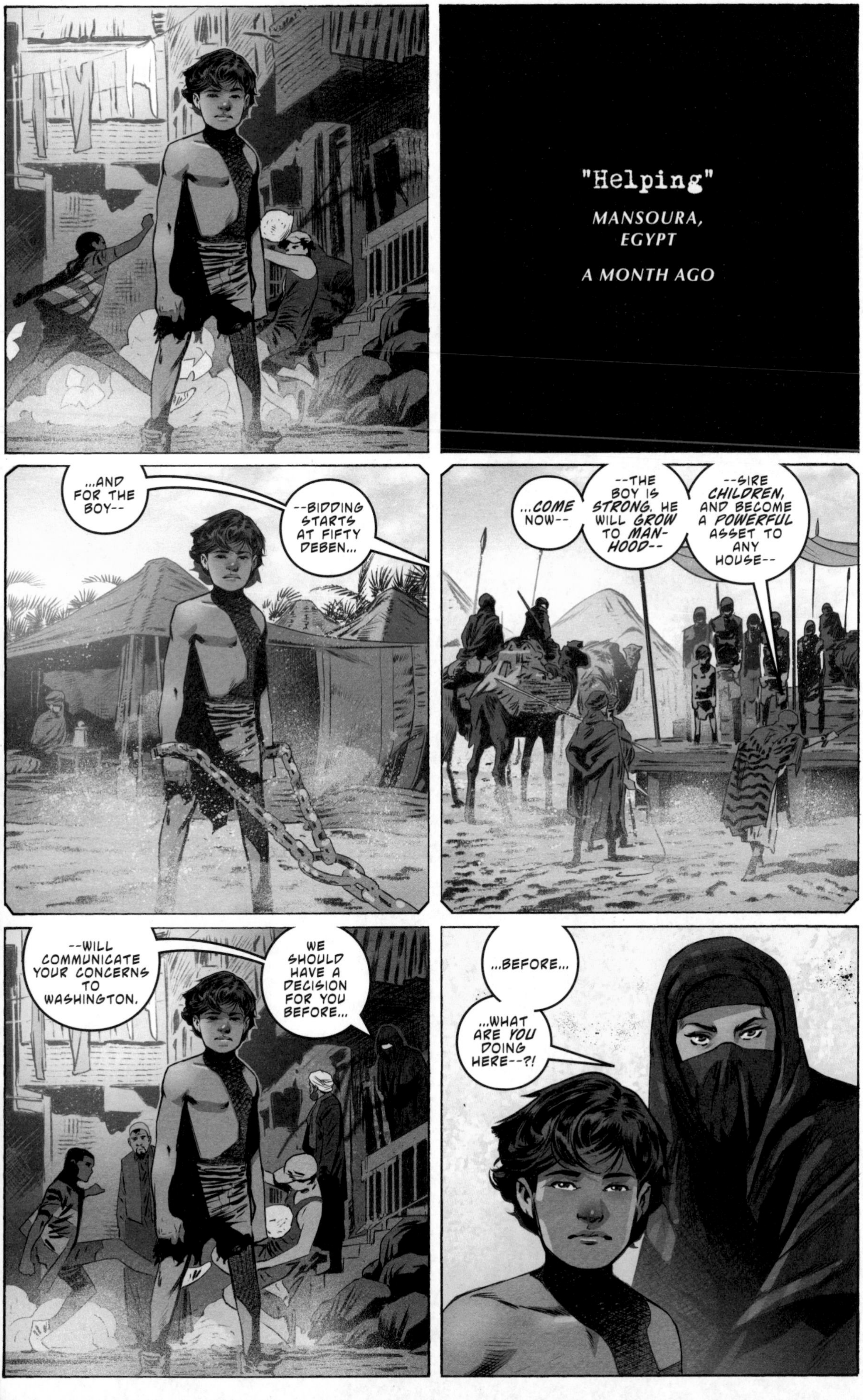
"Helping"
MANSOURA, EGYPT
A MONTH AGO
...AND FOR THE BOY--
--BIDDING STARTS AT FIFTY DEBEN...
...COME NOW--
--THE BOY IS STRONG. HE WILL GROW TO MAN-HOOD--
--SIRE CHILDREN, AND BECOME A POWERFUL ASSET TO ANY HOUSE--
--WILL COMMUNICATE YOUR CONCERNS TO WASHINGTON.
WE SHOULD HAVE A DECISION FOR YOU BEFORE...
...BEFORE...
...WHAT ARE YOU DOING HERE--?!

BLACK ADAM

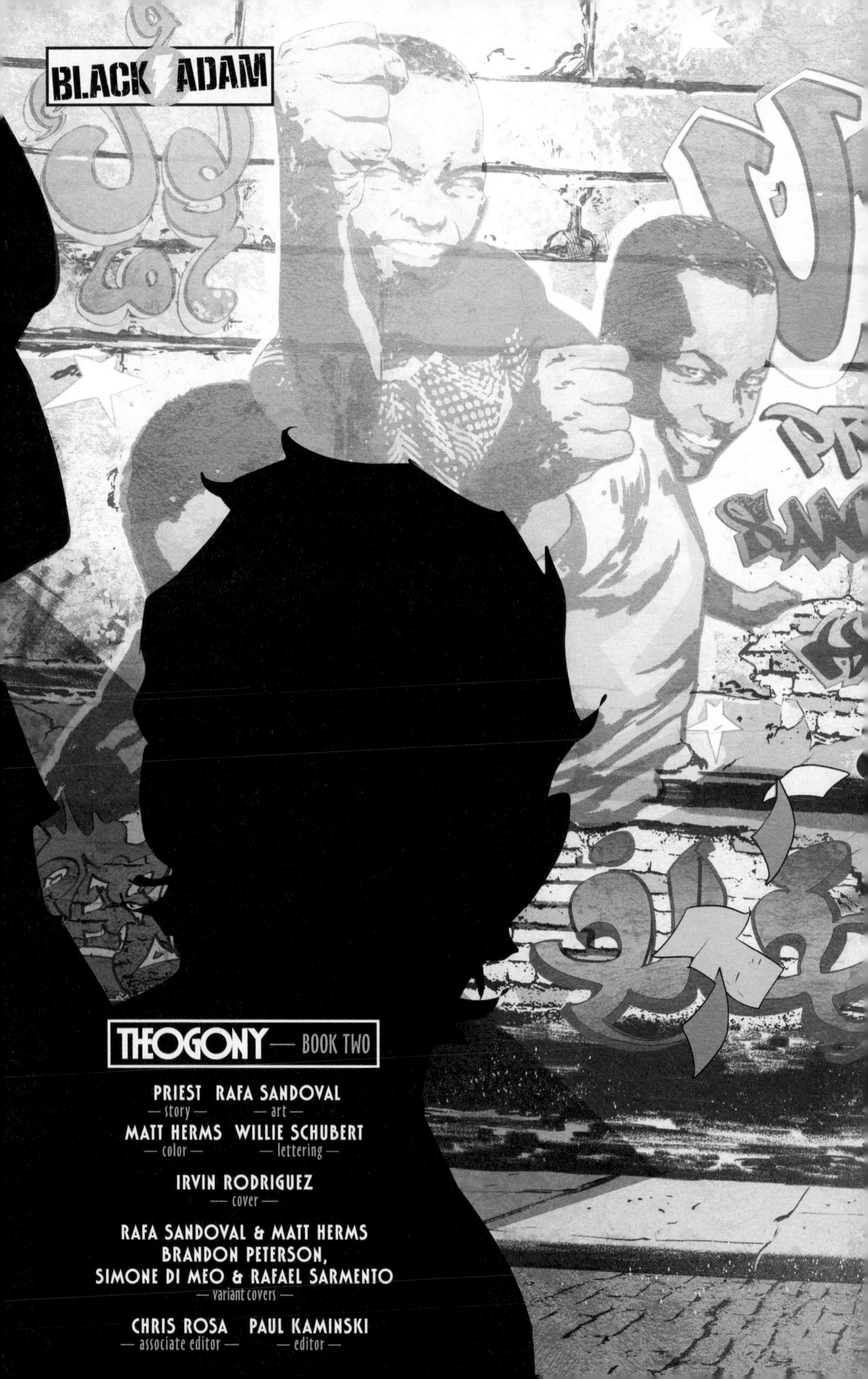

THEOGONY — BOOK TWO

PRIEST — story —
RAFA SANDOVAL — art —
MATT HERMS — color —
WILLIE SCHUBERT — lettering —

IRVIN RODRIGUEZ
— cover —

RAFA SANDOVAL & MATT HERMS
BRANDON PETERSON,
SIMONE DI MEO & RAFAEL SARMENTO
— variant covers —

CHRIS ROSA — associate editor —
PAUL KAMINSKI — editor —

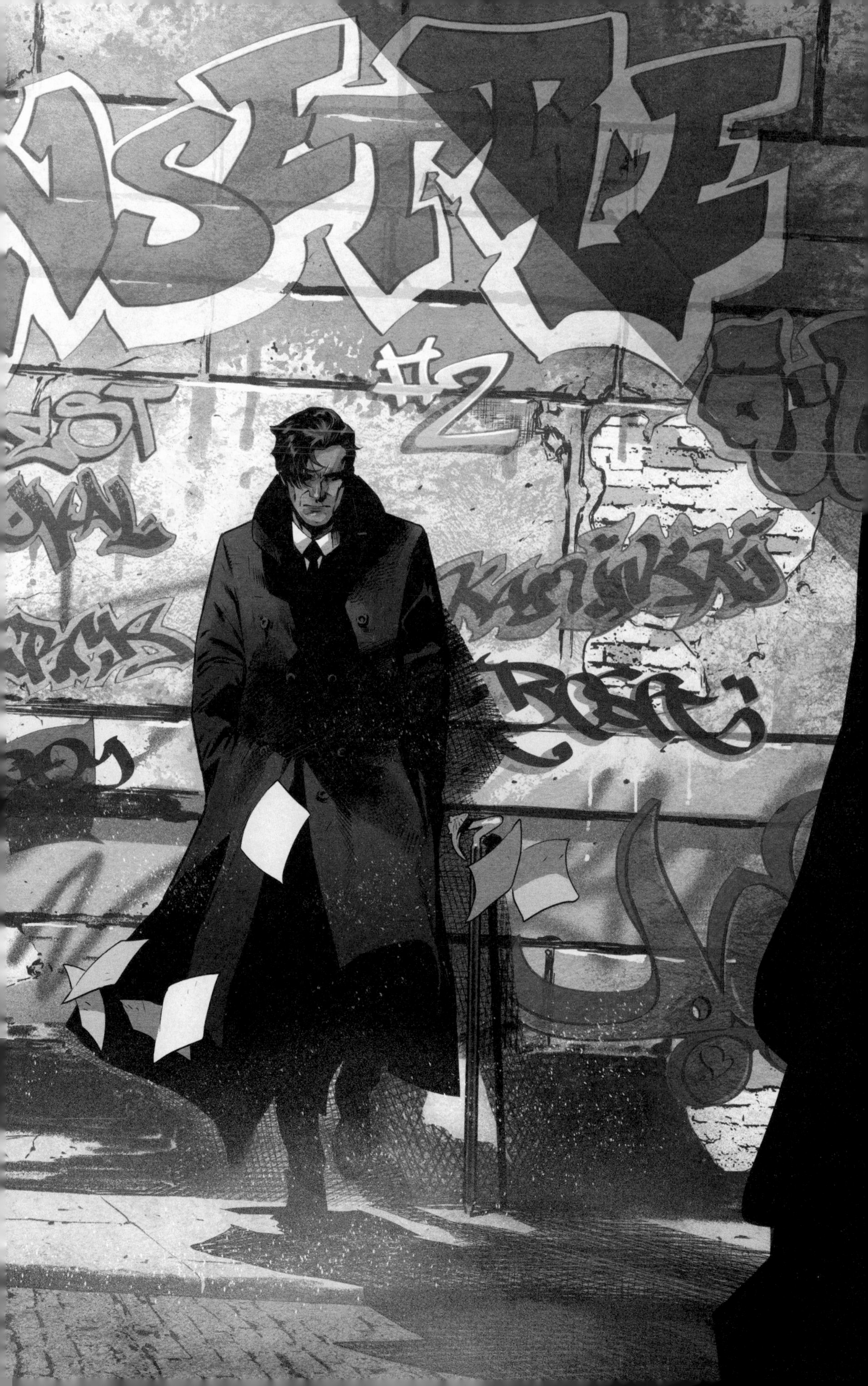
#2

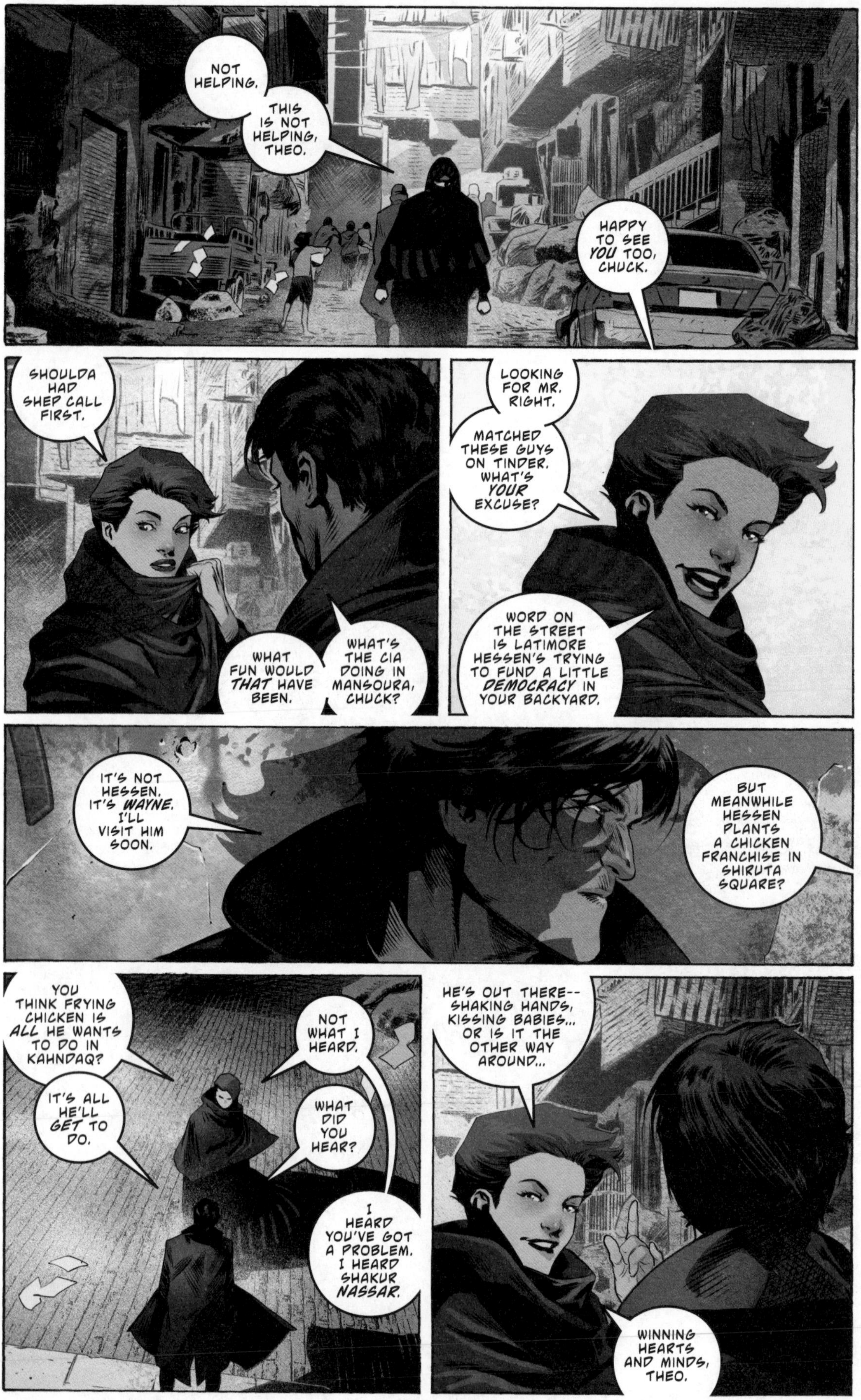
NOT HELPING.
THIS IS NOT HELPING, THEO.
HAPPY TO SEE YOU TOO, CHUCK.
SHOULDA HAD SHEP CALL FIRST.
WHAT FUN WOULD THAT HAVE BEEN.
WHAT'S THE CIA DOING IN MANSOURA, CHUCK?
LOOKING FOR MR. RIGHT.
MATCHED THESE GUYS ON TINDER. WHAT'S YOUR EXCUSE?
WORD ON THE STREET IS LATIMORE HESSEN'S TRYING TO FUND A LITTLE DEMOCRACY IN YOUR BACKYARD.
IT'S NOT HESSEN. IT'S WAYNE. I'LL VISIT HIM SOON.
BUT MEANWHILE HESSEN PLANTS A CHICKEN FRANCHISE IN SHIRUTA SQUARE?
YOU THINK FRYING CHICKEN IS ALL HE WANTS TO DO IN KAHNDAQ?
IT'S ALL HE'LL GET TO DO.
NOT WHAT I HEARD.
WHAT DID YOU HEAR?
I HEARD YOU'VE GOT A PROBLEM. I HEARD SHAKUR NASSAR.
HE'S OUT THERE-- SHAKING HANDS, KISSING BABIES... OR IS IT THE OTHER WAY AROUND...
WINNING HEARTS AND MINDS, THEO.

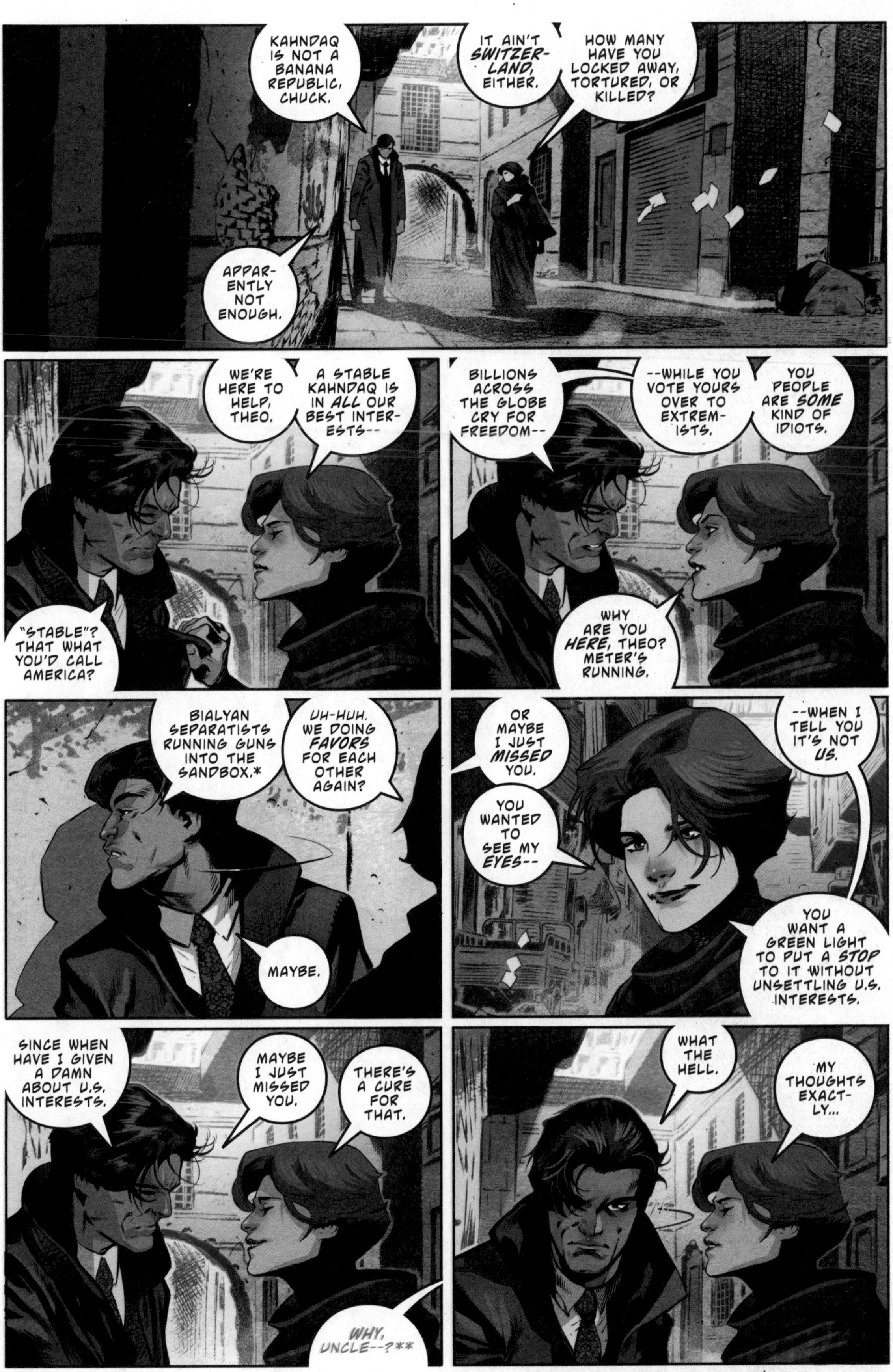
KAHNDAQ IS NOT A BANANA REPUBLIC, CHUCK.
IT AIN'T SWITZERLAND, EITHER.
HOW MANY HAVE YOU LOCKED AWAY, TORTURED, OR KILLED?
APPARENTLY NOT ENOUGH.
WE'RE HERE TO HELP, THEO.
A STABLE KAHNDAQ IS IN ALL OUR BEST INTERESTS--
"STABLE"? THAT WHAT YOU'D CALL AMERICA?
BILLIONS ACROSS THE GLOBE CRY FOR FREEDOM--
--WHILE YOU VOTE YOURS OVER TO EXTREMISTS.
YOU PEOPLE ARE SOME KIND OF IDIOTS.
WHY ARE YOU HERE, THEO? METER'S RUNNING.
BIALYAN SEPARATISTS RUNNING GUNS INTO THE SANDBOX.*
UH-HUH. WE DOING FAVORS FOR EACH OTHER AGAIN?
MAYBE.
OR MAYBE I JUST MISSED YOU.
YOU WANTED TO SEE MY EYES--
--WHEN I TELL YOU IT'S NOT US.
YOU WANT A GREEN LIGHT TO PUT A STOP TO IT WITHOUT UNSETTLING U.S. INTERESTS.
SINCE WHEN HAVE I GIVEN A DAMN ABOUT U.S. INTERESTS.
MAYBE I JUST MISSED YOU.
THERE'S A CURE FOR THAT.
WHY, UNCLE--?**
WHAT THE HELL.
MY THOUGHTS EXACTLY...

*BIALYA=COUNTRY BORDERING KAHNDAQ
SANDBOX=PALESTINIAN TERRITORIES
**TRANSLATED FROM ARABIC

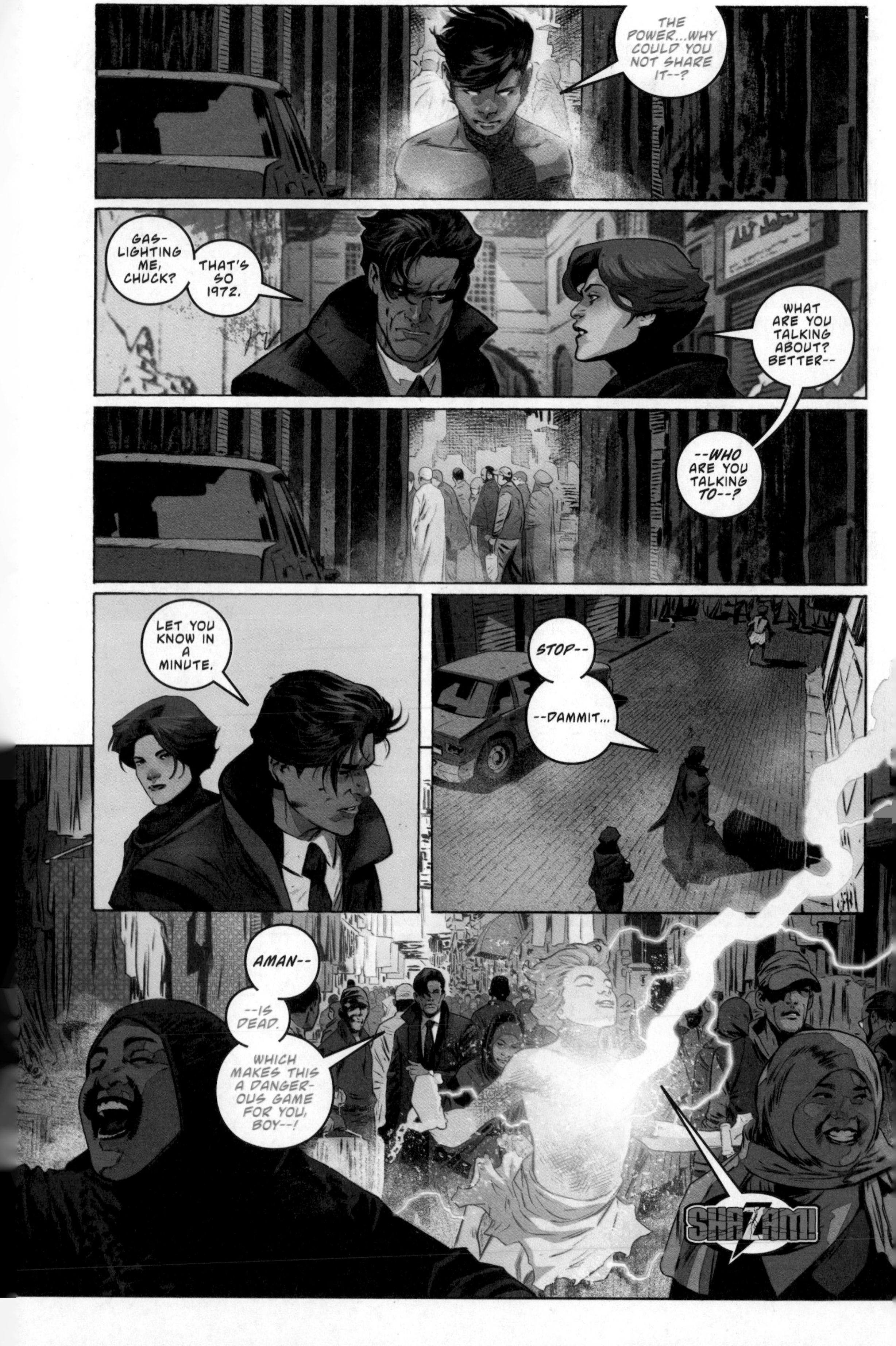
THE POWER...WHY COULD YOU NOT SHARE IT--?
GAS-LIGHTING ME, CHUCK?
THAT'S SO 1972.
WHAT ARE YOU TALKING ABOUT? BETTER--
--WHO ARE YOU TALKING TO--?
LET YOU KNOW IN A MINUTE.
STOP--
--DAMMIT...
AMAN--
--IS DEAD.
WHICH MAKES THIS A DANGER-OUS GAME FOR YOU, BOY--!
SHAZAM!

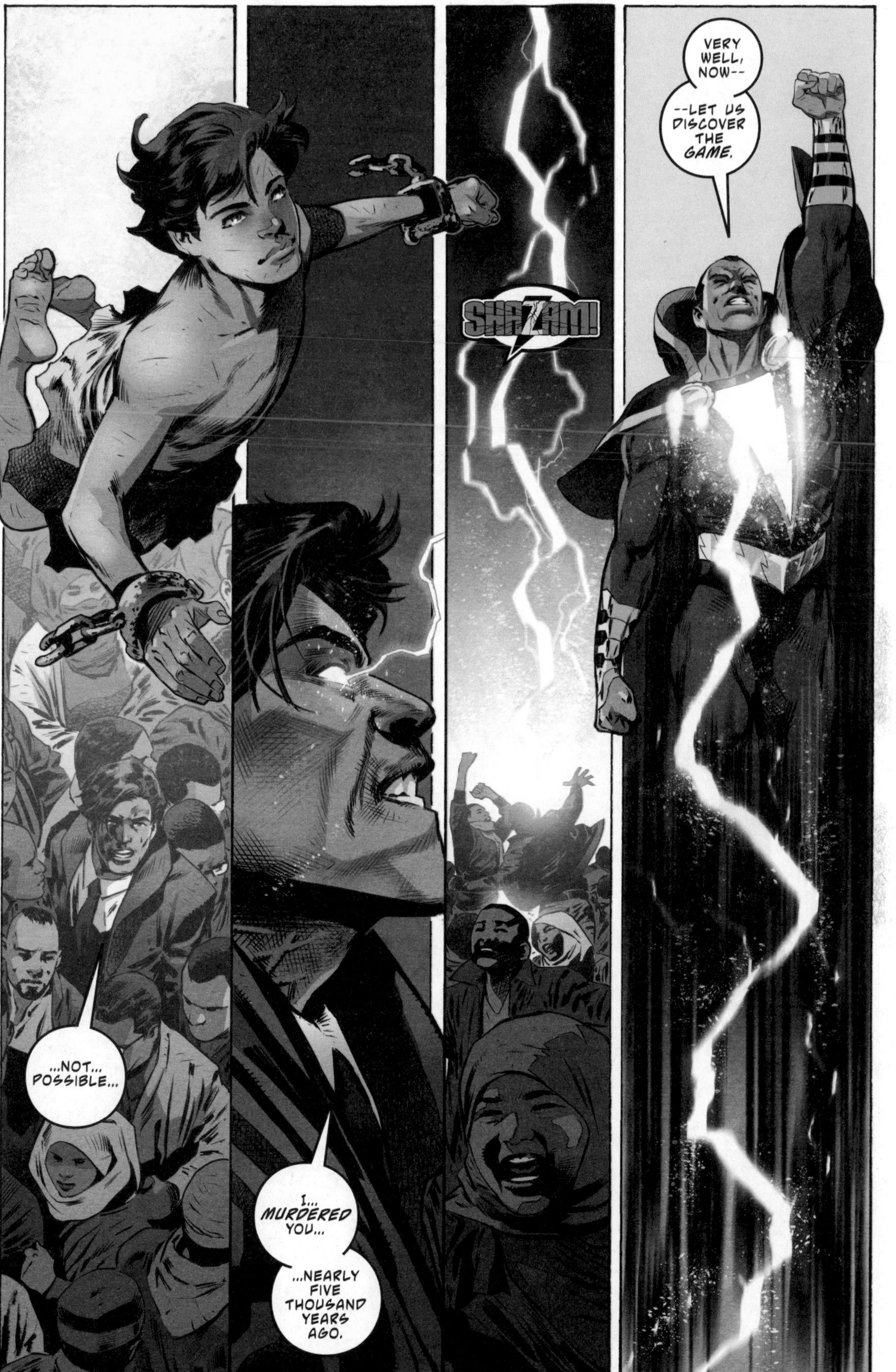
...NOT... POSSIBLE...
I... MURDERED YOU...
...NEARLY FIVE THOUSAND YEARS AGO.
SHAZAM!
VERY WELL, NOW--
--LET US DISCOVER THE GAME.

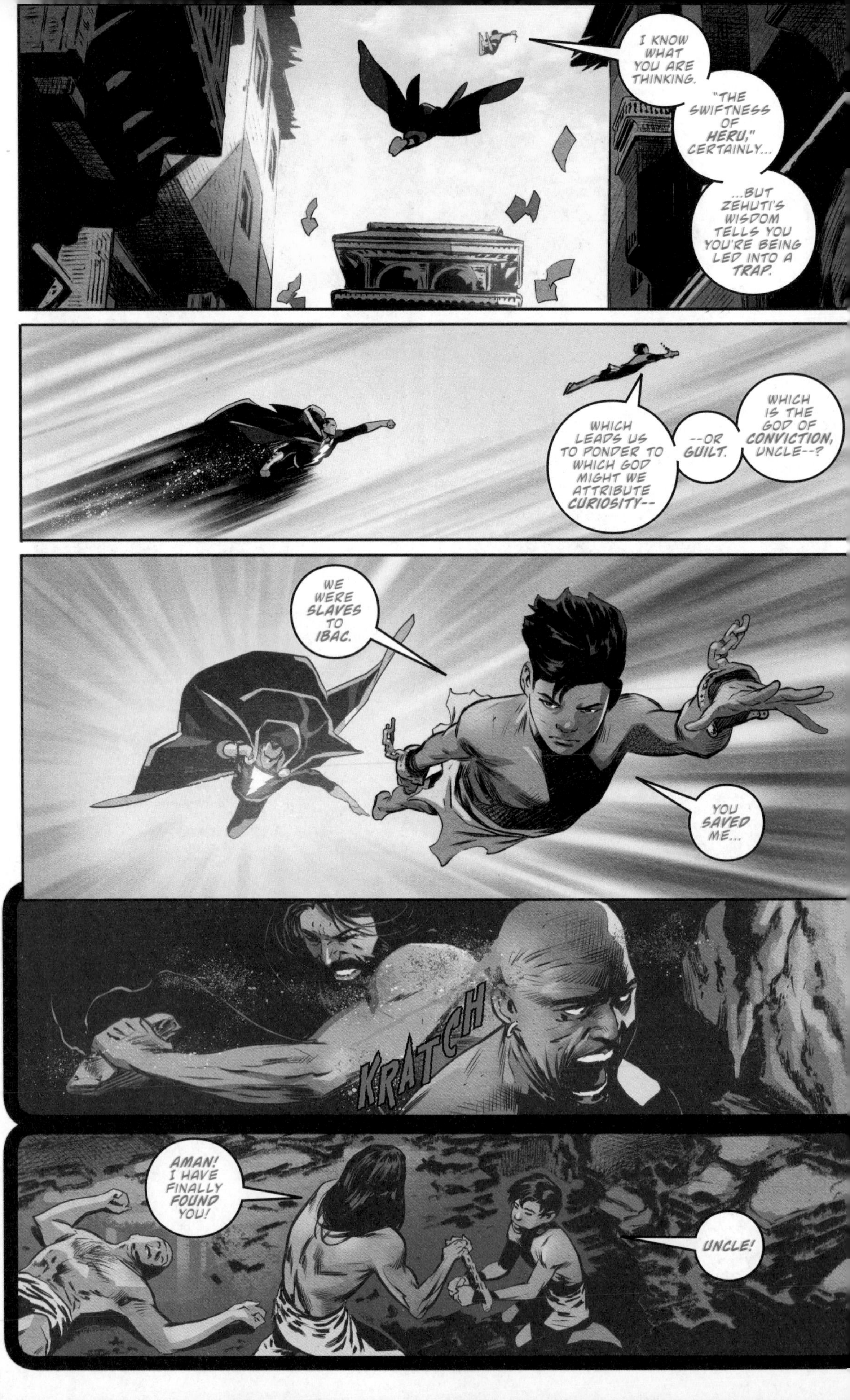
I KNOW WHAT YOU ARE THINKING.
"THE SWIFTNESS OF HERU," CERTAINLY...
...BUT ZEHUTI'S WISDOM TELLS YOU YOU'RE BEING LED INTO A TRAP.
WHICH LEADS US TO PONDER TO WHICH GOD MIGHT WE ATTRIBUTE CURIOSITY--
--OR GUILT.
WHICH IS THE GOD OF CONVICTION, UNCLE--?
WE WERE SLAVES TO IBAC.
YOU SAVED ME...
KRATCH
AMAN! I HAVE FINALLY FOUND YOU!
UNCLE!

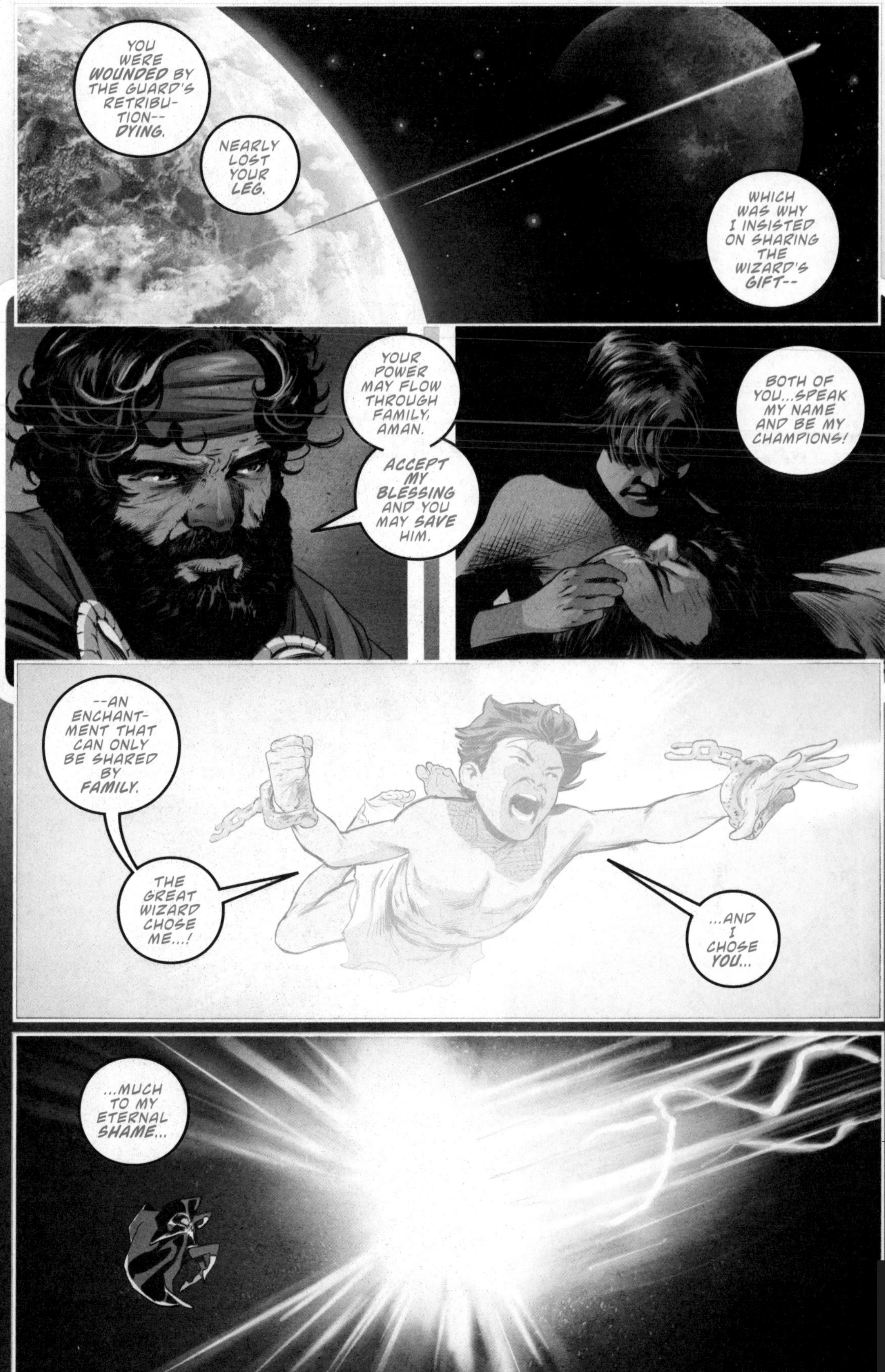
YOU WERE WOUNDED BY THE GUARD'S RETRIBUTION--DYING.
NEARLY LOST YOUR LEG.
WHICH WAS WHY I INSISTED ON SHARING THE WIZARD'S GIFT--
YOUR POWER MAY FLOW THROUGH FAMILY, AMAN.
ACCEPT MY BLESSING AND YOU MAY SAVE HIM.
BOTH OF YOU...SPEAK MY NAME AND BE MY CHAMPIONS!
--AN ENCHANTMENT THAT CAN ONLY BE SHARED BY FAMILY.
THE GREAT WIZARD CHOSE ME...!
...AND I CHOSE YOU...
...MUCH TO MY ETERNAL SHAME...

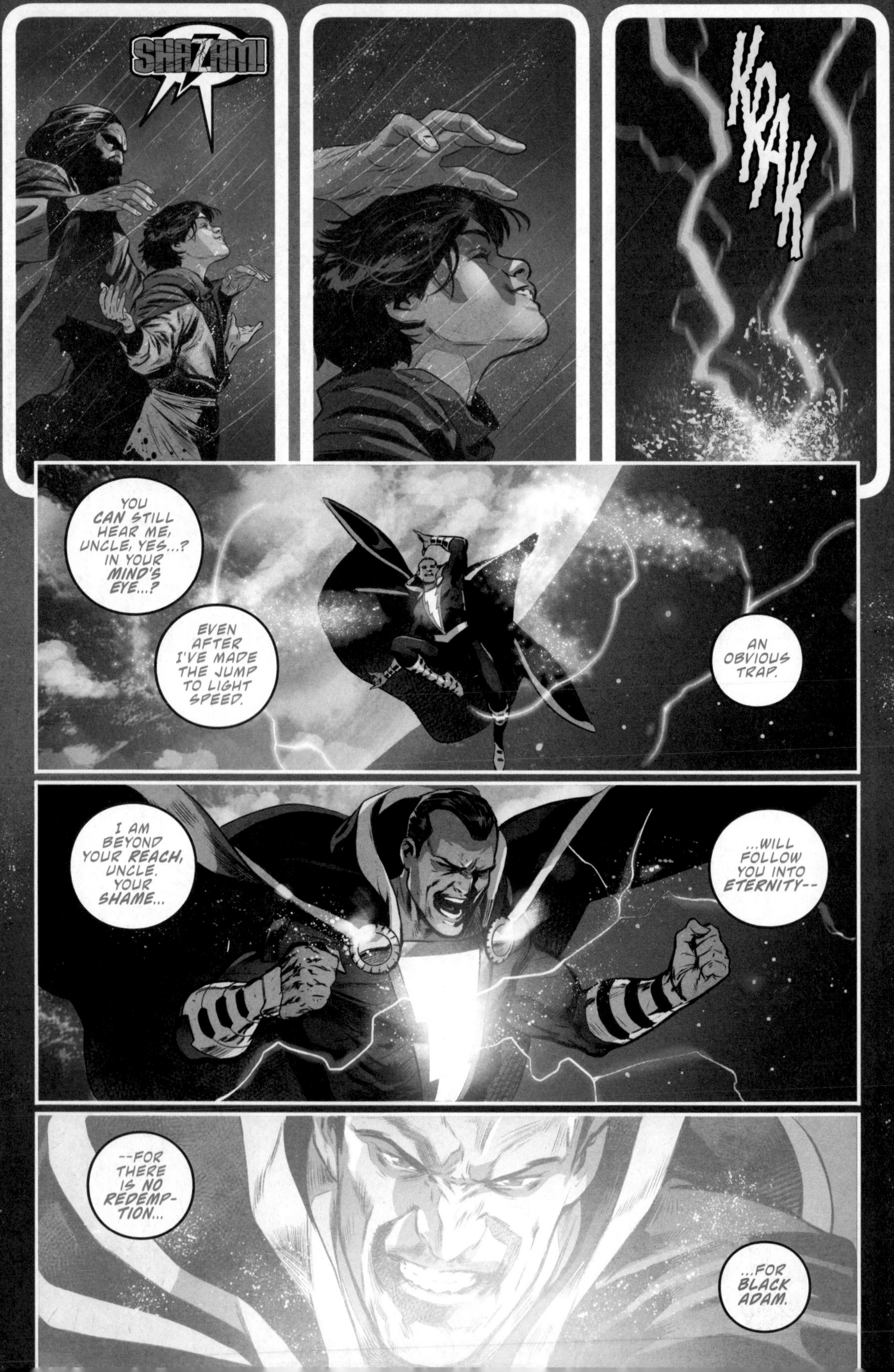

SHAZAM!
KRAK
YOU CAN STILL HEAR ME, UNCLE, YES...? IN YOUR MIND'S EYE...?
EVEN AFTER I'VE MADE THE JUMP TO LIGHT SPEED.
AN OBVIOUS TRAP.
I AM BEYOND YOUR REACH, UNCLE. YOUR SHAME...
...WILL FOLLOW YOU INTO ETERNITY--
--FOR THERE IS NO REDEMP-TION...
...FOR BLACK ADAM.

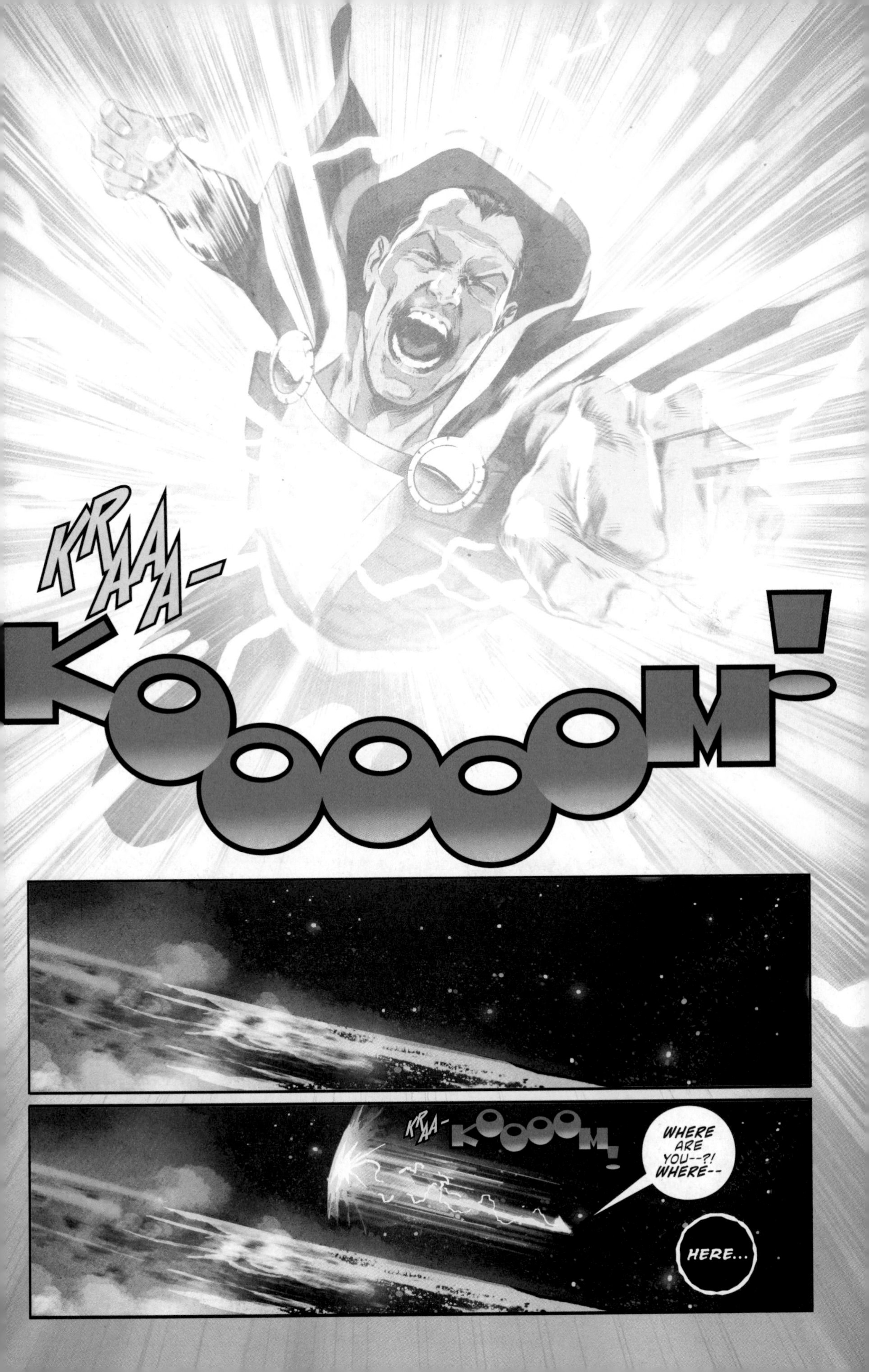

KRAAA-
KOOOOOM!
KRAA-KOOOOOM!
WHERE ARE YOU--?! WHERE--
HERE...

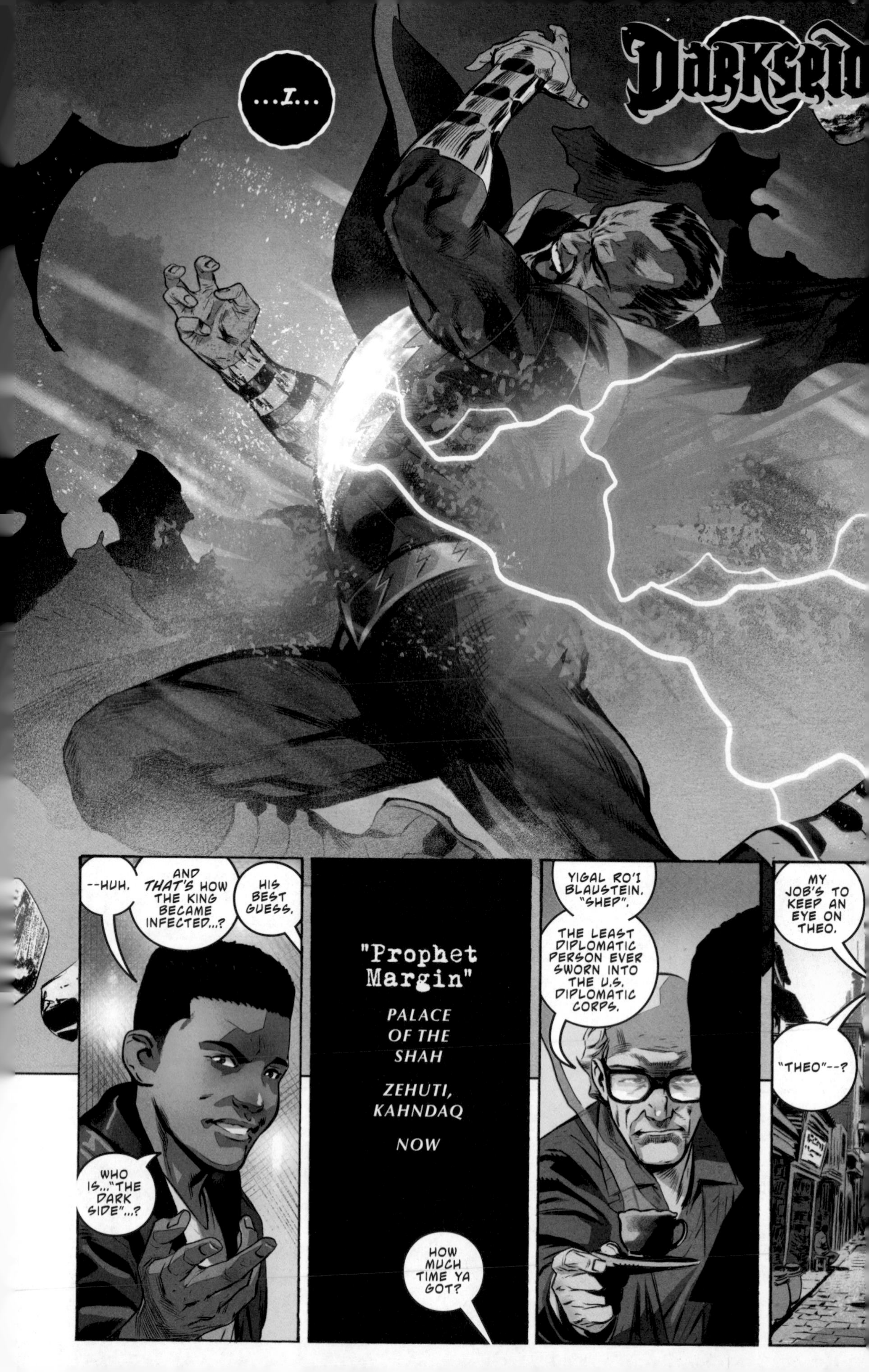
...I...
Darkseid
--HUH.
AND THAT'S HOW THE KING BECAME INFECTED...?
HIS BEST GUESS.
WHO IS..."THE DARK SIDE"...?
"Prophet Margin"
PALACE OF THE SHAH
ZEHUTI, KAHNDAQ
NOW
HOW MUCH TIME YA GOT?
YIGAL RO'I BLAUSTEIN. "SHEP".
THE LEAST DIPLOMATIC PERSON EVER SWORN INTO THE U.S. DIPLOMATIC CORPS.
MY JOB'S TO KEEP AN EYE ON THEO.
"THEO"--?

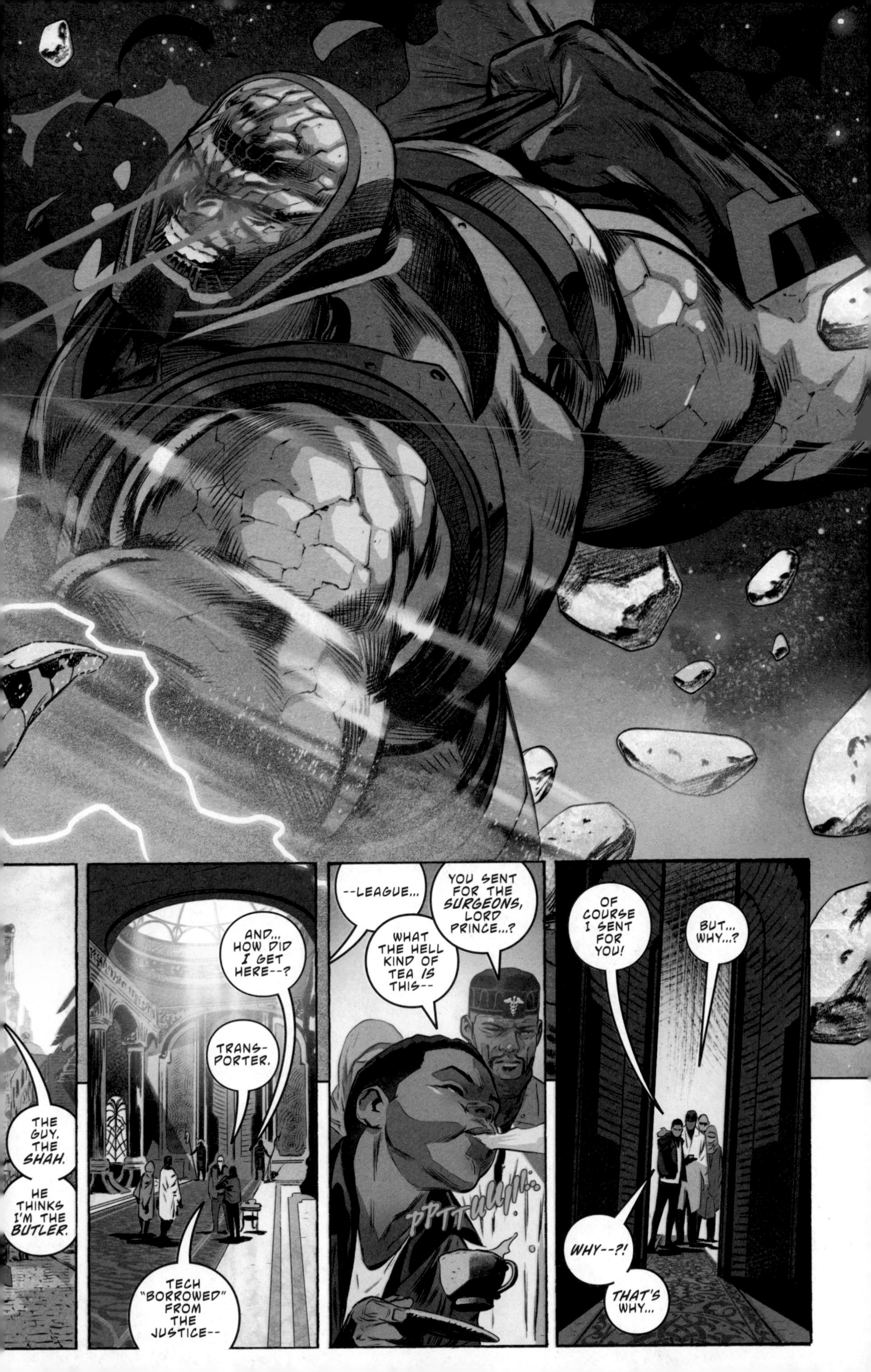
THE GUY. THE SHAH.
HE THINKS I'M THE BUTLER.
AND... HOW DID I GET HERE--?
TRANS-PORTER.
TECH "BORROWED" FROM THE JUSTICE--
--LEAGUE...
YOU SENT FOR THE SURGEONS, LORD PRINCE...?
WHAT THE HELL KIND OF TEA IS THIS--
PPTTTUUUH!!..
OF COURSE I SENT FOR YOU!
BUT... WHY...?
WHY--?!
THAT'S WHY...

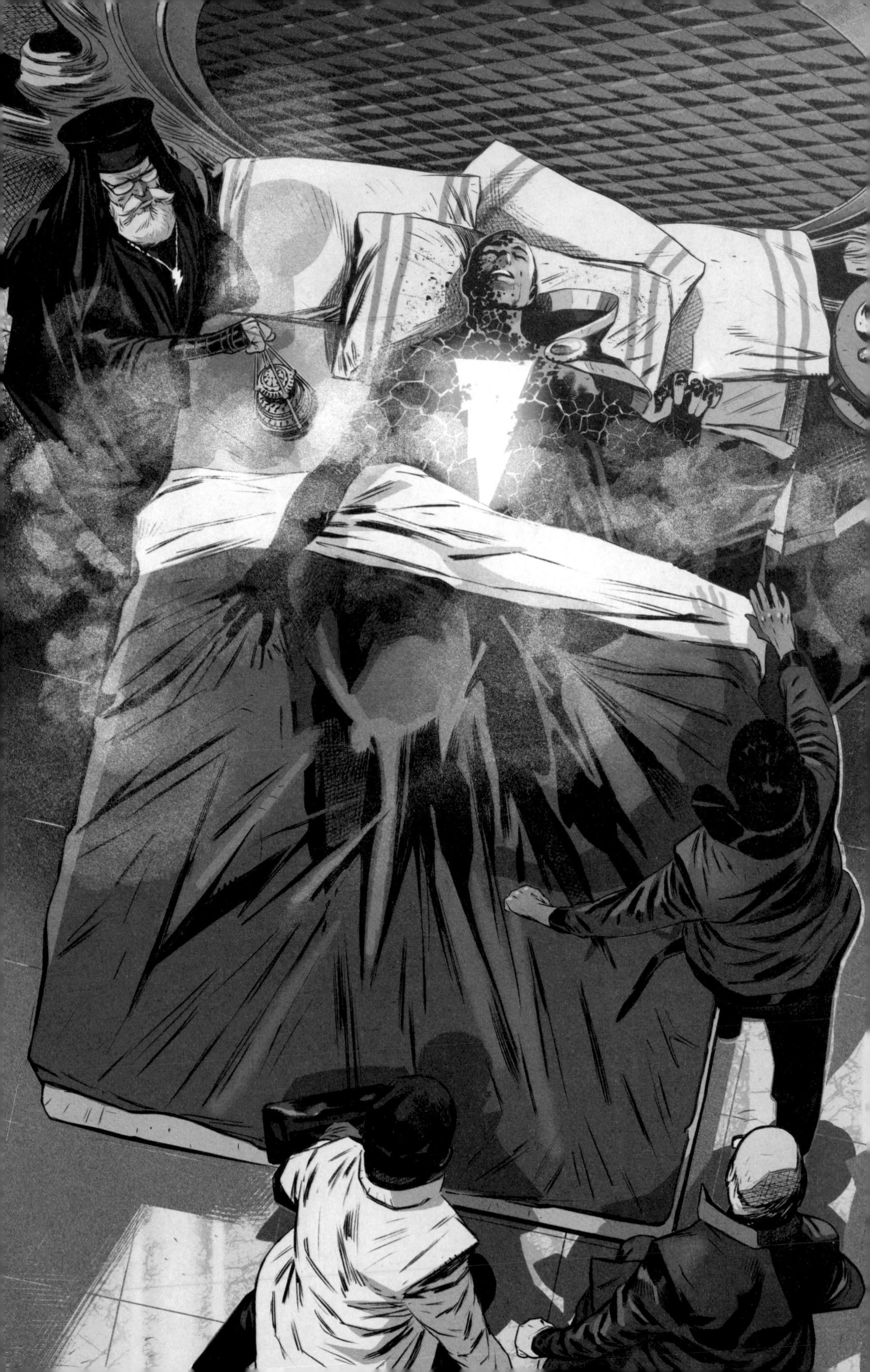

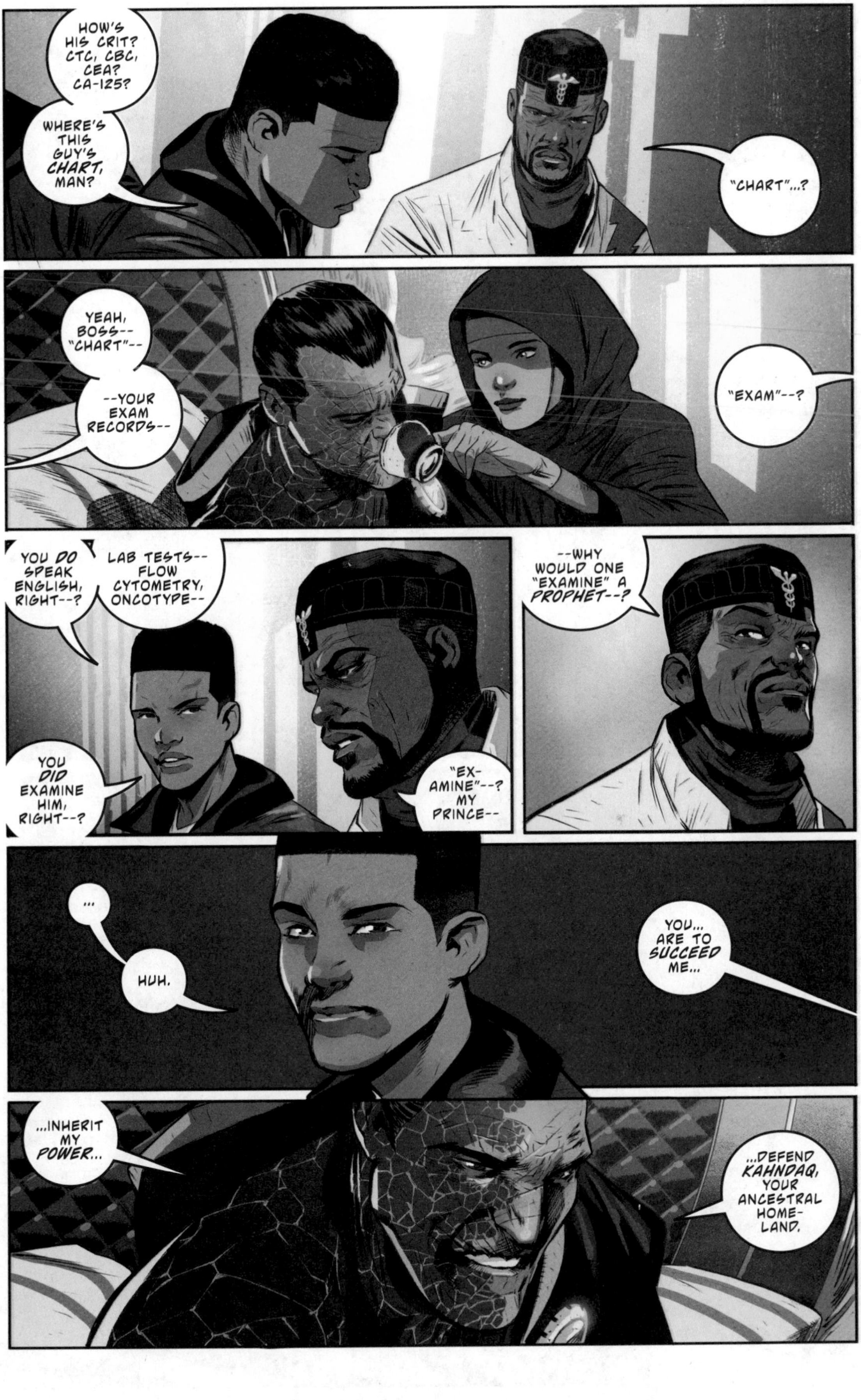
HOW'S HIS CRIT? CTC, CBC, CEA? CA-125?
WHERE'S THIS GUY'S CHART, MAN?
"CHART"...?
YEAH, BOSS-- "CHART"--
--YOUR EXAM RECORDS--
"EXAM"--?
YOU DO SPEAK ENGLISH, RIGHT--?
LAB TESTS-- FLOW CYTOMETRY, ONCOTYPE--
YOU DID EXAMINE HIM, RIGHT--?
"EX-AMINE"--? MY PRINCE--
--WHY WOULD ONE "EXAMINE" A PROPHET--?
...
HUH.
YOU... ARE TO SUCCEED ME...
...INHERIT MY POWER...
...DEFEND KAHNDAQ, YOUR ANCESTRAL HOME-LAND.

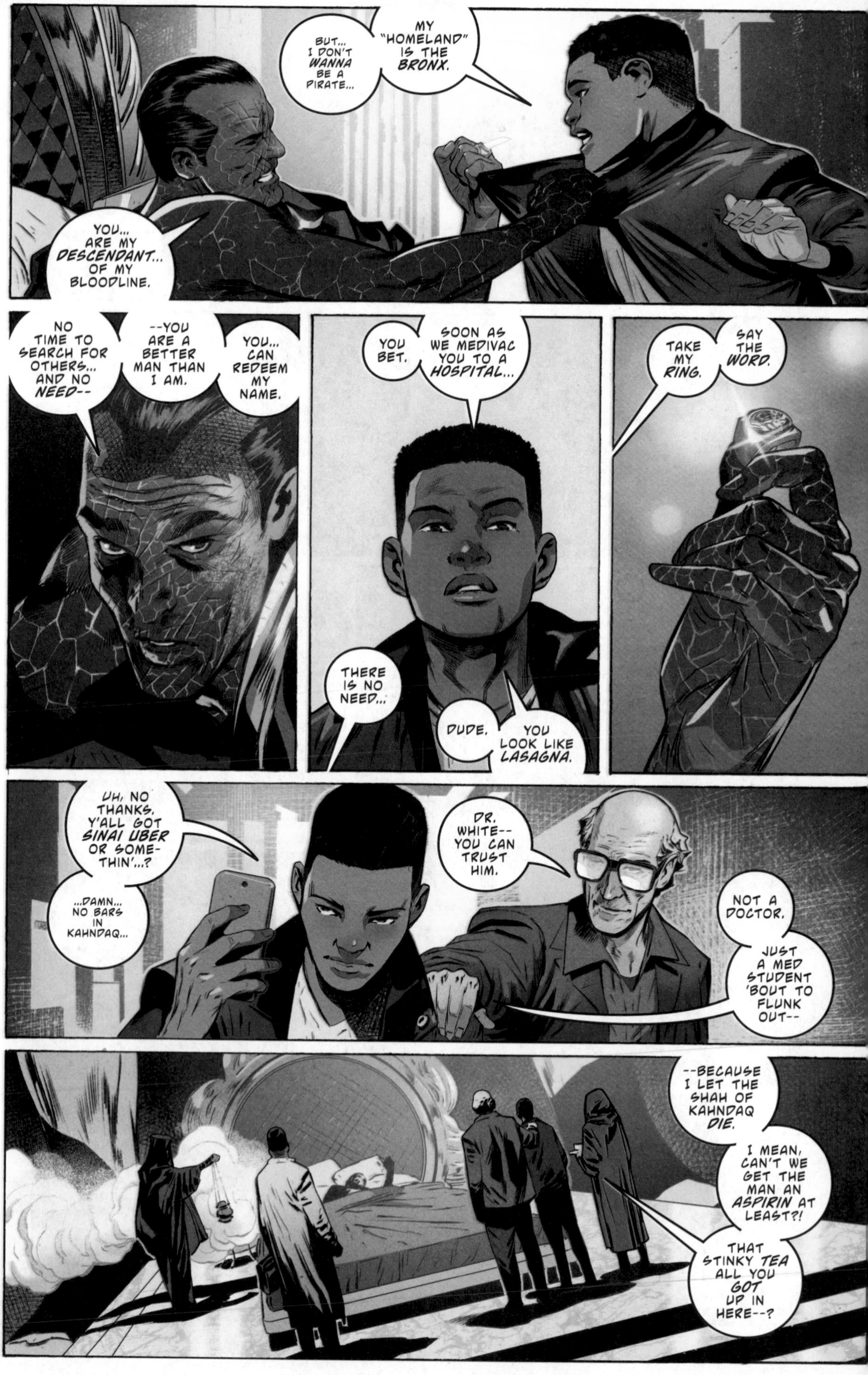
BUT... I DON'T WANNA BE A PIRATE...
MY "HOMELAND" IS THE BRONX.
YOU... ARE MY DESCENDANT... OF MY BLOODLINE.
NO TIME TO SEARCH FOR OTHERS... AND NO NEED--
--YOU ARE A BETTER MAN THAN I AM.
YOU... CAN REDEEM MY NAME.
YOU BET.
SOON AS WE MEDIVAC YOU TO A HOSPITAL...
THERE IS NO NEED...
DUDE.
YOU LOOK LIKE LASAGNA.
TAKE MY RING.
SAY THE WORD.
UH, NO THANKS. Y'ALL GOT SINAI UBER OR SOME-THIN'...?
...DAMN... NO BARS IN KAHNDAQ...
DR. WHITE-- YOU CAN TRUST HIM.
NOT A DOCTOR.
JUST A MED STUDENT 'BOUT TO FLUNK OUT--
--BECAUSE I LET THE SHAH OF KAHNDAQ DIE.
I MEAN, CAN'T WE GET THE MAN AN ASPIRIN AT LEAST?!
THAT STINKY TEA ALL YOU GOT UP IN HERE--?

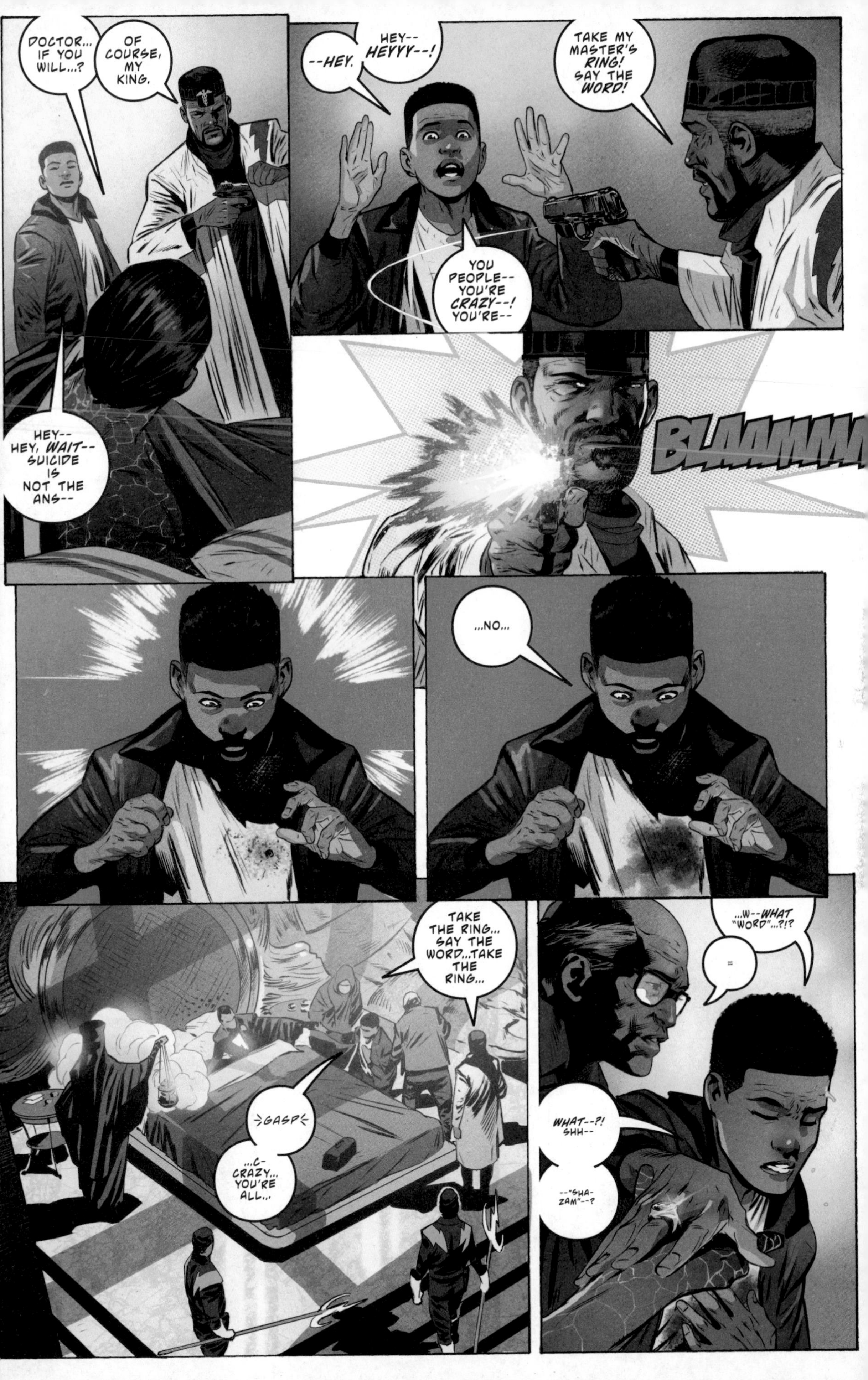
DOCTOR... IF YOU WILL...?
OF COURSE, MY KING.
HEY--HEY, WAIT--SUICIDE IS NOT THE ANS--
--HEY.
HEY--HEYYY--!
TAKE MY MASTER'S RING! SAY THE WORD!
YOU PEOPLE--YOU'RE CRAZY--! YOU'RE--
BLAAMMM
...NO...
TAKE THE RING... SAY THE WORD...TAKE THE RING...
GASP
...C-CRAZY... YOU'RE ALL...
...W--WHAT "WORD"...?!?
WHAT--?! SHH--
--"SHA-ZAM"--?

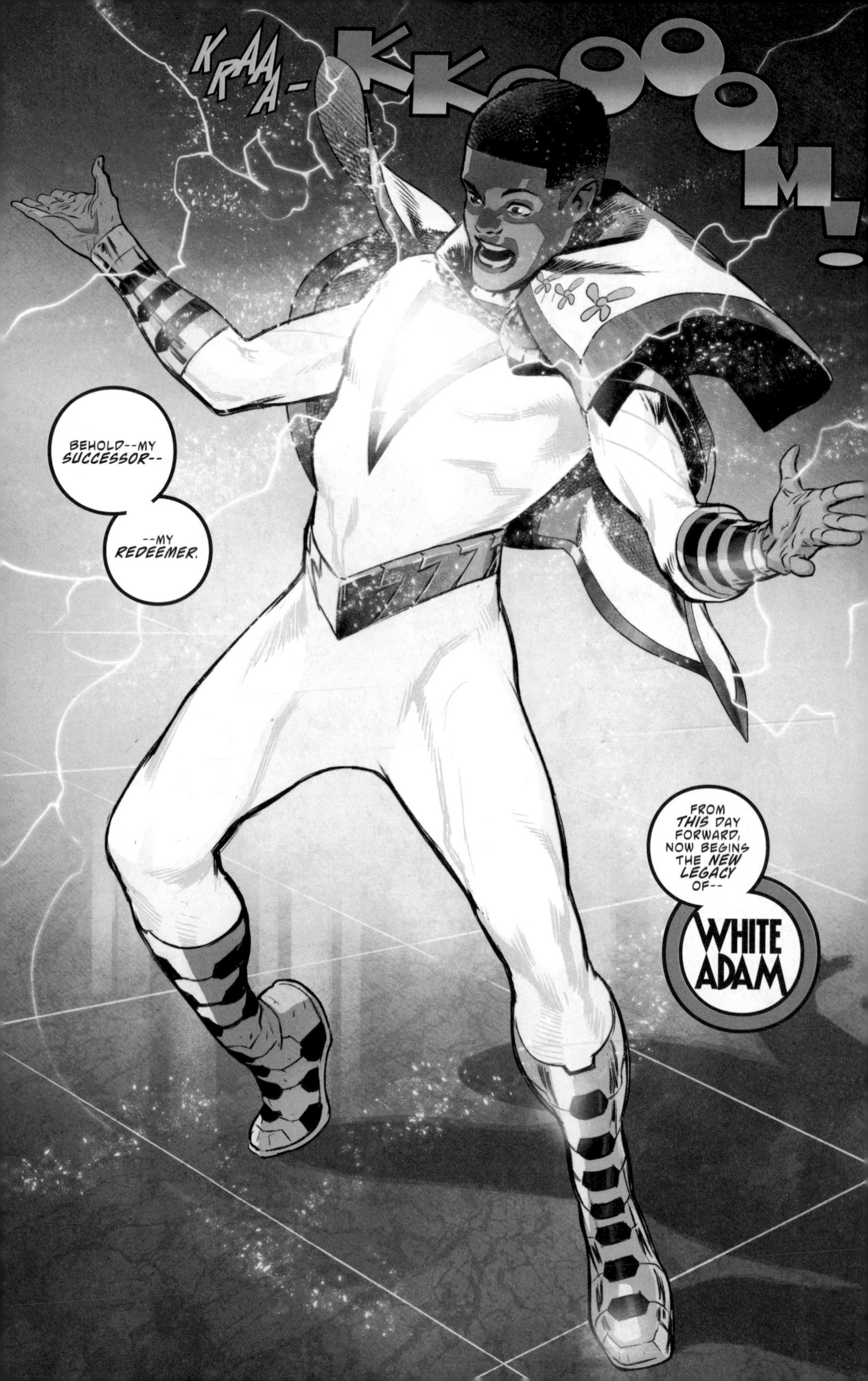
KRAAA-KKOOOOOM!
BEHOLD--MY SUCCESSOR--
--MY REDEEMER.
FROM THIS DAY FORWARD, NOW BEGINS THE NEW LEGACY OF--
WHITE ADAM

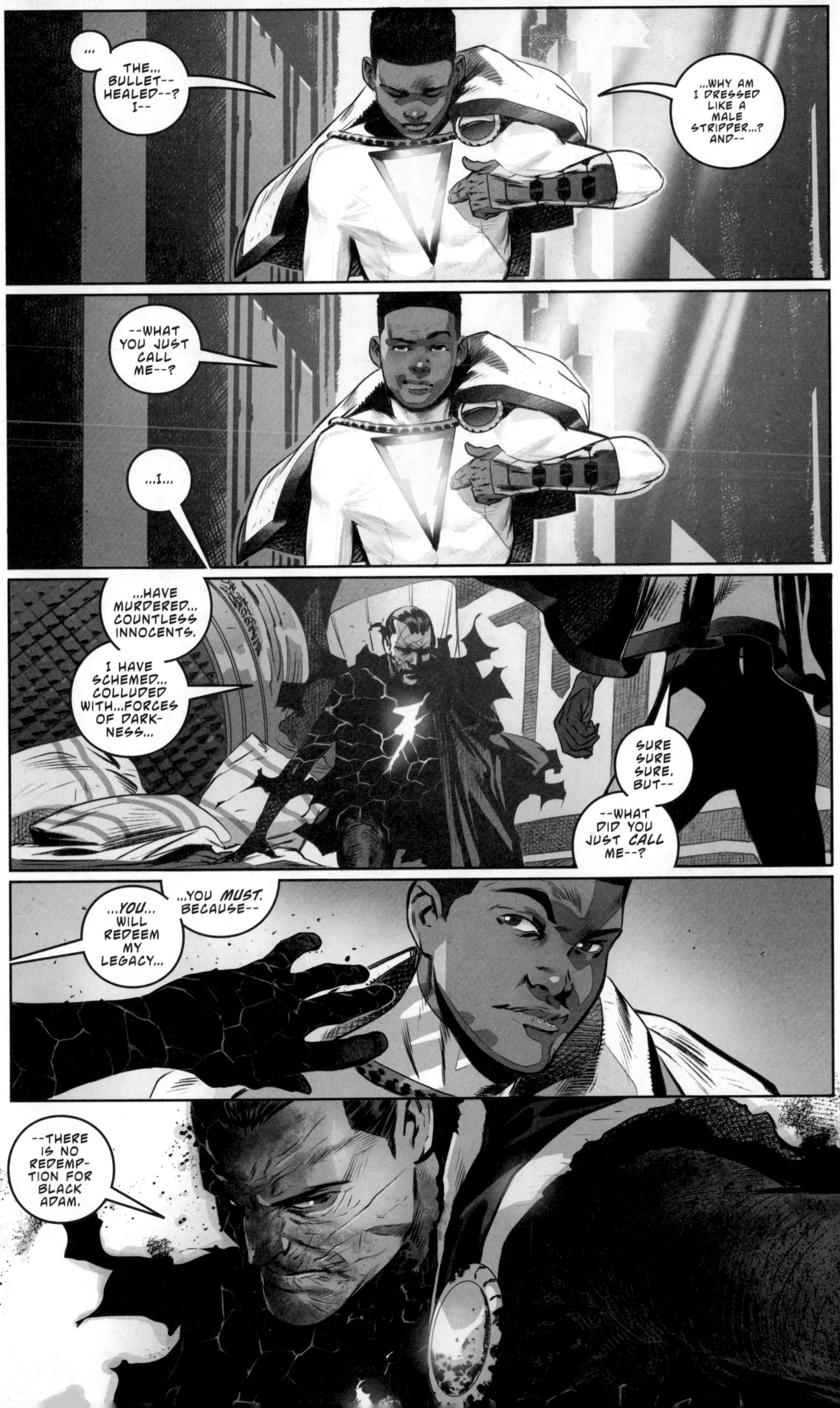
...
THE... BULLET-- HEALED--? I--
...WHY AM I DRESSED LIKE A MALE STRIPPER...? AND--
--WHAT YOU JUST CALL ME--?
...I...
...HAVE MURDERED... COUNTLESS INNOCENTS.
I HAVE SCHEMED... COLLUDED WITH...FORCES OF DARK-NESS...
SURE SURE SURE. BUT--
--WHAT DID YOU JUST *CALL* ME--?
...*YOU*... WILL REDEEM MY LEGACY...
...YOU *MUST*. BECAUSE--
--THERE IS NO REDEMP-TION FOR BLACK ADAM.

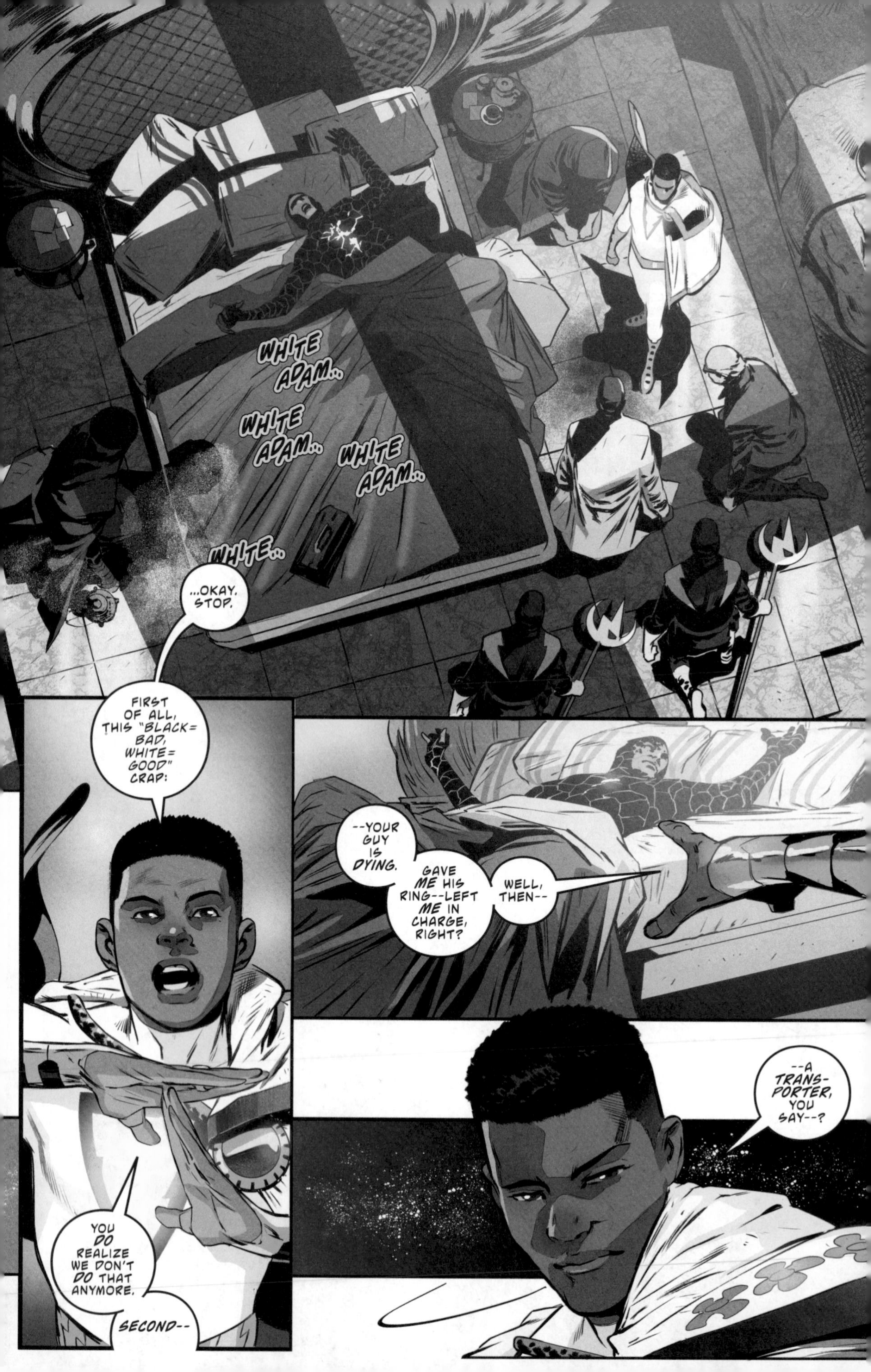

WHITE ADAM..
WHITE ADAM..
WHITE ADAM..
WHITE..
...OKAY. STOP.
FIRST OF ALL, THIS "BLACK= BAD, WHITE= GOOD" CRAP:
YOU DO REALIZE WE DON'T DO THAT ANYMORE.
SECOND--
--YOUR GUY IS DYING.
GAVE ME HIS RING--LEFT ME IN CHARGE, RIGHT?
WELL, THEN--
--A TRANSPORTER, YOU SAY--?

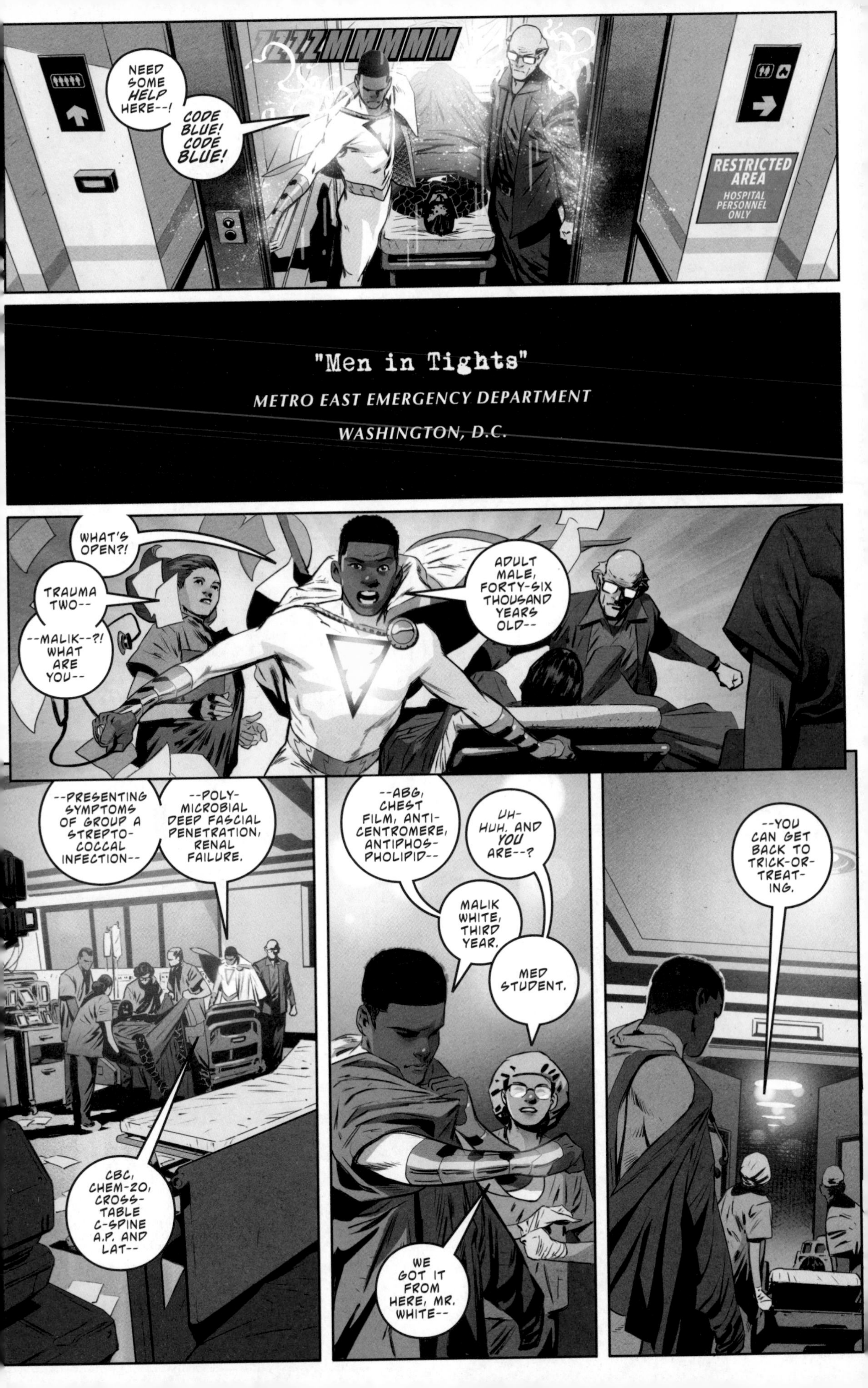
ZZZZMMMMMM
NEED SOME HELP HERE--!
CODE BLUE! CODE BLUE!
RESTRICTED AREA
HOSPITAL PERSONNEL ONLY
"Men in Tights"
METRO EAST EMERGENCY DEPARTMENT
WASHINGTON, D.C.
WHAT'S OPEN?!
TRAUMA TWO--
--MALIK--?! WHAT ARE YOU--
ADULT MALE, FORTY-SIX THOUSAND YEARS OLD--
--PRESENTING SYMPTOMS OF GROUP A STREPTO-COCCAL INFECTION--
--POLY-MICROBIAL DEEP FASCIAL PENETRATION, RENAL FAILURE.
CBC, CHEM-20, CROSS-TABLE C-SPINE A.P. AND LAT--
--ABG, CHEST FILM, ANTI-CENTROMERE, ANTIPHOS-PHOLIPID--
UH-HUH. AND YOU ARE--?
MALIK WHITE, THIRD YEAR.
MED STUDENT.
WE GOT IT FROM HERE, MR. WHITE--
--YOU CAN GET BACK TO TRICK-OR-TREAT-ING.

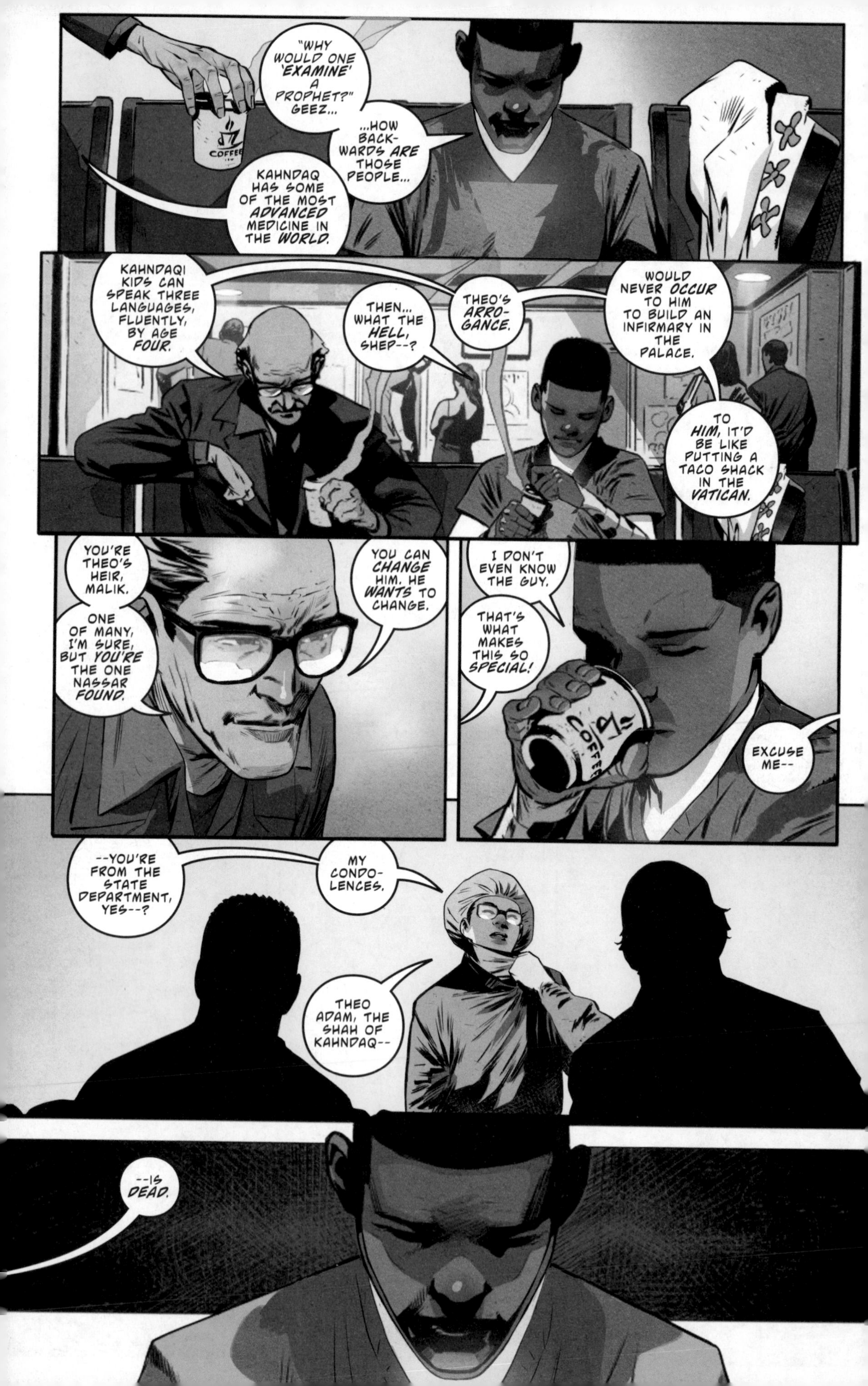
"WHY WOULD ONE 'EXAMINE' A PROPHET?" GEEZ...
...HOW BACKWARDS ARE THOSE PEOPLE...
KAHNDAQ HAS SOME OF THE MOST ADVANCED MEDICINE IN THE WORLD.
KAHNDAQI KIDS CAN SPEAK THREE LANGUAGES, FLUENTLY, BY AGE FOUR.
THEN... WHAT THE HELL, SHEP--?
THEO'S ARROGANCE.
WOULD NEVER OCCUR TO HIM TO BUILD AN INFIRMARY IN THE PALACE.
TO HIM, IT'D BE LIKE PUTTING A TACO SHACK IN THE VATICAN.
YOU'RE THEO'S HEIR, MALIK.
ONE OF MANY, I'M SURE, BUT YOU'RE THE ONE NASSAR FOUND.
YOU CAN CHANGE HIM. HE WANTS TO CHANGE.
I DON'T EVEN KNOW THE GUY.
THAT'S WHAT MAKES THIS SO SPECIAL!
EXCUSE ME--
--YOU'RE FROM THE STATE DEPARTMENT, YES--?
MY CONDOLENCES.
THEO ADAM, THE SHAH OF KAHNDAQ--
--IS DEAD.

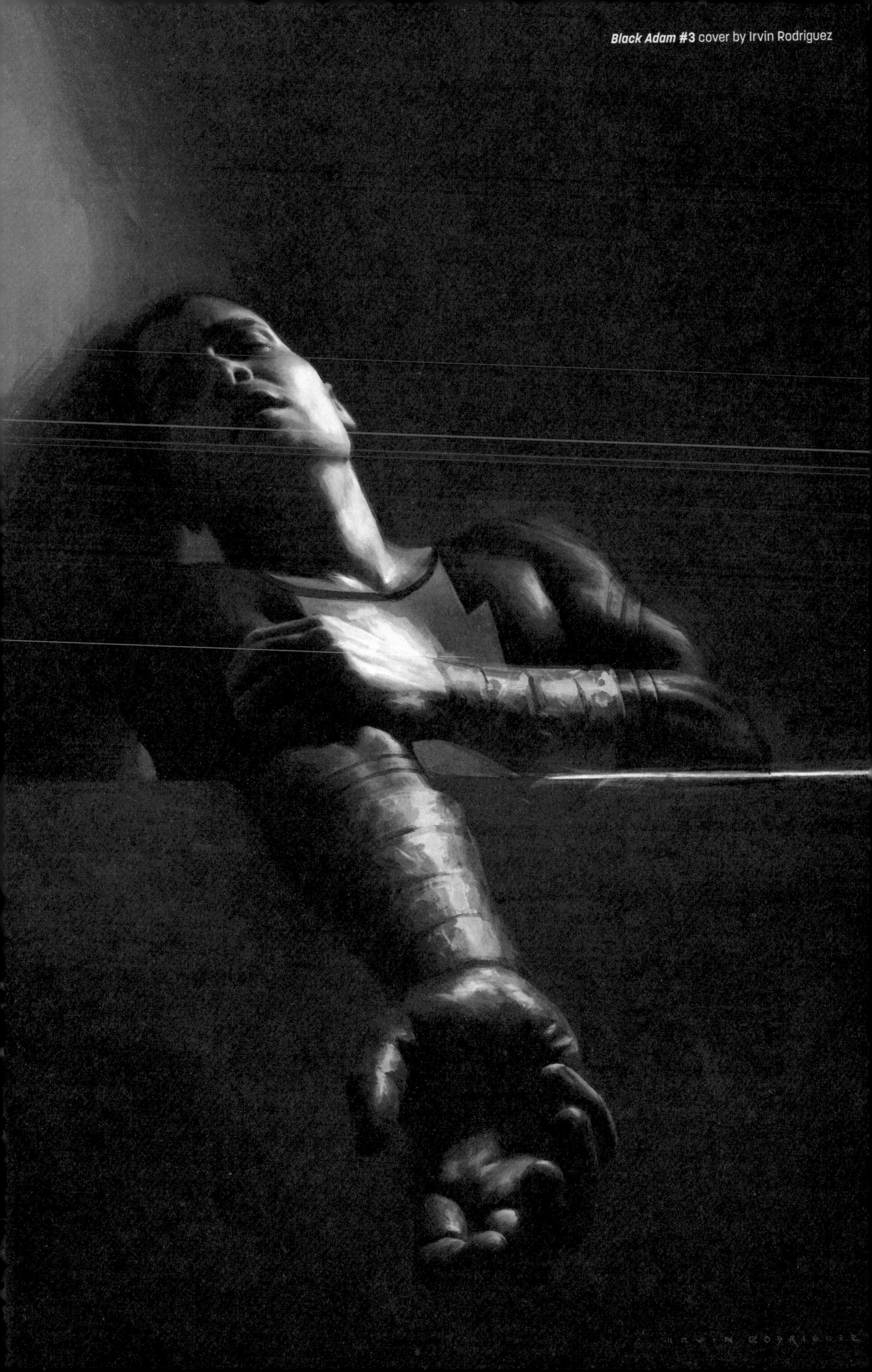

***Black Adam* #3** cover by Irvin Rodriguez

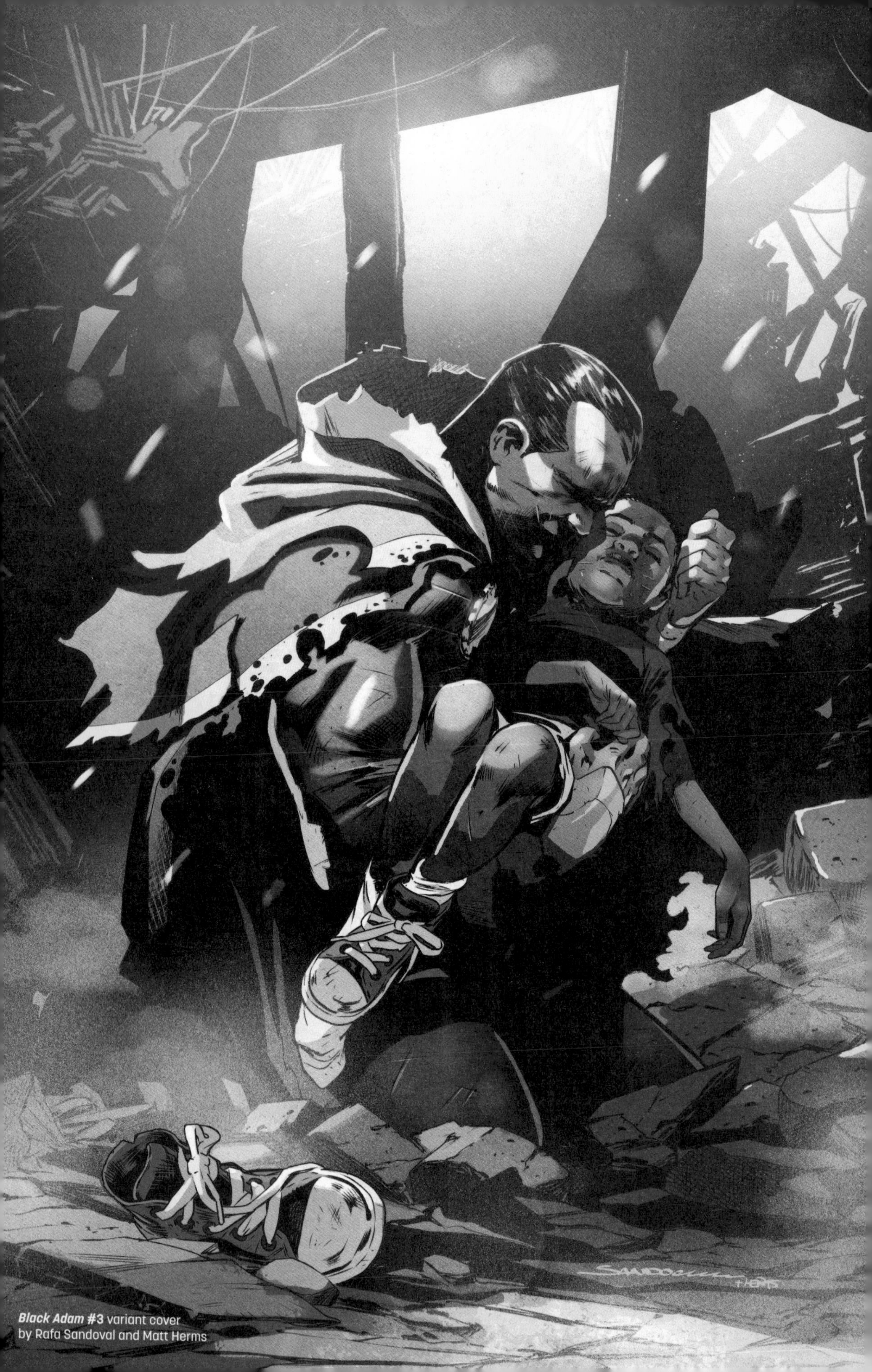
SANDOVAL
+HERMS

Black Adam #3 variant cover
by Rafa Sandoval and Matt Herms

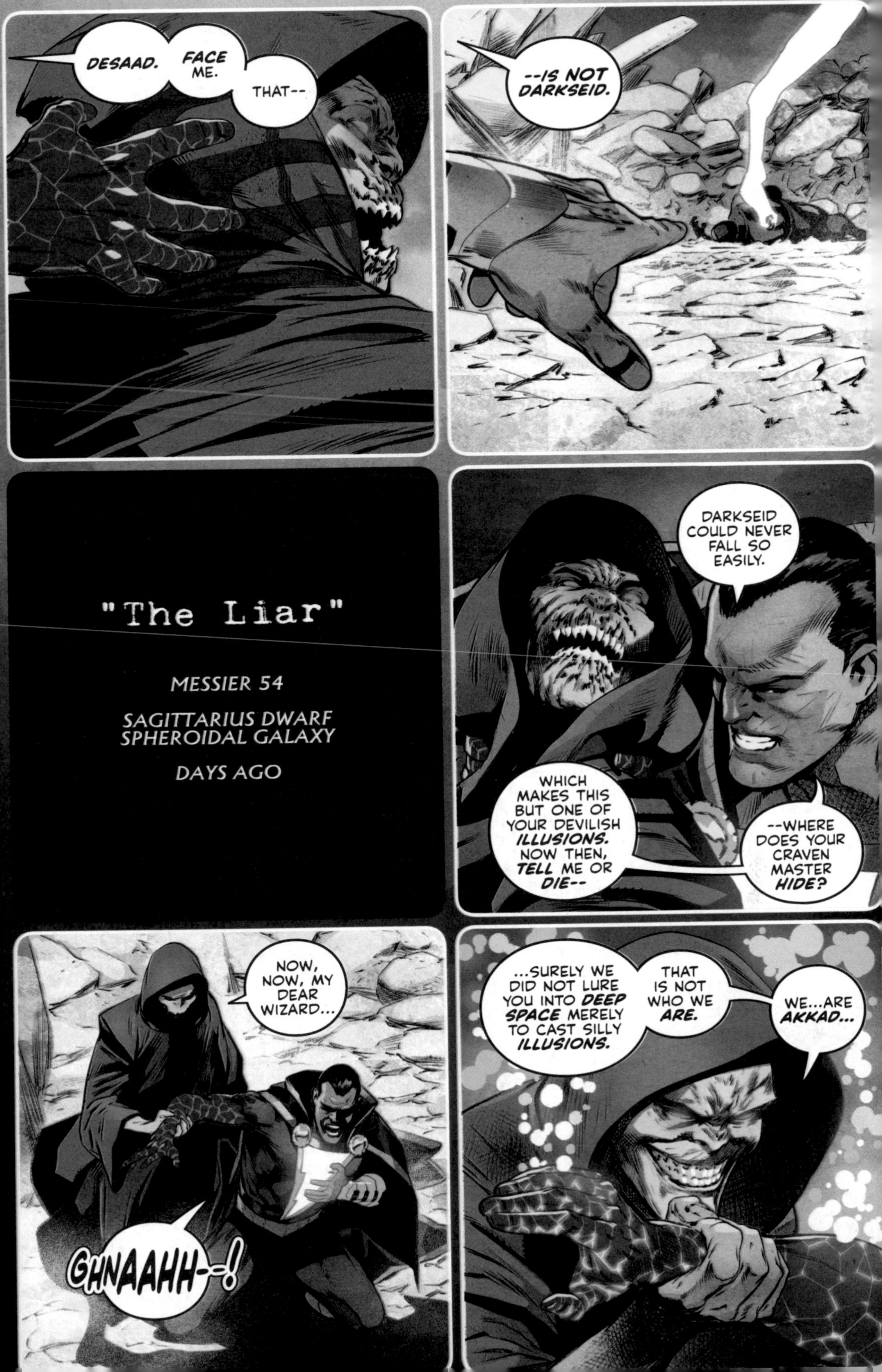
DESAAD.
FACE ME.
THAT--
--IS NOT DARKSEID.
"The Liar"
MESSIER 54
SAGITTARIUS DWARF SPHEROIDAL GALAXY
DAYS AGO
DARKSEID COULD NEVER FALL SO EASILY.
WHICH MAKES THIS BUT ONE OF YOUR DEVILISH ILLUSIONS. NOW THEN, TELL ME OR DIE--
--WHERE DOES YOUR CRAVEN MASTER HIDE?
NOW, NOW, MY DEAR WIZARD...
GHNAAHH--!
...SURELY WE DID NOT LURE YOU INTO DEEP SPACE MERELY TO CAST SILLY ILLUSIONS.
THAT IS NOT WHO WE ARE.
WE...ARE AKKAD...

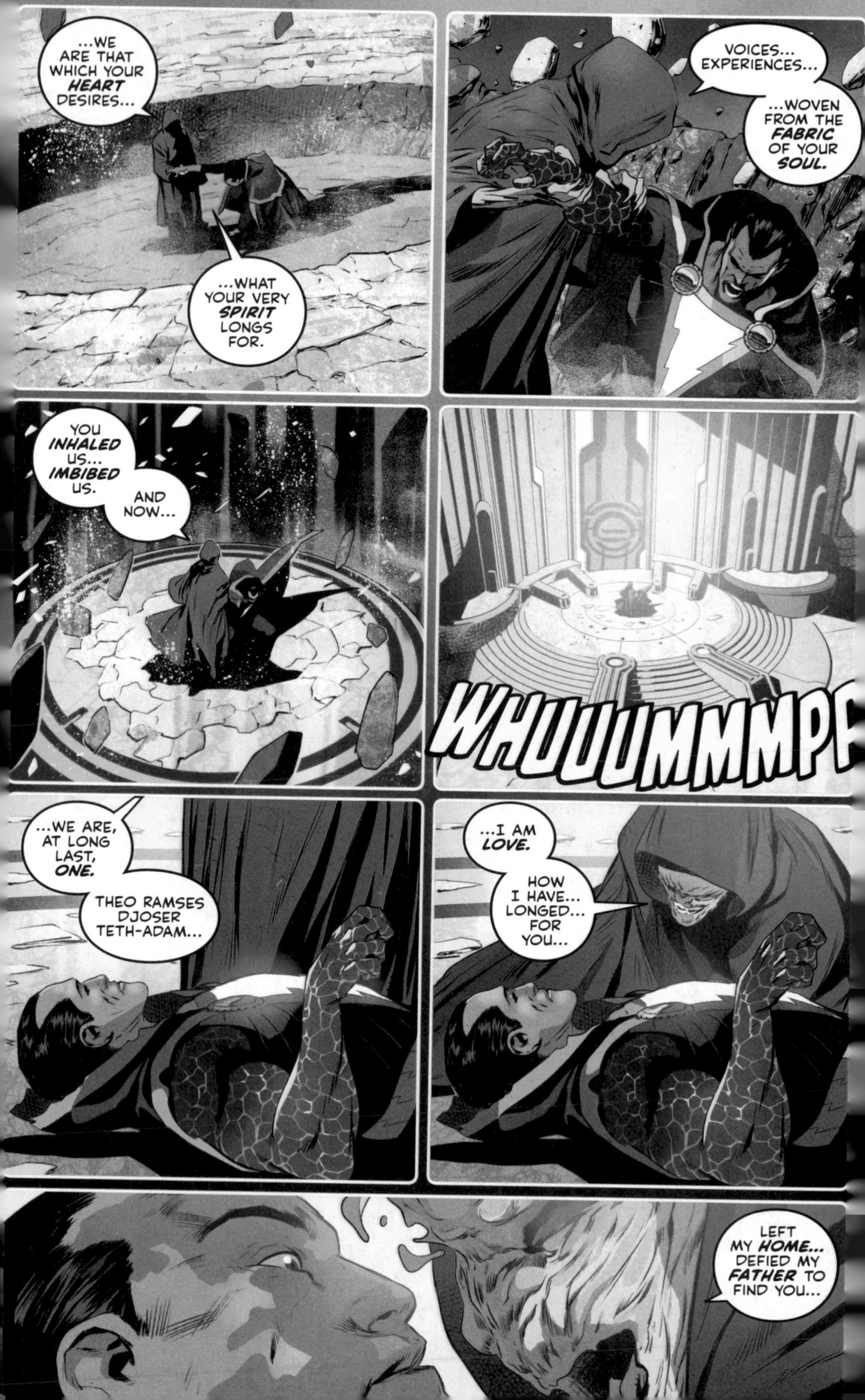
...WE ARE THAT WHICH YOUR HEART DESIRES...
...WHAT YOUR VERY SPIRIT LONGS FOR.
VOICES... EXPERIENCES...
...WOVEN FROM THE FABRIC OF YOUR SOUL.
YOU INHALED US... IMBIBED US.
AND NOW...
WHUUUMMMPF
...WE ARE, AT LONG LAST, ONE.
THEO RAMSES DJOSER TETH-ADAM...
...I AM LOVE.
HOW I HAVE... LONGED... FOR YOU...
LEFT MY HOME... DEFIED MY FATHER TO FIND YOU...

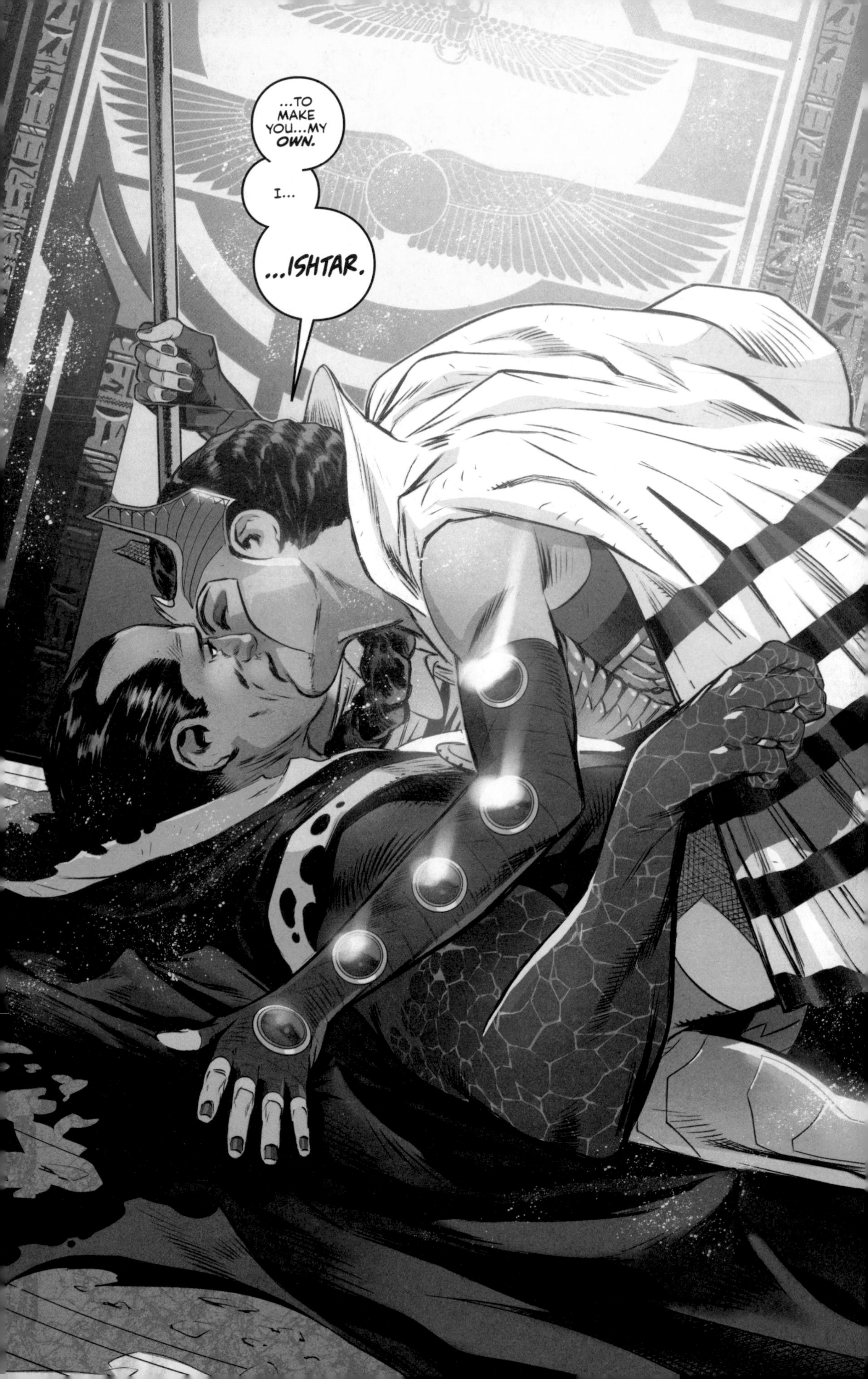
...TO MAKE YOU...MY OWN.
I...
...ISHTAR.

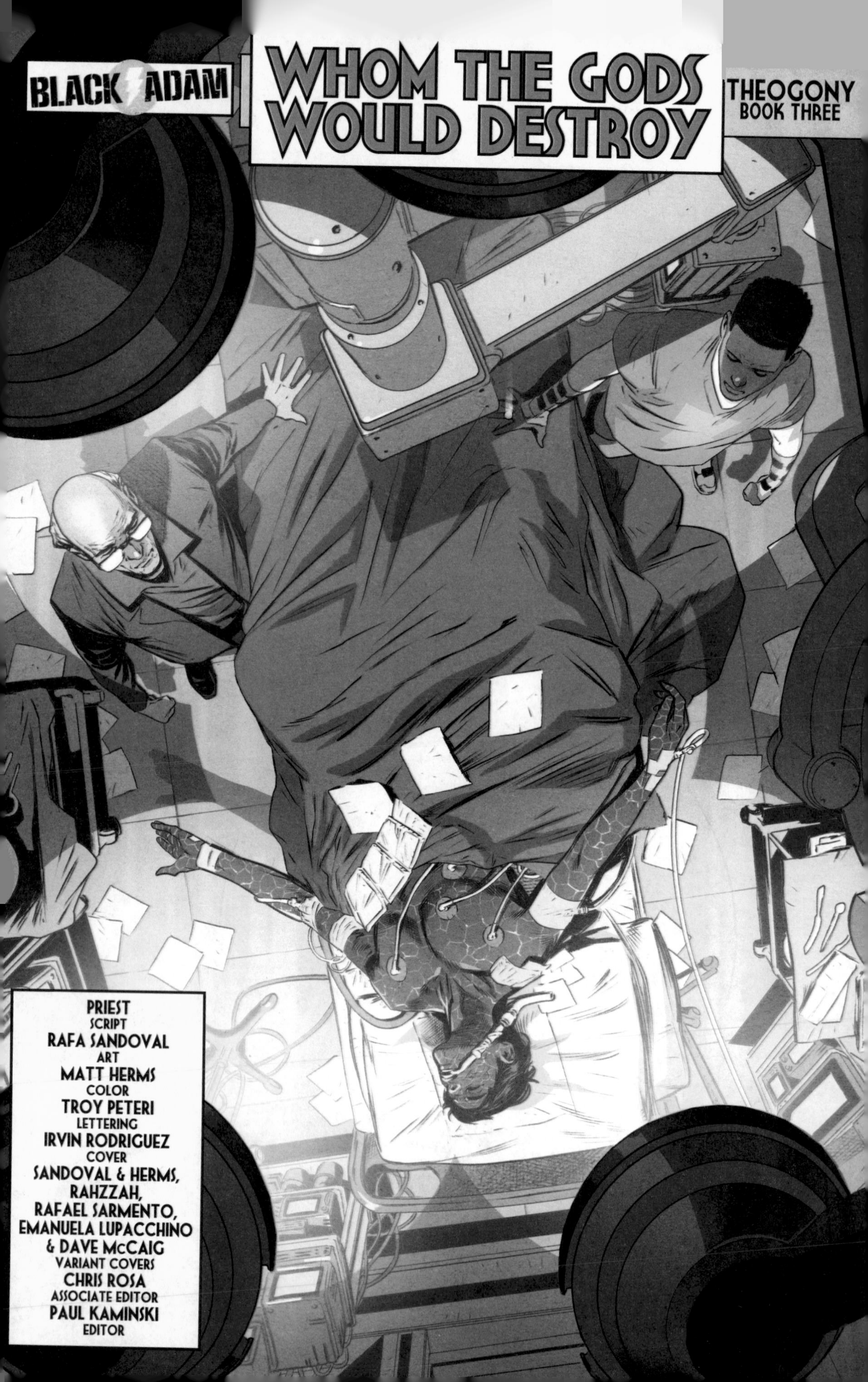

BLACK ADAM
WHOM THE GODS WOULD DESTROY
THEOGONY BOOK THREE
PRIEST SCRIPT
RAFA SANDOVAL ART
MATT HERMS COLOR
TROY PETERI LETTERING
IRVIN RODRIGUEZ COVER
SANDOVAL & HERMS, RAHZZAH, RAFAEL SARMENTO, EMANUELA LUPACCHINO & DAVE McCAIG VARIANT COVERS
CHRIS ROSA ASSOCIATE EDITOR
PAUL KAMINSKI EDITOR

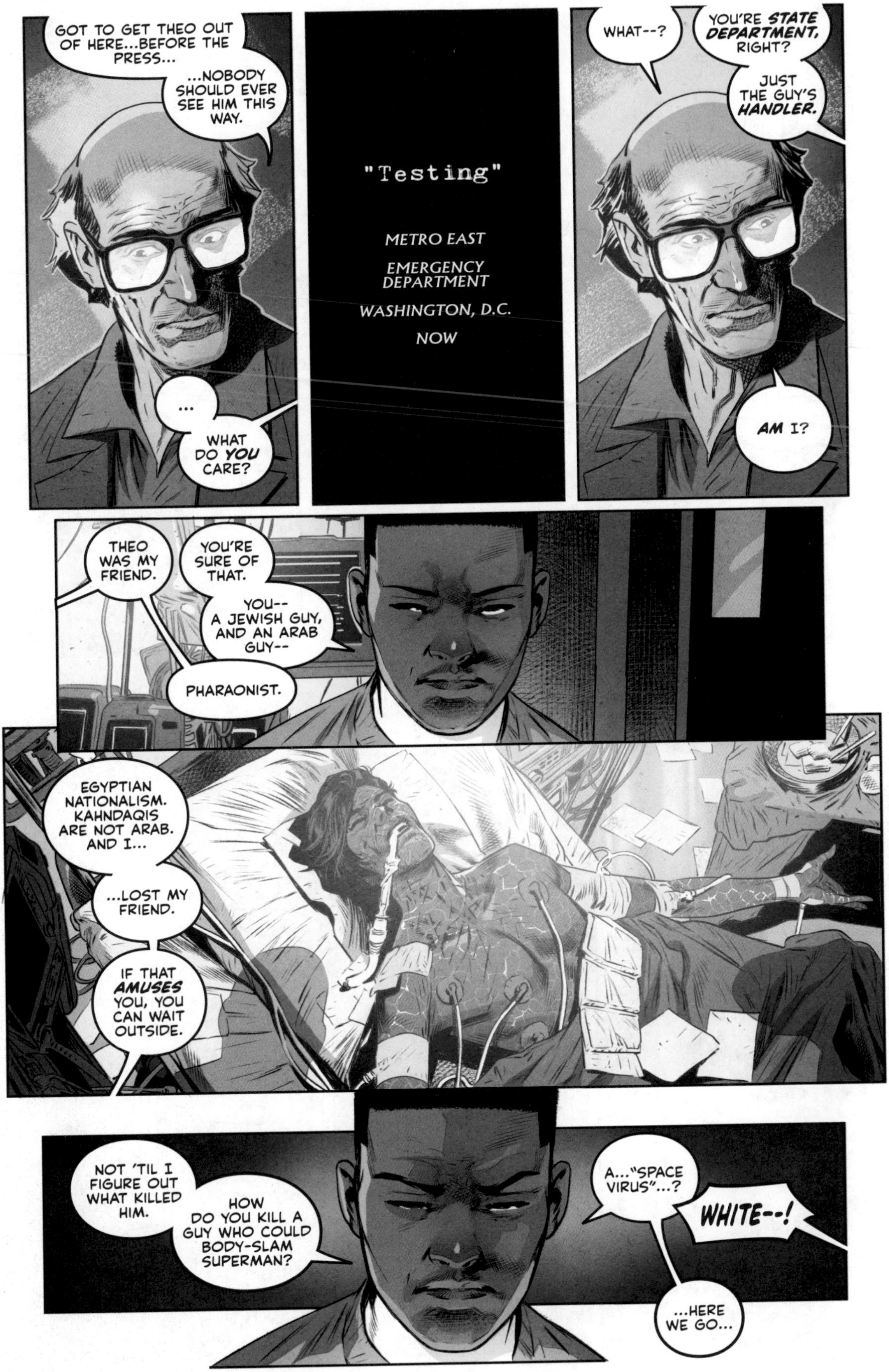
GOT TO GET THEO OUT OF HERE...BEFORE THE PRESS...
...NOBODY SHOULD EVER SEE HIM THIS WAY.
...
WHAT DO *YOU* CARE?
"Testing"
METRO EAST
EMERGENCY DEPARTMENT
WASHINGTON, D.C.
NOW
WHAT--?
YOU'RE *STATE DEPARTMENT,* RIGHT?
JUST THE GUY'S *HANDLER.*
AM I?
THEO WAS MY FRIEND.
YOU'RE SURE OF THAT.
YOU-- A JEWISH GUY, AND AN ARAB GUY--
PHARAONIST.
EGYPTIAN NATIONALISM. KAHNDAQIS ARE NOT ARAB. AND I...
...LOST MY FRIEND.
IF THAT *AMUSES* YOU, YOU CAN WAIT OUTSIDE.
NOT 'TIL I FIGURE OUT WHAT KILLED HIM.
HOW DO YOU KILL A GUY WHO COULD BODY-SLAM SUPERMAN?
A..."SPACE VIRUS"...?
WHITE--!
...HERE WE GO...

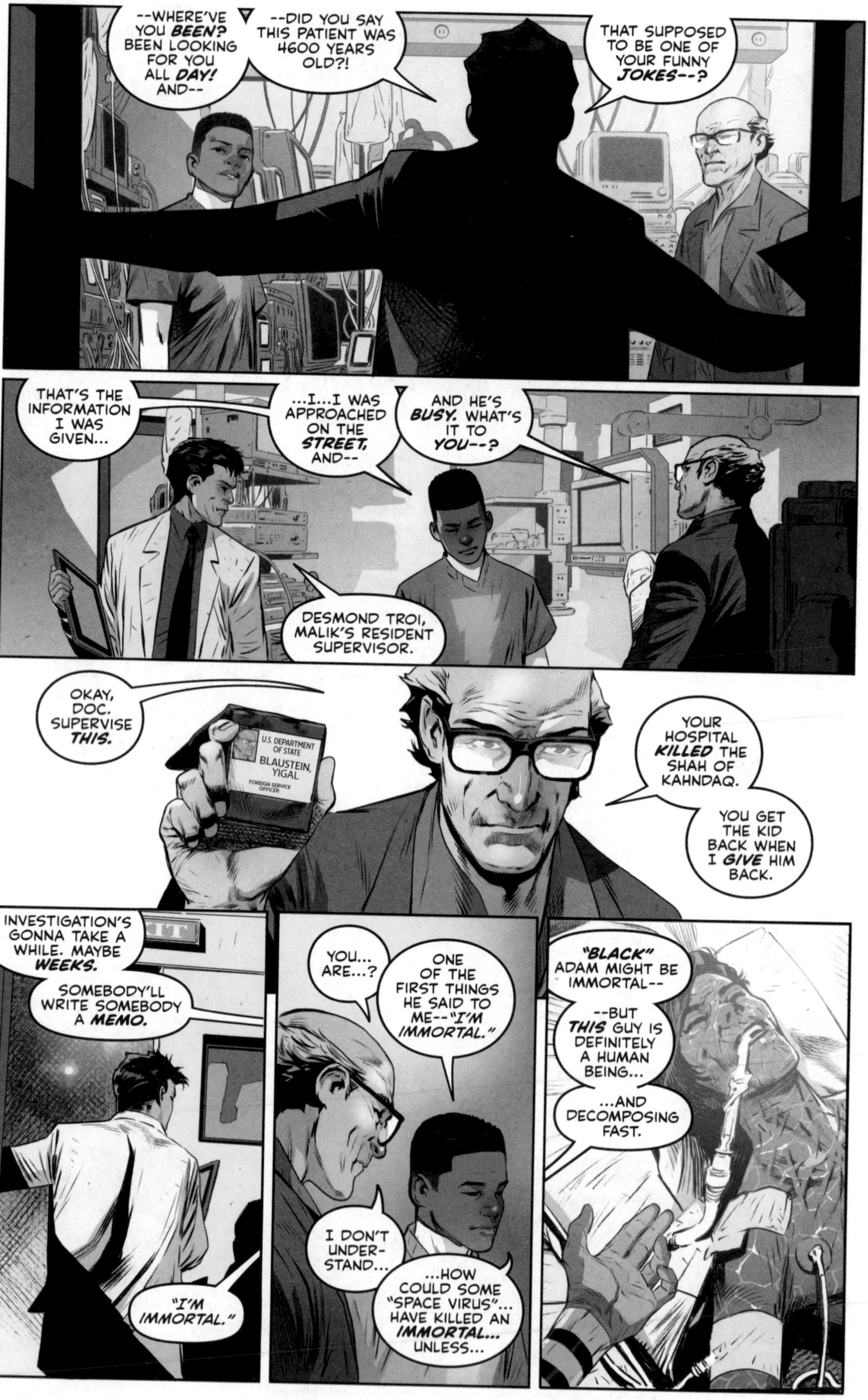
--WHERE'VE YOU BEEN? BEEN LOOKING FOR YOU ALL DAY! AND--
--DID YOU SAY THIS PATIENT WAS 4600 YEARS OLD?!
THAT SUPPOSED TO BE ONE OF YOUR FUNNY JOKES--?
THAT'S THE INFORMATION I WAS GIVEN...
...I...I WAS APPROACHED ON THE STREET, AND--
AND HE'S BUSY. WHAT'S IT TO YOU--?
DESMOND TROI, MALIK'S RESIDENT SUPERVISOR.
OKAY, DOC. SUPERVISE THIS.
U.S. DEPARTMENT OF STATE
BLAUSTEIN, YIGAL
FOREIGN SERVICE OFFICER
YOUR HOSPITAL KILLED THE SHAH OF KAHNDAQ.
YOU GET THE KID BACK WHEN I GIVE HIM BACK.
INVESTIGATION'S GONNA TAKE A WHILE. MAYBE WEEKS.
SOMEBODY'LL WRITE SOMEBODY A MEMO.
"I'M IMMORTAL."
YOU... ARE...?
ONE OF THE FIRST THINGS HE SAID TO ME--"I'M IMMORTAL."
I DON'T UNDER-STAND...
...HOW COULD SOME "SPACE VIRUS"... HAVE KILLED AN IMMORTAL... UNLESS...
"BLACK" ADAM MIGHT BE IMMORTAL--
--BUT THIS GUY IS DEFINITELY A HUMAN BEING...
...AND DECOMPOSING FAST.

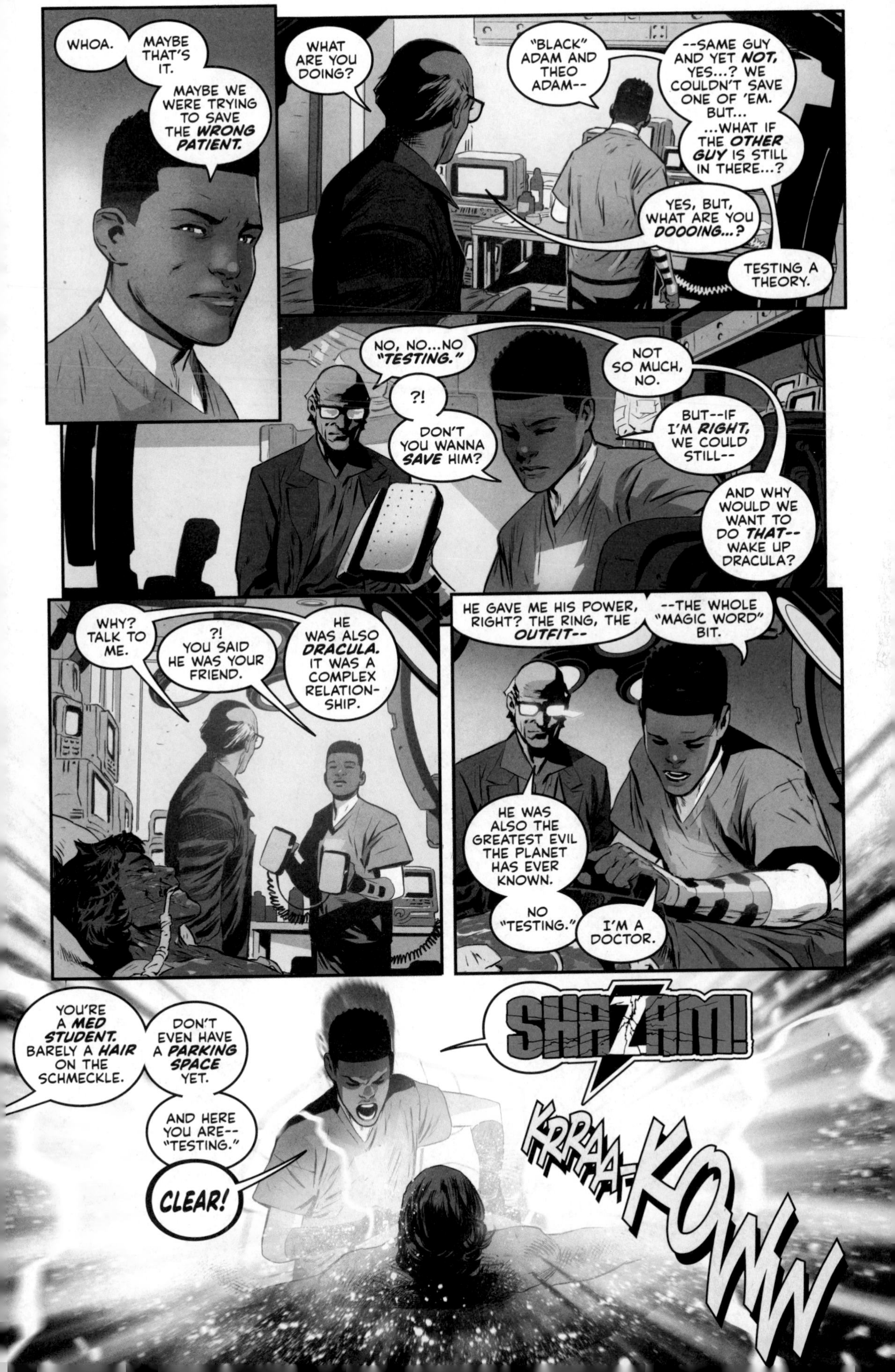

WHOA.
MAYBE THAT'S IT.
MAYBE WE WERE TRYING TO SAVE THE WRONG PATIENT.
WHAT ARE YOU DOING?
"BLACK" ADAM AND THEO ADAM--
--SAME GUY AND YET NOT, YES...? WE COULDN'T SAVE ONE OF 'EM. BUT...
...WHAT IF THE OTHER GUY IS STILL IN THERE...?
YES, BUT, WHAT ARE YOU DOOOING...?
TESTING A THEORY.
NO, NO...NO "TESTING."
NOT SO MUCH, NO.
?!
DON'T YOU WANNA SAVE HIM?
BUT--IF I'M RIGHT, WE COULD STILL--
AND WHY WOULD WE WANT TO DO THAT--WAKE UP DRACULA?
WHY? TALK TO ME.
?! YOU SAID HE WAS YOUR FRIEND.
HE WAS ALSO DRACULA. IT WAS A COMPLEX RELATION-SHIP.
HE GAVE ME HIS POWER, RIGHT? THE RING, THE OUTFIT--
--THE WHOLE "MAGIC WORD" BIT.
HE WAS ALSO THE GREATEST EVIL THE PLANET HAS EVER KNOWN.
NO "TESTING."
I'M A DOCTOR.
YOU'RE A MED STUDENT. BARELY A HAIR ON THE SCHMECKLE.
DON'T EVEN HAVE A PARKING SPACE YET.
AND HERE YOU ARE--"TESTING."
CLEAR!
SHAZAM!
KRRAA-KOWW

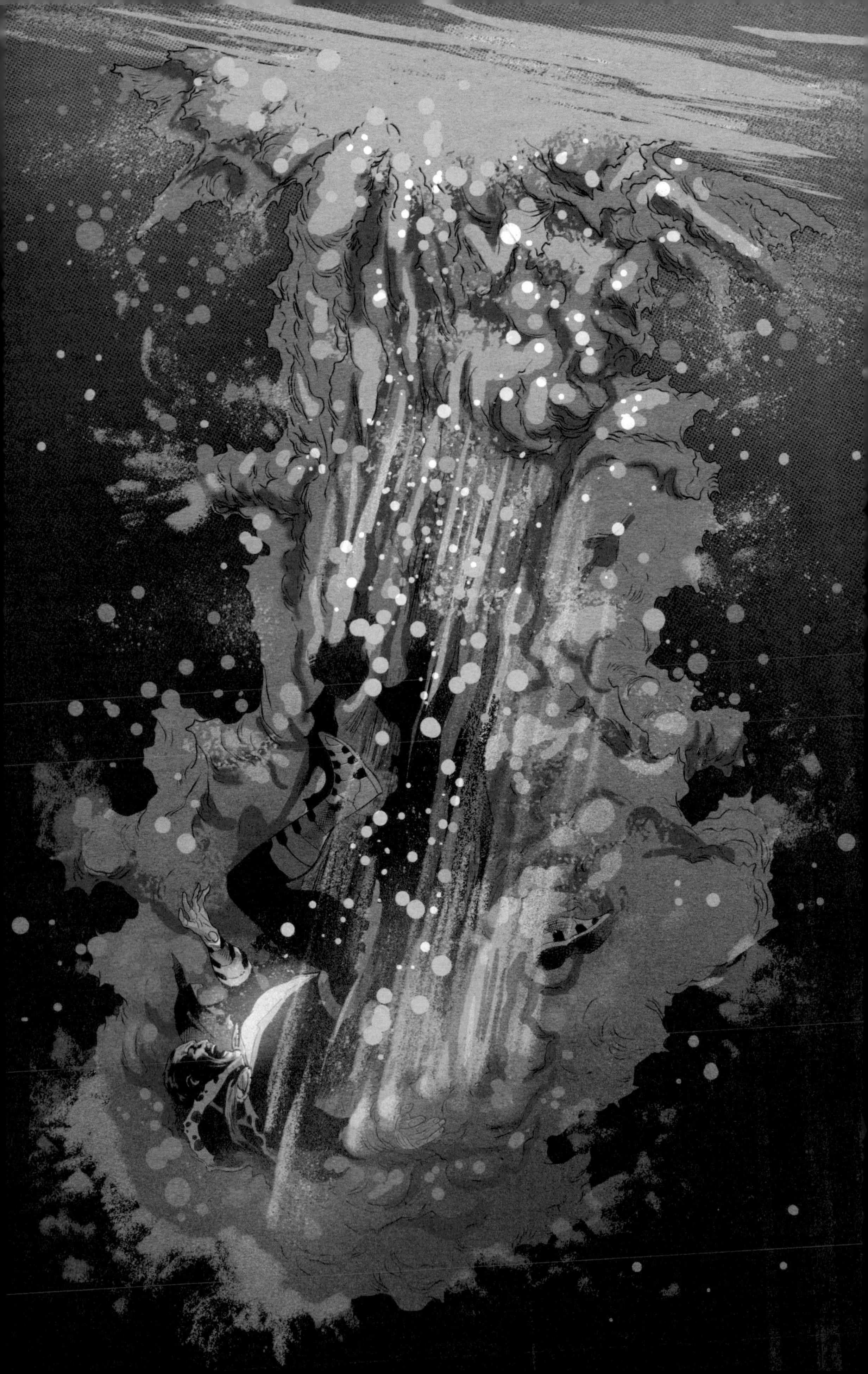

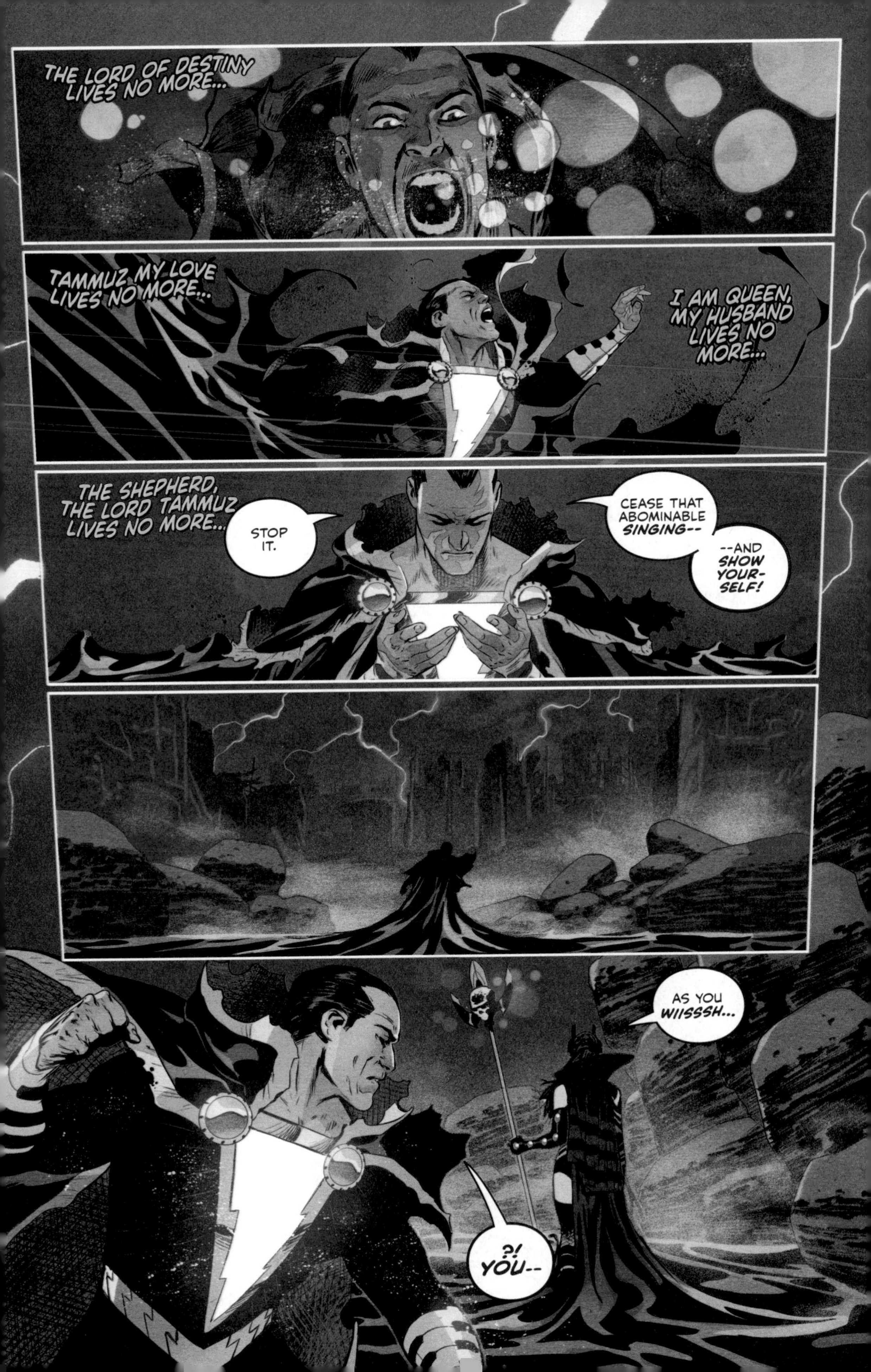
THE LORD OF DESTINY LIVES NO MORE...
TAMMUZ MY LOVE LIVES NO MORE...
I AM QUEEN, MY HUSBAND LIVES NO MORE...
THE SHEPHERD, THE LORD TAMMUZ LIVES NO MORE...
STOP IT.
CEASE THAT ABOMINABLE SINGING--
--AND SHOW YOURSELF!
AS YOU WIISSSH...
?! YOU--

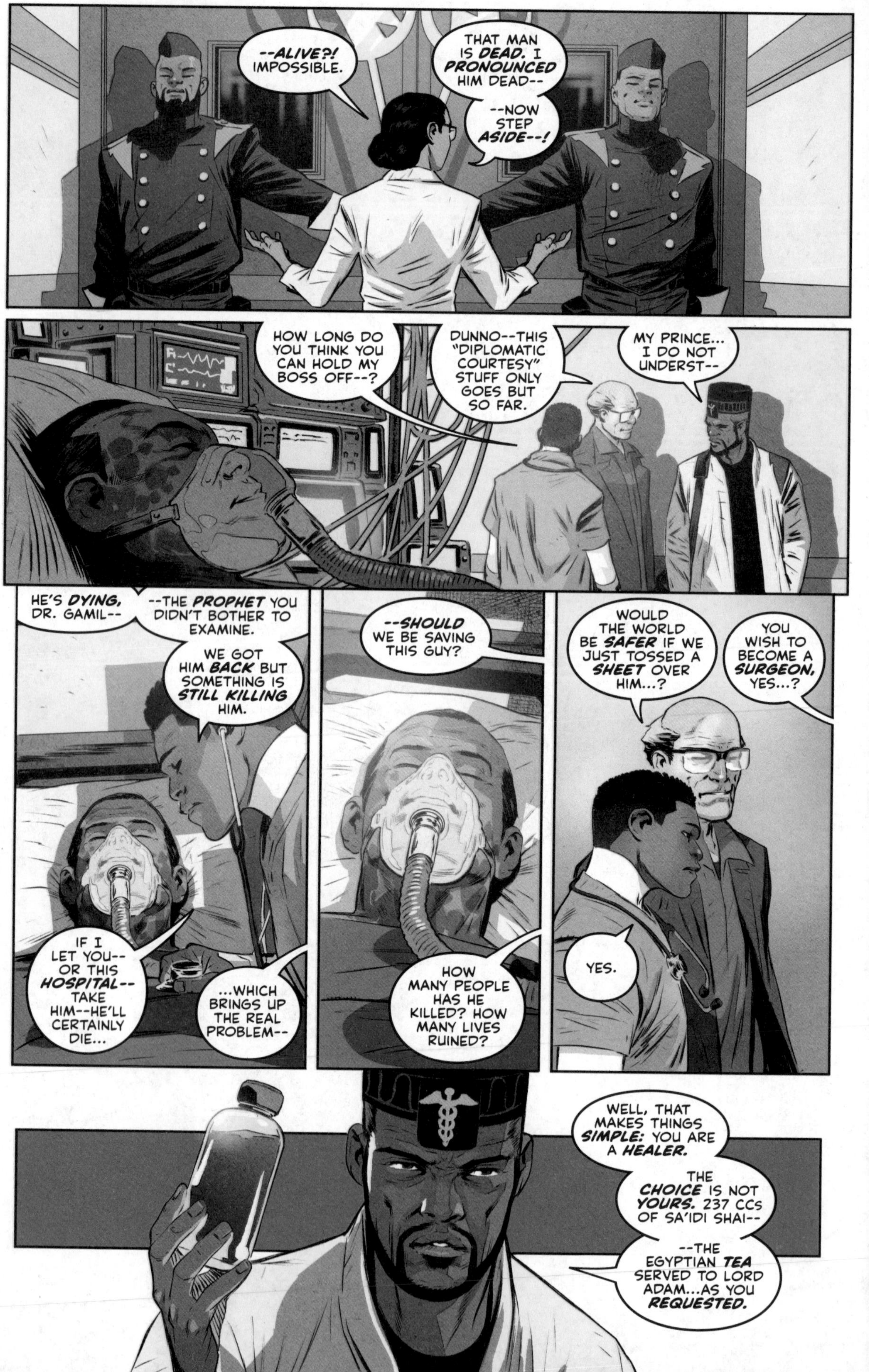

--ALIVE?! IMPOSSIBLE.
THAT MAN IS DEAD. I PRONOUNCED HIM DEAD--
--NOW STEP ASIDE--!
HOW LONG DO YOU THINK YOU CAN HOLD MY BOSS OFF--?
DUNNO--THIS "DIPLOMATIC COURTESY" STUFF ONLY GOES BUT SO FAR.
MY PRINCE... I DO NOT UNDERST--
HE'S DYING, DR. GAMIL--
--THE PROPHET YOU DIDN'T BOTHER TO EXAMINE.
WE GOT HIM BACK BUT SOMETHING IS STILL KILLING HIM.
IF I LET YOU--OR THIS HOSPITAL--TAKE HIM--HE'LL CERTAINLY DIE...
...WHICH BRINGS UP THE REAL PROBLEM--
--SHOULD WE BE SAVING THIS GUY?
HOW MANY PEOPLE HAS HE KILLED? HOW MANY LIVES RUINED?
WOULD THE WORLD BE SAFER IF WE JUST TOSSED A SHEET OVER HIM...?
YOU WISH TO BECOME A SURGEON, YES...?
YES.
WELL, THAT MAKES THINGS SIMPLE: YOU ARE A HEALER.
THE CHOICE IS NOT YOURS. 237 CCs OF SA'IDI SHAI--
--THE EGYPTIAN TEA SERVED TO LORD ADAM...AS YOU REQUESTED.

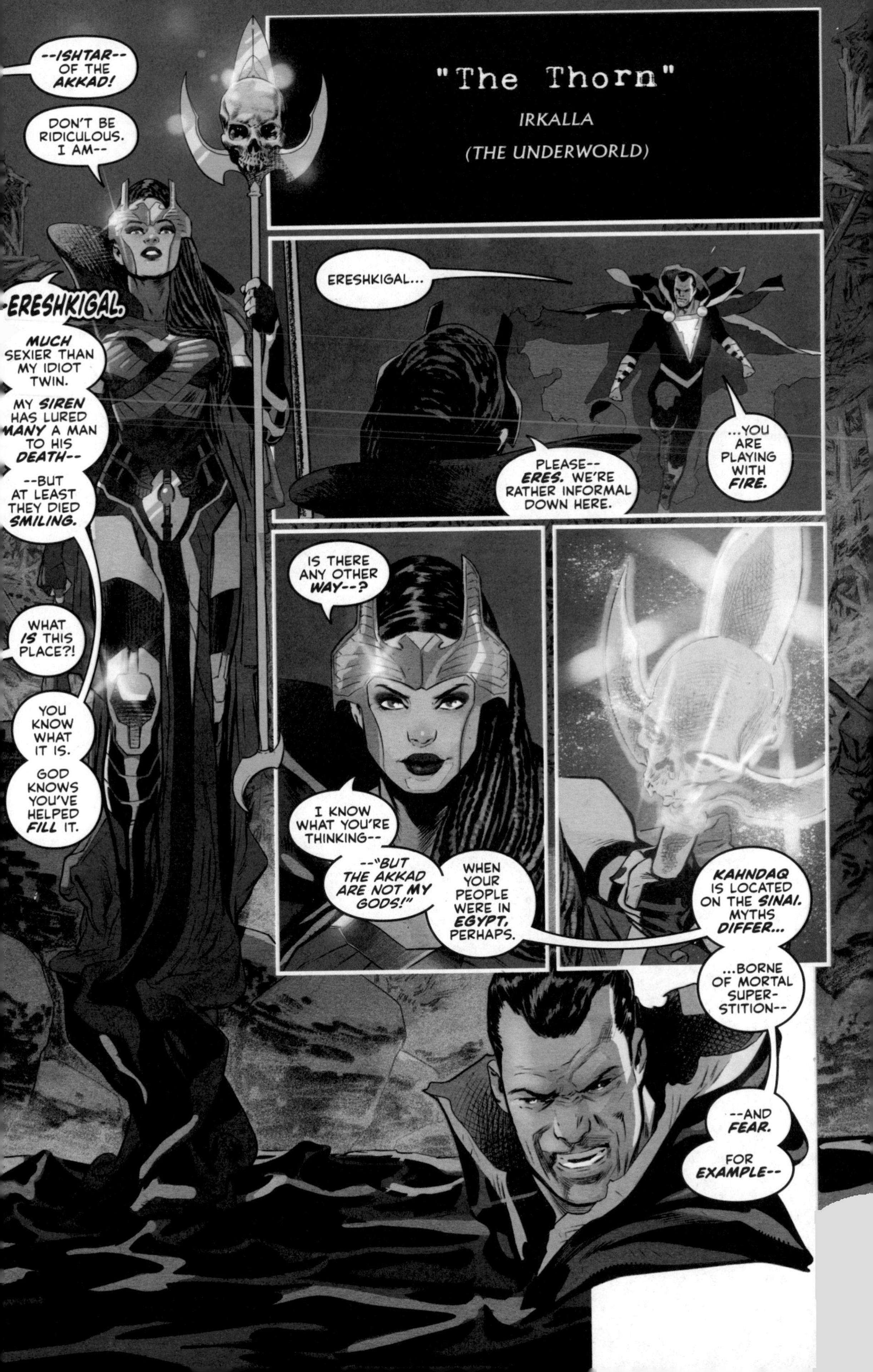
--ISHTAR-- OF THE AKKAD!
DON'T BE RIDICULOUS. I AM--
-ERESHKIGAL.
MUCH SEXIER THAN MY IDIOT TWIN.
MY SIREN HAS LURED MANY A MAN TO HIS DEATH--
--BUT AT LEAST THEY DIED SMILING.
"The Thorn"
IRKALLA
(THE UNDERWORLD)
ERESHKIGAL...
...YOU ARE PLAYING WITH FIRE.
PLEASE-- ERES. WE'RE RATHER INFORMAL DOWN HERE.
WHAT IS THIS PLACE?!
YOU KNOW WHAT IT IS.
GOD KNOWS YOU'VE HELPED FILL IT.
IS THERE ANY OTHER WAY--?
I KNOW WHAT YOU'RE THINKING--
--"BUT THE AKKAD ARE NOT MY GODS!"
WHEN YOUR PEOPLE WERE IN EGYPT, PERHAPS.
KAHNDAQ IS LOCATED ON THE SINAI. MYTHS DIFFER...
...BORNE OF MORTAL SUPER-STITION--
--AND FEAR.
FOR EXAMPLE--

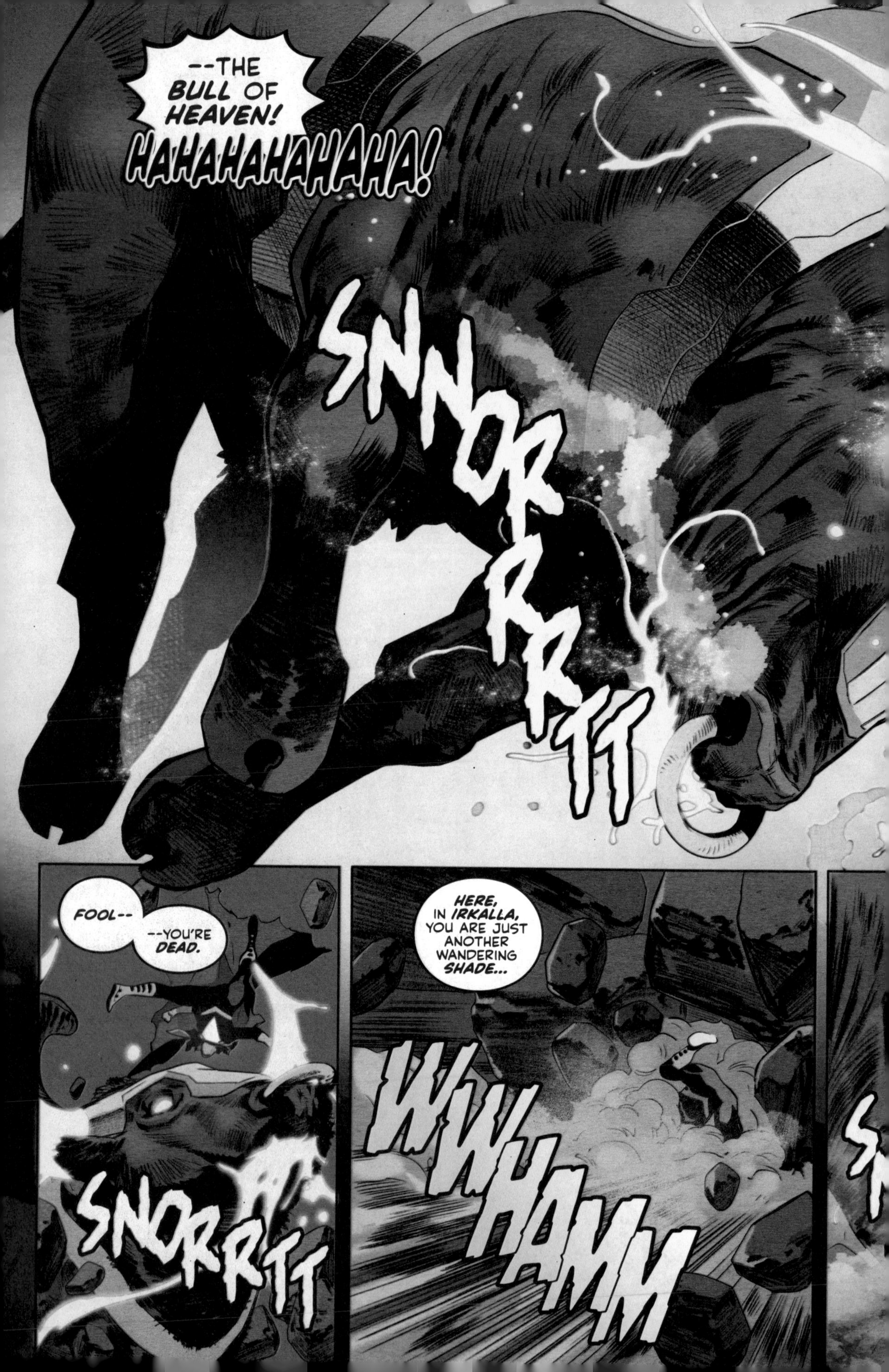
--THE BULL OF HEAVEN!
HAHAHAHAHAHA!
SNNORRRTT
FOOL--
--YOU'RE DEAD.
SNORRTT
HERE, IN IRKALLA, YOU ARE JUST ANOTHER WANDERING SHADE...
WWHAMM

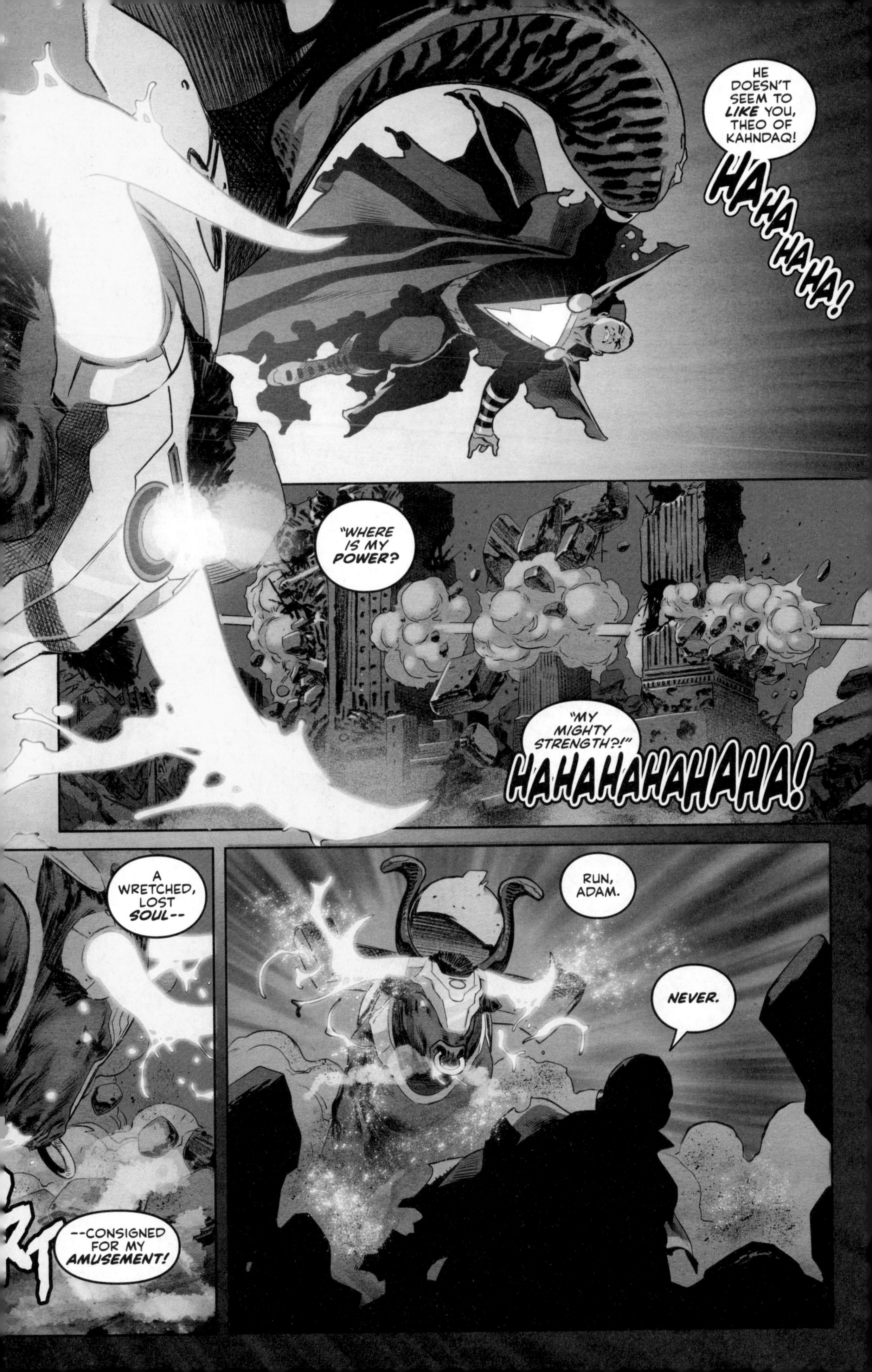
HE DOESN'T SEEM TO LIKE YOU, THEO OF KAHNDAQ!
HAHAHAHAHA!
"WHERE IS MY POWER?
"MY MIGHTY STRENGTH?!"
HAHAHAHAHAHAHA!
A WRETCHED, LOST SOUL--
--CONSIGNED FOR MY AMUSEMENT!
RUN, ADAM.
NEVER.

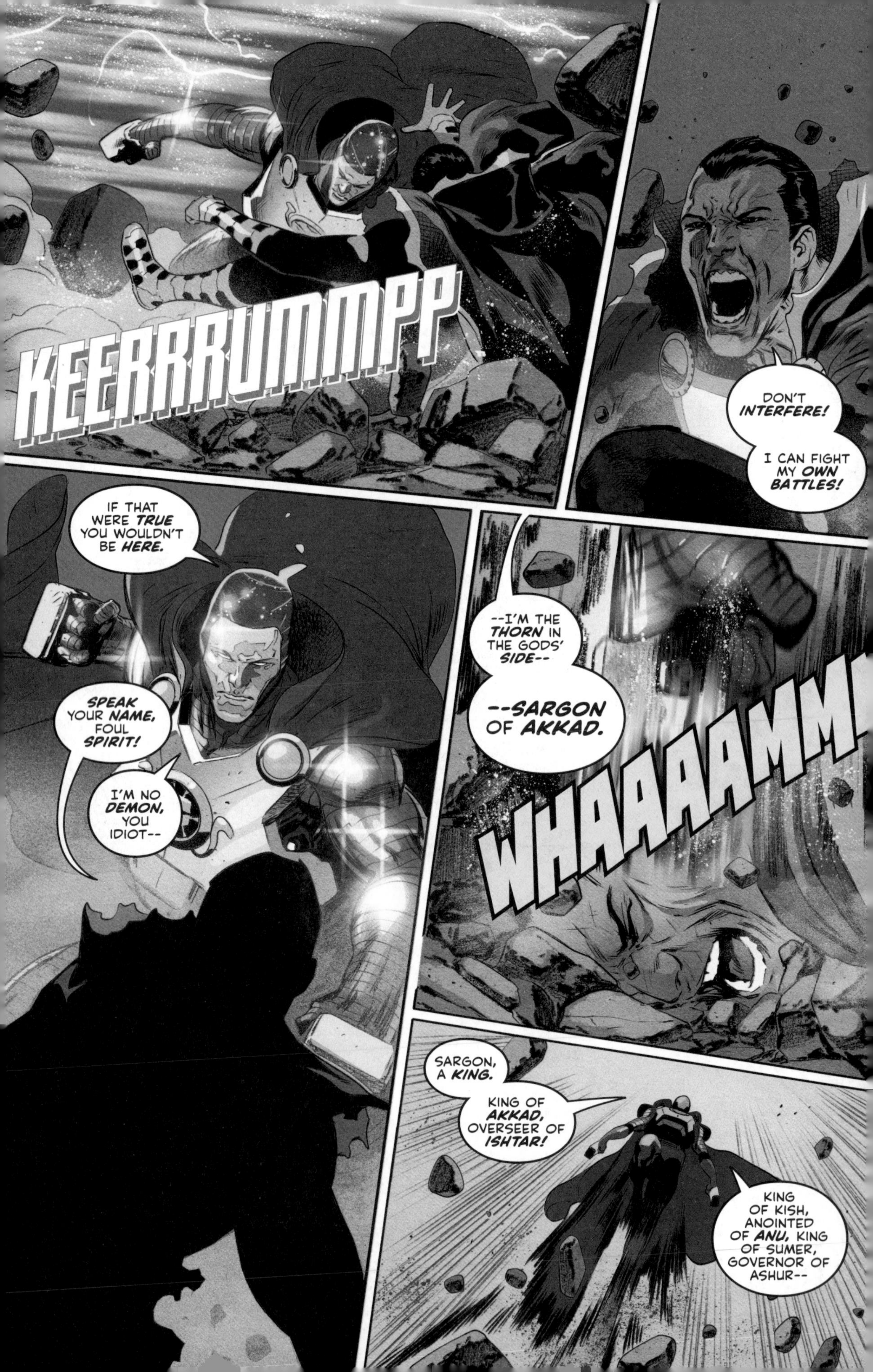
KEERRRUMMMPP
DON'T INTERFERE!
I CAN FIGHT MY OWN BATTLES!
IF THAT WERE TRUE YOU WOULDN'T BE HERE.
SPEAK YOUR NAME, FOUL SPIRIT!
I'M NO DEMON, YOU IDIOT--
--I'M THE THORN IN THE GODS' SIDE--
--SARGON OF AKKAD.
WHAAAAMM
SARGON, A KING.
KING OF AKKAD, OVERSEER OF ISHTAR!
KING OF KISH, ANOINTED OF ANU, KING OF SUMER, GOVERNOR OF ASHUR--

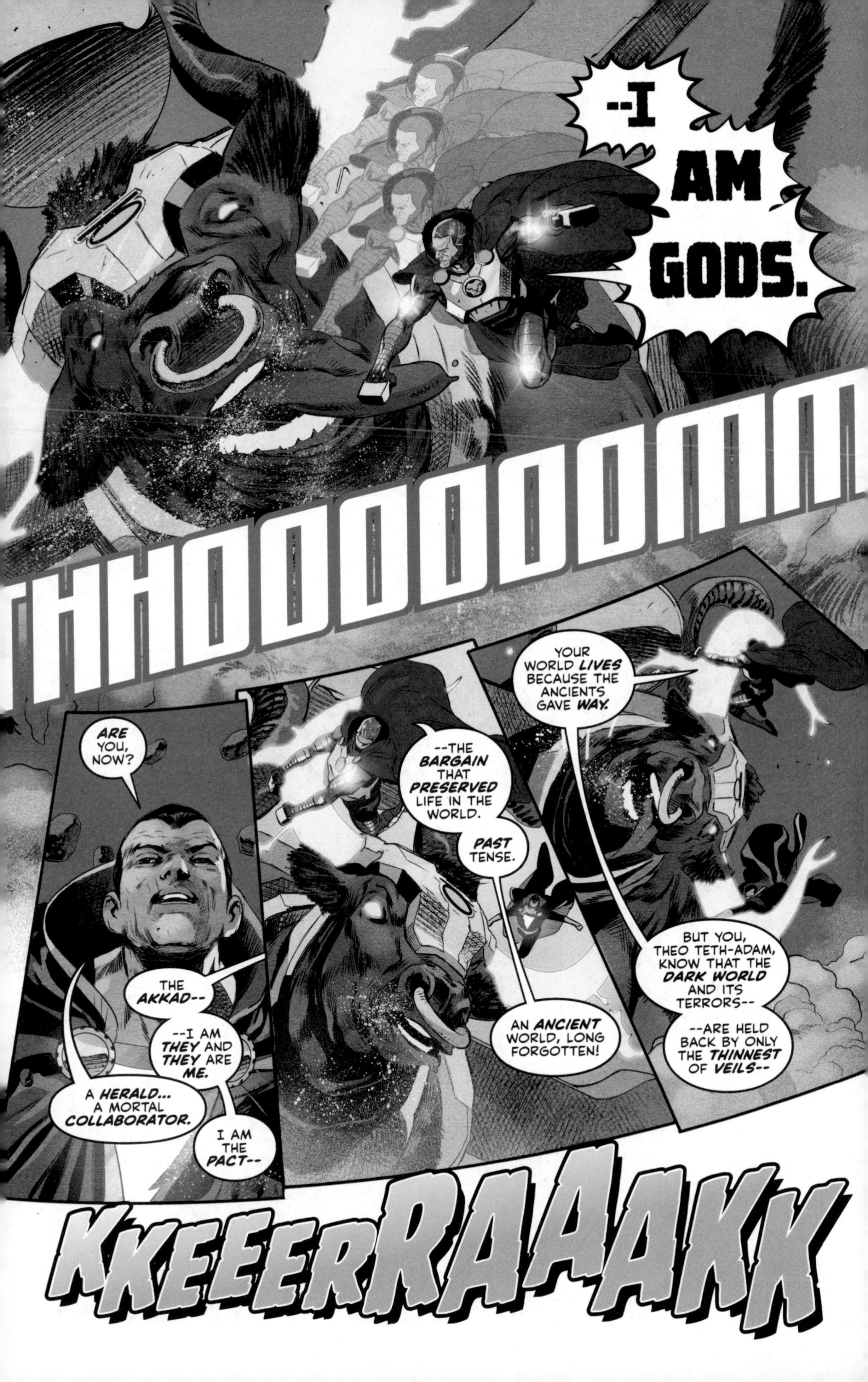
--I AM GODS.
KHOOOOOOMM
ARE YOU, NOW?
THE AKKAD--
--I AM THEY AND THEY ARE ME.
A HERALD... A MORTAL COLLABORATOR.
I AM THE PACT--
--THE BARGAIN THAT PRESERVED LIFE IN THE WORLD.
PAST TENSE.
AN ANCIENT WORLD, LONG FORGOTTEN!
YOUR WORLD LIVES BECAUSE THE ANCIENTS GAVE WAY.
BUT YOU, THEO TETH-ADAM, KNOW THAT THE DARK WORLD AND ITS TERRORS--
--ARE HELD BACK BY ONLY THE THINNEST OF VEILS--
KKEEERRAAAKK

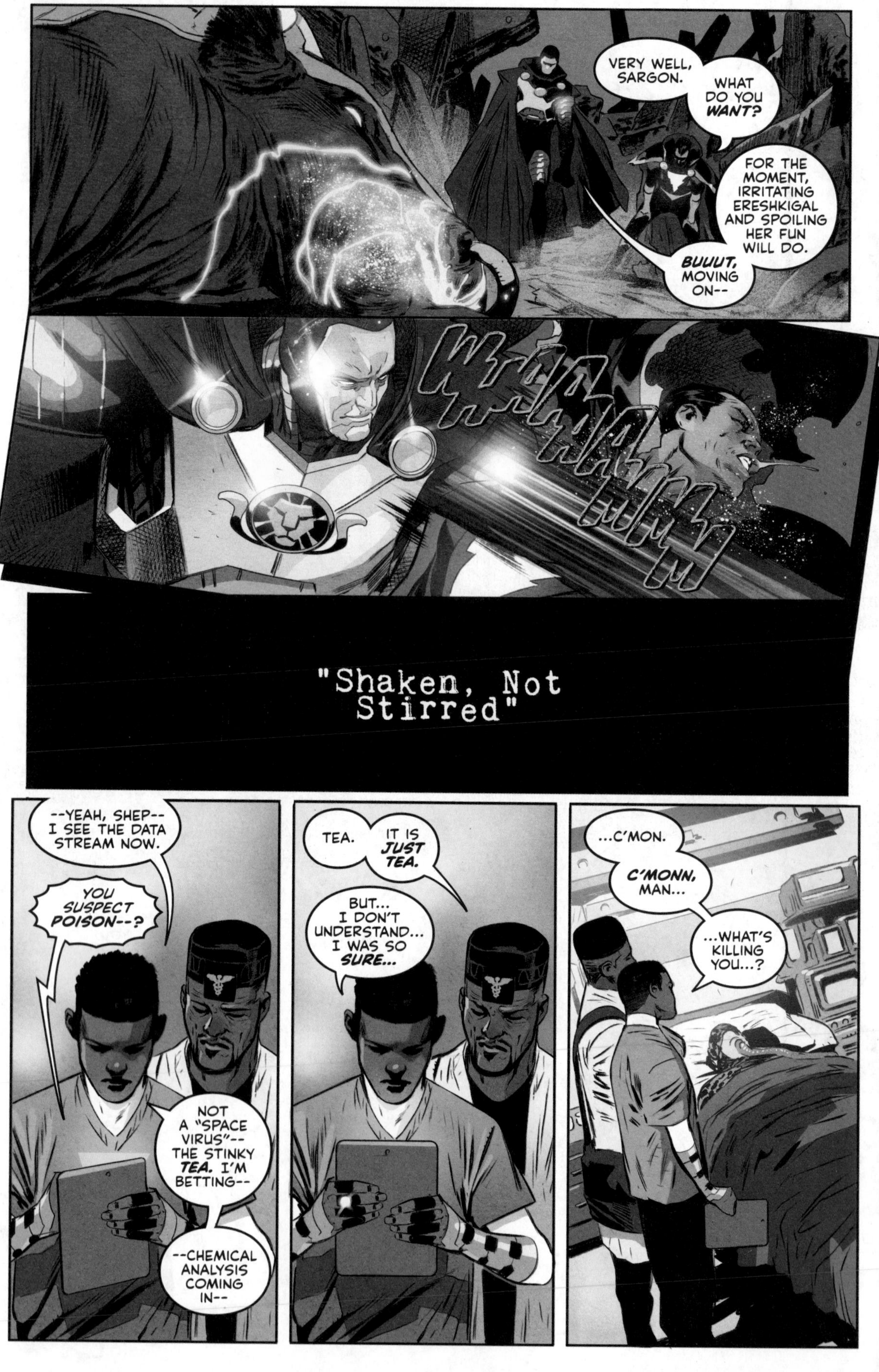
VERY WELL, SARGON.
WHAT DO YOU *WANT?*
FOR THE MOMENT, IRRITATING ERESHKIGAL AND SPOILING HER FUN WILL DO.
BUUUT, MOVING ON--
"Shaken, Not Stirred"
--YEAH, SHEP-- I SEE THE DATA STREAM NOW.
YOU SUSPECT *POISON*--?
NOT A "SPACE VIRUS"-- THE STINKY *TEA.* I'M BETTING--
--CHEMICAL ANALYSIS COMING IN--
TEA.
IT IS *JUST TEA.*
BUT... I DON'T UNDERSTAND... I WAS SO *SURE...*
...C'MON.
C'MONN, MAN...
...WHAT'S KILLING YOU...?

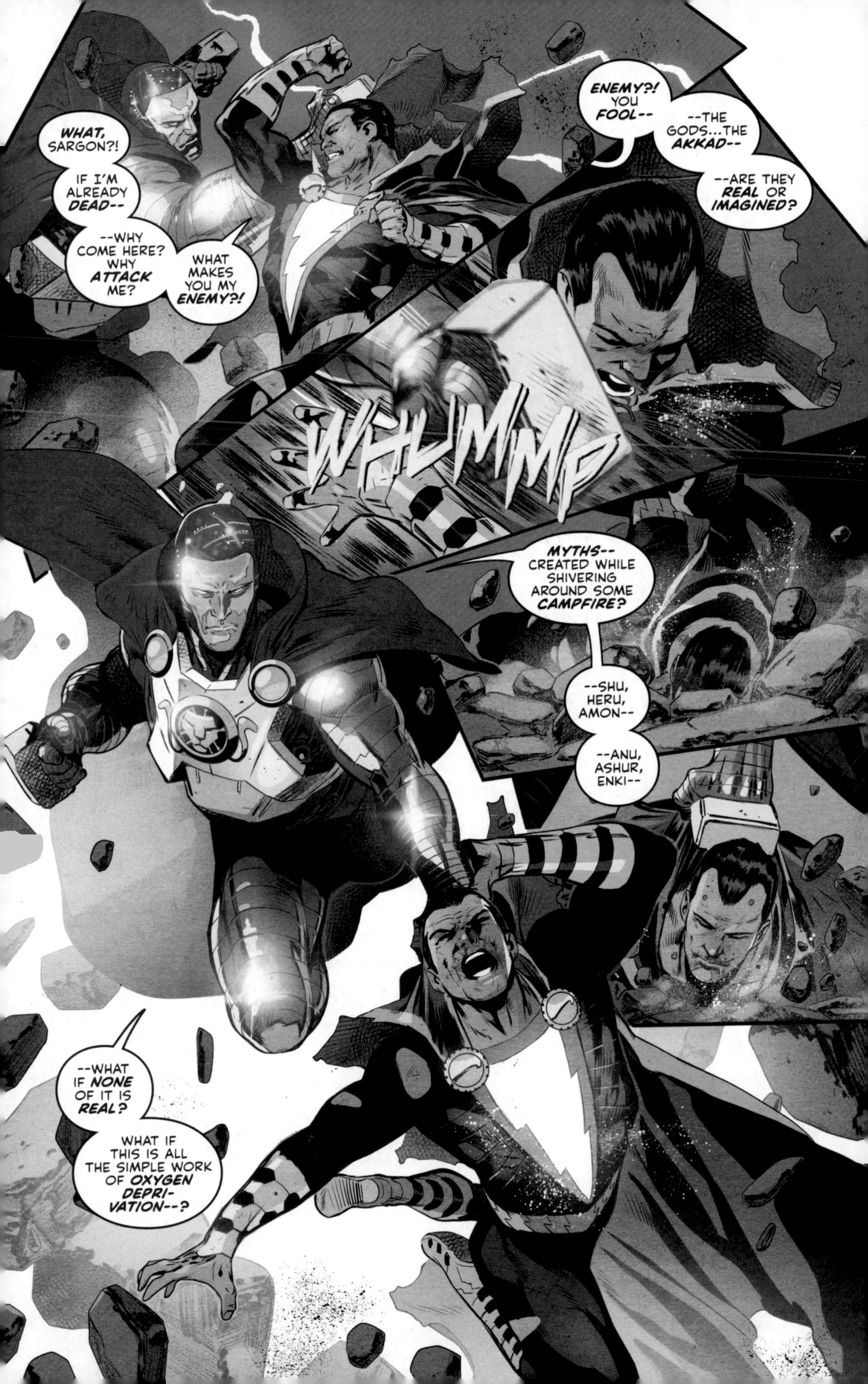
WHAT, SARGON?!
IF I'M ALREADY DEAD--
--WHY COME HERE? WHY ATTACK ME?
WHAT MAKES YOU MY ENEMY?!
ENEMY?! YOU FOOL--
--THE GODS...THE AKKAD--
--ARE THEY REAL OR IMAGINED?
WHUMMP
MYTHS--CREATED WHILE SHIVERING AROUND SOME CAMPFIRE?
--SHU, HERU, AMON--
--ANU, ASHUR, ENKI--
--WHAT IF NONE OF IT IS REAL?
WHAT IF THIS IS ALL THE SIMPLE WORK OF OXYGEN DEPRI-VATION--?

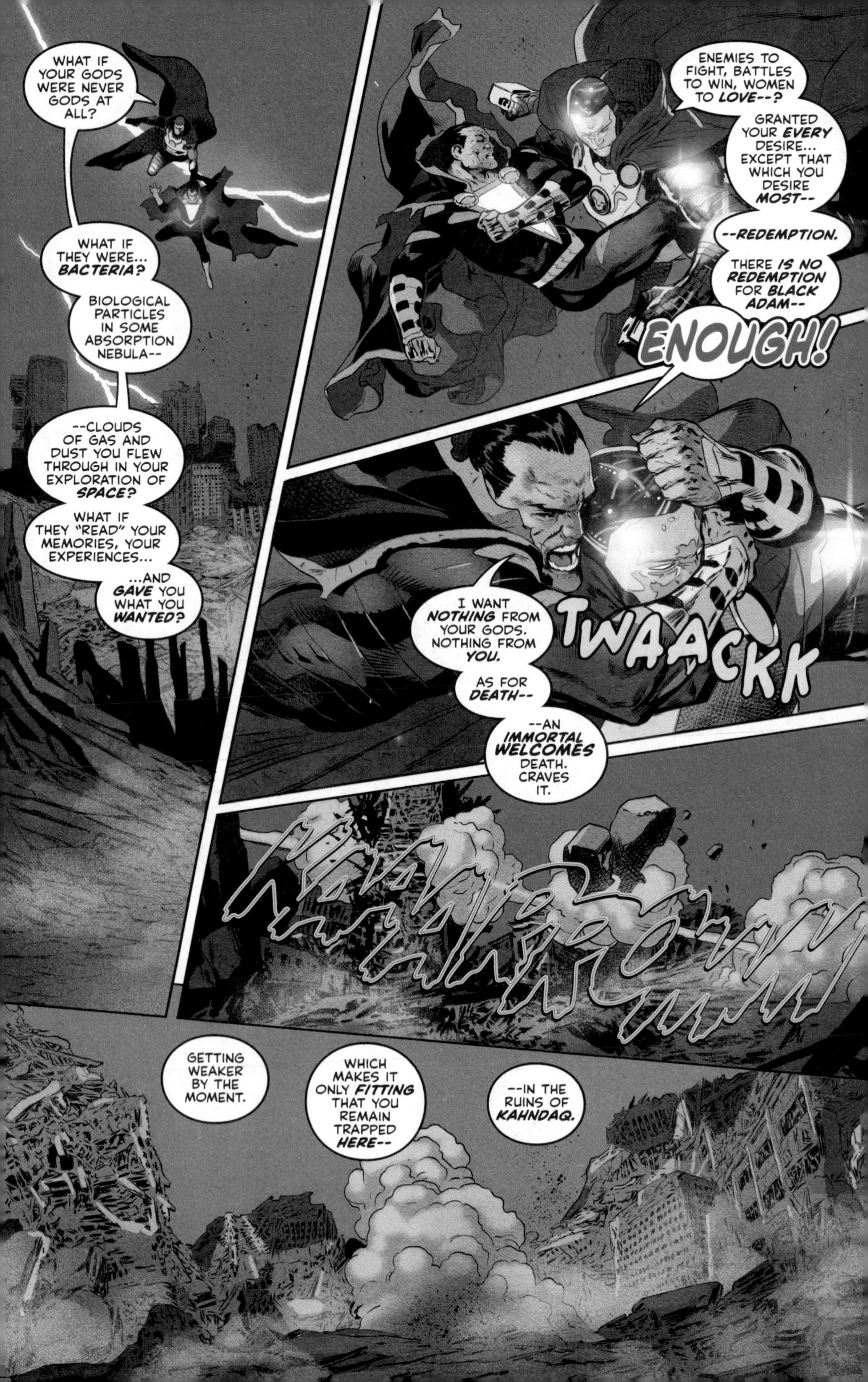

WHAT IF YOUR GODS WERE NEVER GODS AT ALL?
WHAT IF THEY WERE... BACTERIA?
BIOLOGICAL PARTICLES IN SOME ABSORPTION NEBULA--
--CLOUDS OF GAS AND DUST YOU FLEW THROUGH IN YOUR EXPLORATION OF SPACE?
WHAT IF THEY "READ" YOUR MEMORIES, YOUR EXPERIENCES...
...AND GAVE YOU WHAT YOU WANTED?
ENEMIES TO FIGHT, BATTLES TO WIN, WOMEN TO LOVE--?
GRANTED YOUR EVERY DESIRE... EXCEPT THAT WHICH YOU DESIRE MOST--
--REDEMPTION.
THERE IS NO REDEMPTION FOR BLACK ADAM--
ENOUGH!
I WANT NOTHING FROM YOUR GODS. NOTHING FROM YOU.
AS FOR DEATH--
--AN IMMORTAL WELCOMES DEATH. CRAVES IT.
TWAACKK
GETTING WEAKER BY THE MOMENT.
WHICH MAKES IT ONLY FITTING THAT YOU REMAIN TRAPPED HERE--
--IN THE RUINS OF KAHNDAQ.

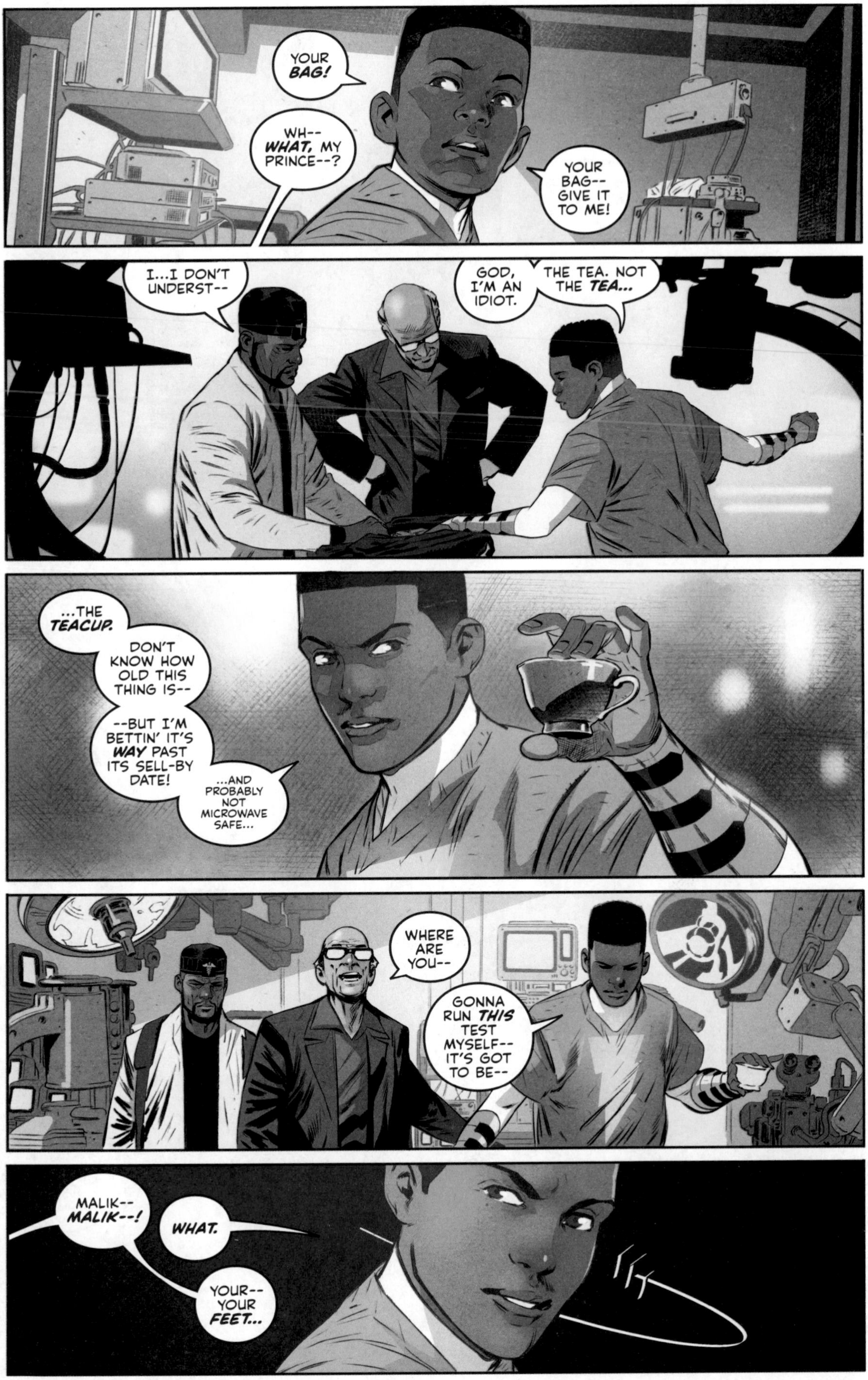

YOUR BAG!
WH-- WHAT, MY PRINCE--?
YOUR BAG-- GIVE IT TO ME!
I...I DON'T UNDERST--
GOD, I'M AN IDIOT.
THE TEA. NOT THE TEA...
...THE TEACUP.
DON'T KNOW HOW OLD THIS THING IS--
--BUT I'M BETTIN' IT'S WAY PAST ITS SELL-BY DATE!
...AND PROBABLY NOT MICROWAVE SAFE...
WHERE ARE YOU--
GONNA RUN THIS TEST MYSELF-- IT'S GOT TO BE--
MALIK-- MALIK--!
WHAT.
YOUR-- YOUR FEET...

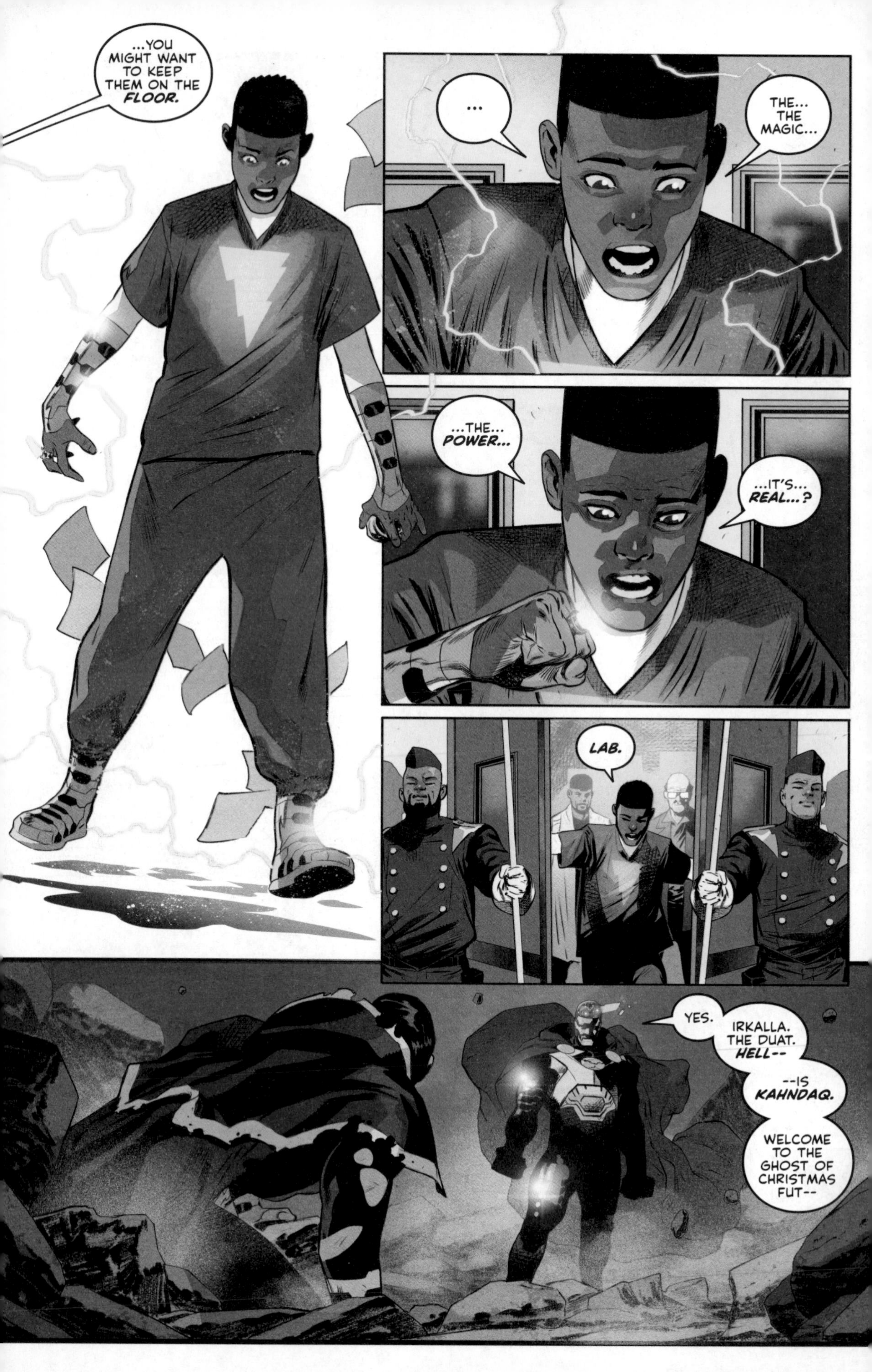
...YOU MIGHT WANT TO KEEP THEM ON THE *FLOOR.*
...
THE... THE MAGIC...
...THE... *POWER...*
...IT'S... *REAL...?*
LAB.
YES.
IRKALLA. THE DUAT. *HELL--*
--IS *KAHNDAQ.*
WELCOME TO THE GHOST OF CHRISTMAS FUT--

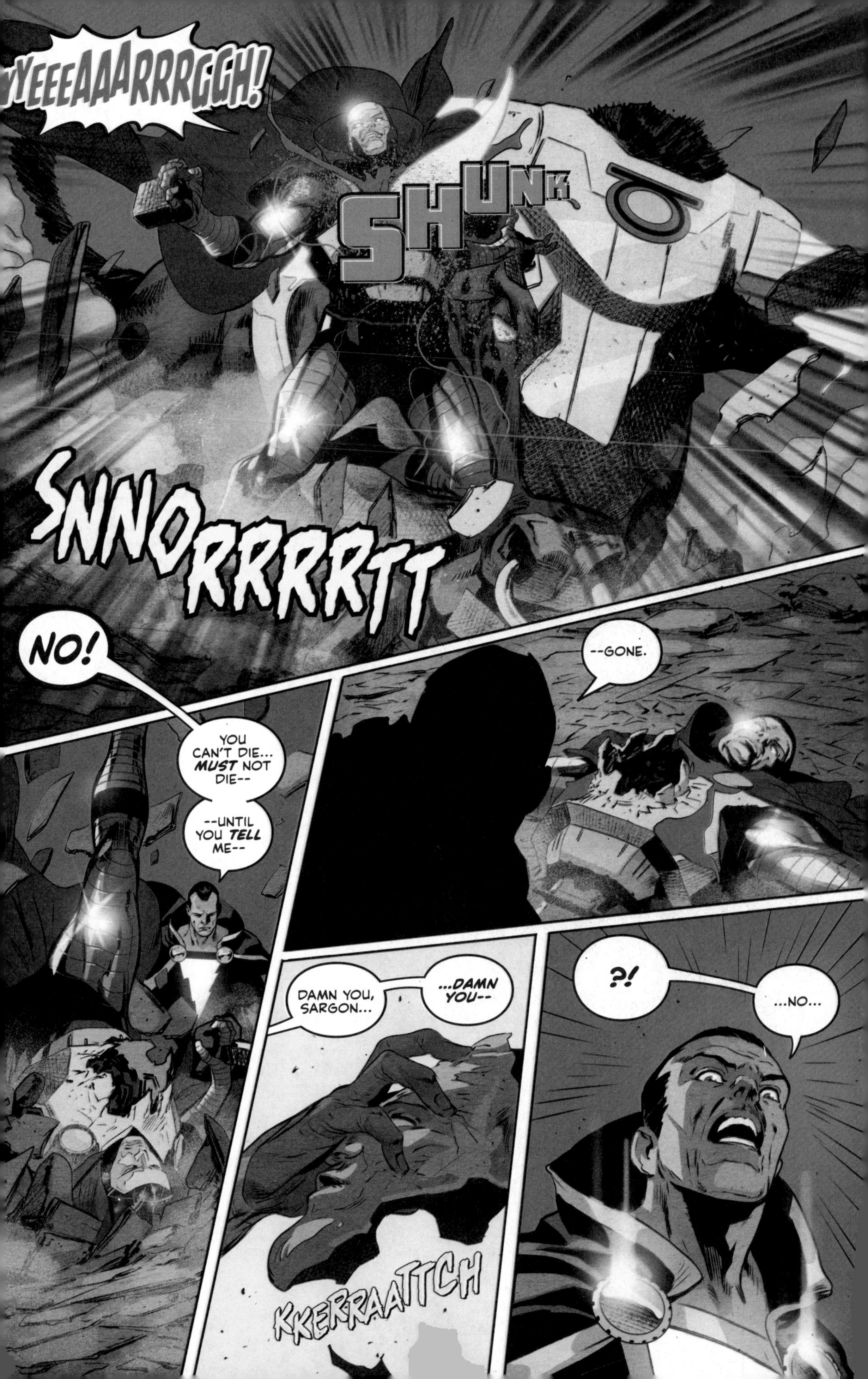
YYEEEAAARRRGGH!
SHUNK
SNNORRRRRTT
NO!
YOU CAN'T DIE... MUST NOT DIE--
--UNTIL YOU TELL ME--
--GONE.
DAMN YOU, SARGON...
...DAMN YOU--
KKERRAATTCH
?!
...NO...

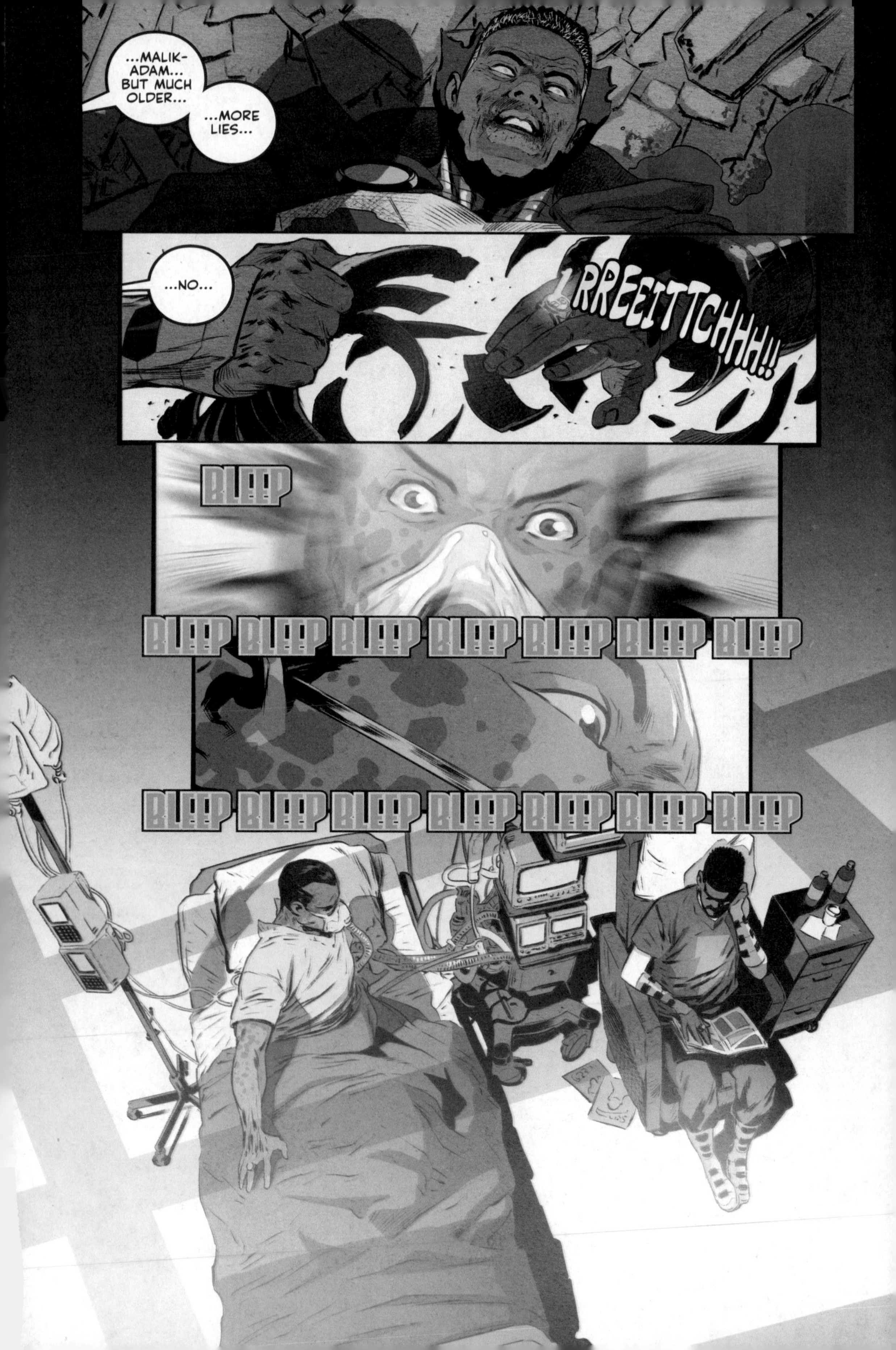
...MALIK-ADAM... BUT MUCH OLDER...
...MORE LIES...
...NO...
RREEITTCHHH!!!
BLEEP
BLEEP BLEEP BLEEP BLEEP BLEEP BLEEP BLEEP
BLEEP BLEEP BLEEP BLEEP BLEEP BLEEP BLEEP

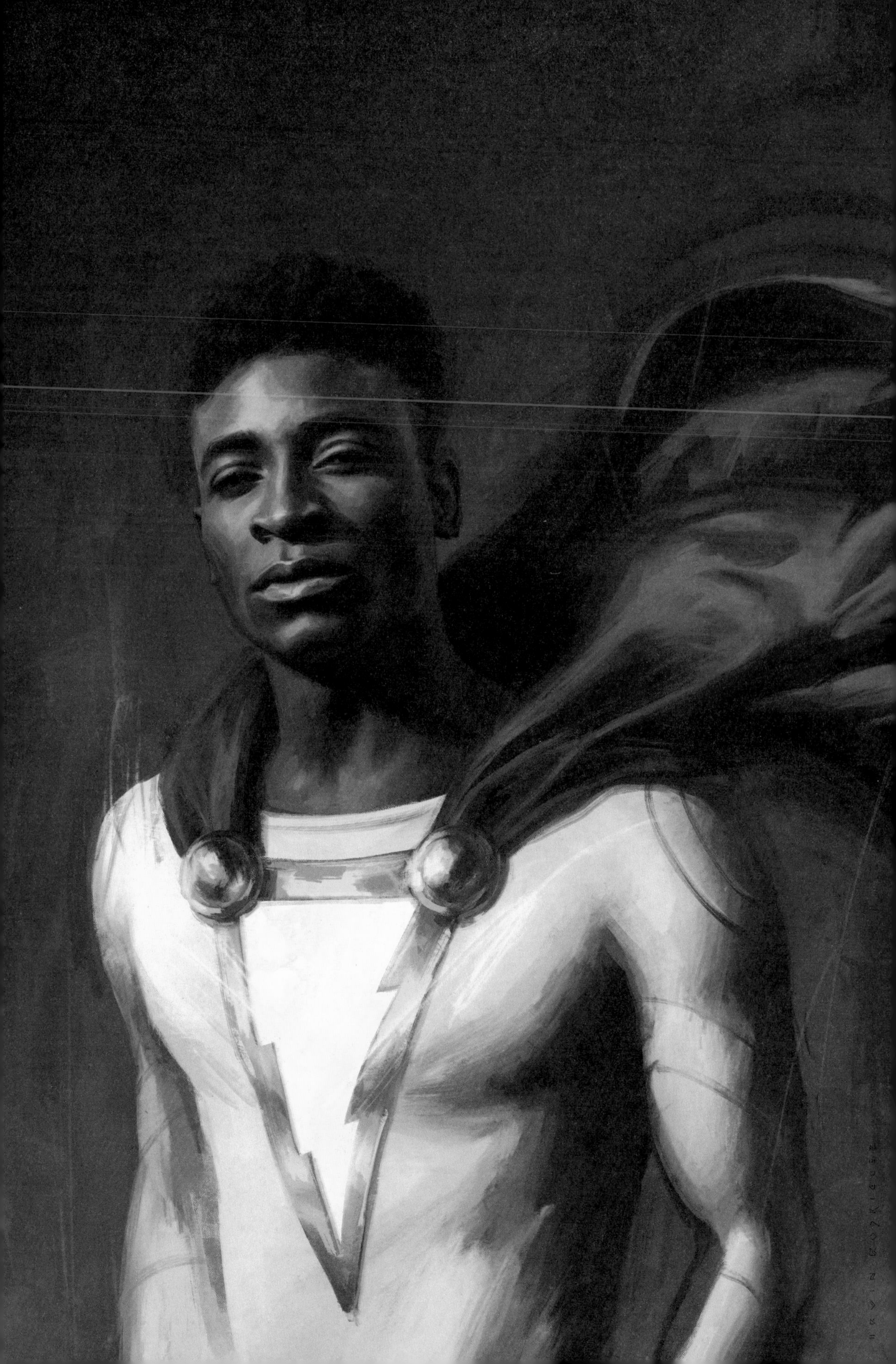

***Black Adam* #4** cover by Irvin Rodriguez

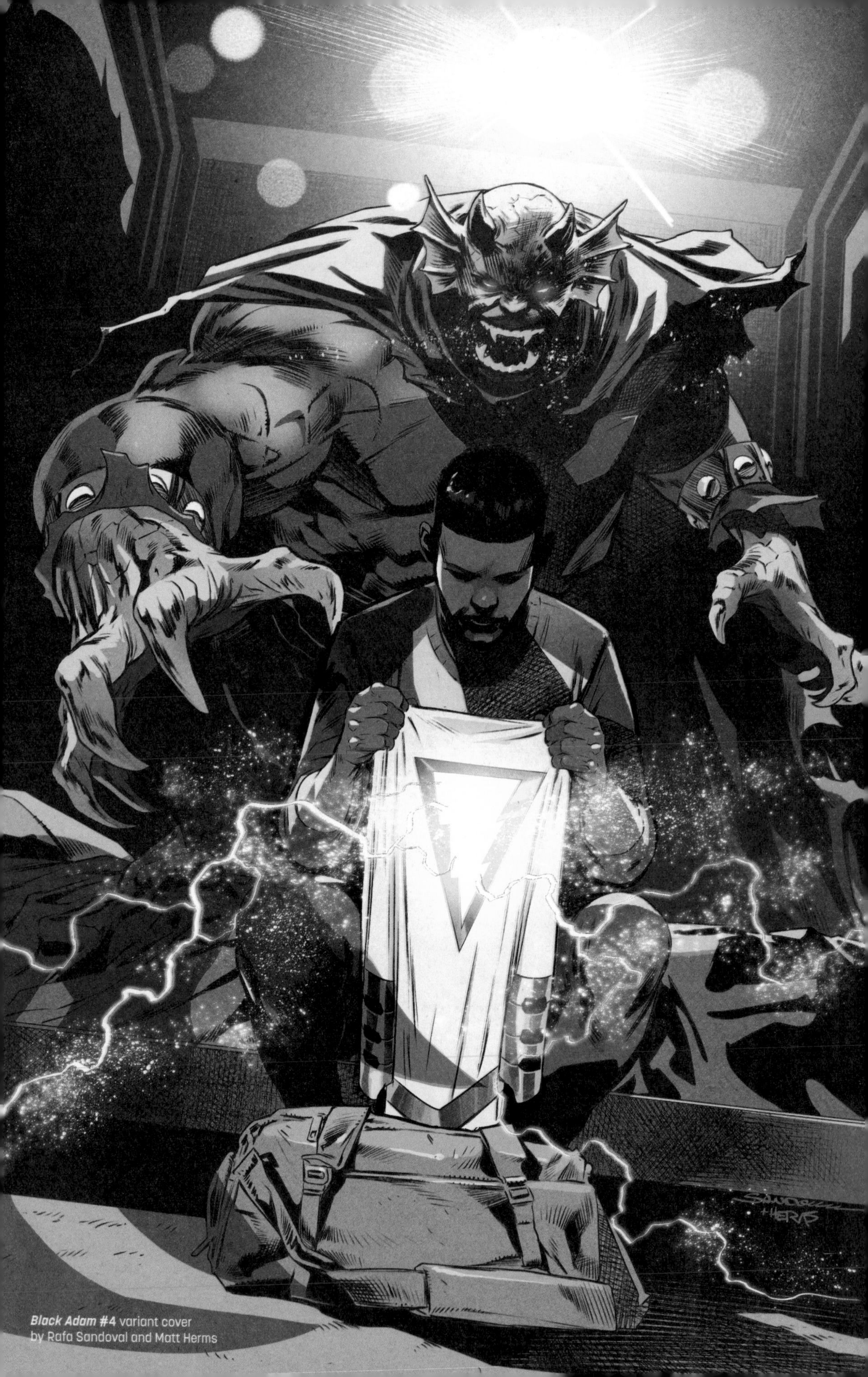

Black Adam #4 variant cover
by Rafa Sandoval and Matt Herms

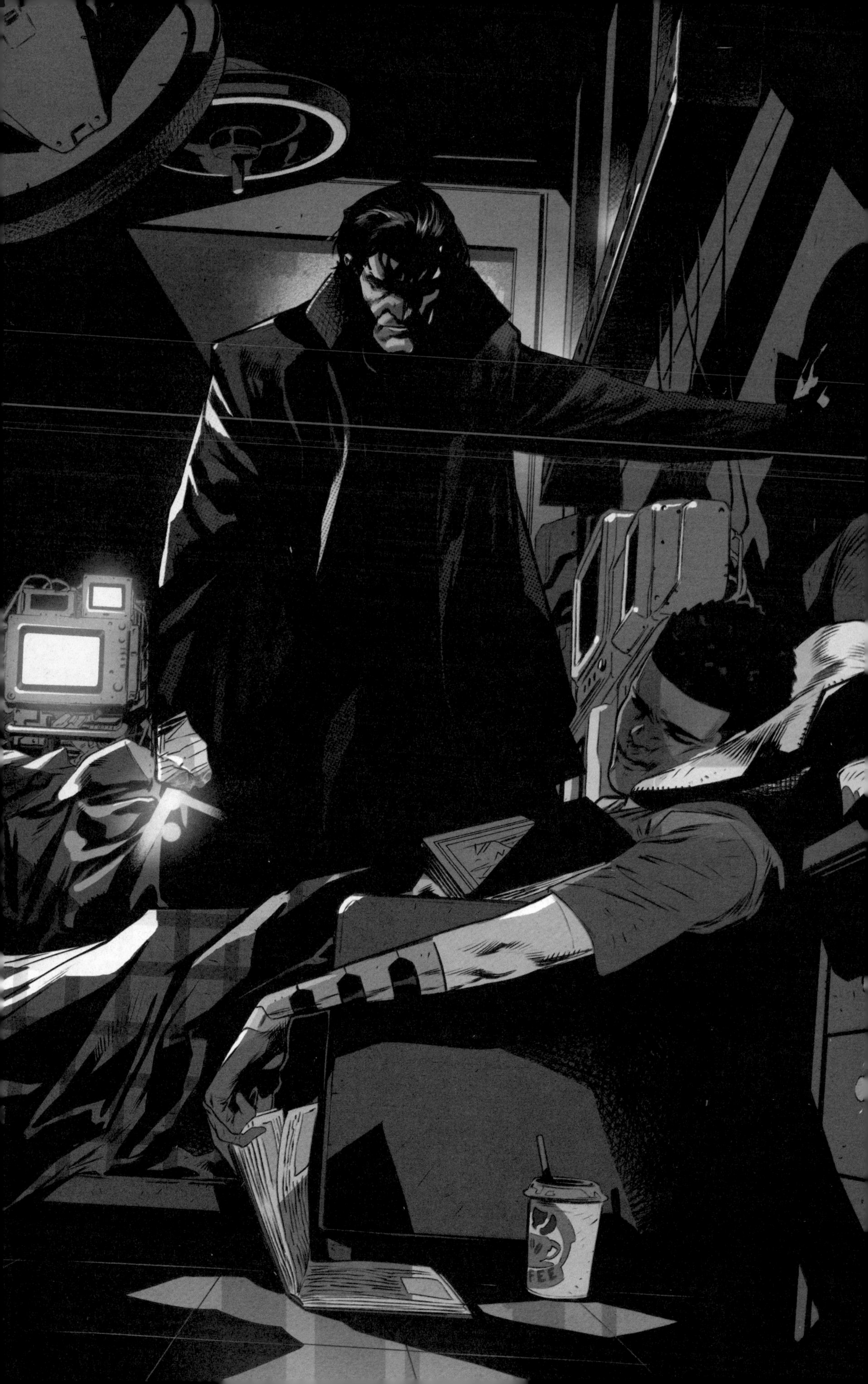

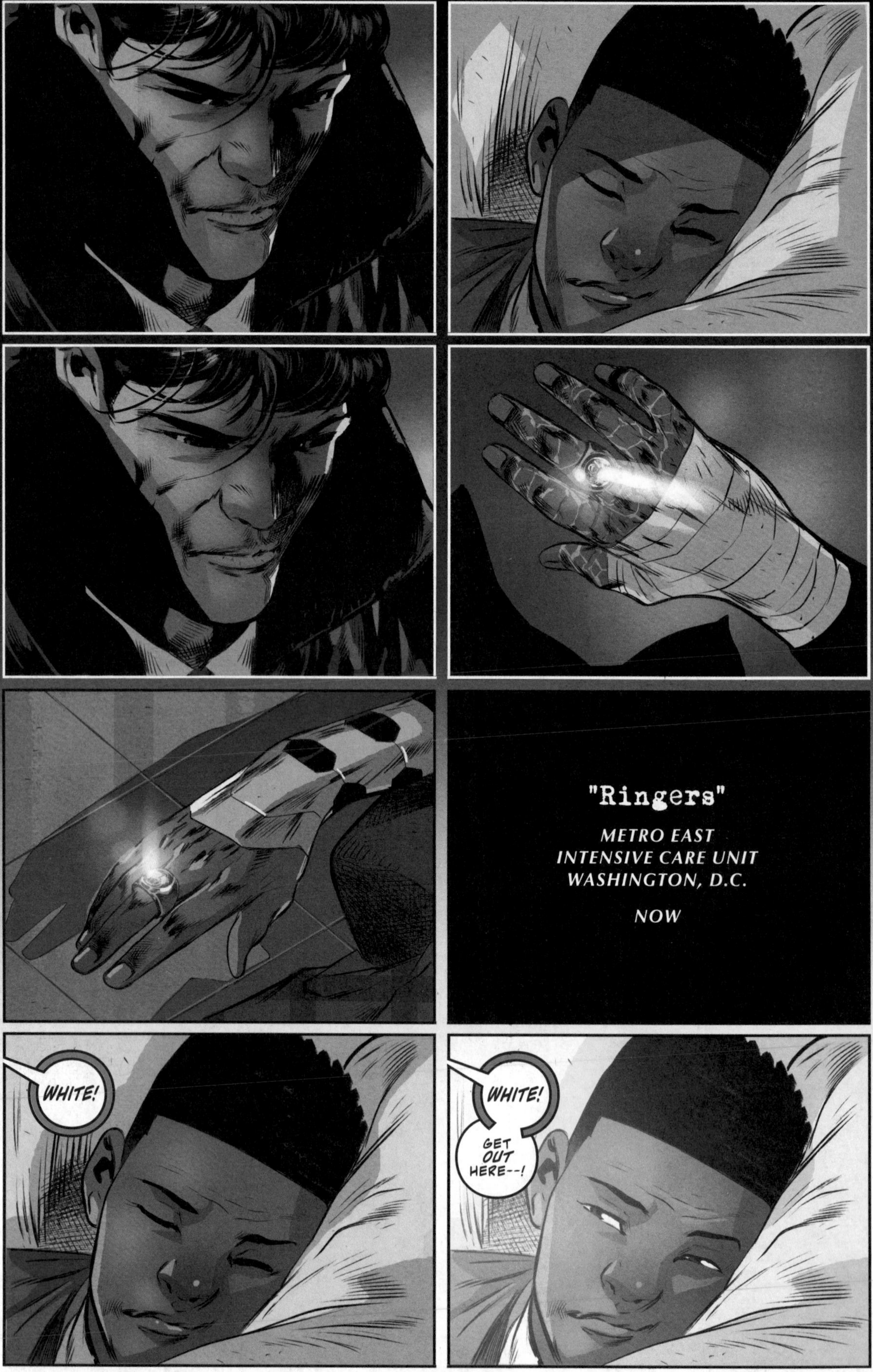
"Ringers"
METRO EAST
INTENSIVE CARE UNIT
WASHINGTON, D.C.
NOW
WHITE!
WHITE!
GET OUT HERE--!

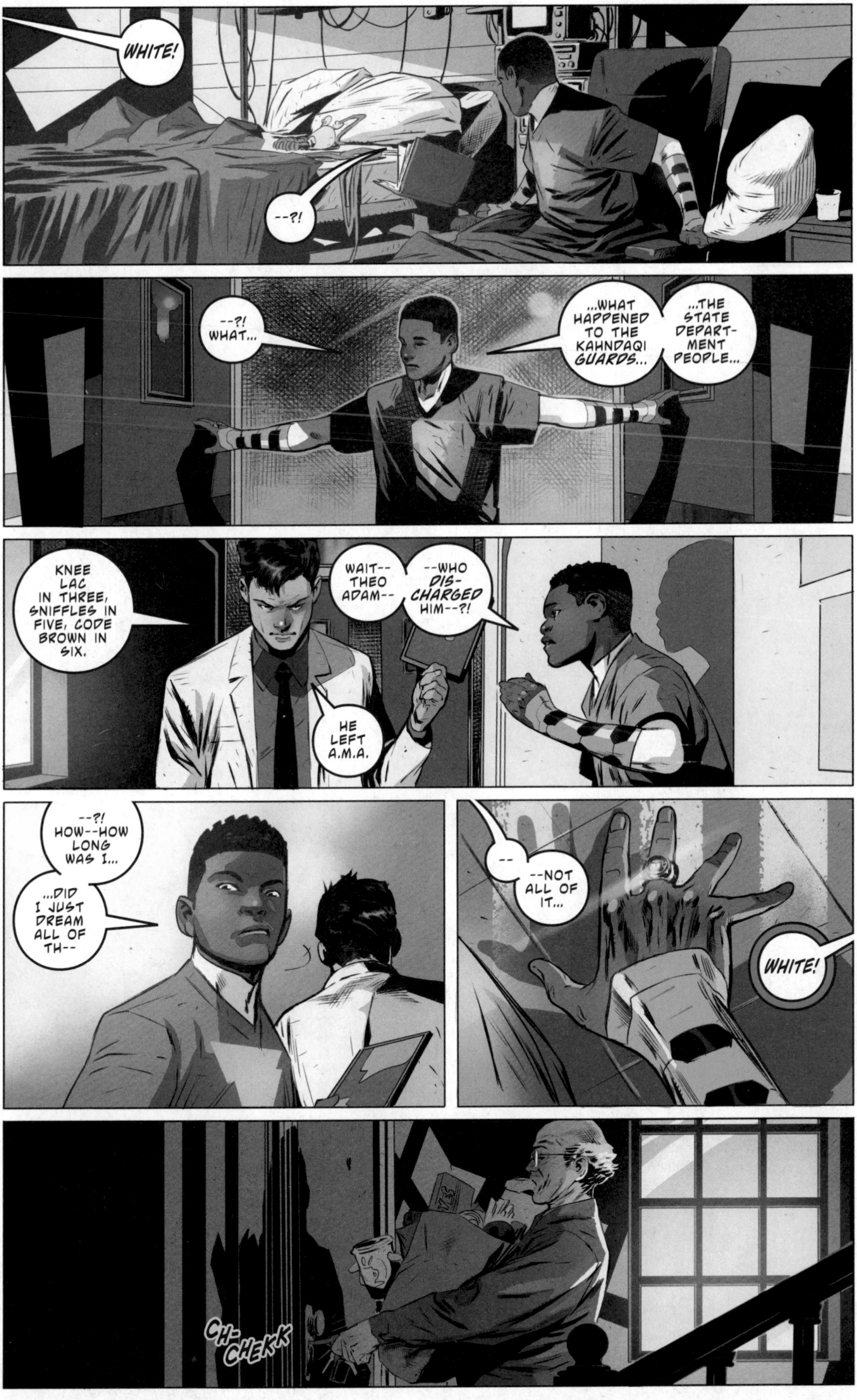
WHITE!
--?!
--?! WHAT...
...WHAT HAPPENED TO THE KAHNDAQI GUARDS...
...THE STATE DEPART-MENT PEOPLE...
KNEE LAC IN THREE, SNIFFLES IN FIVE, CODE BROWN IN SIX.
WAIT-- THEO ADAM--
--WHO DIS-CHARGED HIM--?!
HE LEFT A.M.A.
--?! HOW--HOW LONG WAS I...
...DID I JUST DREAM ALL OF TH--
--
--NOT ALL OF IT...
WHITE!
CH-CHEKK

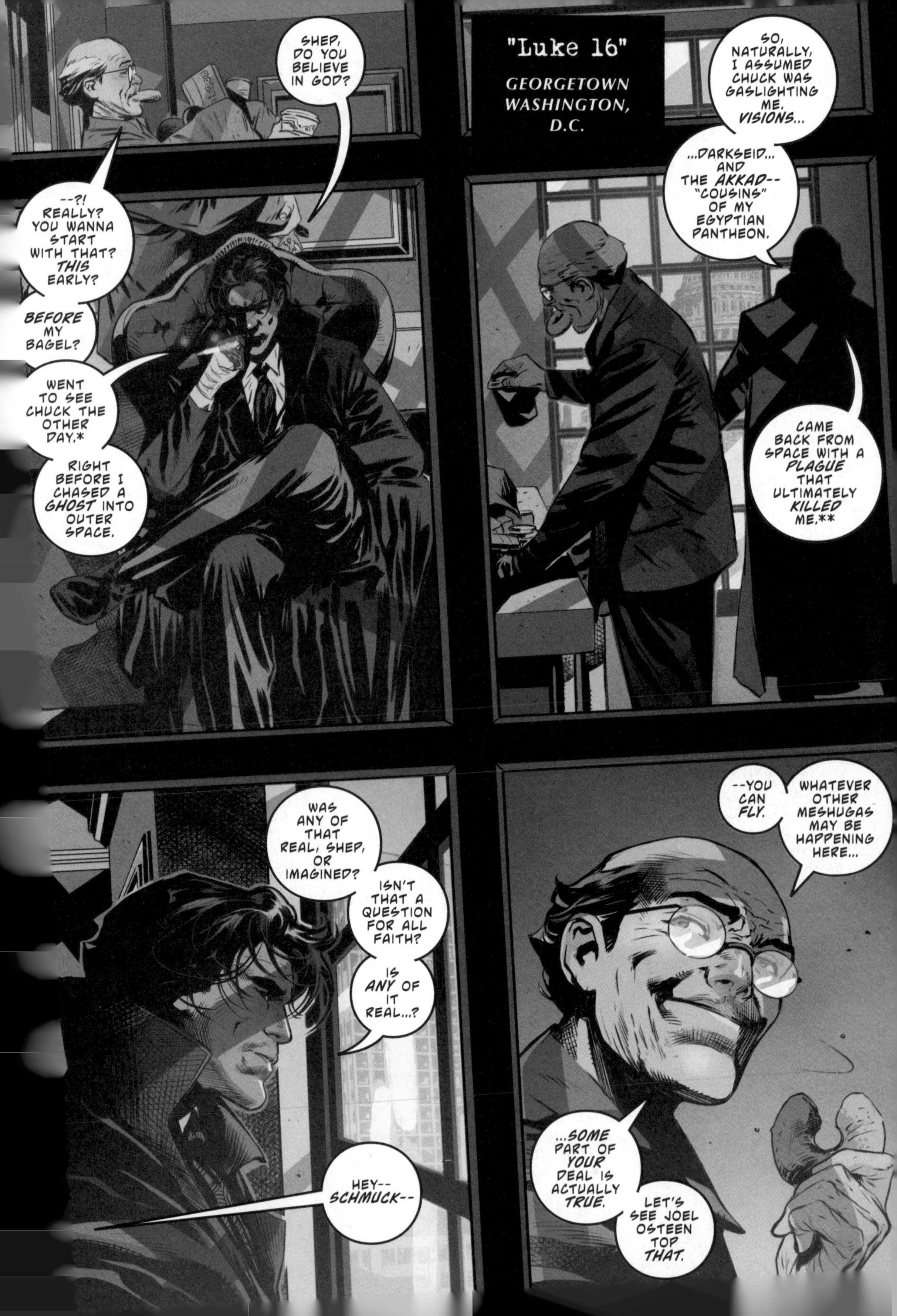

"Luke 16"
GEORGETOWN WASHINGTON, D.C.
SHEP, DO YOU BELIEVE IN GOD?
--?! REALLY? YOU WANNA START WITH THAT? THIS EARLY?
BEFORE MY BAGEL?
WENT TO SEE CHUCK THE OTHER DAY.*
RIGHT BEFORE I CHASED A GHOST INTO OUTER SPACE.
SO, NATURALLY, I ASSUMED CHUCK WAS GASLIGHTING ME. VISIONS...
...DARKSEID... AND THE AKKAD-- "COUSINS" OF MY EGYPTIAN PANTHEON.
CAME BACK FROM SPACE WITH A PLAGUE THAT ULTIMATELY KILLED ME.**
WAS ANY OF THAT REAL, SHEP, OR IMAGINED?
ISN'T THAT A QUESTION FOR ALL FAITH?
IS ANY OF IT REAL...?
HEY-- SCHMUCK--
--YOU CAN FLY.
WHATEVER OTHER MESHUGAS MAY BE HAPPENING HERE...
...SOME PART OF YOUR DEAL IS ACTUALLY TRUE.
LET'S SEE JOEL OSTEEN TOP THAT.

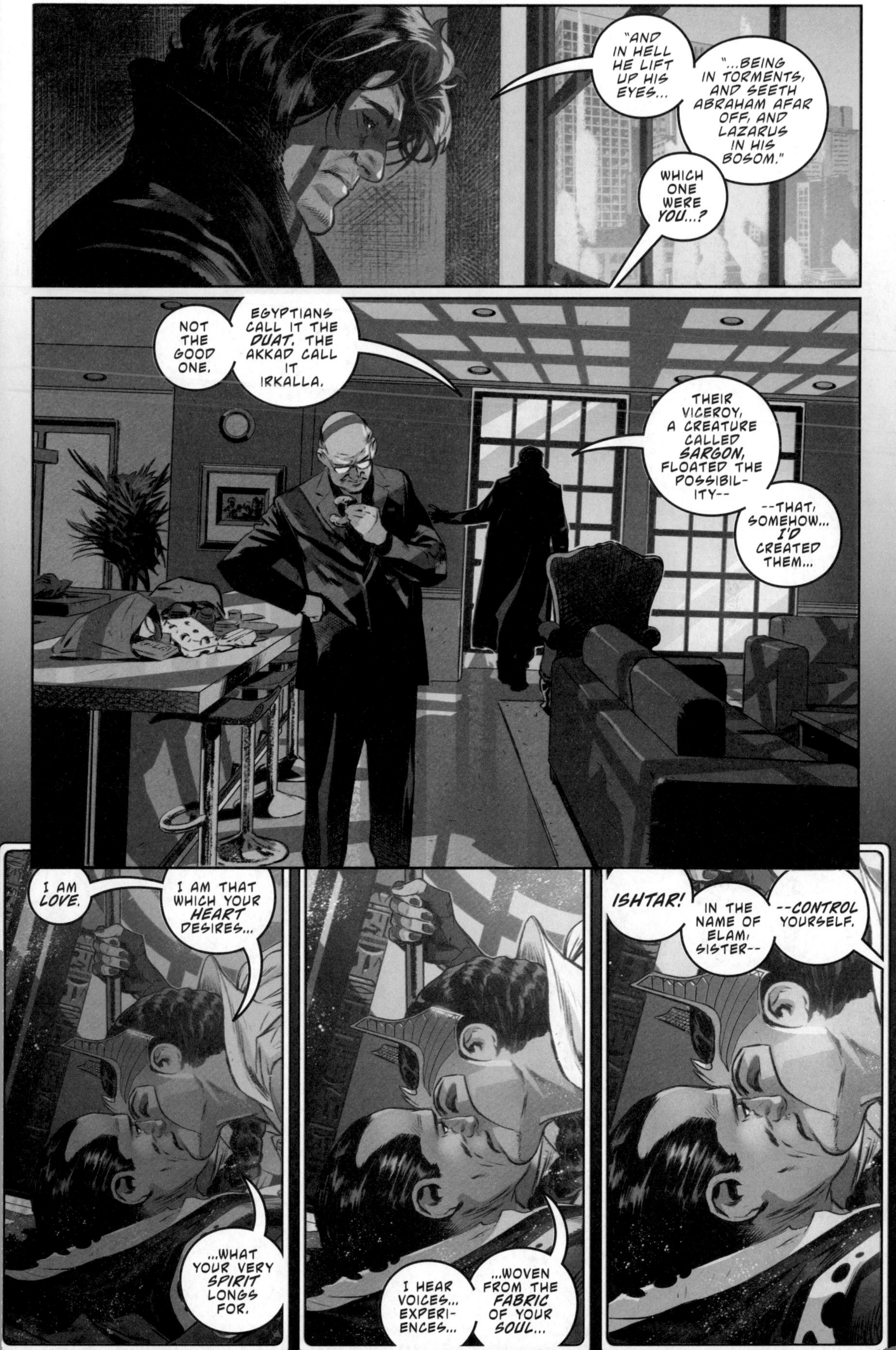
"AND IN HELL HE LIFT UP HIS EYES...
"...BEING IN TORMENTS, AND SEETH ABRAHAM AFAR OFF, AND LAZARUS IN HIS BOSOM."
WHICH ONE WERE YOU...?
NOT THE GOOD ONE.
EGYPTIANS CALL IT THE DUAT. THE AKKAD CALL IT IRKALLA.
THEIR VICEROY, A CREATURE CALLED SARGON, FLOATED THE POSSIBIL-ITY--
--THAT, SOMEHOW... I'D CREATED THEM...
I AM LOVE.
I AM THAT WHICH YOUR HEART DESIRES...
...WHAT YOUR VERY SPIRIT LONGS FOR.
I HEAR VOICES... EXPERI-ENCES...
...WOVEN FROM THE FABRIC OF YOUR SOUL...
ISHTAR!
IN THE NAME OF ELAM, SISTER--
--CONTROL YOURSELF.

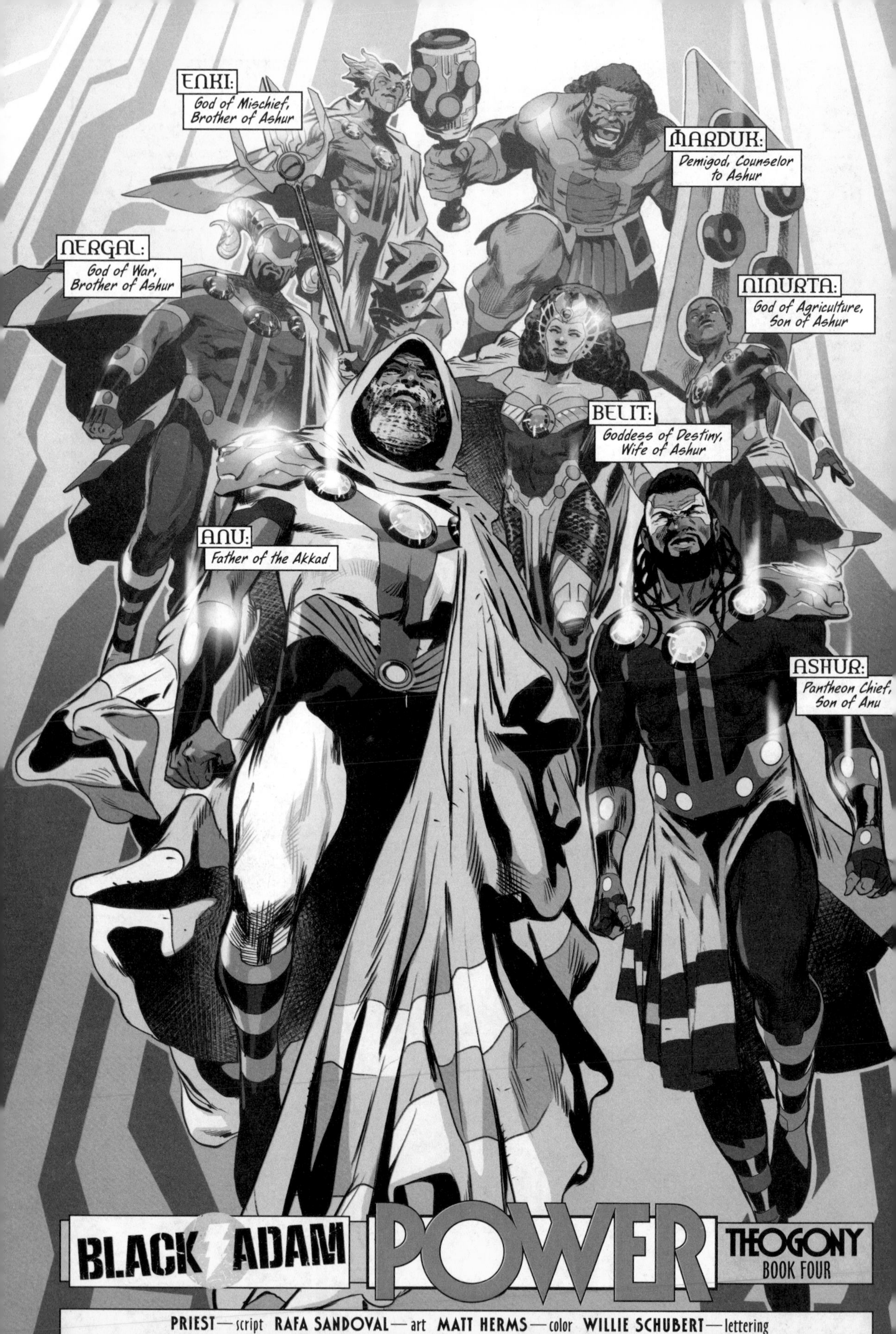
ENKI:
God of Mischief, Brother of Ashur
MARDUK:
Demigod, Counselor to Ashur
NERGAL:
God of War, Brother of Ashur
NINURTA:
God of Agriculture, Son of Ashur
BELIT:
Goddess of Destiny, Wife of Ashur
ANU:
Father of the Akkad
ASHUR:
Pantheon Chief, Son of Anu

BLACK ADAM POWER

THEOGONY
BOOK FOUR

PRIEST—script RAFA SANDOVAL—art MATT HERMS—color WILLIE SCHUBERT—lettering
IRVIN RODRIGUEZ—cover RAFA SANDOVAL & MATT HERMS, TAURIN CLARKE, PAMELA HOOGEBOOM—variant covers
CHRIS ROSA—associate editor PAUL KAMINSKI—editor

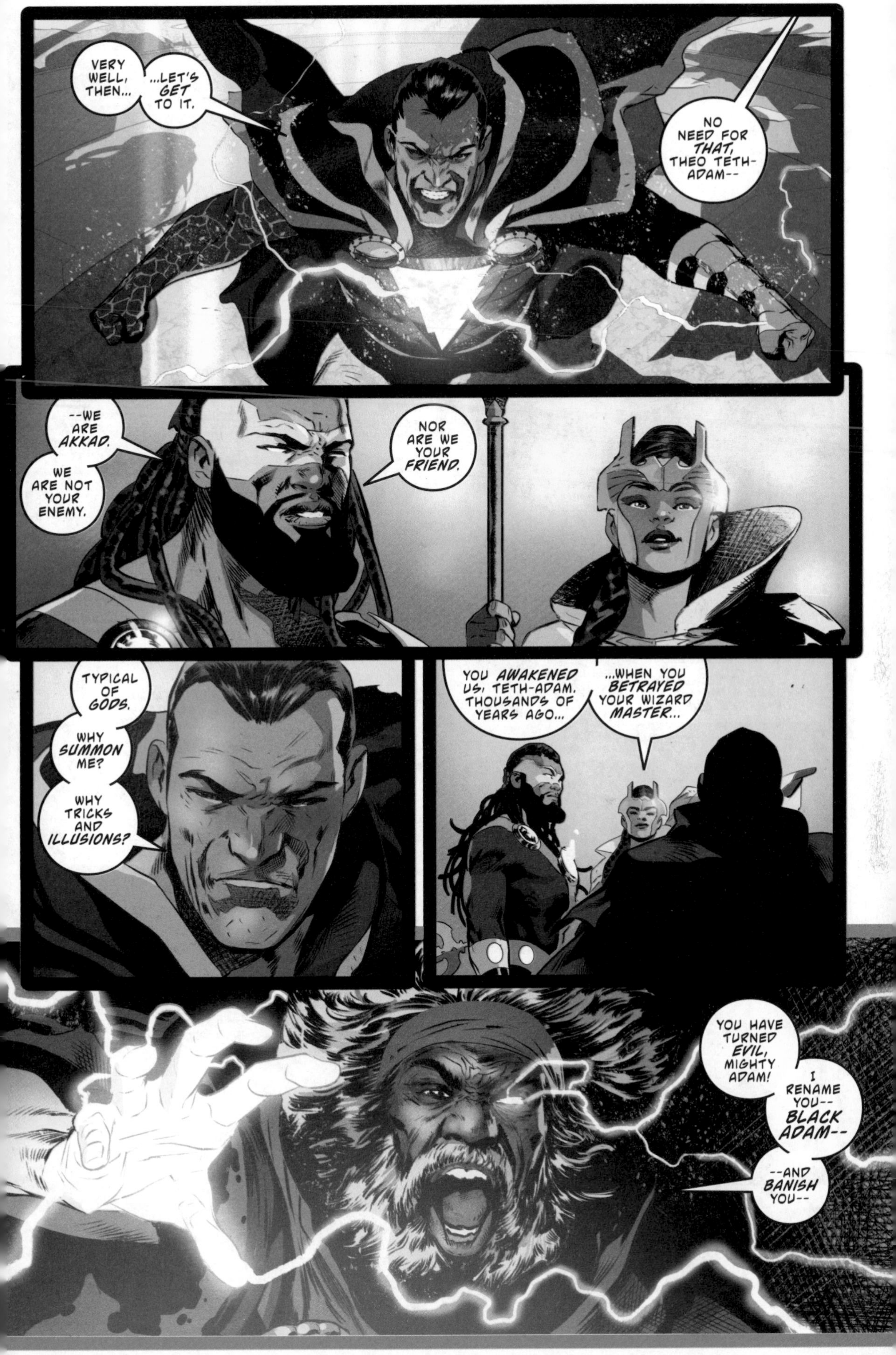
VERY WELL, THEN...
...LET'S GET TO IT.
NO NEED FOR THAT, THEO TETH-ADAM--
--WE ARE AKKAD.
WE ARE NOT YOUR ENEMY.
NOR ARE WE YOUR FRIEND.
TYPICAL OF GODS.
WHY SUMMON ME?
WHY TRICKS AND ILLUSIONS?
YOU AWAKENED US, TETH-ADAM. THOUSANDS OF YEARS AGO...
...WHEN YOU BETRAYED YOUR WIZARD MASTER...
YOU HAVE TURNED EVIL, MIGHTY ADAM!
I RENAME YOU--BLACK ADAM--
--AND BANISH YOU--

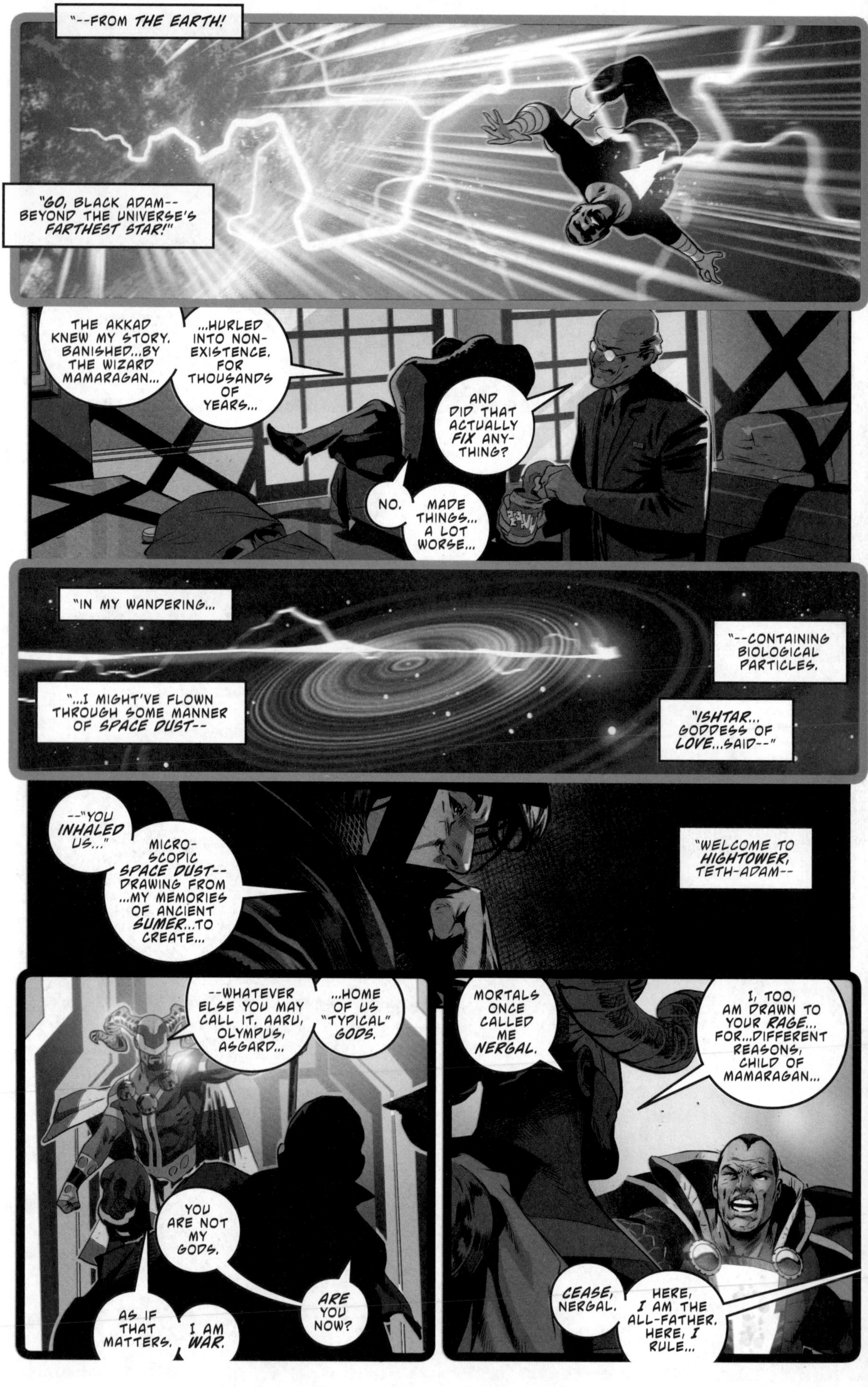
"--FROM THE EARTH!
"GO, BLACK ADAM-- BEYOND THE UNIVERSE'S FARTHEST STAR!"
THE AKKAD KNEW MY STORY. BANISHED...BY THE WIZARD MAMARAGAN...
...HURLED INTO NON-EXISTENCE. FOR THOUSANDS OF YEARS...
AND DID THAT ACTUALLY FIX ANYTHING?
NO.
MADE THINGS... A LOT WORSE...
"IN MY WANDERING...
"...I MIGHT'VE FLOWN THROUGH SOME MANNER OF SPACE DUST--
"--CONTAINING BIOLOGICAL PARTICLES.
"ISHTAR... GODDESS OF LOVE...SAID--"
--"YOU INHALED US..."
MICRO-SCOPIC SPACE DUST-- DRAWING FROM ...MY MEMORIES OF ANCIENT SUMER...TO CREATE...
"WELCOME TO HIGHTOWER, TETH-ADAM--
--WHATEVER ELSE YOU MAY CALL IT. AARU, OLYMPUS, ASGARD...
...HOME OF US "TYPICAL" GODS.
YOU ARE NOT MY GODS.
ARE YOU NOW?
AS IF THAT MATTERS.
I AM WAR.
MORTALS ONCE CALLED ME NERGAL.
I, TOO, AM DRAWN TO YOUR RAGE... FOR...DIFFERENT REASONS, CHILD OF MAMARAGAN...
CEASE, NERGAL.
HERE, I AM THE ALL-FATHER. HERE, I RULE...

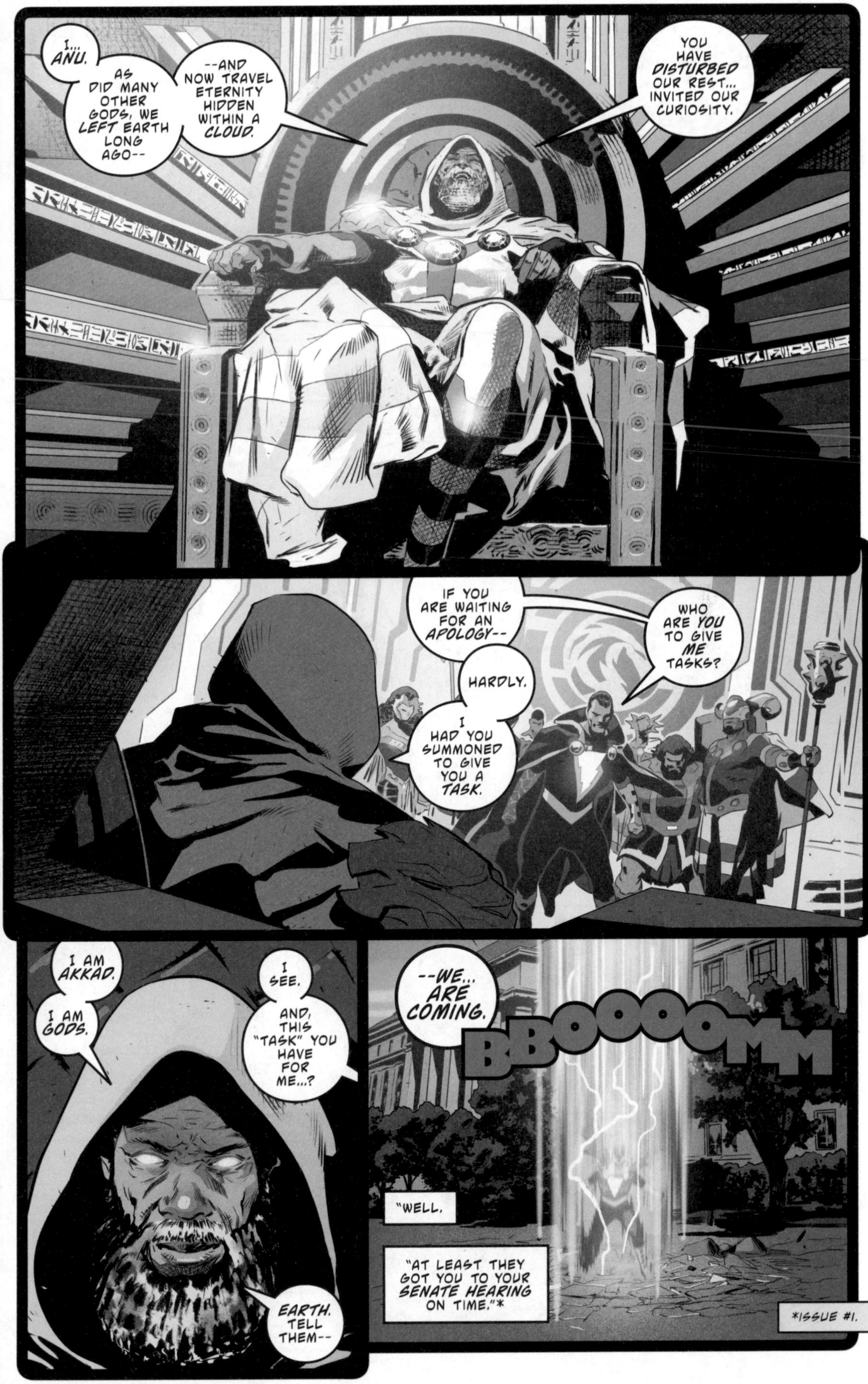
I... ANU.
AS DID MANY OTHER GODS, WE LEFT EARTH LONG AGO--
--AND NOW TRAVEL ETERNITY HIDDEN WITHIN A CLOUD.
YOU HAVE DISTURBED OUR REST... INVITED OUR CURIOSITY.
IF YOU ARE WAITING FOR AN APOLOGY--
HARDLY.
I HAD YOU SUMMONED TO GIVE YOU A TASK.
WHO ARE YOU TO GIVE ME TASKS?
I AM AKKAD.
I AM GODS.
I SEE.
AND, THIS "TASK" YOU HAVE FOR ME...?
EARTH. TELL THEM--
--WE... ARE COMING.
BBOOOOOMM
"WELL.
"AT LEAST THEY GOT YOU TO YOUR SENATE HEARING ON TIME."*
*ISSUE #1.

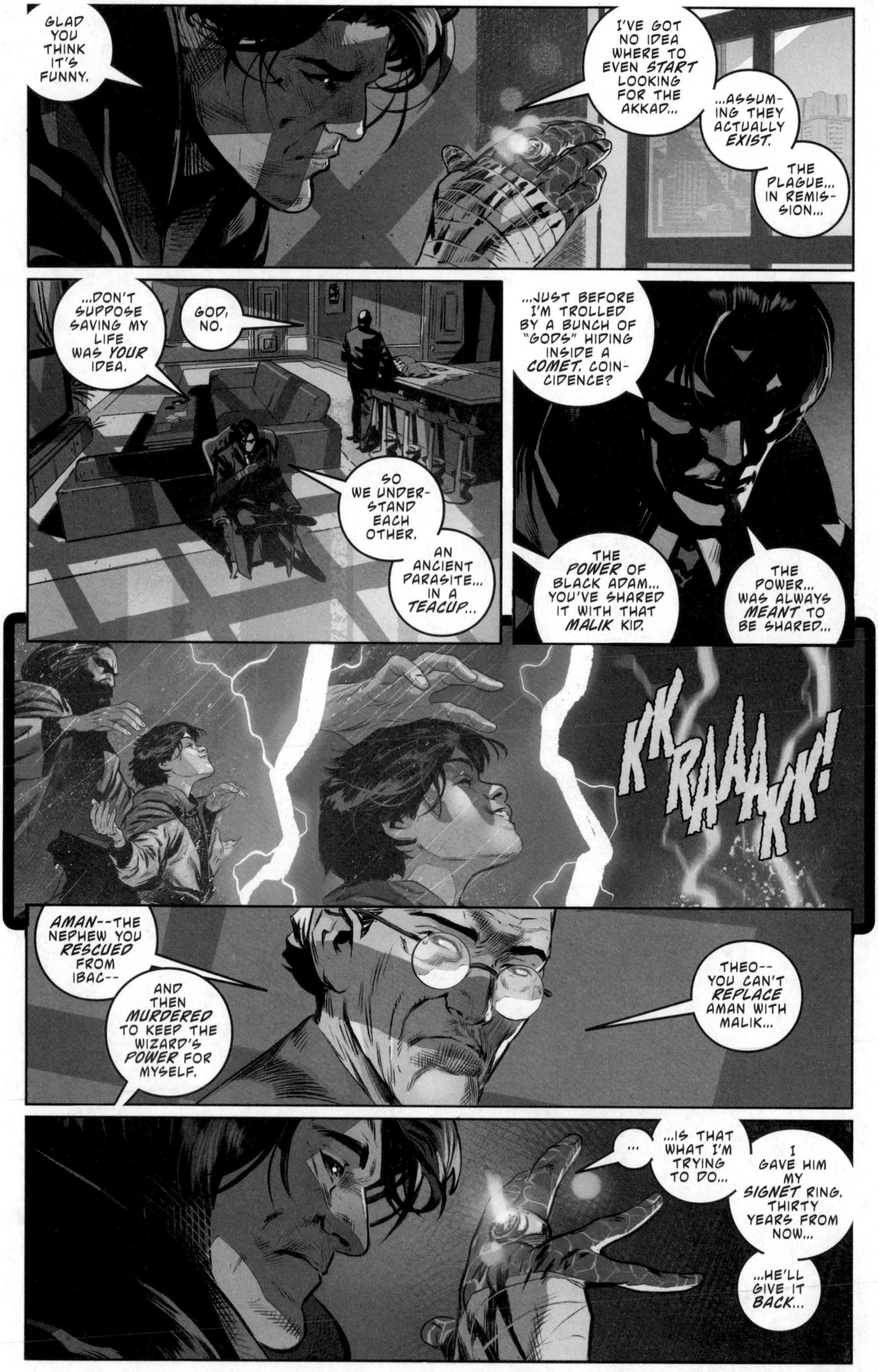
GLAD YOU THINK IT'S FUNNY.
I'VE GOT NO IDEA WHERE TO EVEN START LOOKING FOR THE AKKAD...
...ASSUMING THEY ACTUALLY EXIST.
THE PLAGUE... IN REMISSION...
...DON'T SUPPOSE SAVING MY LIFE WAS YOUR IDEA.
GOD, NO.
SO WE UNDERSTAND EACH OTHER.
AN ANCIENT PARASITE... IN A TEACUP...
...JUST BEFORE I'M TROLLED BY A BUNCH OF "GODS" HIDING INSIDE A COMET. COINCIDENCE?
THE POWER OF BLACK ADAM... YOU'VE SHARED IT WITH THAT MALIK KID.
THE POWER... WAS ALWAYS MEANT TO BE SHARED...
KKRAAAKK!
AMAN--THE NEPHEW YOU RESCUED FROM IBAC--
AND THEN MURDERED TO KEEP THE WIZARD'S POWER FOR MYSELF.
THEO--YOU CAN'T REPLACE AMAN WITH MALIK...
...
...IS THAT WHAT I'M TRYING TO DO...
I GAVE HIM MY SIGNET RING. THIRTY YEARS FROM NOW...
...HE'LL GIVE IT BACK...

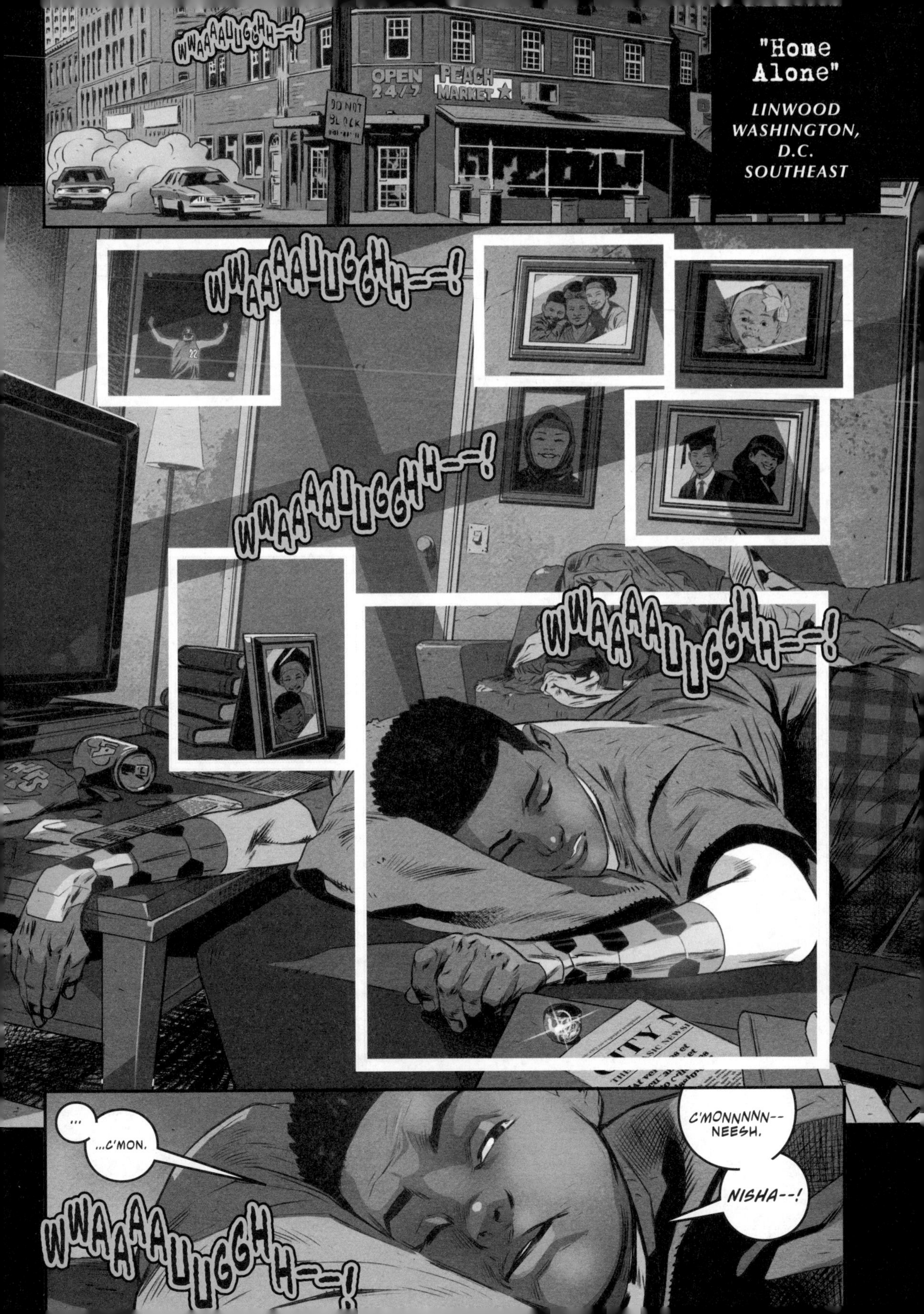
WWAAAAUGGHH--!
OPEN 24/7
PEACH MARKET
DO NOT BLOCK
"Home Alone"
LINWOOD WASHINGTON, D.C. SOUTHEAST
WWAAAAUUGGHH--!
WWAAAAUUGGHH--!
WWAAAAUUGGHH--!
...
...C'MON.
C'MONNNNN-- NEESH.
NISHA--!
WWAAAAUUGGHH--!

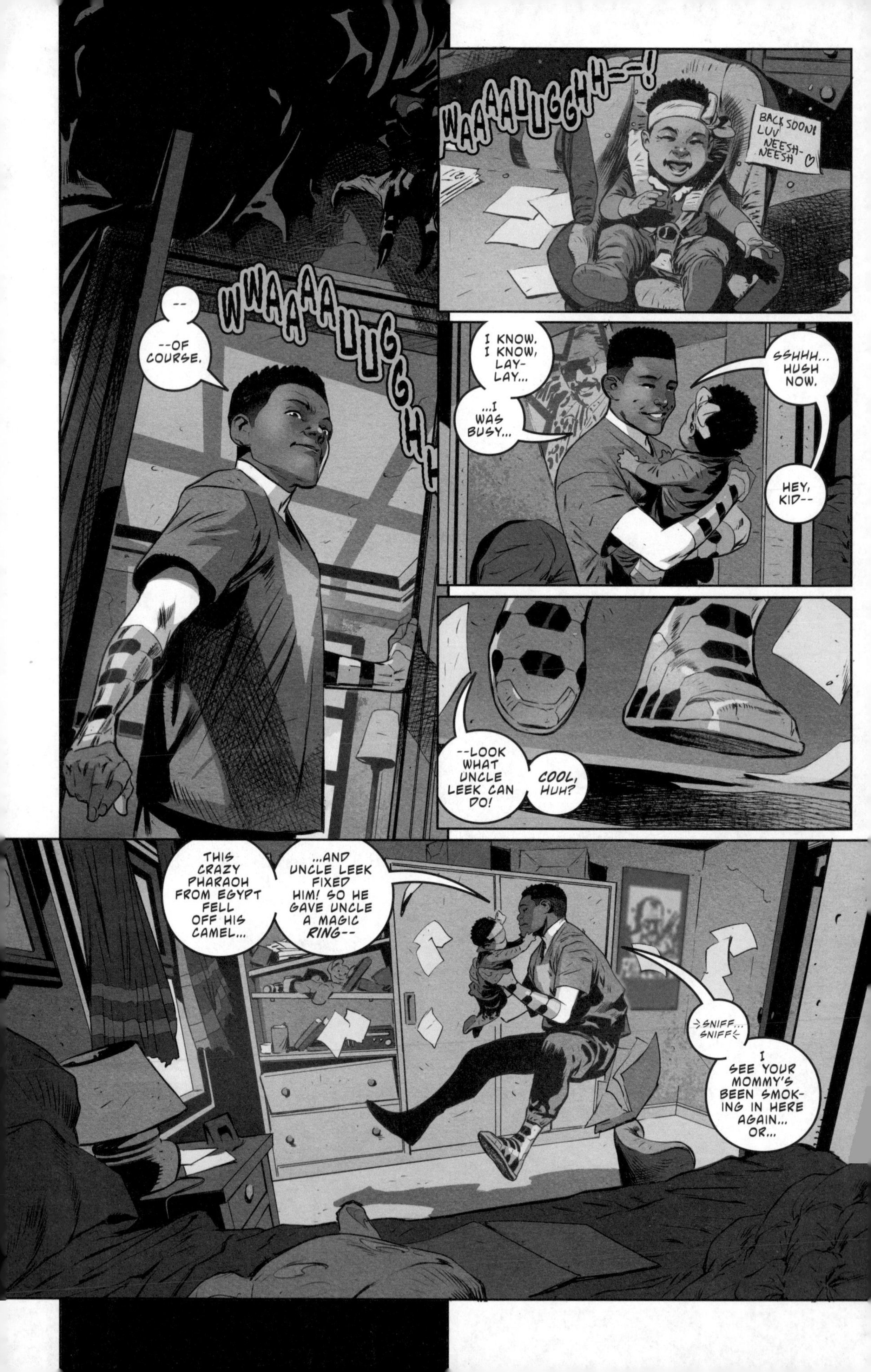WAAAAUGGHH--!
BACK SOON! LUV NEESH-NEESH
WWAAAAAUUGGHH
--
--OF COURSE.
I KNOW. I KNOW, LAY-LAY...
...I WAS BUSY...
SSHHH... HUSH NOW.
HEY, KID--
--LOOK WHAT UNCLE LEEK CAN DO!
COOL, HUH?
THIS CRAZY PHARAOH FROM EGYPT FELL OFF HIS CAMEL...
...AND UNCLE LEEK FIXED HIM! SO HE GAVE UNCLE A MAGIC RING--
SNIFF... SNIFF
I SEE YOUR MOMMY'S BEEN SMOKING IN HERE AGAIN... OR...

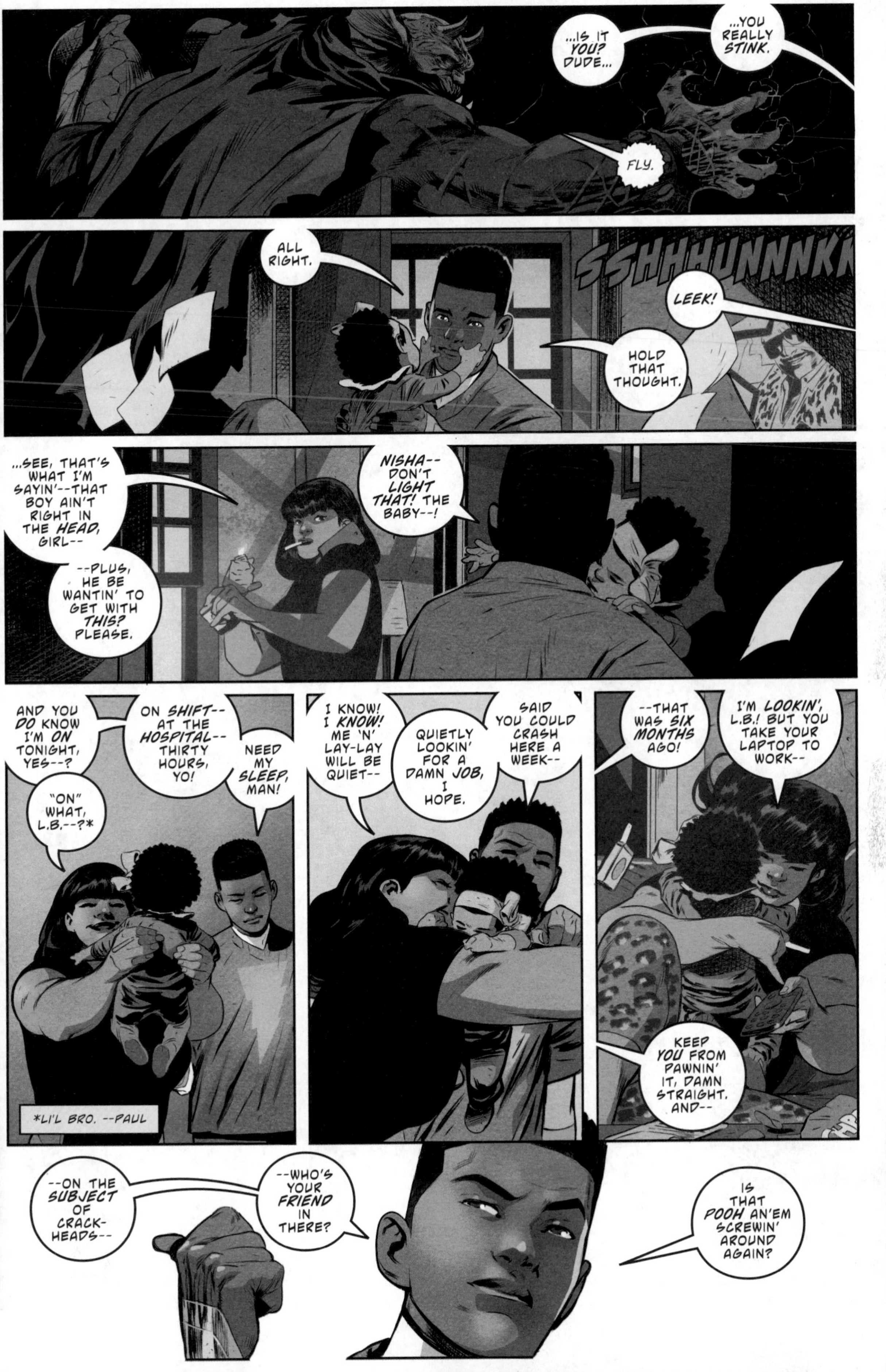

...IS IT YOU? DUDE...
...YOU REALLY STINK.
FLY.
ALL RIGHT.
SSHHHUNNNKK
LEEK!
HOLD THAT THOUGHT.
...SEE, THAT'S WHAT I'M SAYIN'--THAT BOY AIN'T RIGHT IN THE HEAD, GIRL--
--PLUS, HE BE WANTIN' TO GET WITH THIS? PLEASE.
NISHA--DON'T LIGHT THAT! THE BABY--!
AND YOU DO KNOW I'M ON TONIGHT, YES--?
"ON" WHAT, L.B.--?*
ON SHIFT--AT THE HOSPITAL--THIRTY HOURS, YO!
NEED MY SLEEP, MAN!
*LI'L BRO. --PAUL
I KNOW! I KNOW! ME 'N' LAY-LAY WILL BE QUIET--
QUIETLY LOOKIN' FOR A DAMN JOB, I HOPE.
SAID YOU COULD CRASH HERE A WEEK--
--THAT WAS SIX MONTHS AGO!
I'M LOOKIN', L.B.! BUT YOU TAKE YOUR LAPTOP TO WORK--
KEEP YOU FROM PAWNIN' IT, DAMN STRAIGHT. AND--
--ON THE SUBJECT OF CRACK-HEADS--
--WHO'S YOUR FRIEND IN THERE?
IS THAT POOH AN'EM SCREWIN' AROUND AGAIN?

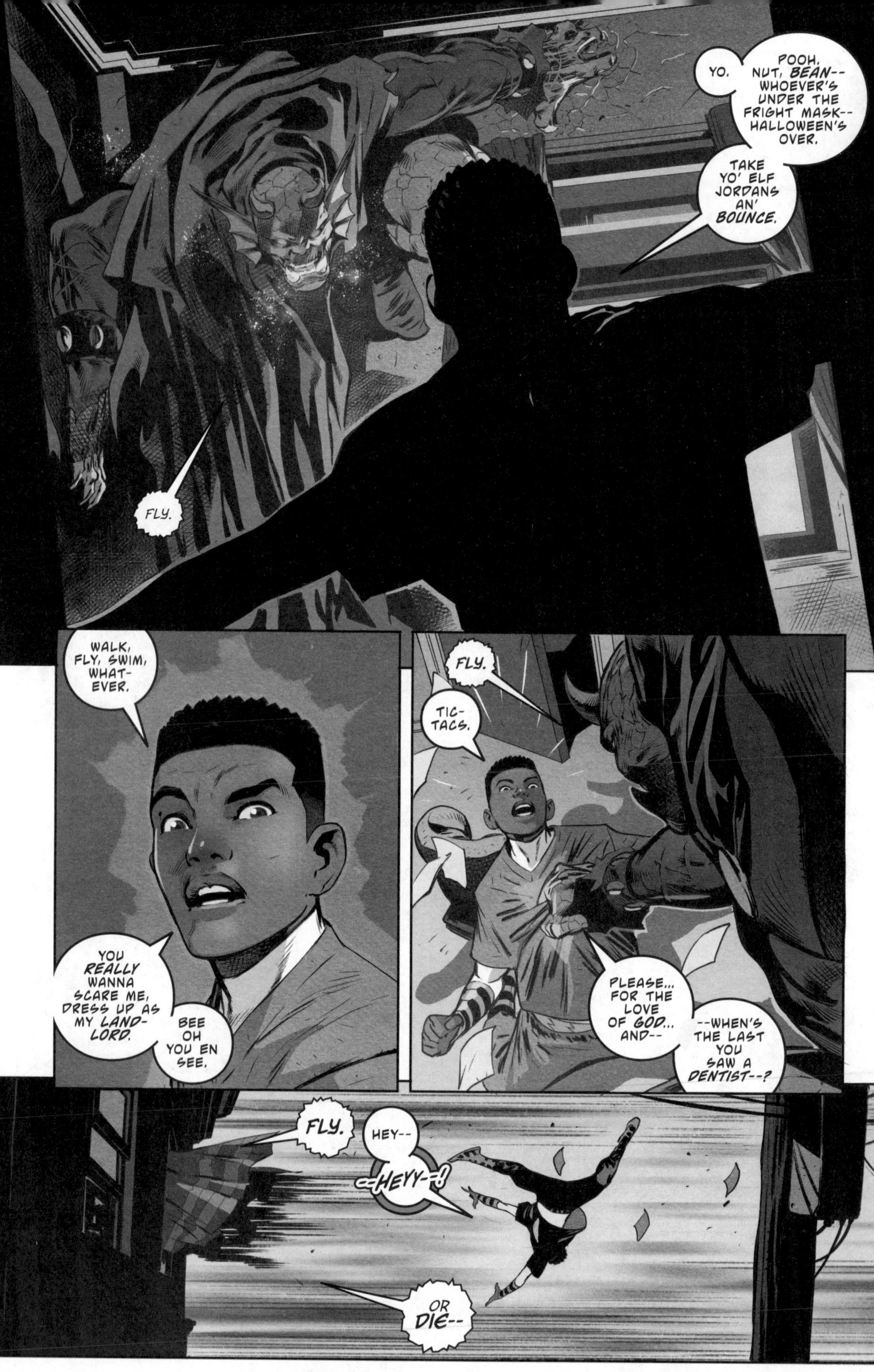
YO.
POOH, NUT, BEAN-- WHOEVER'S UNDER THE FRIGHT MASK-- HALLOWEEN'S OVER.
TAKE YO' ELF JORDANS AN' BOUNCE.
FLY.
WALK, FLY, SWIM, WHAT-EVER.
YOU REALLY WANNA SCARE ME, DRESS UP AS MY LAND-LORD.
BEE OH YOU EN SEE.
FLY.
TIC-TACS.
PLEASE... FOR THE LOVE OF GOD... AND--
--WHEN'S THE LAST YOU SAW A DENTIST--?
FLY.
HEY--
--HEYY--!
OR DIE--

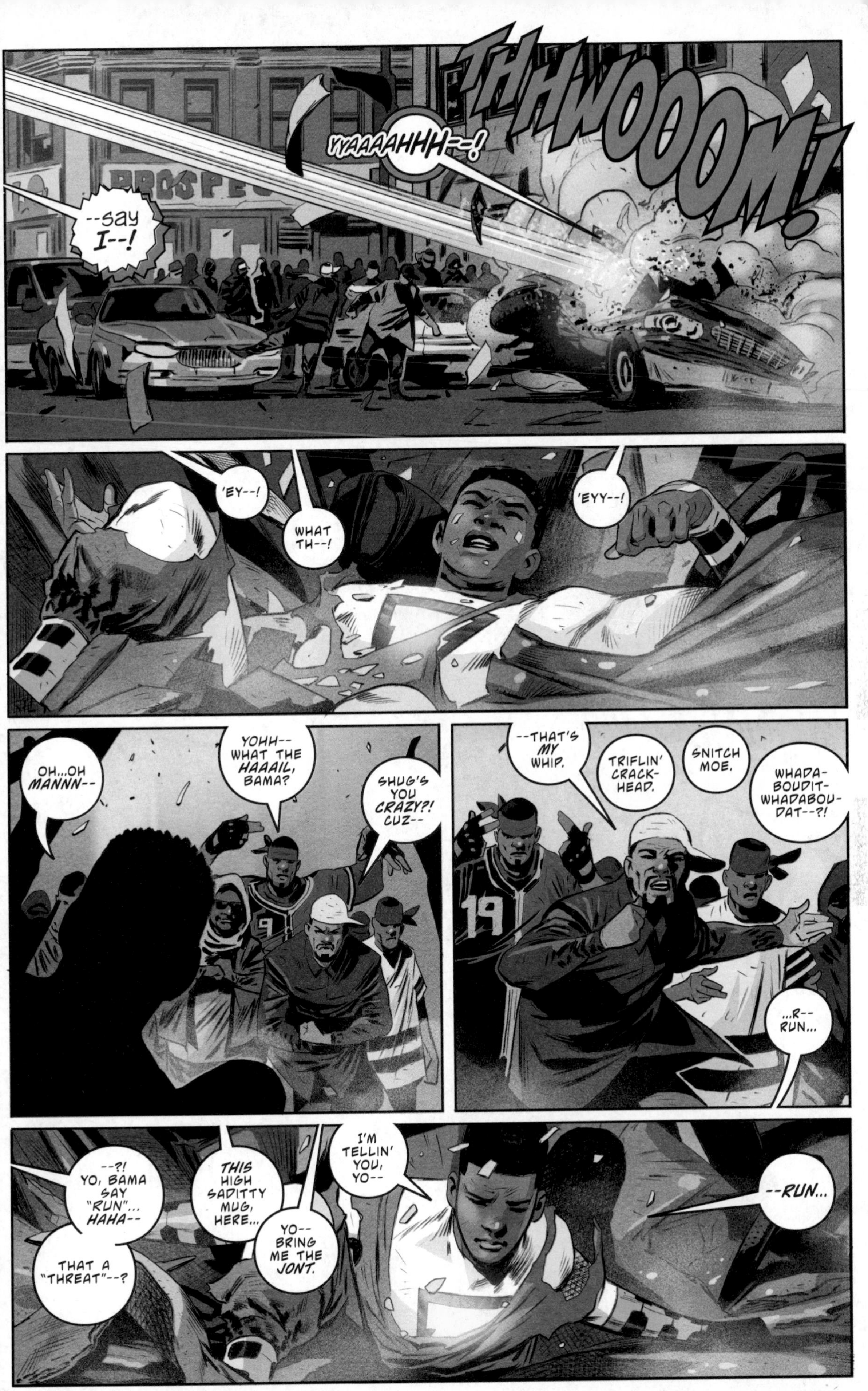
THHWOOOM!
YYAAAAHHH--!
--say I--!
'EY--!
WHAT TH--!
'EYY--!
OH...OH MANNN--
YOHH-- WHAT THE HAAAIL, BAMA?
SHUG'S YOU CRAZY?! CUZ--
--THAT'S MY WHIP.
TRIFLIN' CRACK-HEAD.
SNITCH MOE.
WHADA-BOUDIT-WHADABOU-DAT--?!
...R-- RUN...
--?! YO, BAMA SAY "RUN"... HAHA--
THAT A "THREAT"--?
THIS HIGH SADITTY MUG, HERE...
I'M TELLIN' YOU, YO--
YO-- BRING ME THE JONT.
--RUN...

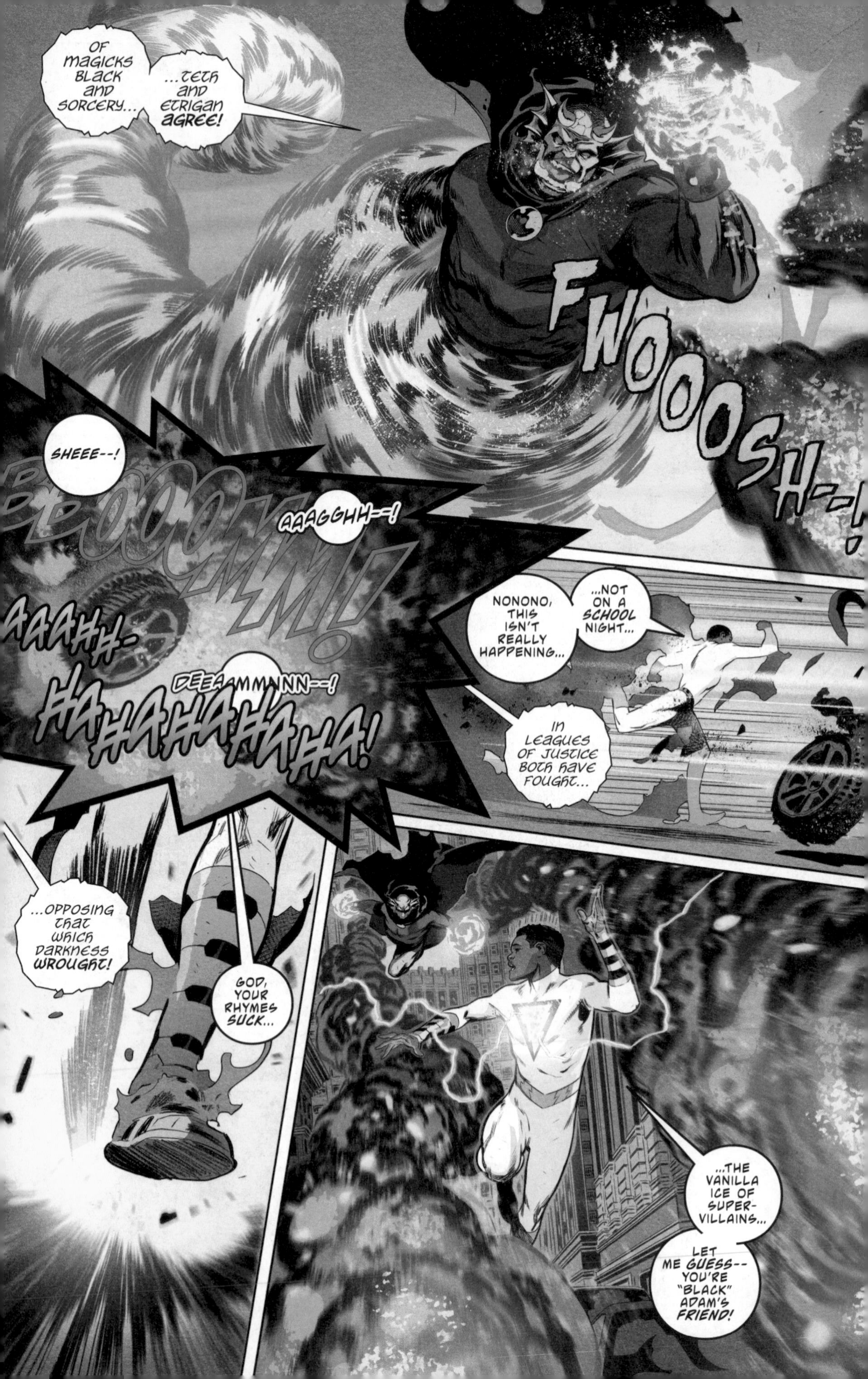

OF MAGICKS BLACK AND SORCERY...
...TETH AND ETRIGAN AGREE!
FWOOOOSH--!
SHEEE--!
BLOOOOMM!
AAAGGHH--!
AAAHH-HAHAHAHAHAHAHA!
DEEAAMMNNN--!
NONONO, THIS ISN'T REALLY HAPPENING...
...NOT ON A SCHOOL NIGHT...
IN LEAGUES OF JUSTICE BOTH HAVE FOUGHT...
...OPPOSING THAT WHICH DARKNESS WROUGHT!
GOD, YOUR RHYMES SUCK...
...THE VANILLA ICE OF SUPER-VILLAINS...
LET ME GUESS--YOU'RE "BLACK" ADAM'S FRIEND!

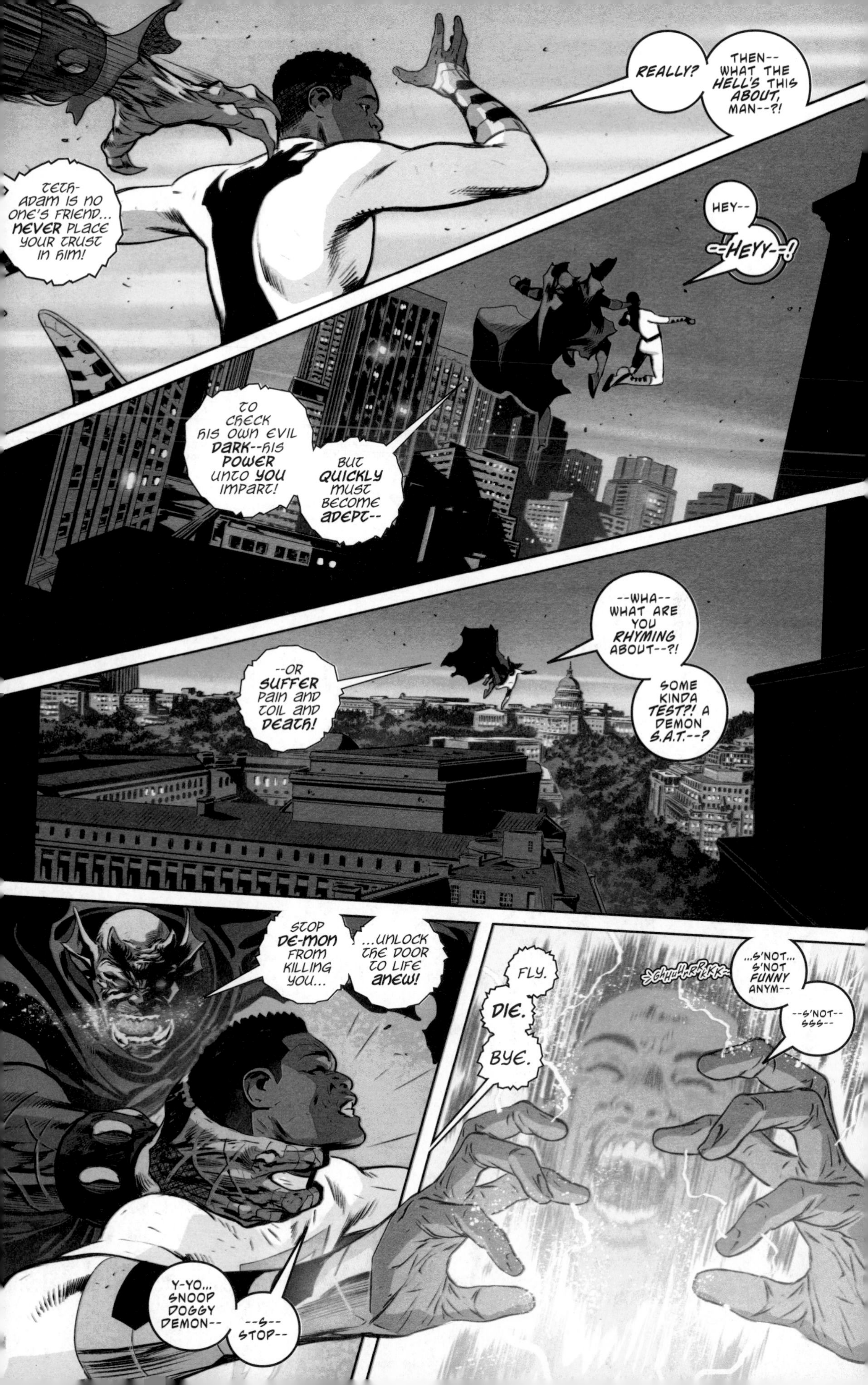

REALLY?
THEN-- WHAT THE HELL'S THIS ABOUT, MAN--?!
TETH-ADAM IS NO ONE'S FRIEND... NEVER PLACE YOUR TRUST IN HIM!
HEY--
--HEYY--!
TO CHECK HIS OWN EVIL DARK--HIS POWER UNTO YOU IMPART!
BUT QUICKLY MUST BECOME ADEPT--
--WHA-- WHAT ARE YOU RHYMING ABOUT--?!
SOME KINDA TEST?! A DEMON S.A.T.--?
--OR SUFFER PAIN AND TOIL AND DEATH!
STOP DE-MON FROM KILLING YOU...
...UNLOCK THE DOOR TO LIFE ANEW!
Y-YO... SNOOP DOGGY DEMON--
--S-- STOP--
FLY.
DIE.
BYE.
...S'NOT... S'NOT FUNNY ANYM--
--S'NOT-- SSS--

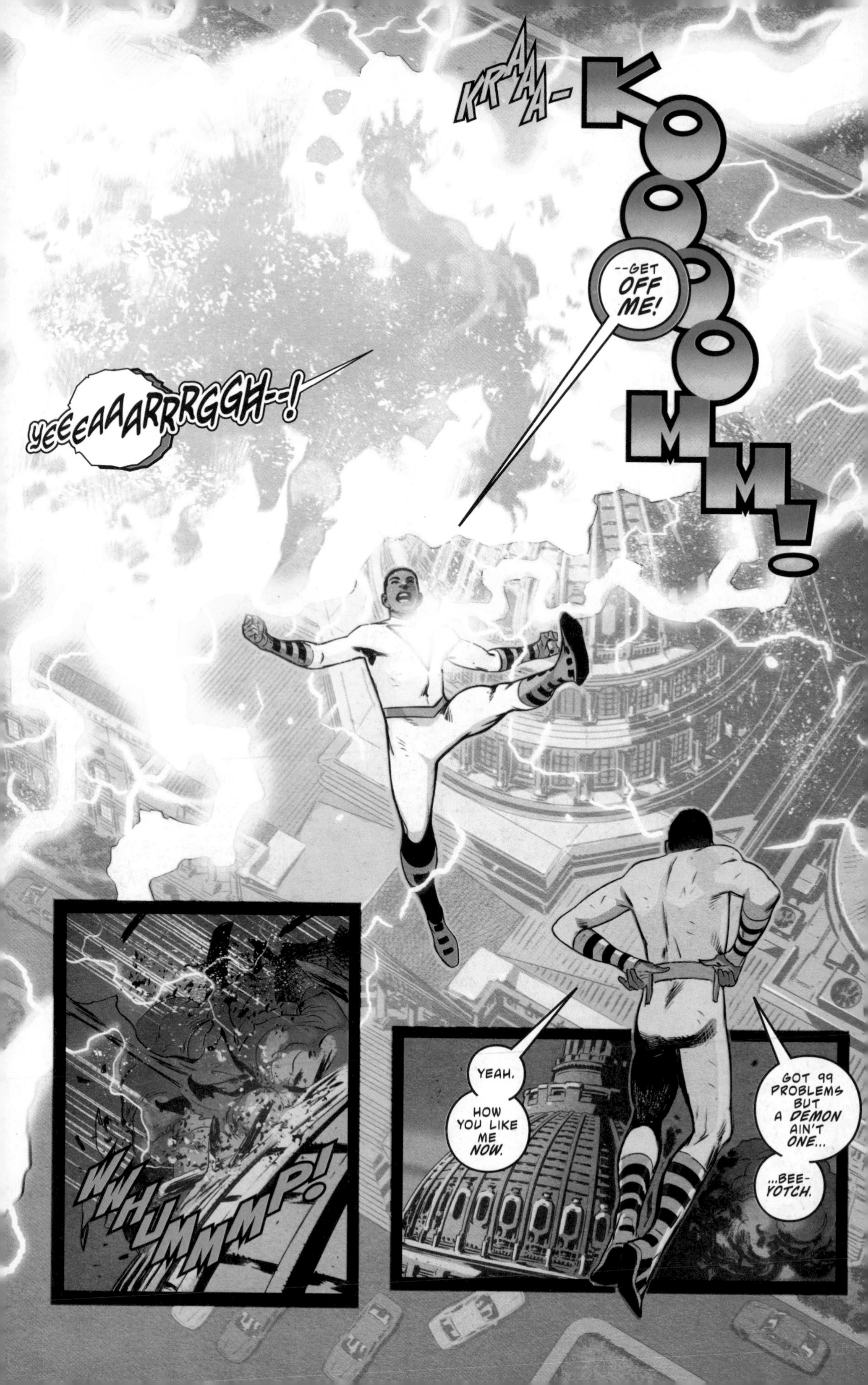
KRAAA-KOOOOOMM!
--GET OFF ME!
YEEEAAARRRGGH--!
WWHUMMMMP!
YEAH.
HOW YOU LIKE ME NOW.
GOT 99 PROBLEMS BUT A DEMON AIN'T ONE...
...BEE-YOTCH.

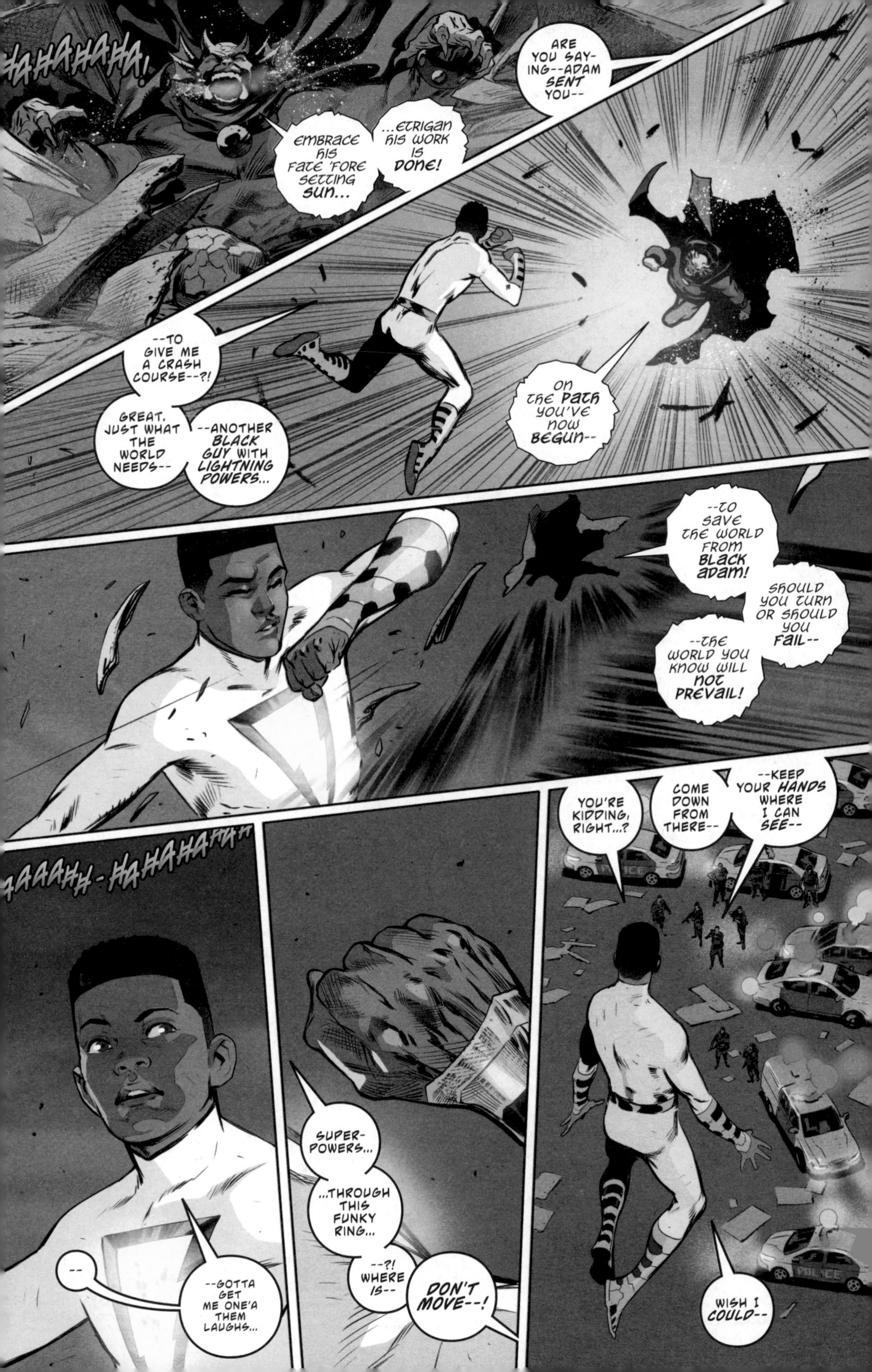
HAHAHAHA!
ARE YOU SAYING--ADAM SENT YOU--
EMBRACE HIS FATE 'FORE SETTING SUN...
...ETRIGAN HIS WORK IS DONE!
--TO GIVE ME A CRASH COURSE--?!
GREAT. JUST WHAT THE WORLD NEEDS--
--ANOTHER BLACK GUY WITH LIGHTNING POWERS...
ON THE PATH YOU'VE NOW BEGUN--
--TO SAVE THE WORLD FROM BLACK ADAM!
SHOULD YOU TURN OR SHOULD YOU FAIL--
--THE WORLD YOU KNOW WILL NOT PREVAIL!
AAAAH-HAHAHAHA
--
--GOTTA GET ME ONE'A THEM LAUGHS...
SUPER-POWERS...
...THROUGH THIS FUNKY RING...
--?! WHERE IS--
DON'T MOVE--!
YOU'RE KIDDING, RIGHT...?
COME DOWN FROM THERE--
--KEEP YOUR HANDS WHERE I CAN SEE--
WISH I COULD--

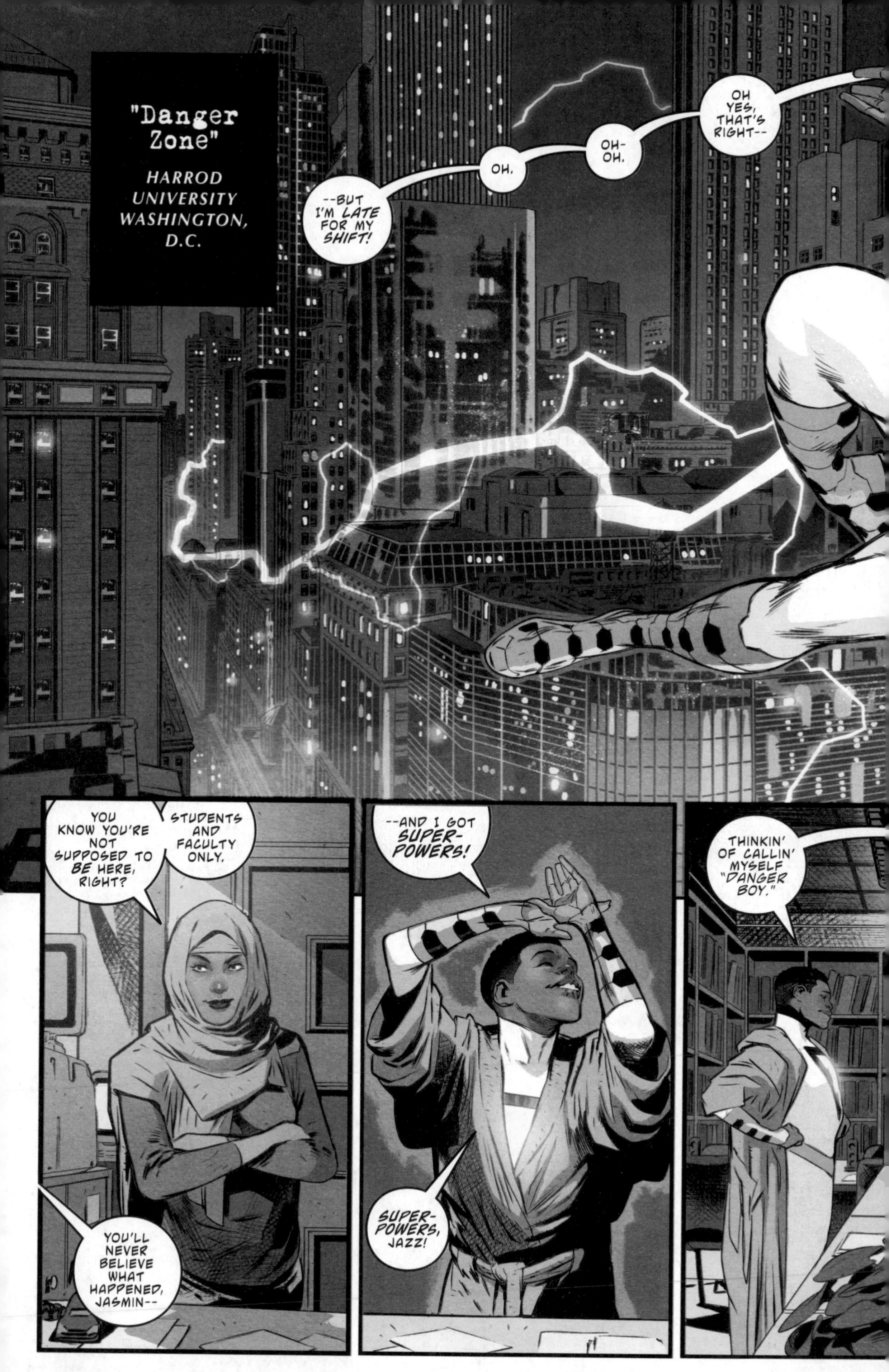
"Danger Zone"
HARROD UNIVERSITY WASHINGTON, D.C.
--BUT I'M LATE FOR MY SHIFT!
OH.
OH-OH.
OH YES, THAT'S RIGHT--
YOU KNOW YOU'RE NOT SUPPOSED TO BE HERE, RIGHT?
STUDENTS AND FACULTY ONLY.
YOU'LL NEVER BELIEVE WHAT HAPPENED, JASMIN--
--AND I GOT SUPER-POWERS!
SUPER-POWERS, JAZZ!
THINKIN' OF CALLIN' MYSELF "DANGER BOY."

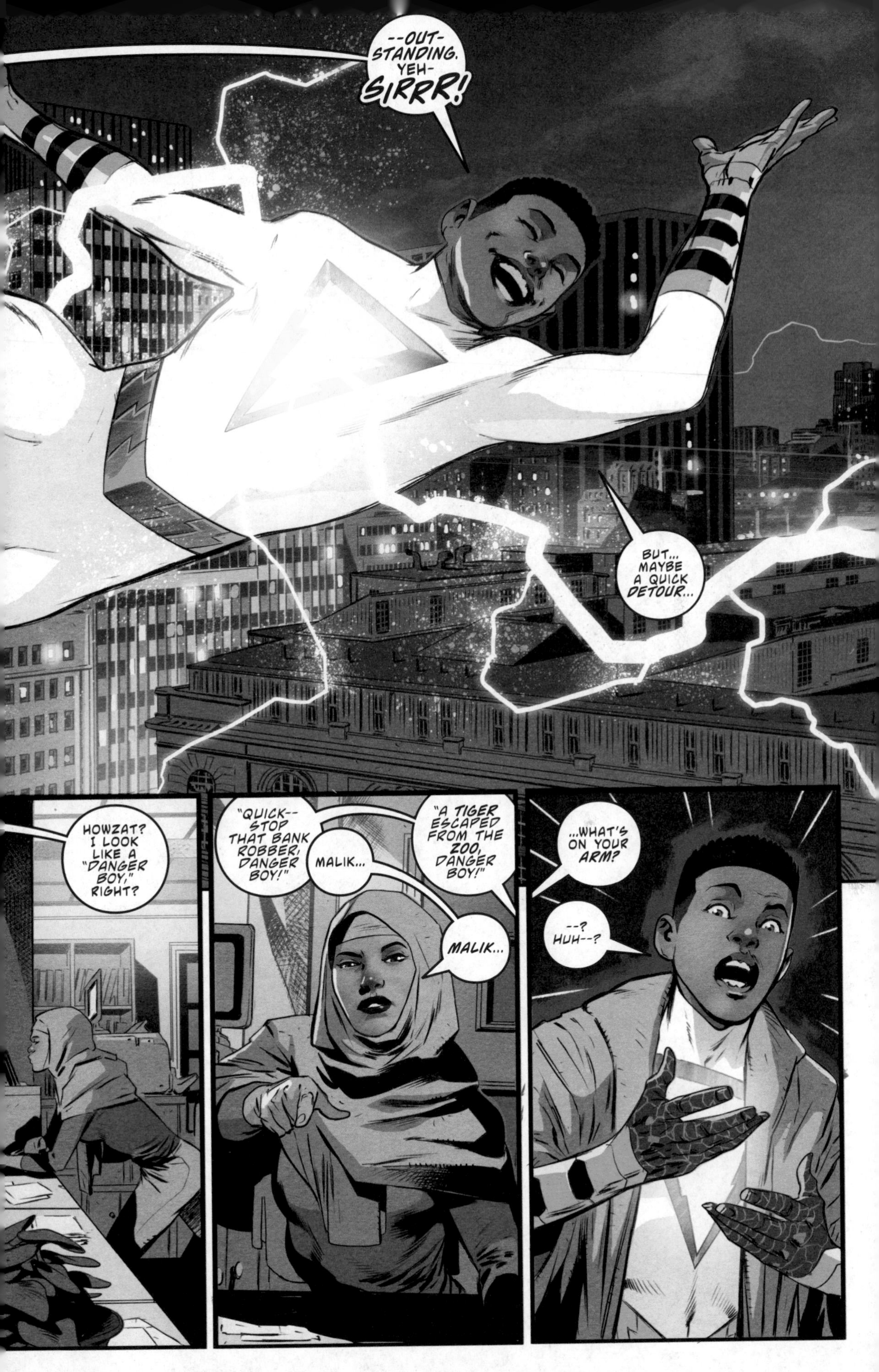
--OUT-STANDING. YEH-SIRRR!
BUT... MAYBE A QUICK DETOUR...
HOWZAT? I LOOK LIKE A "DANGER BOY," RIGHT?
"QUICK--STOP THAT BANK ROBBER, DANGER BOY!"
"A TIGER ESCAPED FROM THE ZOO, DANGER BOY!"
MALIK...
MALIK...
...WHAT'S ON YOUR ARM?
--? HUH--?

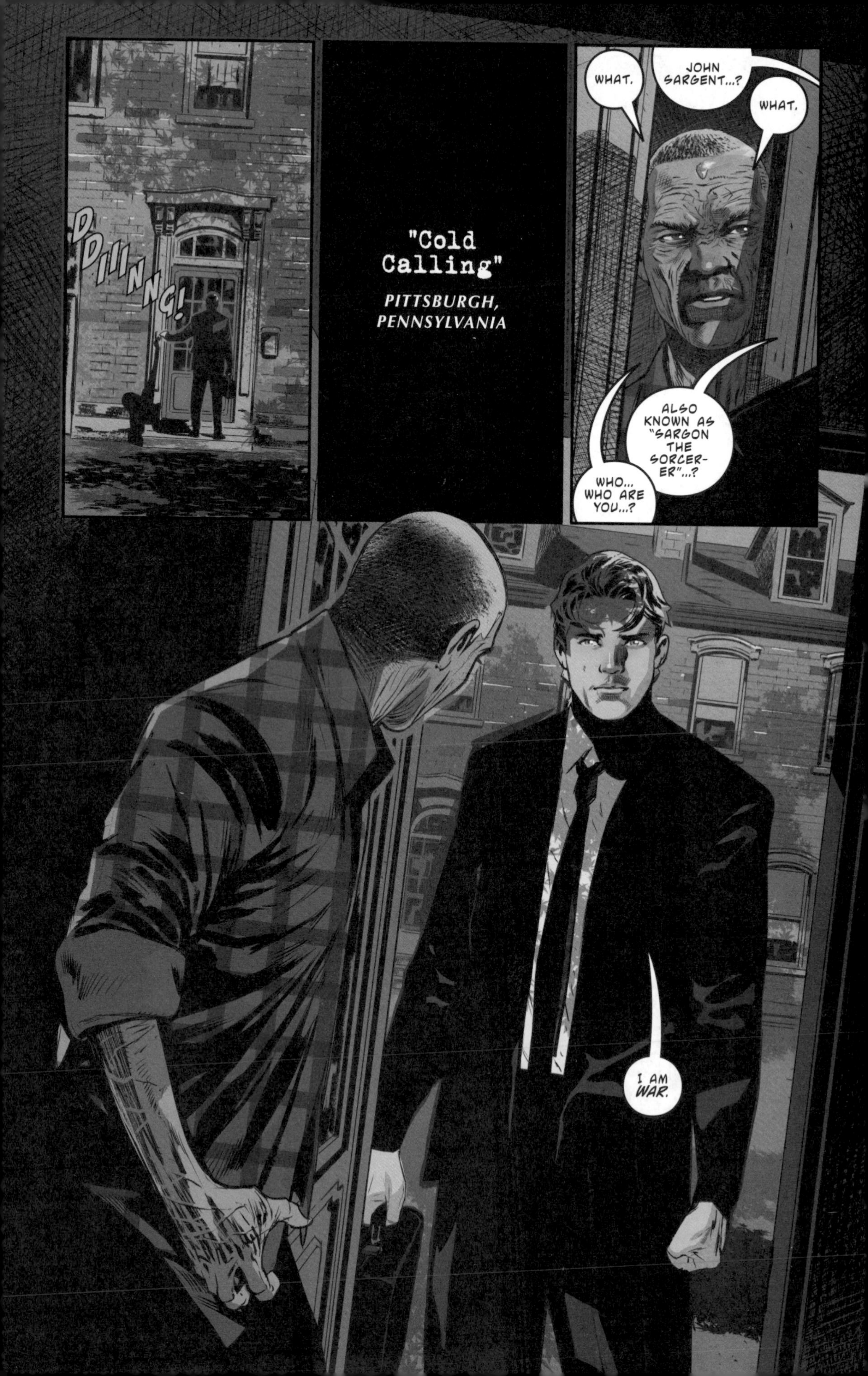

DDIIING!
"Cold Calling"
PITTSBURGH, PENNSYLVANIA
WHAT.
JOHN SARGENT...?
WHAT.
ALSO KNOWN AS "SARGON THE SORCERER"...?
WHO... WHO ARE YOU...?
I AM WAR.

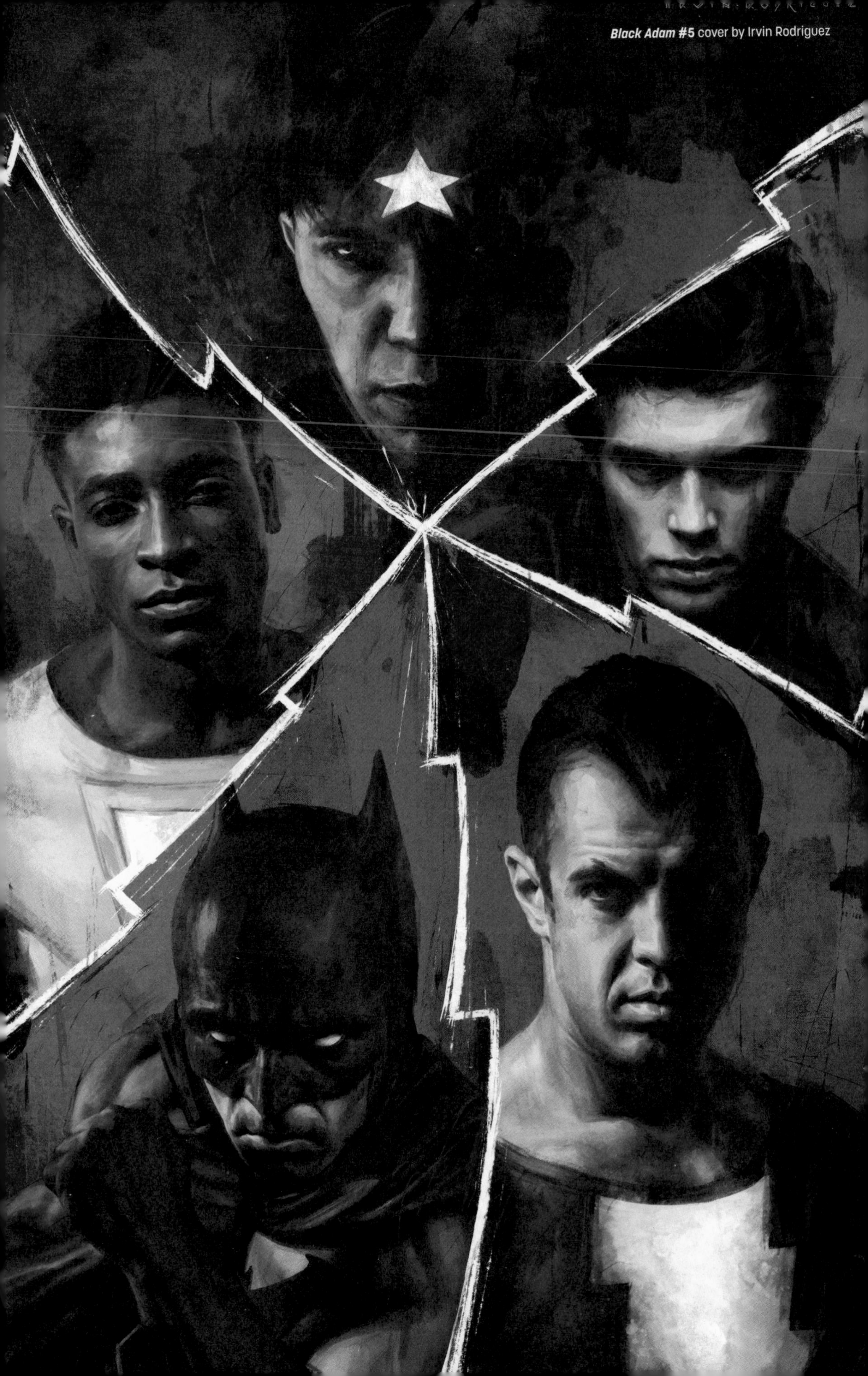

***Black Adam* #5** cover by Irvin Rodriguez

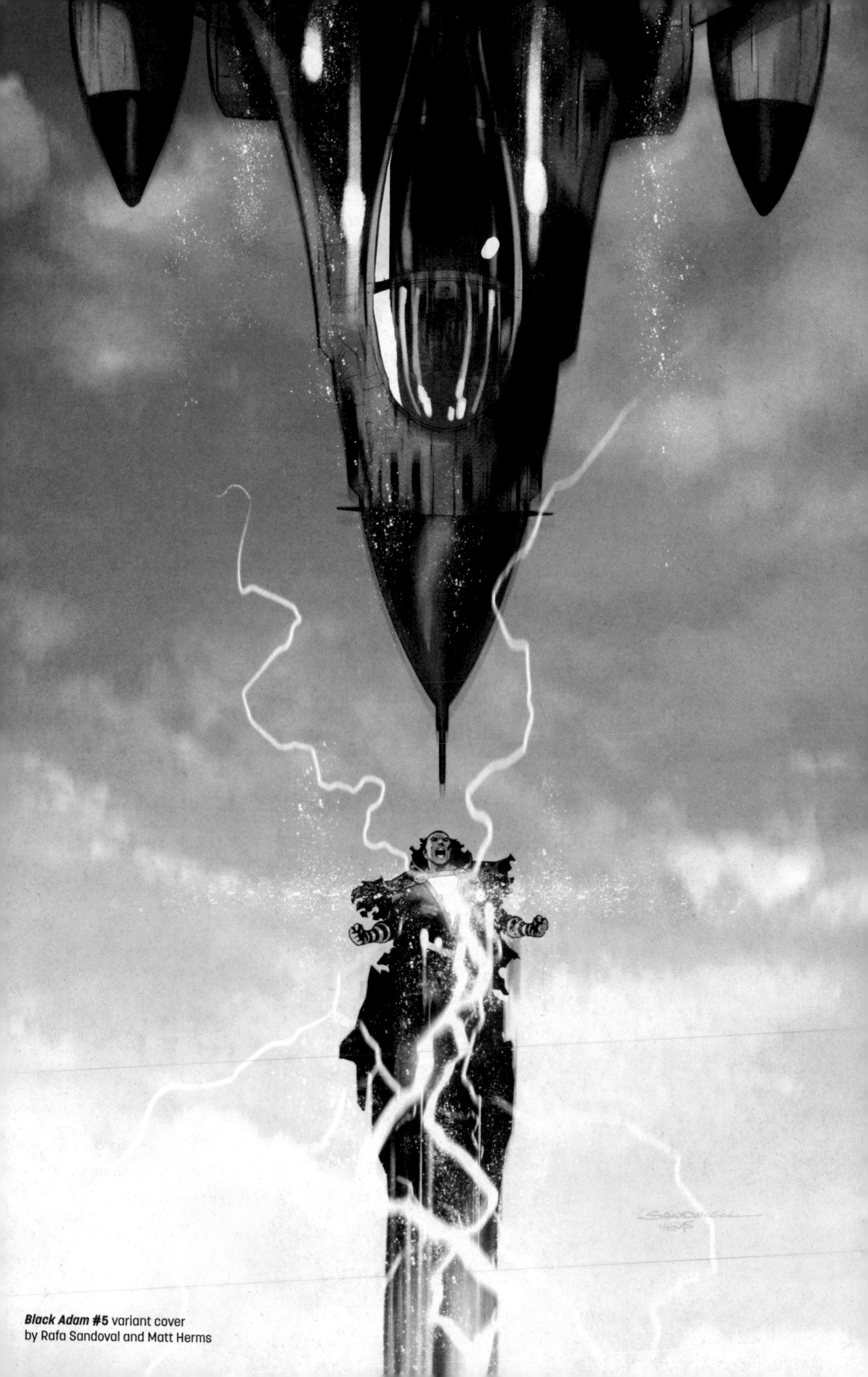

***Black Adam* #5** variant cover
by Rafa Sandoval and Matt Herms

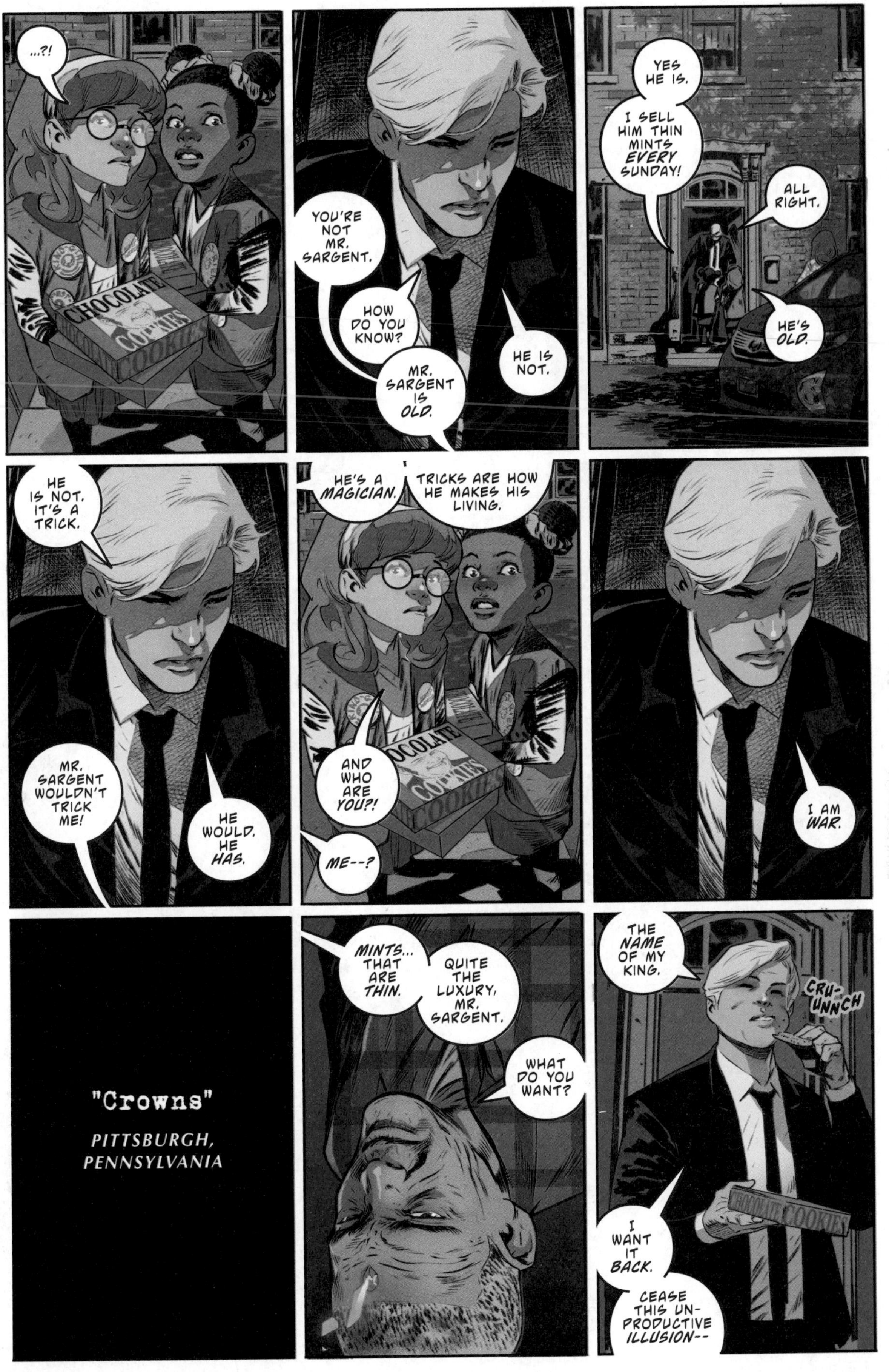
...?!
YOU'RE NOT MR. SARGENT.
HOW DO YOU KNOW?
MR. SARGENT IS OLD.
HE IS NOT.
YES HE IS.
I SELL HIM THIN MINTS EVERY SUNDAY!
ALL RIGHT.
HE'S OLD.
HE IS NOT. IT'S A TRICK.
MR. SARGENT WOULDN'T TRICK ME!
HE WOULD. HE HAS.
HE'S A MAGICIAN.
TRICKS ARE HOW HE MAKES HIS LIVING.
AND WHO ARE YOU?!
ME--?
I AM WAR.
"Crowns"
PITTSBURGH, PENNSYLVANIA
MINTS... THAT ARE THIN.
QUITE THE LUXURY, MR. SARGENT.
WHAT DO YOU WANT?
THE NAME OF MY KING.
CRU-UNNCH
I WANT IT BACK.
CEASE THIS UN-PRODUCTIVE ILLUSION--

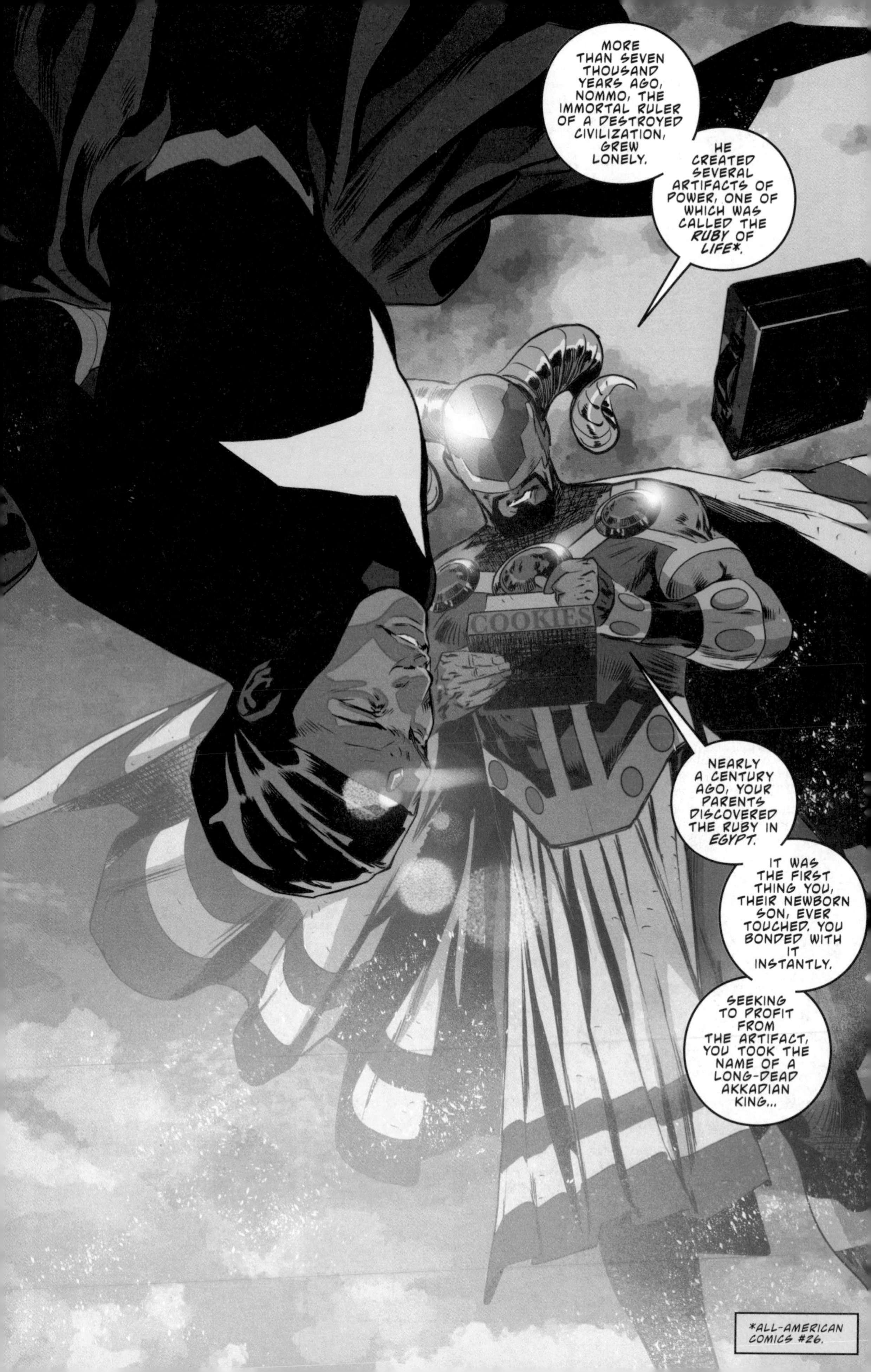
MORE THAN SEVEN THOUSAND YEARS AGO, NOMMO, THE IMMORTAL RULER OF A DESTROYED CIVILIZATION, GREW LONELY.
HE CREATED SEVERAL ARTIFACTS OF POWER, ONE OF WHICH WAS CALLED THE *RUBY OF LIFE**.
COOKIES
NEARLY A CENTURY AGO, YOUR PARENTS DISCOVERED THE RUBY IN *EGYPT*.
IT WAS THE FIRST THING YOU, THEIR NEWBORN SON, EVER TOUCHED. YOU BONDED WITH IT INSTANTLY.
SEEKING TO PROFIT FROM THE ARTIFACT, YOU TOOK THE NAME OF A LONG-DEAD AKKADIAN KING...
*ALL-AMERICAN COMICS #26.

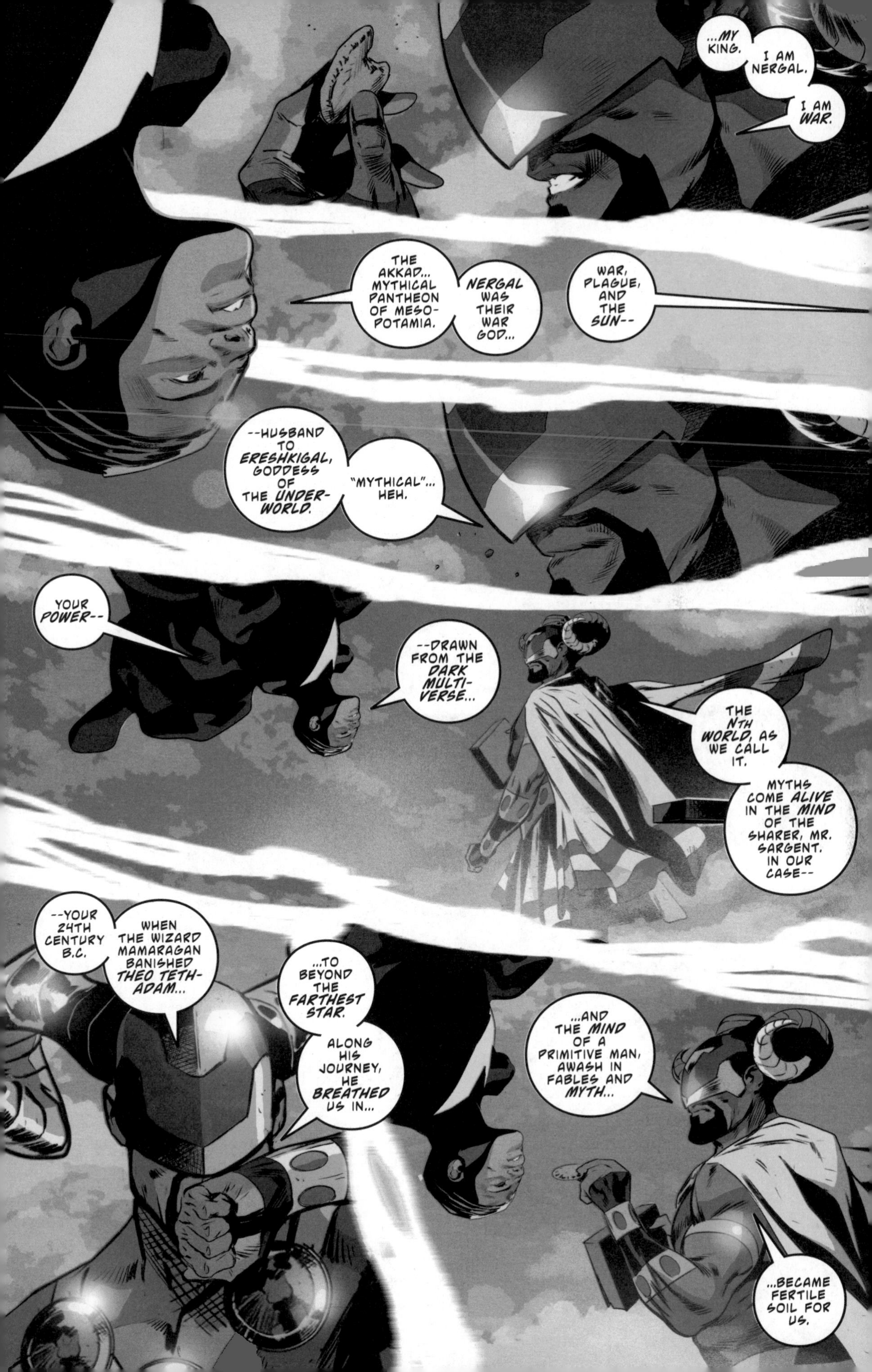
...MY KING.
I AM NERGAL.
I AM WAR.
THE AKKAD... MYTHICAL PANTHEON OF MESO-POTAMIA.
NERGAL WAS THEIR WAR GOD...
WAR, PLAGUE, AND THE SUN--
--HUSBAND TO ERESHKIGAL, GODDESS OF THE UNDER-WORLD.
"MYTHICAL"... HEH.
YOUR POWER--
--DRAWN FROM THE DARK MULTI-VERSE...
THE Nth WORLD, AS WE CALL IT.
MYTHS COME ALIVE IN THE MIND OF THE SHARER, MR. SARGENT. IN OUR CASE--
--YOUR 24TH CENTURY B.C.
WHEN THE WIZARD MAMARAGAN BANISHED THEO TETH-ADAM...
...TO BEYOND THE FARTHEST STAR.
ALONG HIS JOURNEY, HE BREATHED US IN...
...AND THE MIND OF A PRIMITIVE MAN, AWASH IN FABLES AND MYTH...
...BECAME FERTILE SOIL FOR US.

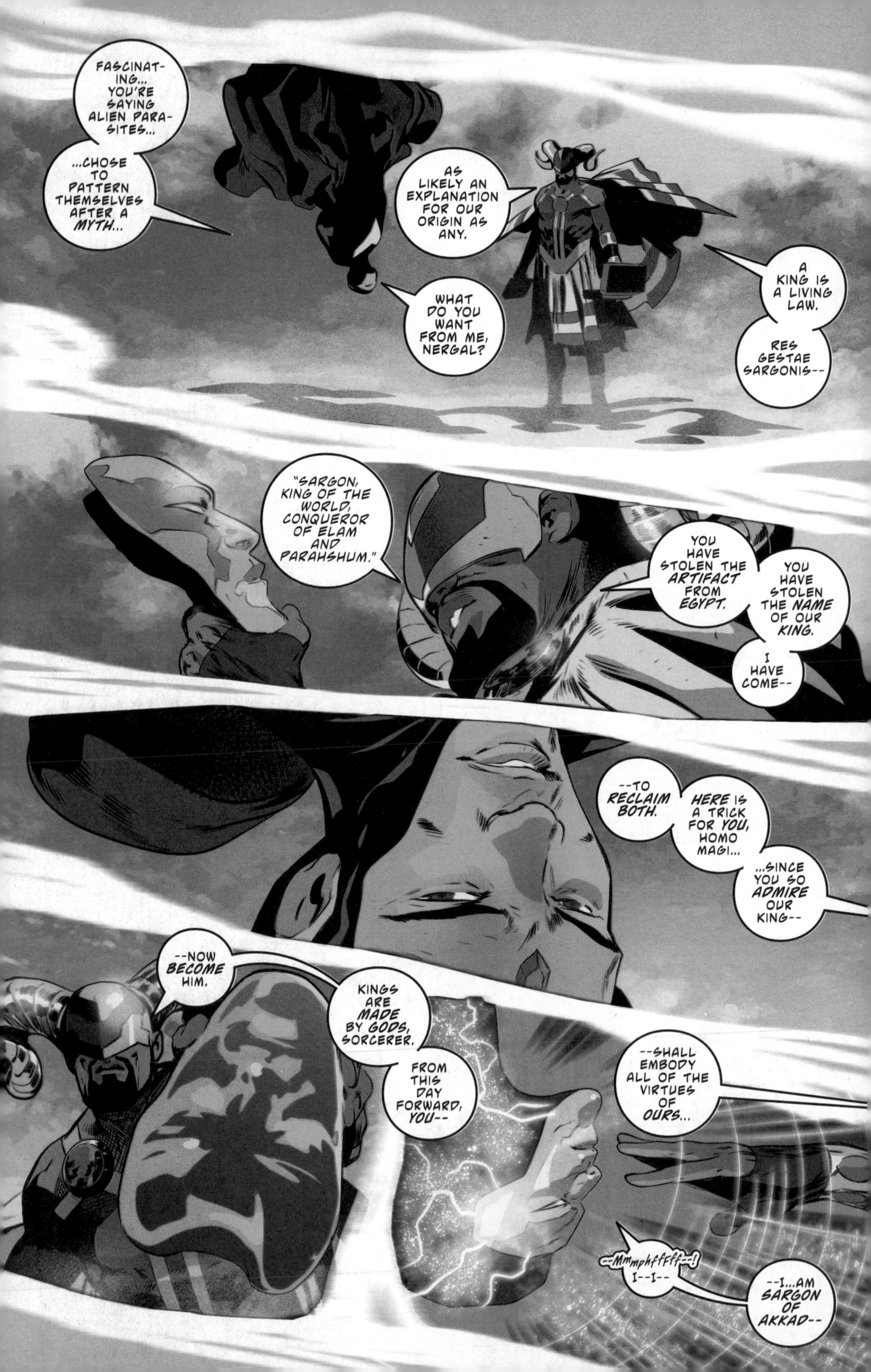
FASCINATING... YOU'RE SAYING ALIEN PARASITES...
...CHOSE TO PATTERN THEMSELVES AFTER A MYTH...
AS LIKELY AN EXPLANATION FOR OUR ORIGIN AS ANY.
WHAT DO YOU WANT FROM ME, NERGAL?
A KING IS A LIVING LAW.
RES GESTAE SARGONIS--
"SARGON, KING OF THE WORLD, CONQUEROR OF ELAM AND PARAHSHUM."
YOU HAVE STOLEN THE ARTIFACT FROM EGYPT.
YOU HAVE STOLEN THE NAME OF OUR KING.
I HAVE COME--
--TO RECLAIM BOTH.
HERE IS A TRICK FOR YOU, HOMO MAGI...
...SINCE YOU SO ADMIRE OUR KING--
--NOW BECOME HIM.
KINGS ARE MADE BY GODS, SORCERER.
FROM THIS DAY FORWARD, YOU--
--SHALL EMBODY ALL OF THE VIRTUES OF OURS...
--Mmmphffff--! I--I--
--I...AM SARGON OF AKKAD--

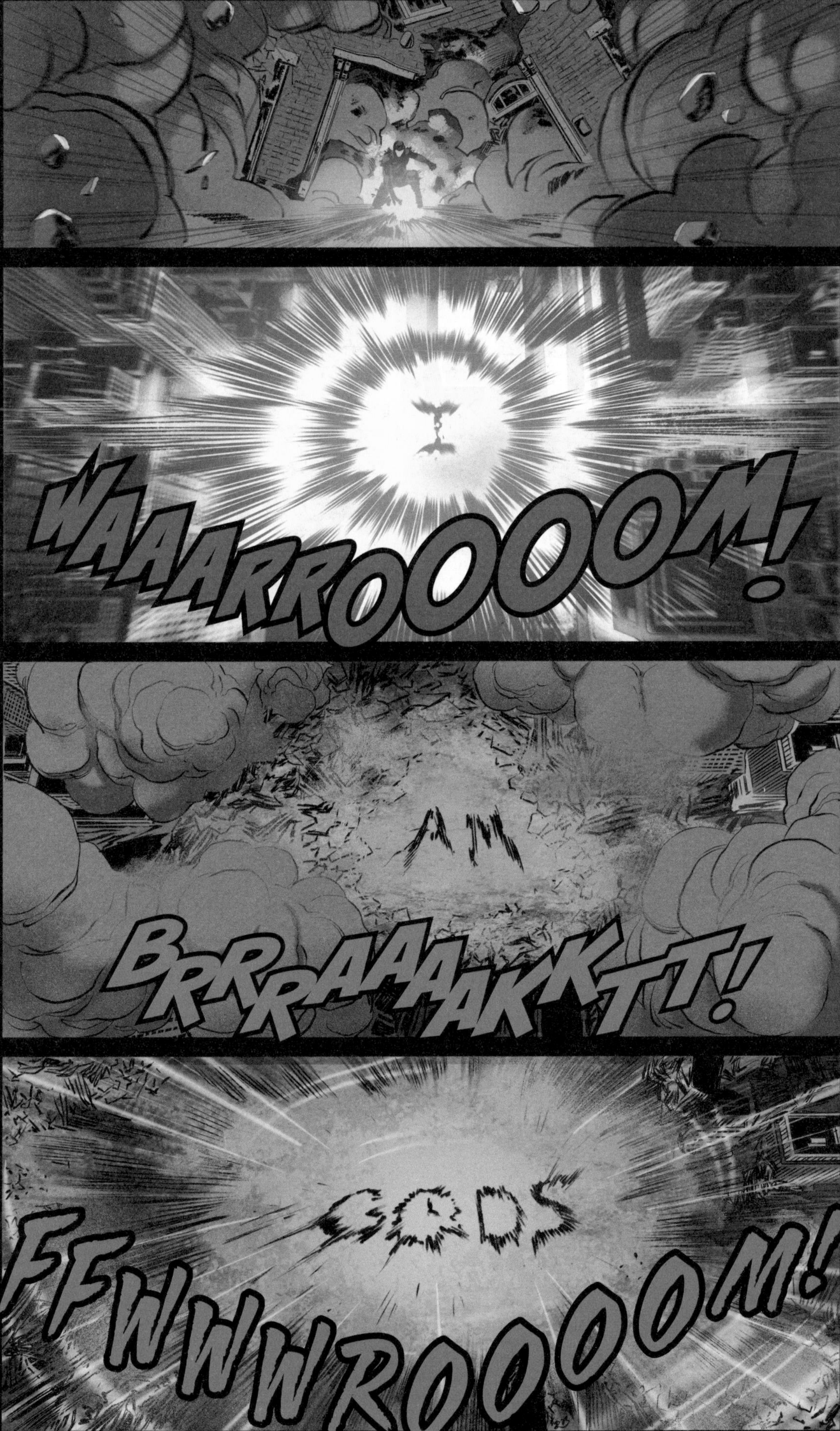
WAAARROOOOOM!
AM
BRRRAAAAKKTT!
GODS
FFWWWROOOOOM!

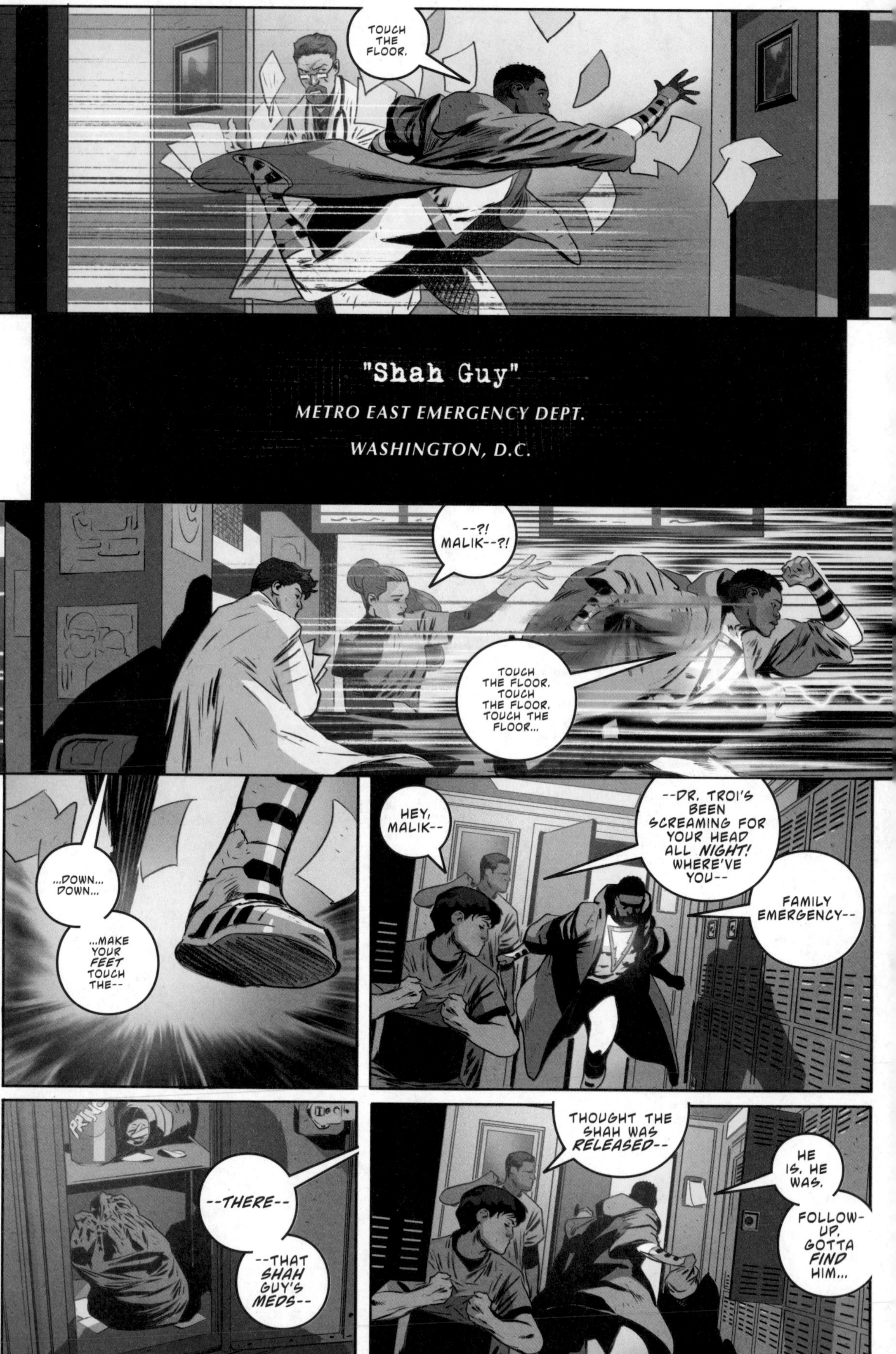
TOUCH THE FLOOR.
"Shah Guy"
METRO EAST EMERGENCY DEPT.
WASHINGTON, D.C.
--?! MALIK--?!
TOUCH THE FLOOR. TOUCH THE FLOOR. TOUCH THE FLOOR...
...DOWN... DOWN...
...MAKE YOUR FEET TOUCH THE--
HEY, MALIK--
--DR. TROI'S BEEN SCREAMING FOR YOUR HEAD ALL NIGHT! WHERE'VE YOU--
FAMILY EMERGENCY--
--THERE--
--THAT SHAH GUY'S MEDS--
THOUGHT THE SHAH WAS RELEASED--
HE IS. HE WAS.
FOLLOW-UP. GOTTA FIND HIM...

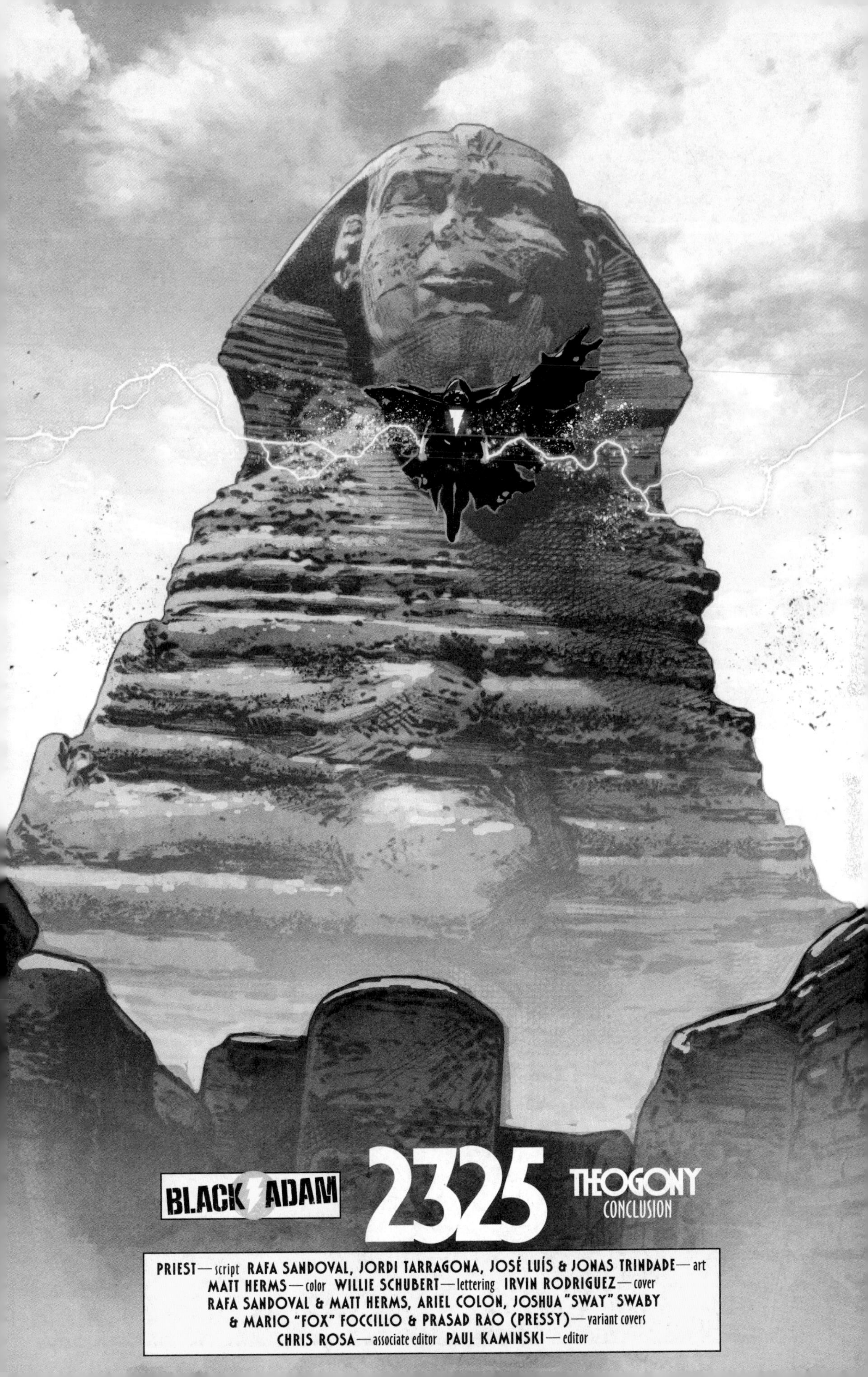
BLACK ADAM
2325
THEOGONY
CONCLUSION
PRIEST—script RAFA SANDOVAL, JORDI TARRAGONA, JOSÉ LUÍS & JONAS TRINDADE—art
MATT HERMS—color WILLIE SCHUBERT—lettering IRVIN RODRIGUEZ—cover
RAFA SANDOVAL & MATT HERMS, ARIEL COLON, JOSHUA "SWAY" SWABY
& MARIO "FOX" FOCCILLO & PRASAD RAO (PRESSY)—variant covers
CHRIS ROSA—associate editor PAUL KAMINSKI—editor

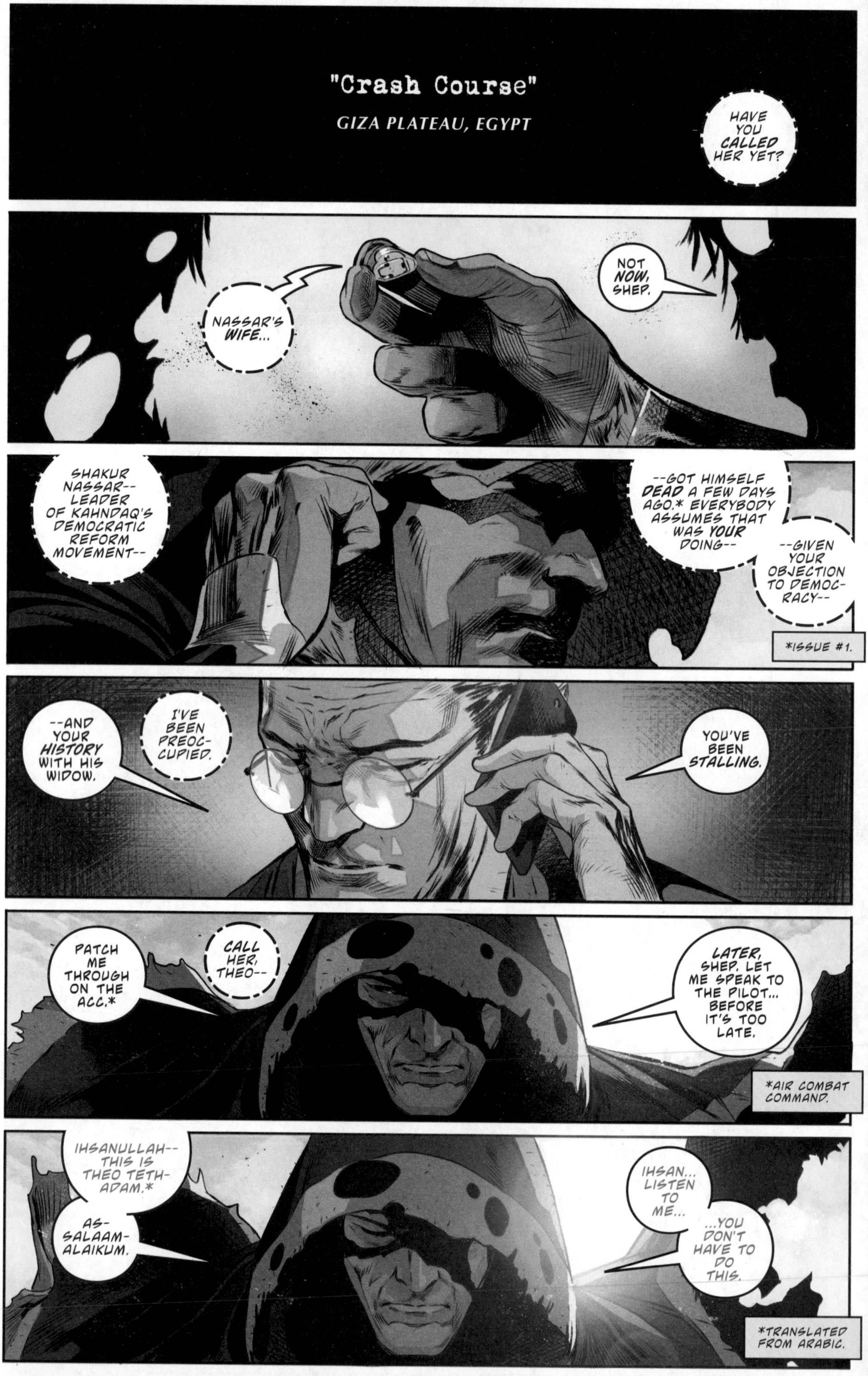
"Crash Course"
GIZA PLATEAU, EGYPT
HAVE YOU CALLED HER YET?
NASSAR'S WIFE...
NOT NOW, SHEP.
SHAKUR NASSAR-- LEADER OF KAHNDAQ'S DEMOCRATIC REFORM MOVEMENT--
--GOT HIMSELF DEAD A FEW DAYS AGO.* EVERYBODY ASSUMES THAT WAS YOUR DOING--
--GIVEN YOUR OBJECTION TO DEMOC-RACY--
*ISSUE #1.
--AND YOUR HISTORY WITH HIS WIDOW.
I'VE BEEN PREOC-CUPIED.
YOU'VE BEEN STALLING.
PATCH ME THROUGH ON THE ACC.*
CALL HER, THEO--
LATER, SHEP. LET ME SPEAK TO THE PILOT... BEFORE IT'S TOO LATE.
*AIR COMBAT COMMAND.
IHSANULLAH-- THIS IS THEO TETH-ADAM.*
AS-SALAAM-ALAIKUM.
IHSAN... LISTEN TO ME...
...YOU DON'T HAVE TO DO THIS.
*TRANSLATED FROM ARABIC.

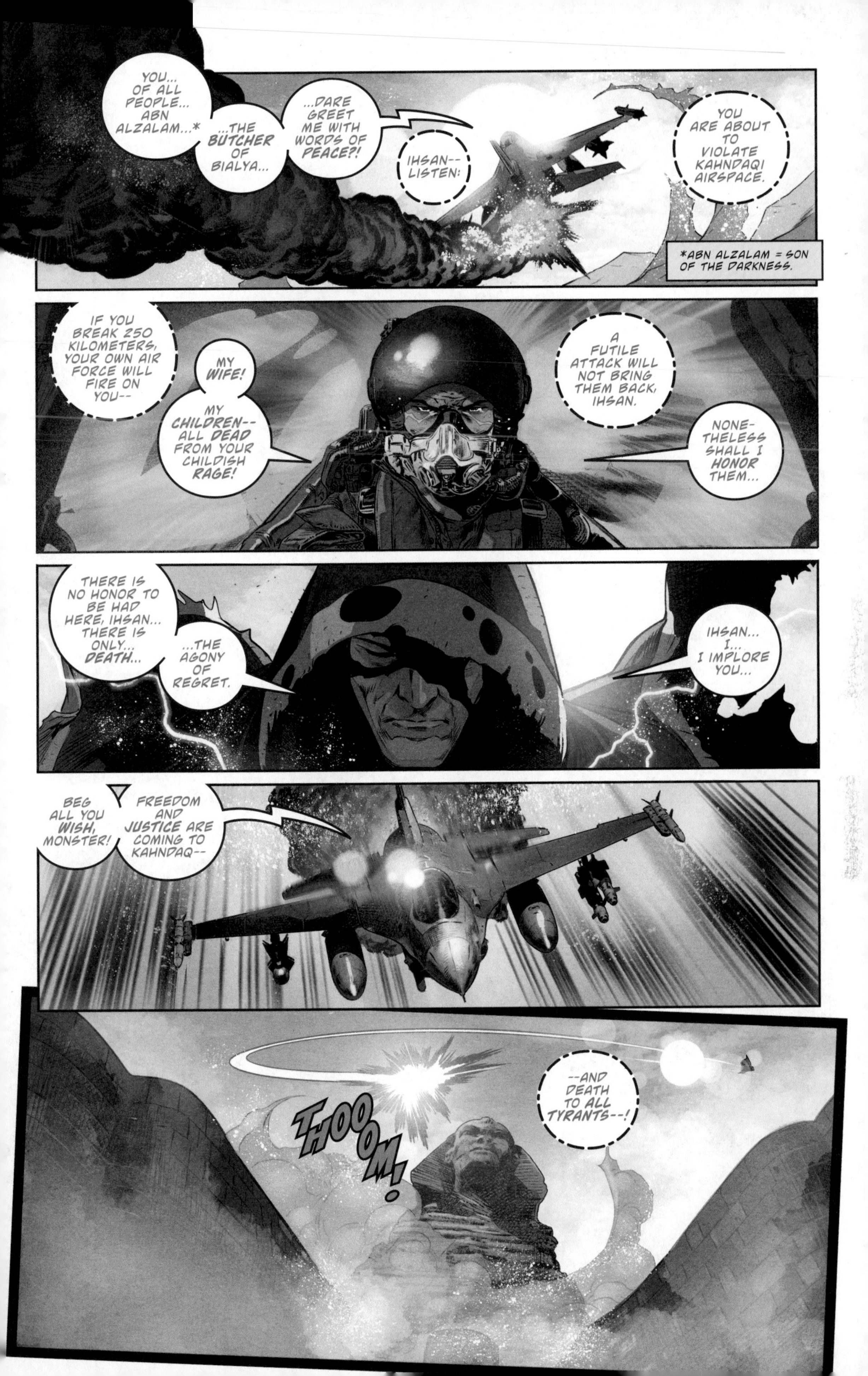
YOU... OF ALL PEOPLE... ABN ALZALAM...*
...THE BUTCHER OF BIALYA...
...DARE GREET ME WITH WORDS OF PEACE?!
IHSAN-- LISTEN:
YOU ARE ABOUT TO VIOLATE KAHNDAQI AIRSPACE.
*ABN ALZALAM = SON OF THE DARKNESS.
IF YOU BREAK 250 KILOMETERS, YOUR OWN AIR FORCE WILL FIRE ON YOU--
MY WIFE!
MY CHILDREN-- ALL DEAD FROM YOUR CHILDISH RAGE!
A FUTILE ATTACK WILL NOT BRING THEM BACK, IHSAN.
NONE-THELESS SHALL I HONOR THEM...
THERE IS NO HONOR TO BE HAD HERE, IHSAN... THERE IS ONLY... DEATH...
...THE AGONY OF REGRET.
IHSAN... I... I IMPLORE YOU...
BEG ALL YOU WISH, MONSTER!
FREEDOM AND JUSTICE ARE COMING TO KAHNDAQ--
THOOOM!
--AND DEATH TO ALL TYRANTS--!

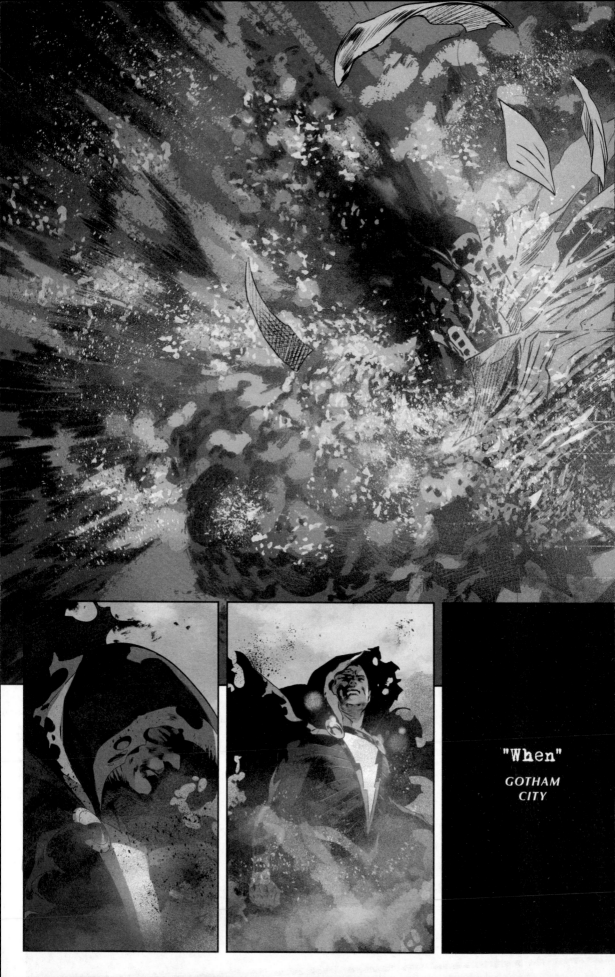

"When"

*GOTHAM
CITY*

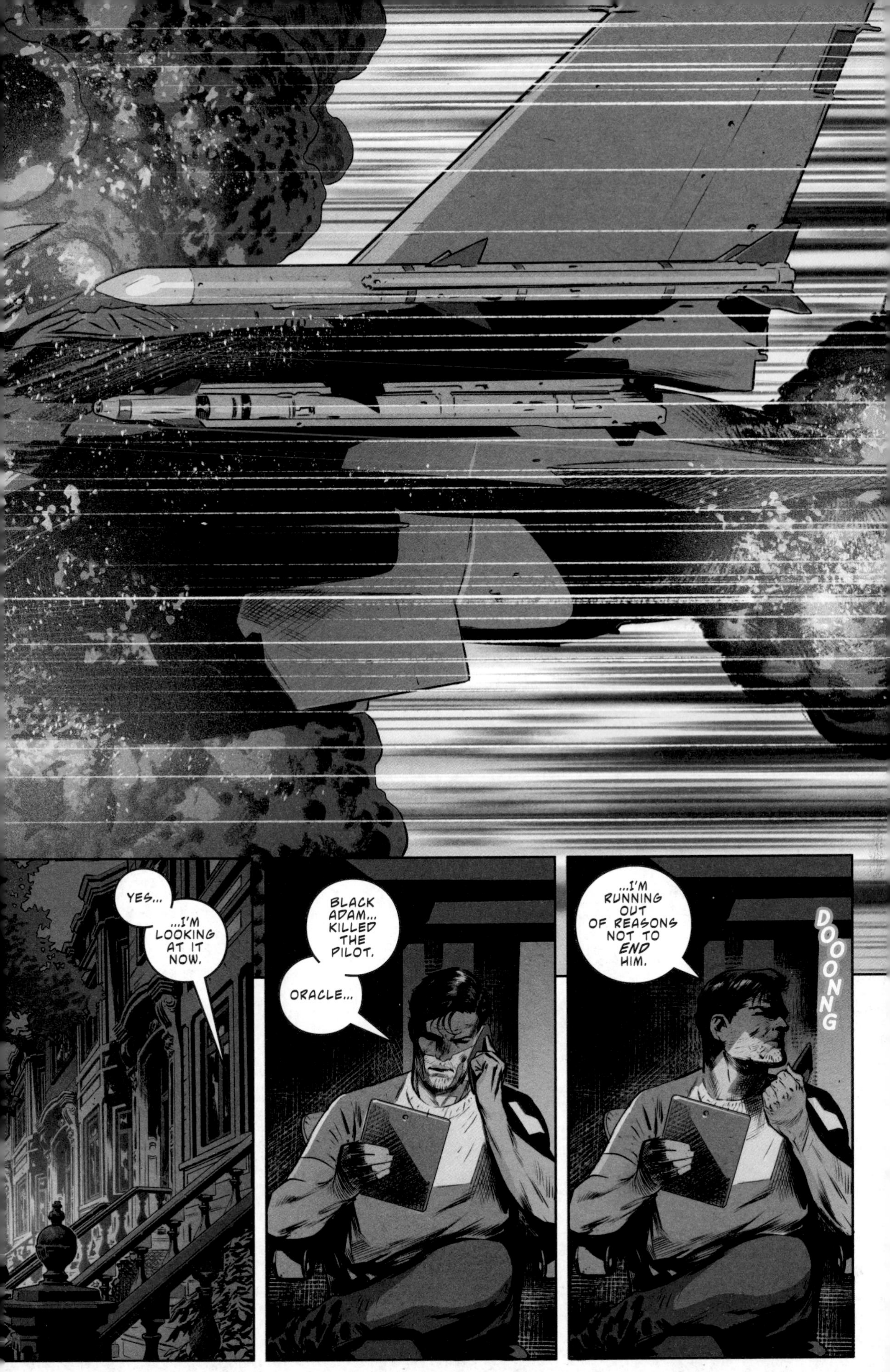
YES...
...I'M LOOKING AT IT NOW.
BLACK ADAM... KILLED THE PILOT.
ORACLE...
...I'M RUNNING OUT OF REASONS NOT TO *END* HIM.
DOOOONG

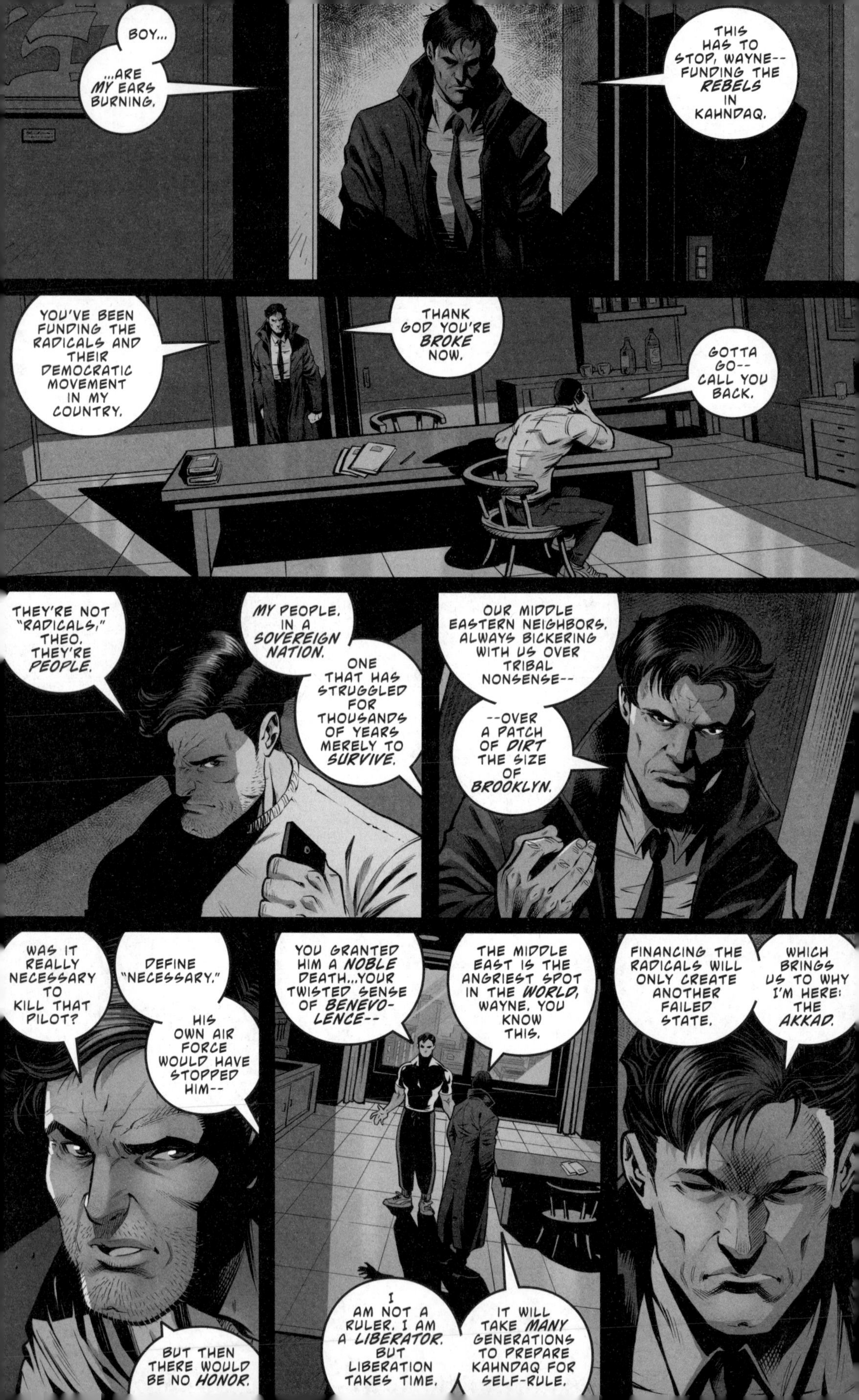
BOY...
...ARE MY EARS BURNING.
THIS HAS TO STOP, WAYNE-- FUNDING THE REBELS IN KAHNDAQ.
YOU'VE BEEN FUNDING THE RADICALS AND THEIR DEMOCRATIC MOVEMENT IN MY COUNTRY.
THANK GOD YOU'RE BROKE NOW.
GOTTA GO-- CALL YOU BACK.
THEY'RE NOT "RADICALS," THEO. THEY'RE PEOPLE.
MY PEOPLE. IN A SOVEREIGN NATION.
ONE THAT HAS STRUGGLED FOR THOUSANDS OF YEARS MERELY TO SURVIVE.
OUR MIDDLE EASTERN NEIGHBORS, ALWAYS BICKERING WITH US OVER TRIBAL NONSENSE--
--OVER A PATCH OF DIRT THE SIZE OF BROOKLYN.
WAS IT REALLY NECESSARY TO KILL THAT PILOT?
DEFINE "NECESSARY."
HIS OWN AIR FORCE WOULD HAVE STOPPED HIM--
BUT THEN THERE WOULD BE NO HONOR.
YOU GRANTED HIM A NOBLE DEATH...YOUR TWISTED SENSE OF BENEVO-LENCE--
THE MIDDLE EAST IS THE ANGRIEST SPOT IN THE WORLD, WAYNE. YOU KNOW THIS.
I AM NOT A RULER. I AM A LIBERATOR. BUT LIBERATION TAKES TIME.
IT WILL TAKE MANY GENERATIONS TO PREPARE KAHNDAQ FOR SELF-RULE.
FINANCING THE RADICALS WILL ONLY CREATE ANOTHER FAILED STATE.
WHICH BRINGS US TO WHY I'M HERE: THE AKKAD.

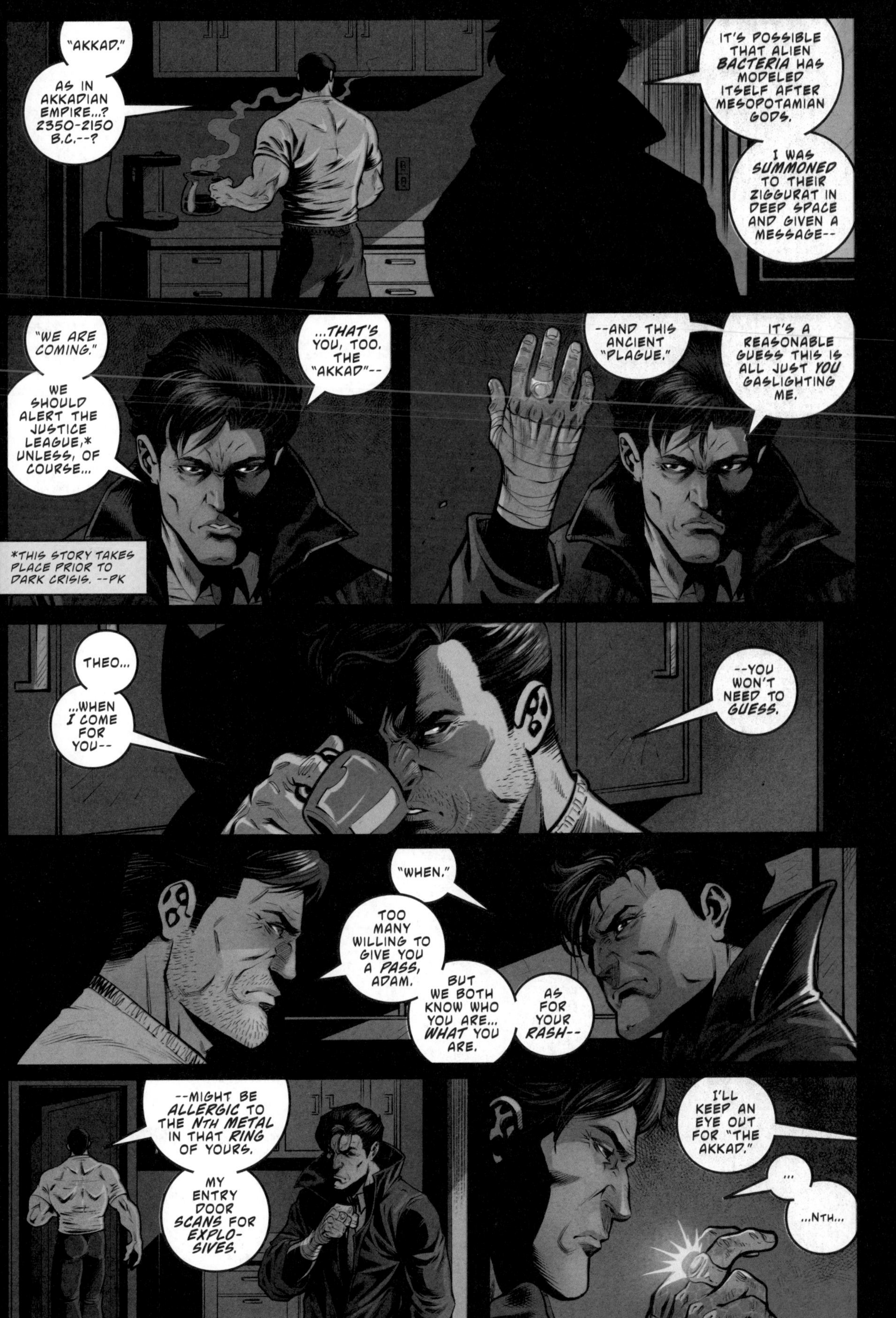
"AKKAD."
AS IN AKKADIAN EMPIRE...? 2350-2150 B.C.--?
IT'S POSSIBLE THAT ALIEN *BACTERIA* HAS MODELED ITSELF AFTER MESOPOTAMIAN GODS.
I WAS *SUMMONED* TO THEIR ZIGGURAT IN DEEP SPACE AND GIVEN A MESSAGE--
"WE ARE COMING."
WE SHOULD ALERT THE JUSTICE LEAGUE,* UNLESS, OF COURSE...
...*THAT'S* YOU, TOO. THE "AKKAD"--
*THIS STORY TAKES PLACE PRIOR TO DARK CRISIS. --PK
--AND THIS ANCIENT "PLAGUE."
IT'S A REASONABLE GUESS THIS IS ALL JUST *YOU* GASLIGHTING ME.
THEO...
...WHEN *I* COME FOR YOU--
--YOU WON'T NEED TO *GUESS.*
"WHEN."
TOO MANY WILLING TO GIVE YOU A *PASS,* ADAM.
BUT WE BOTH KNOW WHO YOU ARE... *WHAT* YOU ARE.
AS FOR YOUR *RASH*--
--MIGHT BE *ALLERGIC* TO THE *Nth METAL* IN THAT *RING* OF YOURS.
MY ENTRY DOOR *SCANS* FOR *EXPLO-SIVES.*
I'LL KEEP AN EYE OUT FOR "THE AKKAD."
...
...Nth...

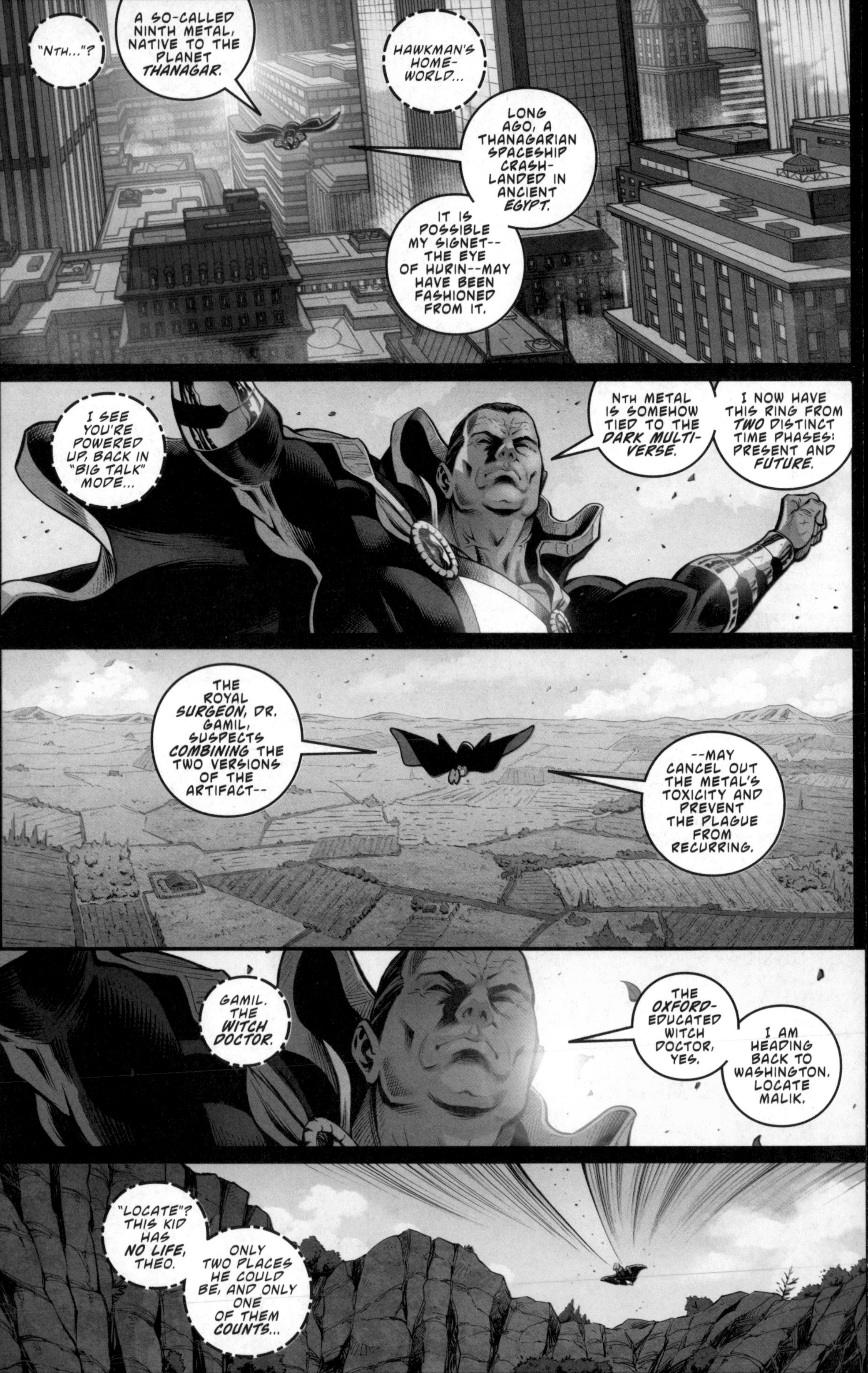
"NTH..."?
A SO-CALLED NINTH METAL, NATIVE TO THE PLANET THANAGAR.
HAWKMAN'S HOME-WORLD...
LONG AGO, A THANAGARIAN SPACESHIP CRASH-LANDED IN ANCIENT EGYPT.
IT IS POSSIBLE MY SIGNET--THE EYE OF HURIN--MAY HAVE BEEN FASHIONED FROM IT.
I SEE YOU'RE POWERED UP, BACK IN "BIG TALK" MODE...
NTH METAL IS SOMEHOW TIED TO THE DARK MULTI-VERSE.
I NOW HAVE THIS RING FROM TWO DISTINCT TIME PHASES: PRESENT AND FUTURE.
THE ROYAL SURGEON, DR. GAMIL, SUSPECTS COMBINING THE TWO VERSIONS OF THE ARTIFACT--
--MAY CANCEL OUT THE METAL'S TOXICITY AND PREVENT THE PLAGUE FROM RECURRING.
GAMIL. THE WITCH DOCTOR.
THE OXFORD-EDUCATED WITCH DOCTOR, YES.
I AM HEADING BACK TO WASHINGTON. LOCATE MALIK.
"LOCATE"? THIS KID HAS NO LIFE, THEO.
ONLY TWO PLACES HE COULD BE, AND ONLY ONE OF THEM COUNTS...

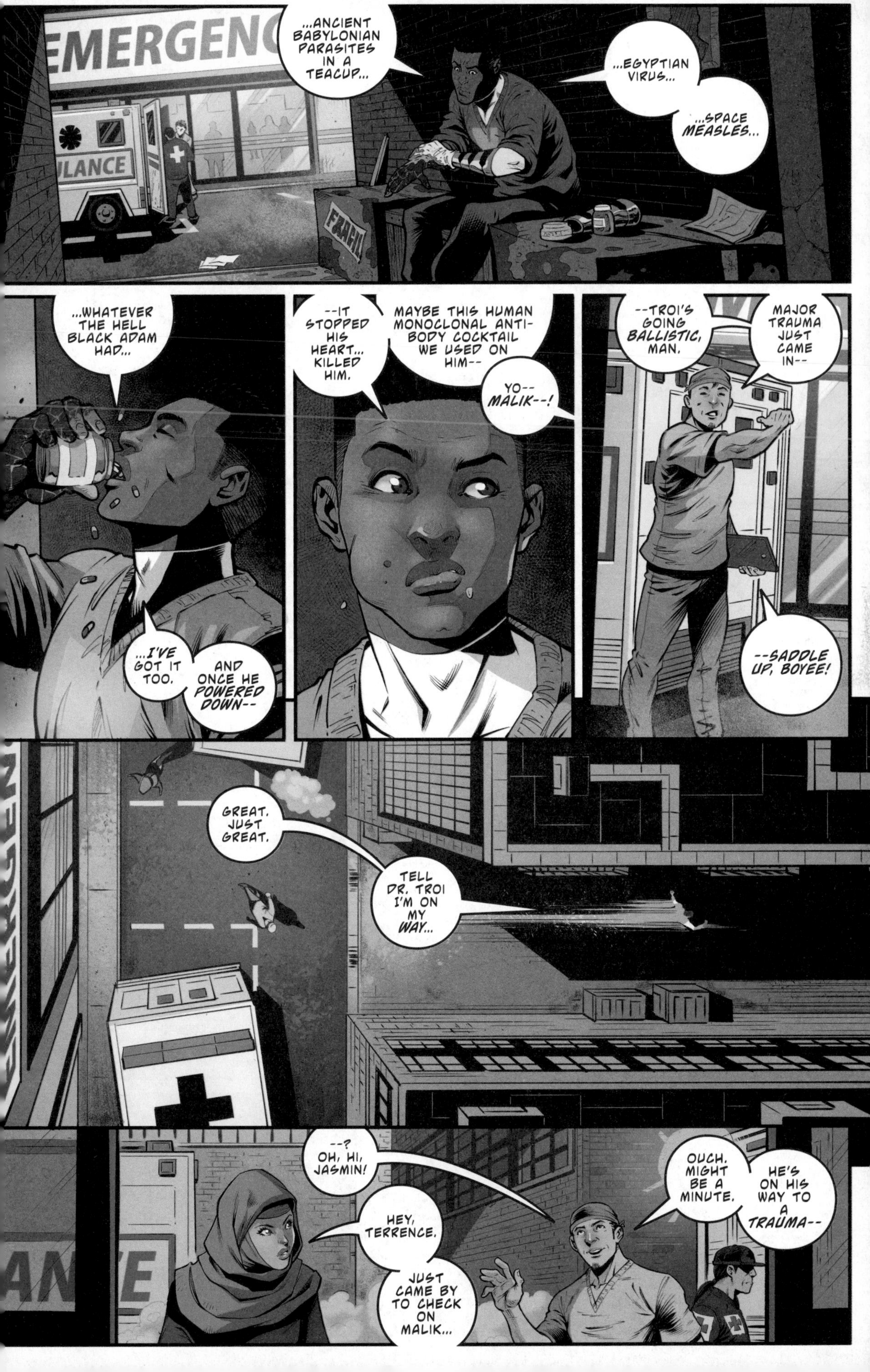
EMERGENC
ULANCE
...ANCIENT BABYLONIAN PARASITES IN A TEACUP...
...EGYPTIAN VIRUS...
...SPACE MEASLES...
...WHATEVER THE HELL BLACK ADAM HAD...
...I'VE GOT IT TOO.
AND ONCE HE POWERED DOWN--
--IT STOPPED HIS HEART... KILLED HIM.
MAYBE THIS HUMAN MONOCLONAL ANTI-BODY COCKTAIL WE USED ON HIM--
YO-- MALIK--!
--TROI'S GOING BALLISTIC, MAN.
MAJOR TRAUMA JUST CAME IN--
--SADDLE UP, BOYEE!
GREAT. JUST GREAT.
TELL DR. TROI I'M ON MY WAY...
--? OH, HI, JASMIN!
HEY, TERRENCE.
JUST CAME BY TO CHECK ON MALIK...
OUCH. MIGHT BE A MINUTE.
HE'S ON HIS WAY TO A TRAUMA--

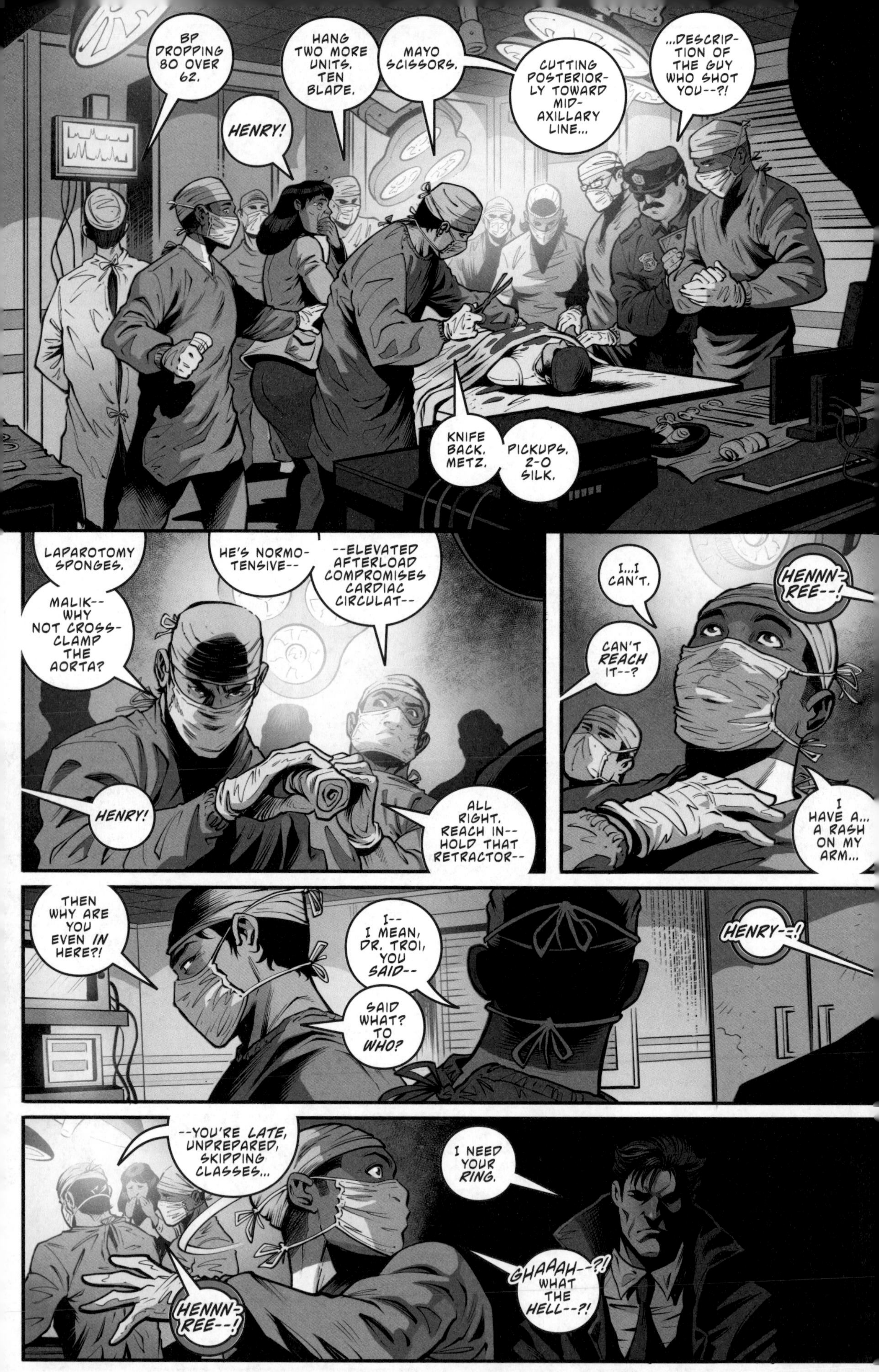
BP DROPPING 80 OVER 62.
HENRY!
HANG TWO MORE UNITS. TEN BLADE.
MAYO SCISSORS.
CUTTING POSTERIORLY TOWARD MID-AXILLARY LINE...
...DESCRIPTION OF THE GUY WHO SHOT YOU--?!
KNIFE BACK. METZ.
PICKUPS. 2-0 SILK.
LAPAROTOMY SPONGES.
HE'S NORMOTENSIVE--
--ELEVATED AFTERLOAD COMPROMISES CARDIAC CIRCULAT--
MALIK--WHY NOT CROSS-CLAMP THE AORTA?
HENRY!
ALL RIGHT. REACH IN--HOLD THAT RETRACTOR--
I...I CAN'T.
HENNN-REE--!
CAN'T REACH IT--?
I HAVE A... A RASH ON MY ARM...
THEN WHY ARE YOU EVEN IN HERE?!
I--I MEAN, DR. TROI, YOU SAID--
SAID WHAT? TO WHO?
HENRY--!
--YOU'RE LATE, UNPREPARED, SKIPPING CLASSES...
I NEED YOUR RING.
HENNN-REE--!
GHAAAH--?! WHAT THE HELL--?!

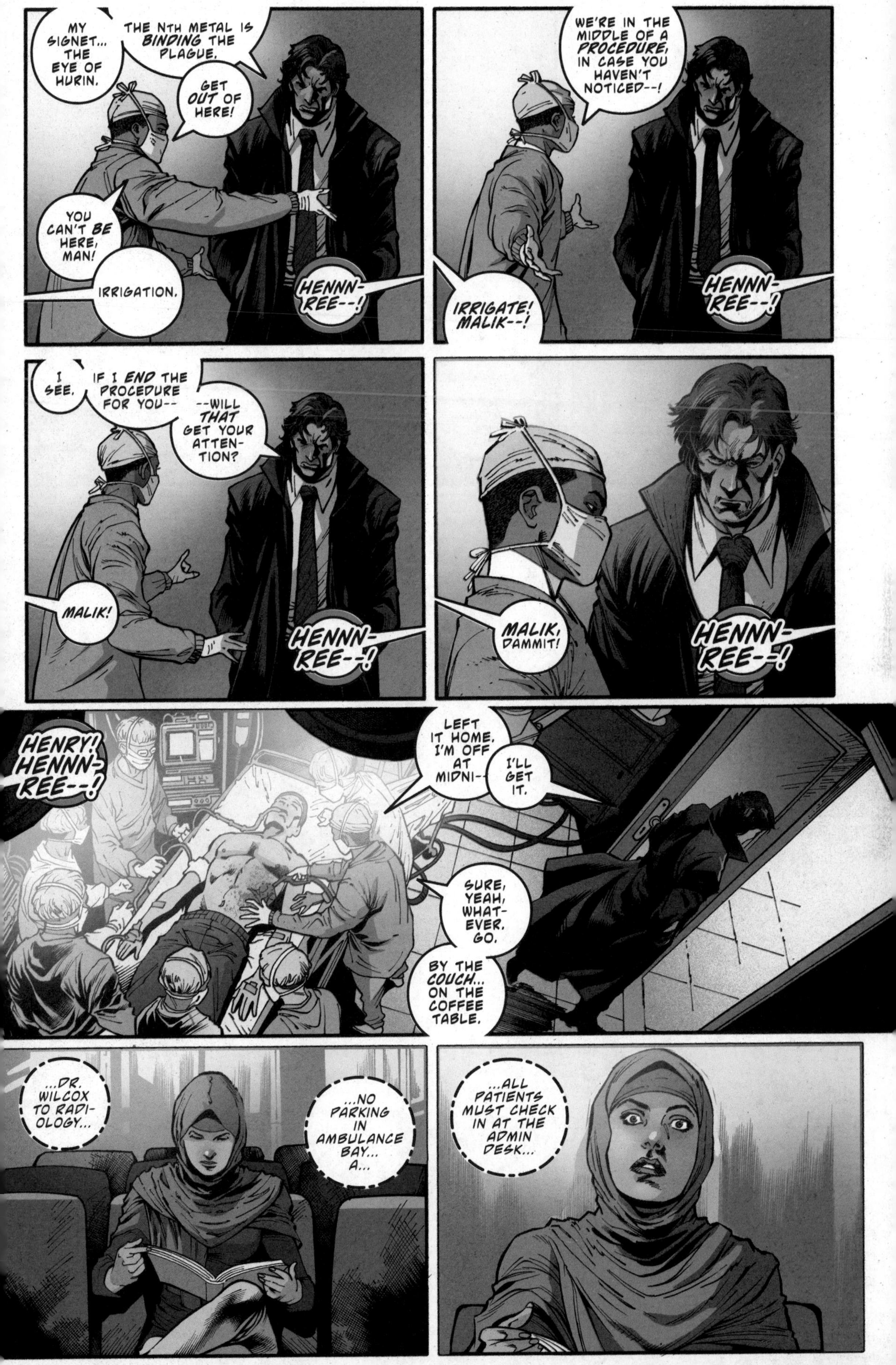
MY SIGNET... THE EYE OF HURIN.
THE Nth METAL IS BINDING THE PLAGUE.
GET OUT OF HERE!
YOU CAN'T BE HERE, MAN!
IRRIGATION.
HENNN-REE--!
WE'RE IN THE MIDDLE OF A PROCEDURE, IN CASE YOU HAVEN'T NOTICED--!
IRRIGATE! MALIK--!
HENNN-REE--!
I SEE.
IF I END THE PROCEDURE FOR YOU--
--WILL THAT GET YOUR ATTENTION?
MALIK!
HENNN-REE--!
MALIK, DAMMIT!
HENNN-REE--!
HENRY! HENNN-REE--!
LEFT IT HOME. I'M OFF AT MIDNI--
I'LL GET IT.
SURE, YEAH, WHATEVER. GO.
BY THE COUCH... ON THE COFFEE TABLE.
...DR. WILCOX TO RADIOLOGY...
...NO PARKING IN AMBULANCE BAY... A...
...ALL PATIENTS MUST CHECK IN AT THE ADMIN DESK...

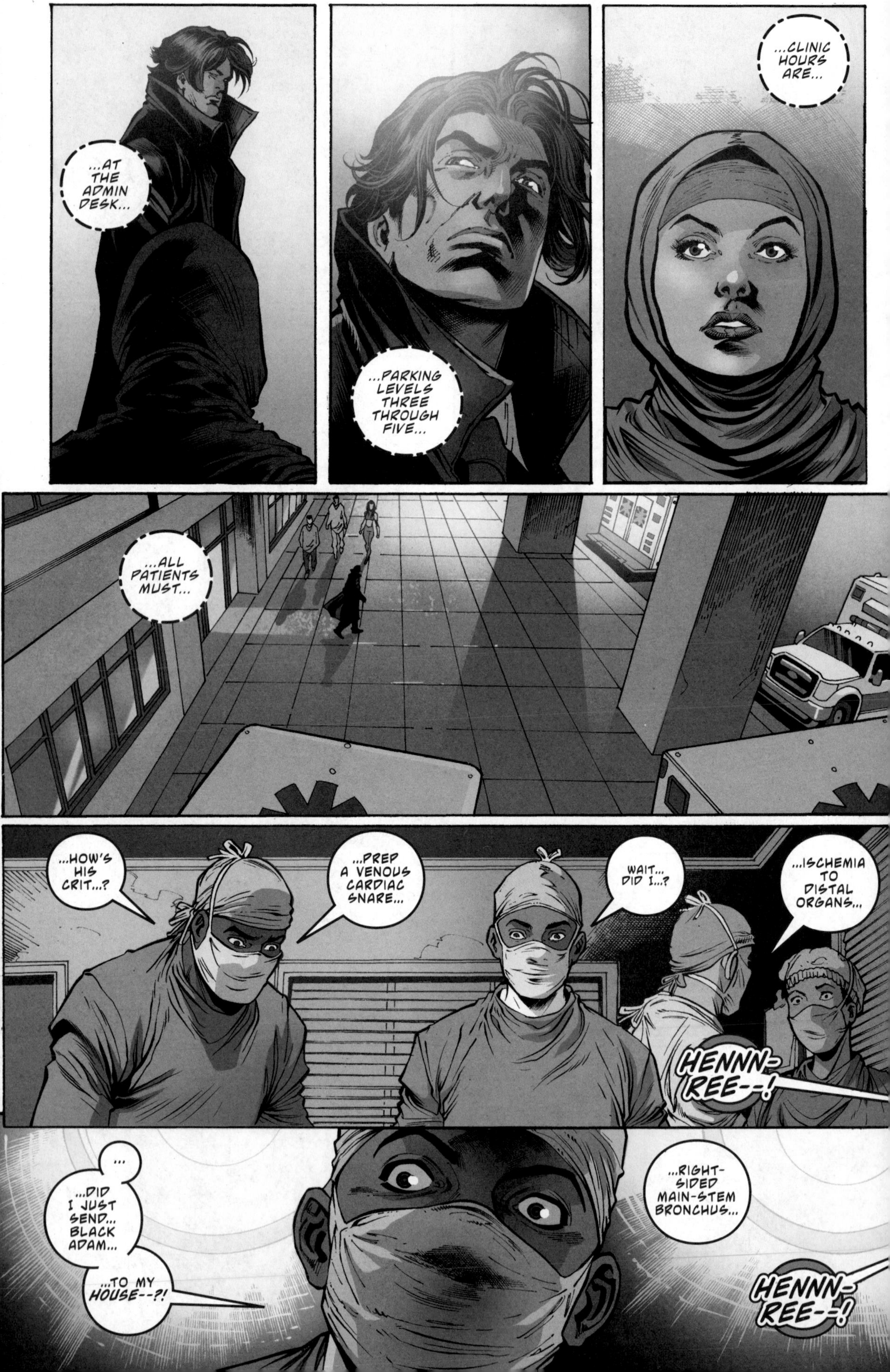
...AT THE ADMIN DESK...
...PARKING LEVELS THREE THROUGH FIVE...
...CLINIC HOURS ARE...
...ALL PATIENTS MUST...
...HOW'S HIS CRIT...?
...PREP A VENOUS CARDIAC SNARE...
WAIT... DID I...?
...ISCHEMIA TO DISTAL ORGANS...
HENNN-REE--!
...
...DID I JUST SEND... BLACK ADAM...
...TO MY HOUSE--?!
...RIGHT-SIDED MAIN-STEM BRONCHUS...
HENNN-REE--!

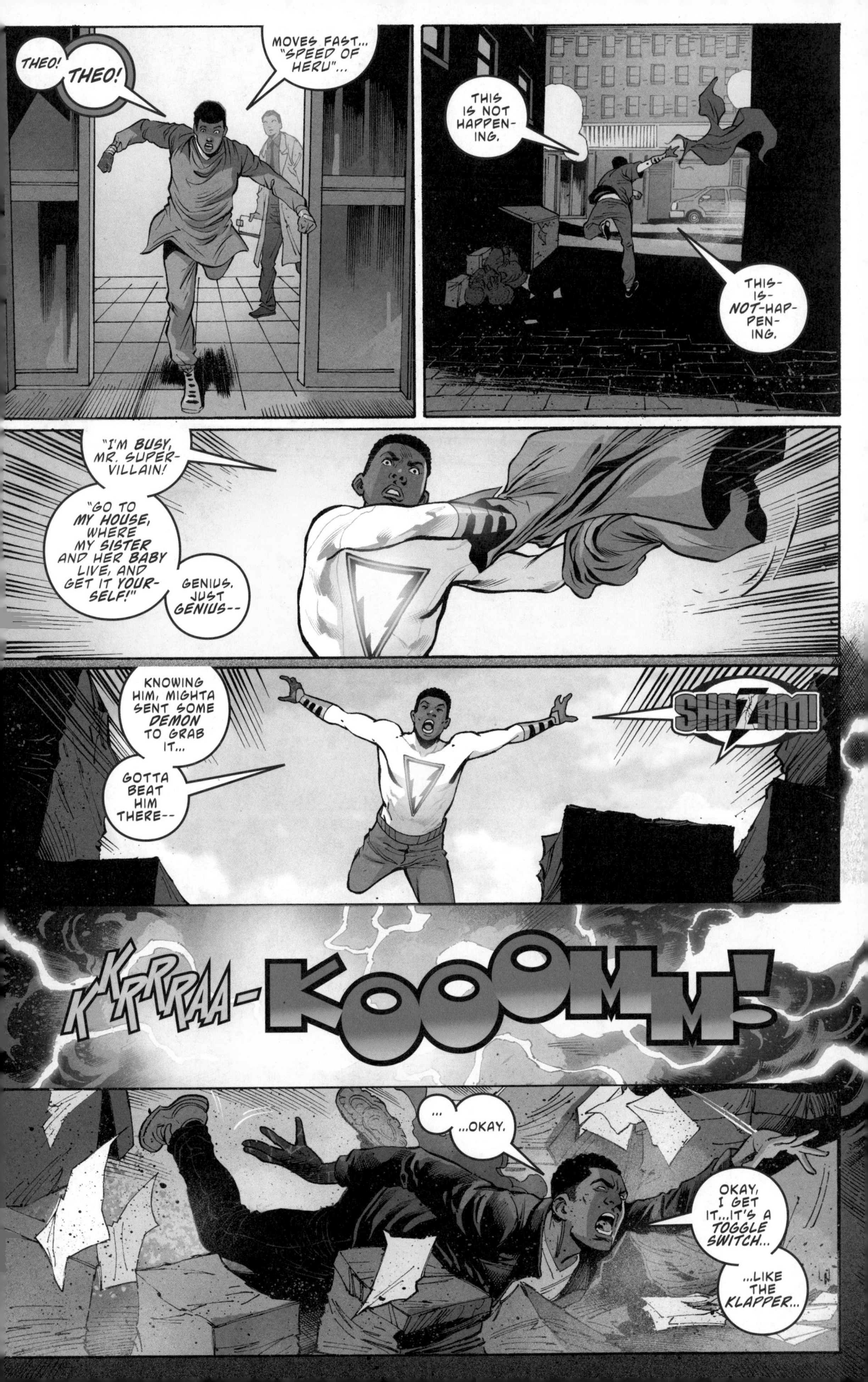
THEO!
THEO!
MOVES FAST... "SPEED OF HERU"...
THIS IS NOT HAPPENING.
THIS-IS-NOT-HAPPENING.
"I'M BUSY, MR. SUPER-VILLAIN!
"GO TO MY HOUSE, WHERE MY SISTER AND HER BABY LIVE, AND GET IT YOURSELF!"
GENIUS. JUST GENIUS--
KNOWING HIM, MIGHTA SENT SOME DEMON TO GRAB IT...
GOTTA BEAT HIM THERE--
SHAZAM!
KKRRRAA-KOOOOMMM!
...
...OKAY.
OKAY, I GET IT...IT'S A TOGGLE SWITCH...
...LIKE THE KLAPPER...

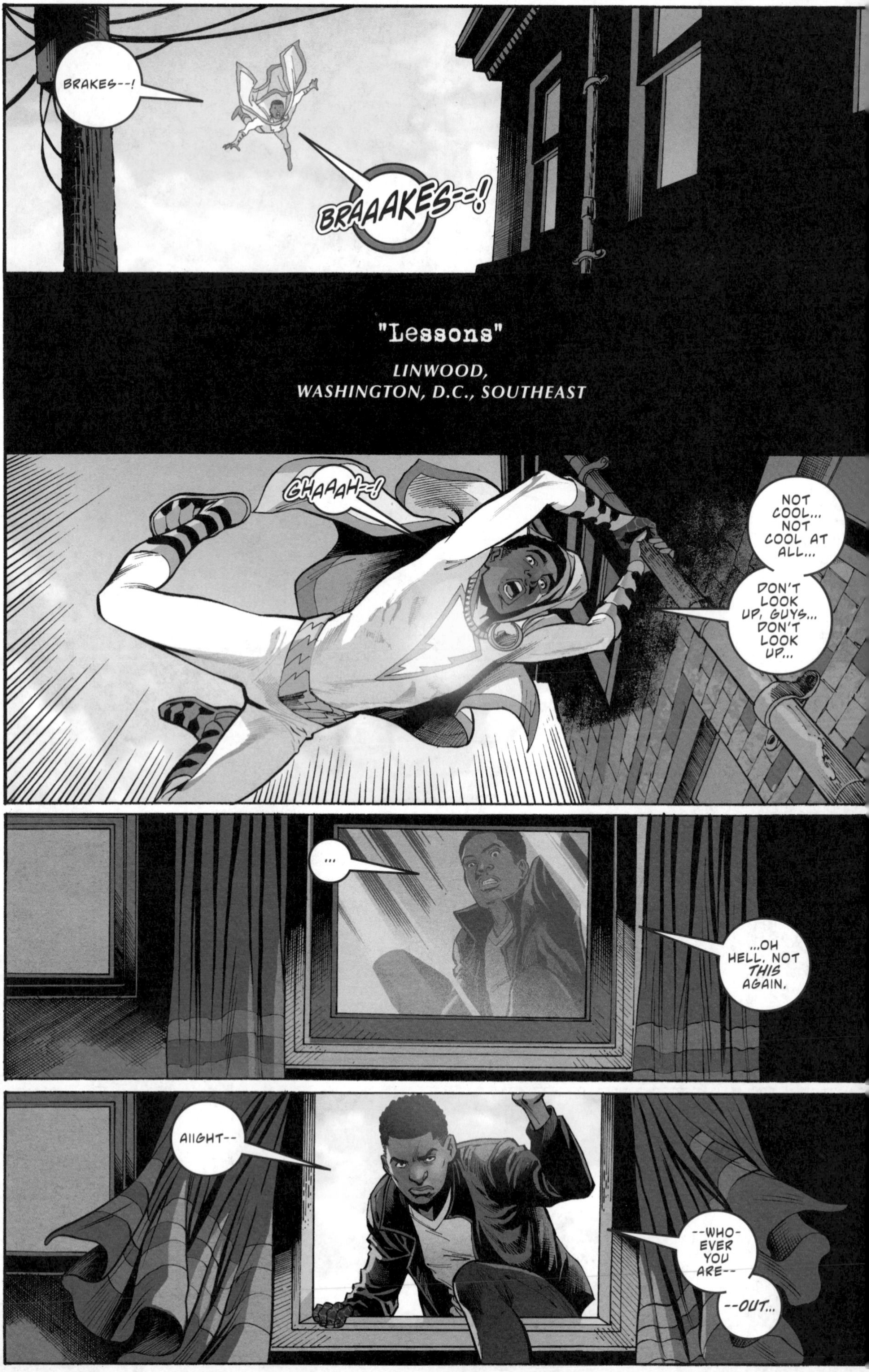
BRAKES--!
BRAAAKES--!
"Lessons"
LINWOOD,
WASHINGTON, D.C., SOUTHEAST
GHAAAH--!
NOT COOL... NOT COOL AT ALL...
DON'T LOOK UP, GUYS... DON'T LOOK UP...
...
...OH HELL, NOT THIS AGAIN.
AIIGHT--
--WHO-EVER YOU ARE--
--OUT...

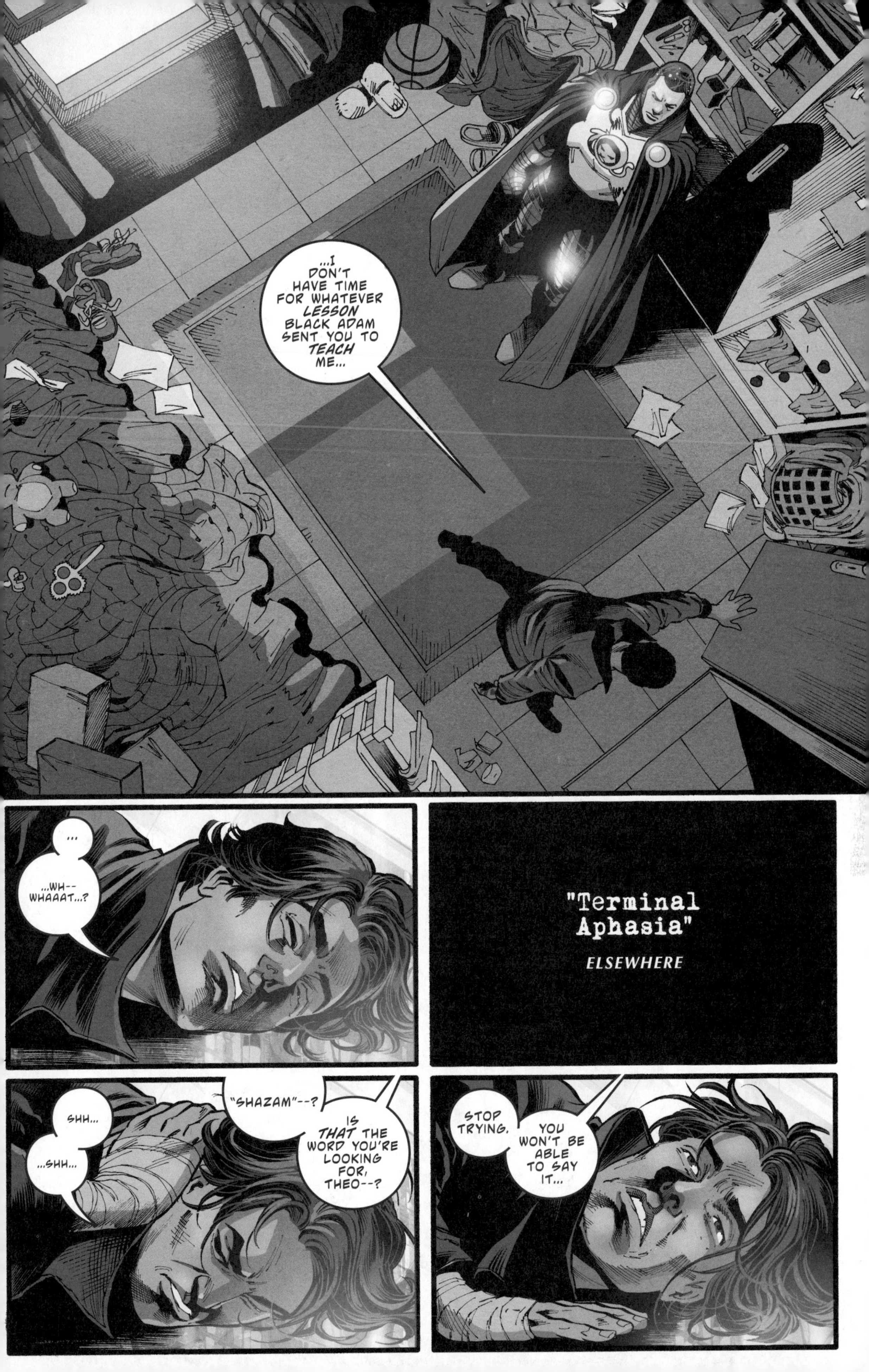
...I DON'T HAVE TIME FOR WHATEVER LESSON BLACK ADAM SENT YOU TO TEACH ME...
...
...WH--WHAAAT...?
"Terminal Aphasia"
ELSEWHERE
SHH...
...SHH...
"SHAZAM"--?
IS THAT THE WORD YOU'RE LOOKING FOR, THEO--?
STOP TRYING.
YOU WON'T BE ABLE TO SAY IT...

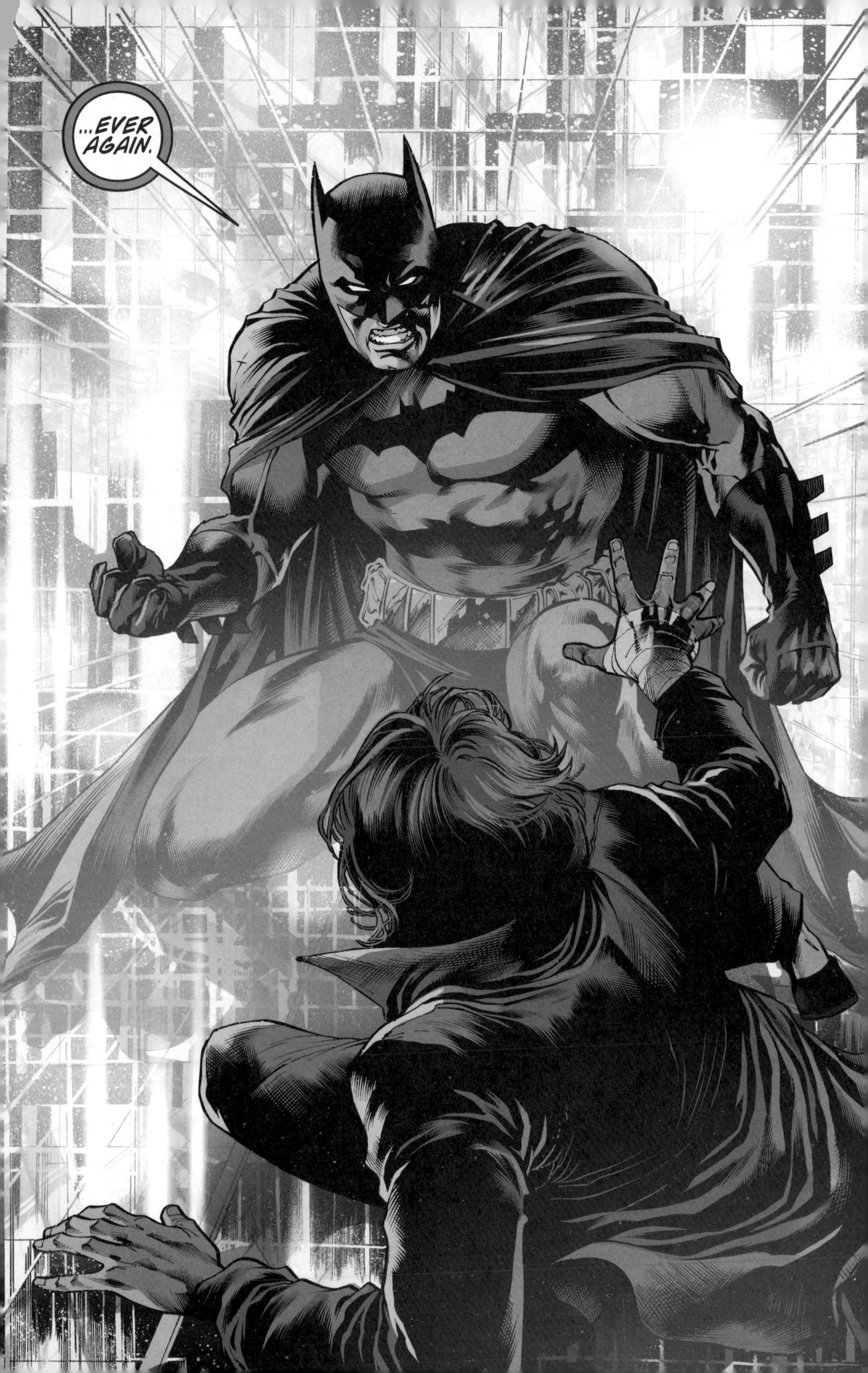
...EVER AGAIN.

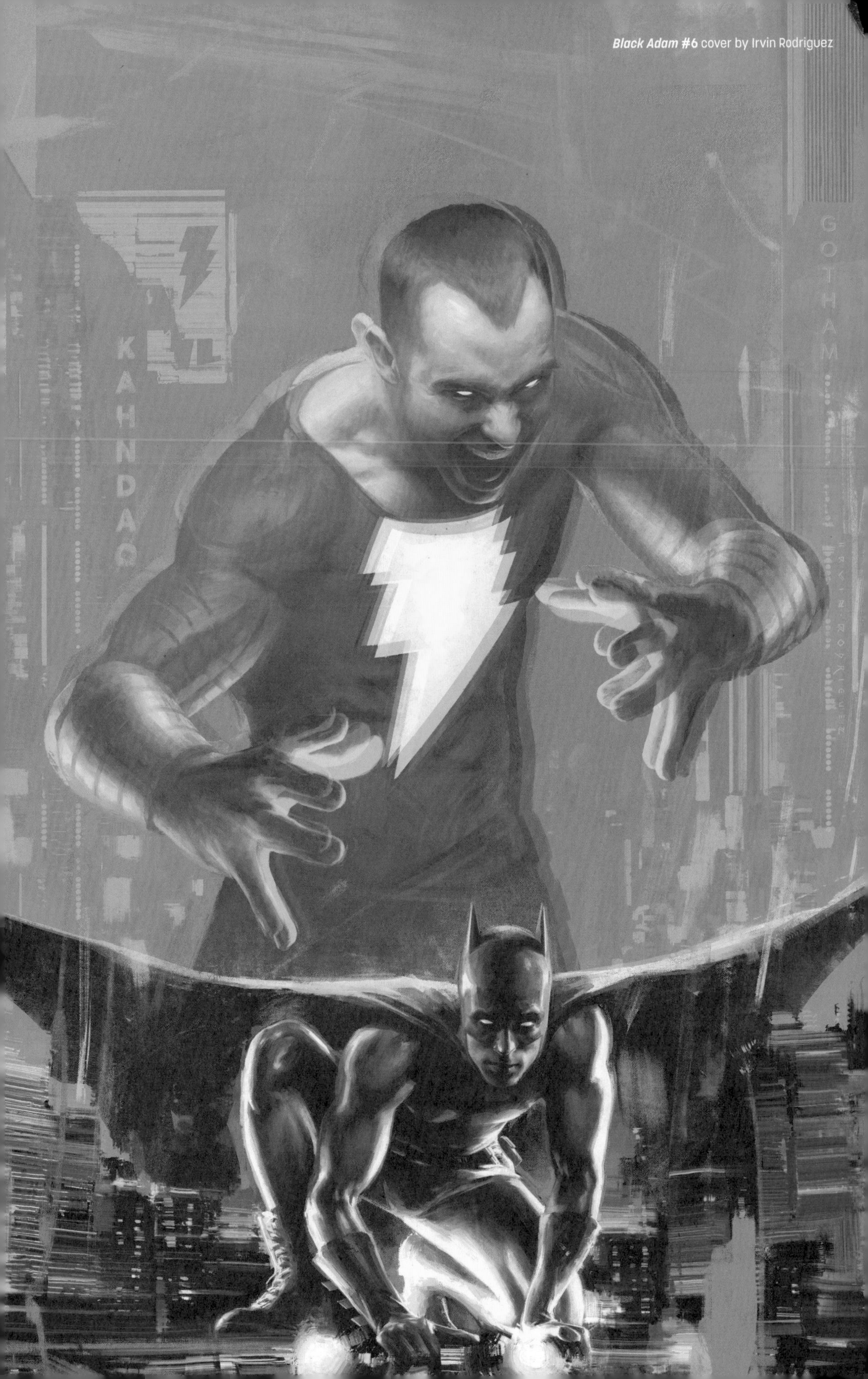
KAHNDAQ
GOTHAM

Black Adam **#6** cover by Irvin Rodriguez

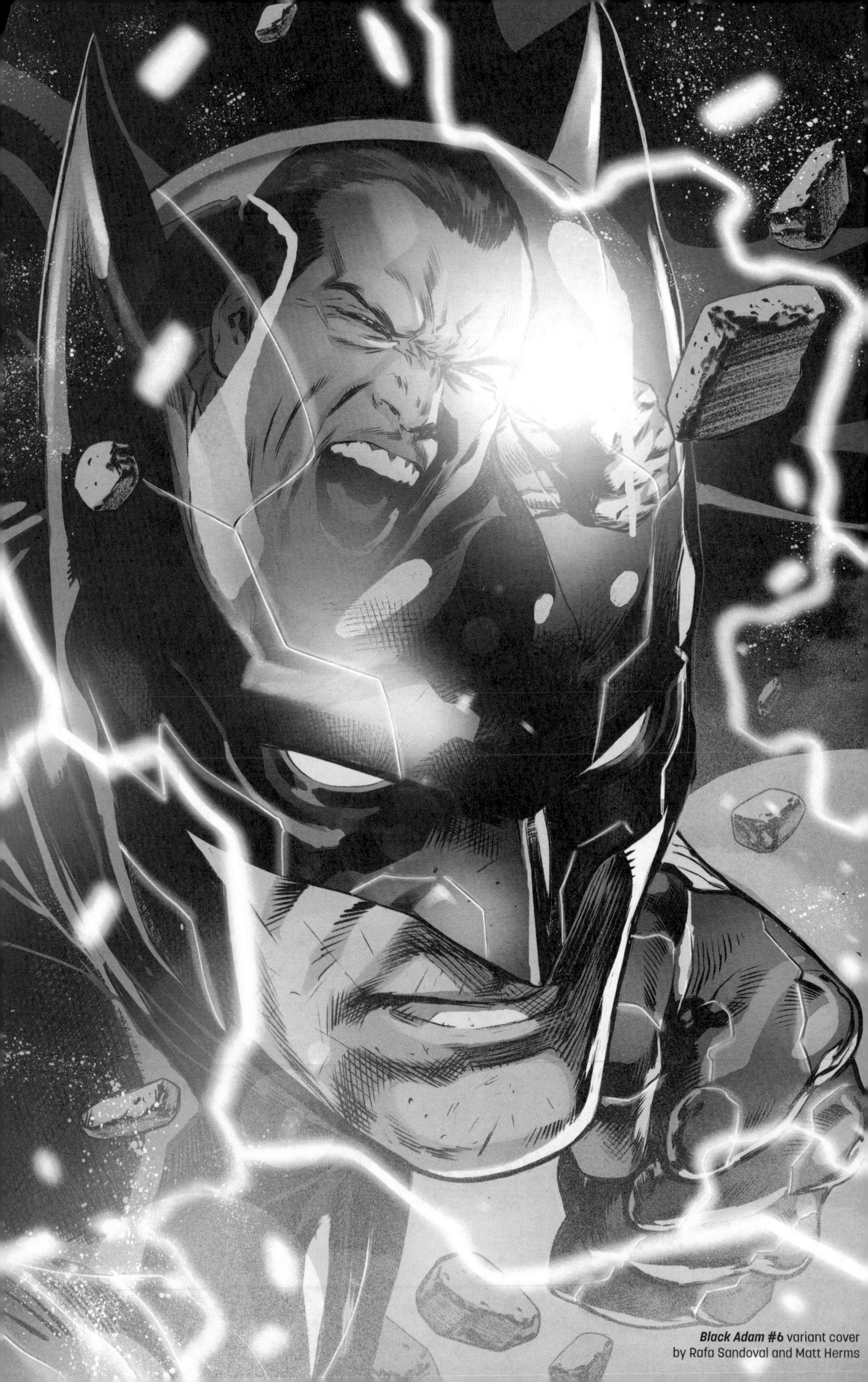

Black Adam #6 variant cover
by Rafa Sandoval and Matt Herms

YOU HAD NEVER SEEN RAIN. YOU'D HEARD OF IT, BUT NEVER ACTUALLY SEEN IT.

"'FOR EVEN THOUGH A MAN HAS NOT BEFORE BEEN TOLD IT HE CAN AT ONCE SEE, IF HE HAVE SENSE...

"'...THAT THAT EGYPT TO WHICH THE GREEKS SAIL IS LAND ACQUIRED BY THE EGYPTIANS...

"'...GIVEN THEM BY THE RIVER.' HERODOTUS, BOOK II CHAPTER FIVE.

"THE NILE... A FORCE THAT DESTROYED THE CIVILIZATIONS IT NURTURED.

"EN-NADDAHA PULLS HER VICTIMS INTO THE NILE AND DROWNS THEM.

"IS THAT WHAT HAPPENED TO YOUR FATHER, THEO? WHY HE LEFT YOU 4,600 YEARS AGO...?

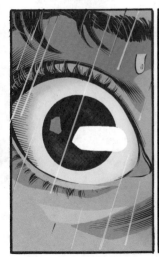

"Aegyptiaca"

MEMPHIS, EGYPT

26TH CENTURY B.C.E.

"LEFT YOU AND YOUR MOTHER WITH HIS *DEBTS*...? WHY YOU BOTH BECAME SLAVES?

"REMEMBER WHAT THEY DID TO YOU, WHAT THEY DID TO YOUR *MOTHER*...

"DOES THE RAIN EXPLAIN THE BLACKNESS INSIDE YOU, THEO...?

"GOOD. LET'S BEGIN...

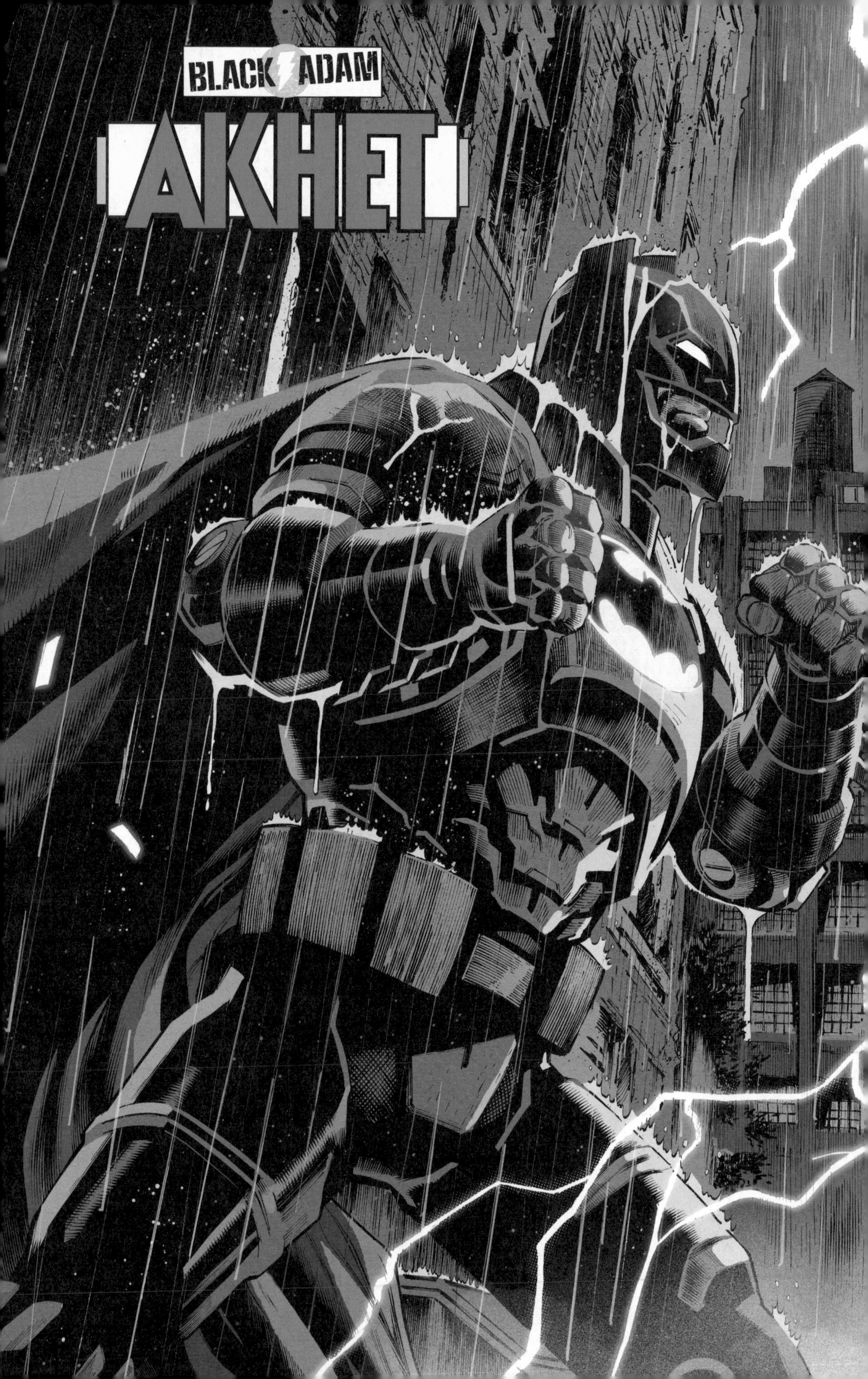
BLACK ADAM
AKHET

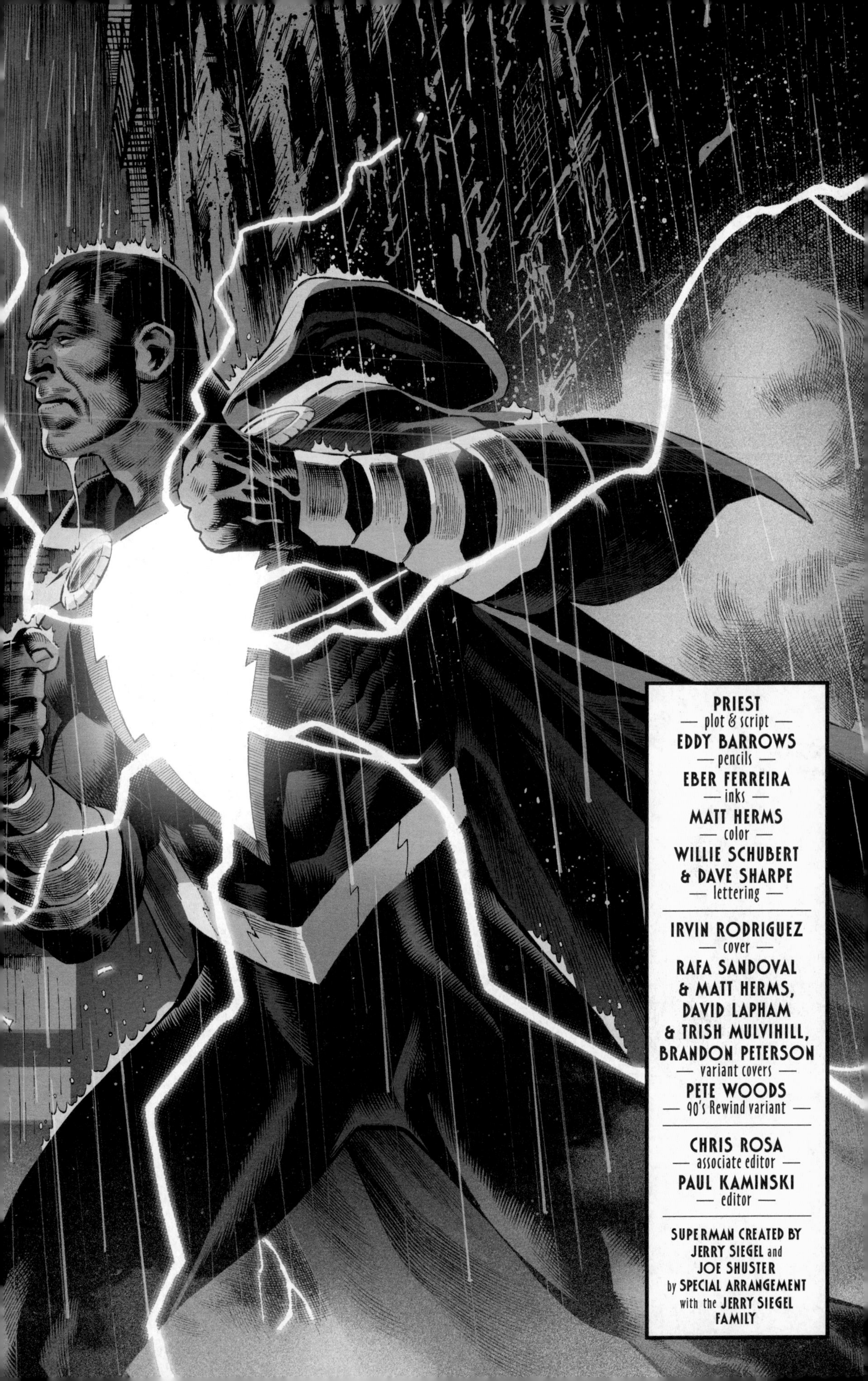
PRIEST
— plot & script —
EDDY BARROWS
— pencils —
EBER FERREIRA
— inks —
MATT HERMS
— color —
WILLIE SCHUBERT
& DAVE SHARPE
— lettering —
IRVIN RODRIGUEZ
— cover —
RAFA SANDOVAL
& MATT HERMS,
DAVID LAPHAM
& TRISH MULVIHILL,
BRANDON PETERSON
— variant covers —
PETE WOODS
— 90's Rewind variant —
CHRIS ROSA
— associate editor —
PAUL KAMINSKI
— editor —
SUPERMAN CREATED BY
JERRY SIEGEL and
JOE SHUSTER
by SPECIAL ARRANGEMENT
with the JERRY SIEGEL
FAMILY

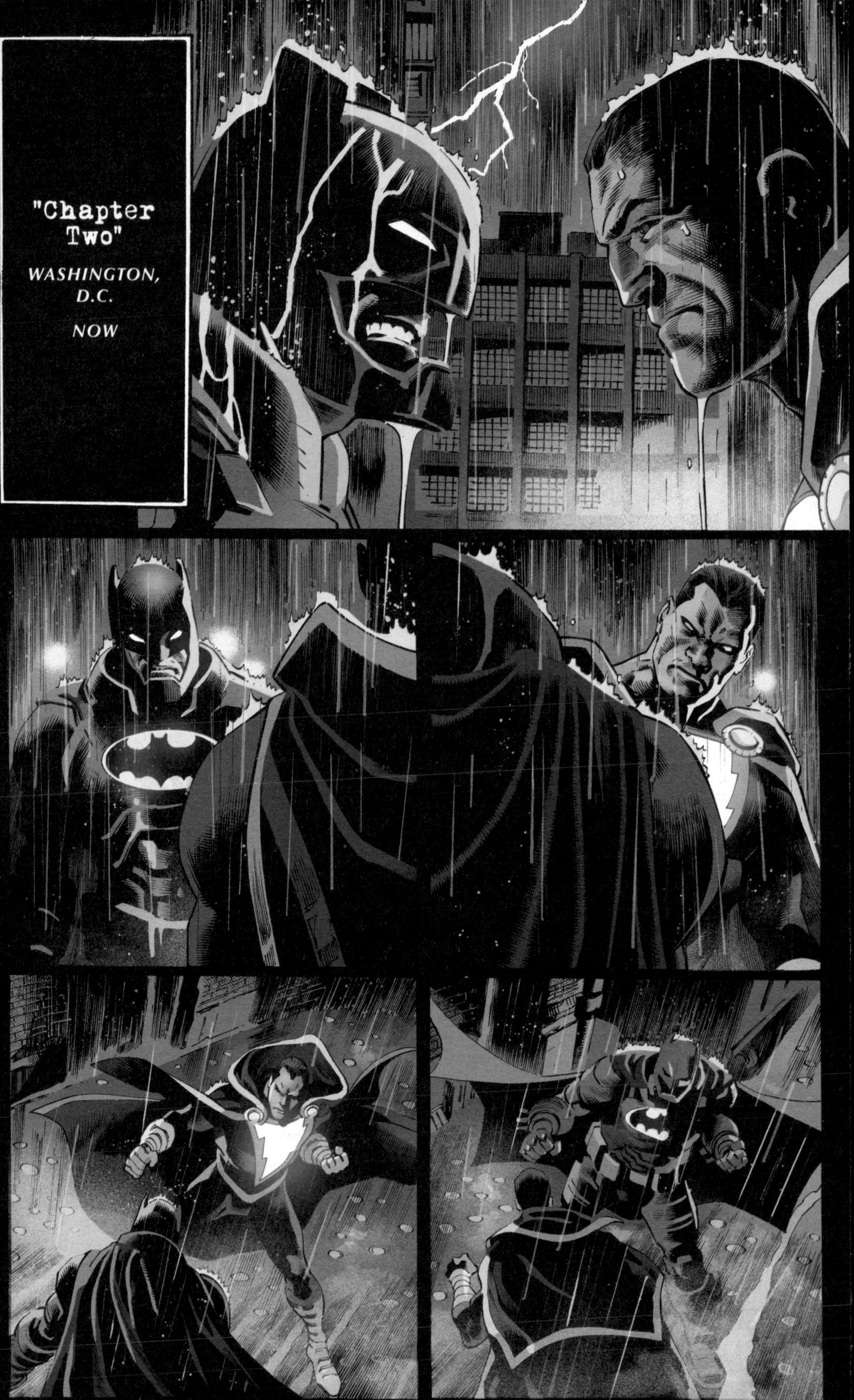
"Chapter Two"
WASHINGTON, D.C.
NOW

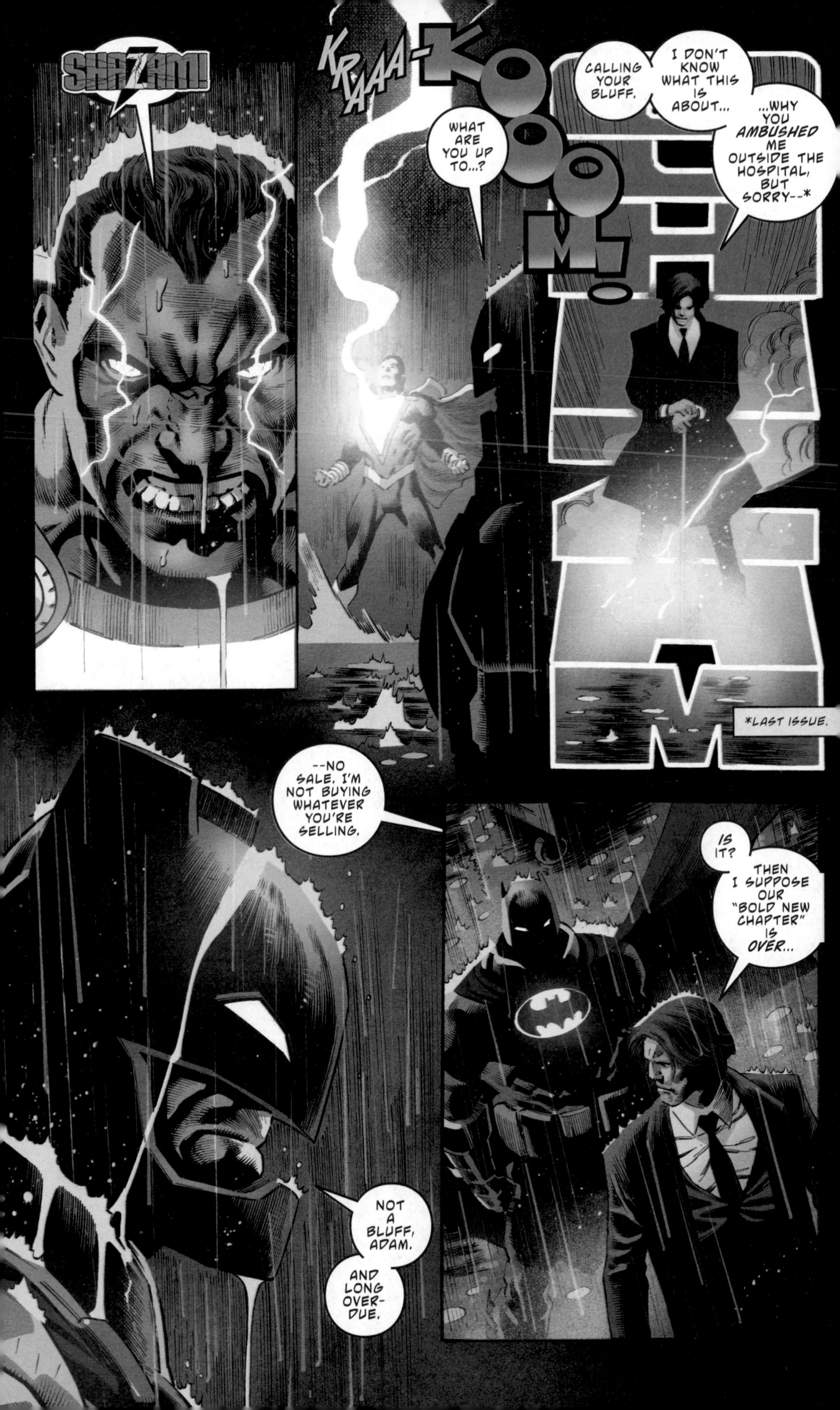
SHAZAM!
KRAAA-KOOOOM!
WHAT ARE YOU UP TO...?
CALLING YOUR BLUFF.
I DON'T KNOW WHAT THIS IS ABOUT...
...WHY YOU AMBUSHED ME OUTSIDE THE HOSPITAL, BUT SORRY--*
*LAST ISSUE.
--NO SALE. I'M NOT BUYING WHATEVER YOU'RE SELLING.
NOT A BLUFF, ADAM.
AND LONG OVERDUE.
IS IT?
THEN I SUPPOSE OUR "BOLD NEW CHAPTER" IS OVER...

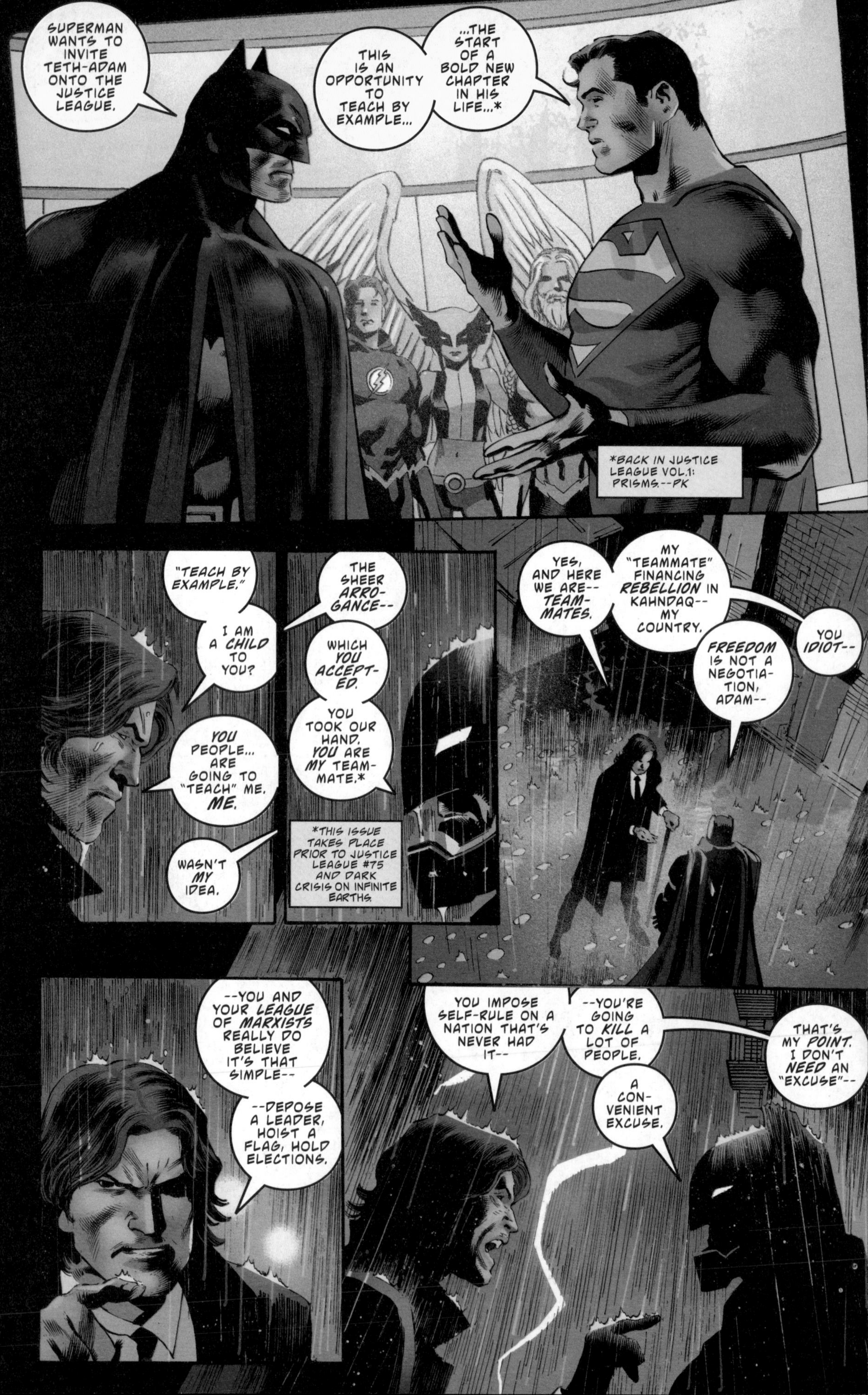

SUPERMAN WANTS TO INVITE TETH-ADAM ONTO THE JUSTICE LEAGUE.
THIS IS AN OPPORTUNITY TO TEACH BY EXAMPLE...
...THE START OF A BOLD NEW CHAPTER IN HIS LIFE...*
*BACK IN JUSTICE LEAGUE VOL.1: PRISMS.--PK
"TEACH BY EXAMPLE."
I AM A CHILD TO YOU?
YOU PEOPLE... ARE GOING TO "TEACH" ME. ME.
WASN'T MY IDEA.
THE SHEER ARROGANCE--
WHICH YOU ACCEPTED.
YOU TOOK OUR HAND. YOU ARE MY TEAMMATE.*
*THIS ISSUE TAKES PLACE PRIOR TO JUSTICE LEAGUE #75 AND DARK CRISIS ON INFINITE EARTHS.
YES, AND HERE WE ARE-- TEAMMATES.
MY "TEAMMATE" FINANCING REBELLION IN KAHNDAQ-- MY COUNTRY.
FREEDOM IS NOT A NEGOTIATION, ADAM--
YOU IDIOT--
--YOU AND YOUR LEAGUE OF MARXISTS REALLY DO BELIEVE IT'S THAT SIMPLE--
--DEPOSE A LEADER, HOIST A FLAG, HOLD ELECTIONS.
YOU IMPOSE SELF-RULE ON A NATION THAT'S NEVER HAD IT--
--YOU'RE GOING TO KILL A LOT OF PEOPLE.
A CONVENIENT EXCUSE.
THAT'S MY POINT. I DON'T NEED AN "EXCUSE"--

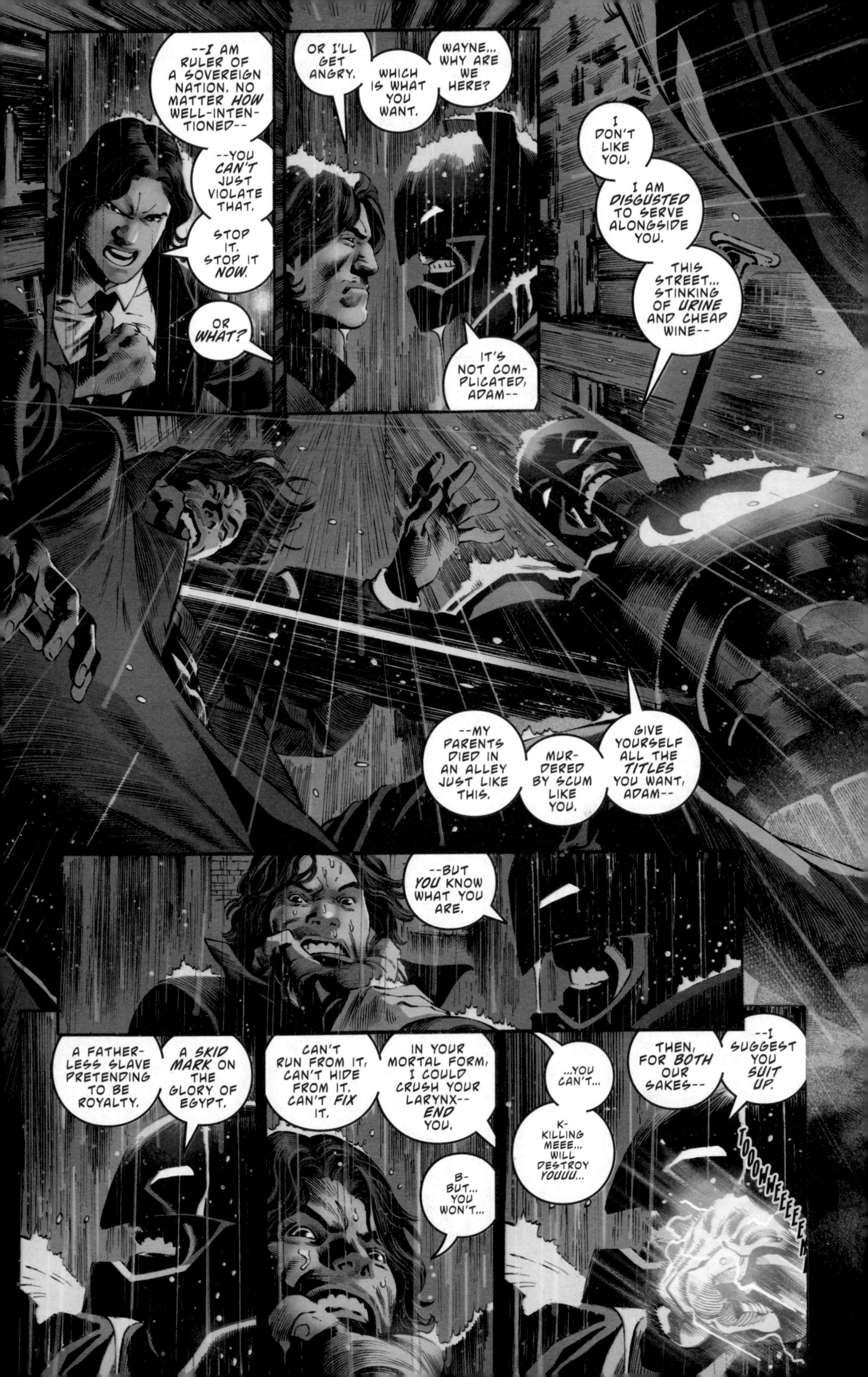
--I AM RULER OF A SOVEREIGN NATION. NO MATTER HOW WELL-INTENTIONED--
--YOU CAN'T JUST VIOLATE THAT.
STOP IT. STOP IT NOW.
OR WHAT?
OR I'LL GET ANGRY.
WHICH IS WHAT YOU WANT.
WAYNE... WHY ARE WE HERE?
IT'S NOT COMPLICATED, ADAM--
I DON'T LIKE YOU.
I AM DISGUSTED TO SERVE ALONGSIDE YOU.
THIS STREET... STINKING OF URINE AND CHEAP WINE--
--MY PARENTS DIED IN AN ALLEY JUST LIKE THIS.
MURDERED BY SCUM LIKE YOU.
GIVE YOURSELF ALL THE TITLES YOU WANT, ADAM--
--BUT YOU KNOW WHAT YOU ARE.
A FATHERLESS SLAVE PRETENDING TO BE ROYALTY.
A SKID MARK ON THE GLORY OF EGYPT.
CAN'T RUN FROM IT, CAN'T HIDE FROM IT. CAN'T FIX IT.
IN YOUR MORTAL FORM, I COULD CRUSH YOUR LARYNX-- END YOU.
B-BUT... YOU WON'T...
...YOU CAN'T...
K-KILLING MEEE... WILL DESTROY YOUUU...
THEN, FOR BOTH OUR SAKES--
--I SUGGEST YOU SUIT UP.
TOOOHHHEEEEEN

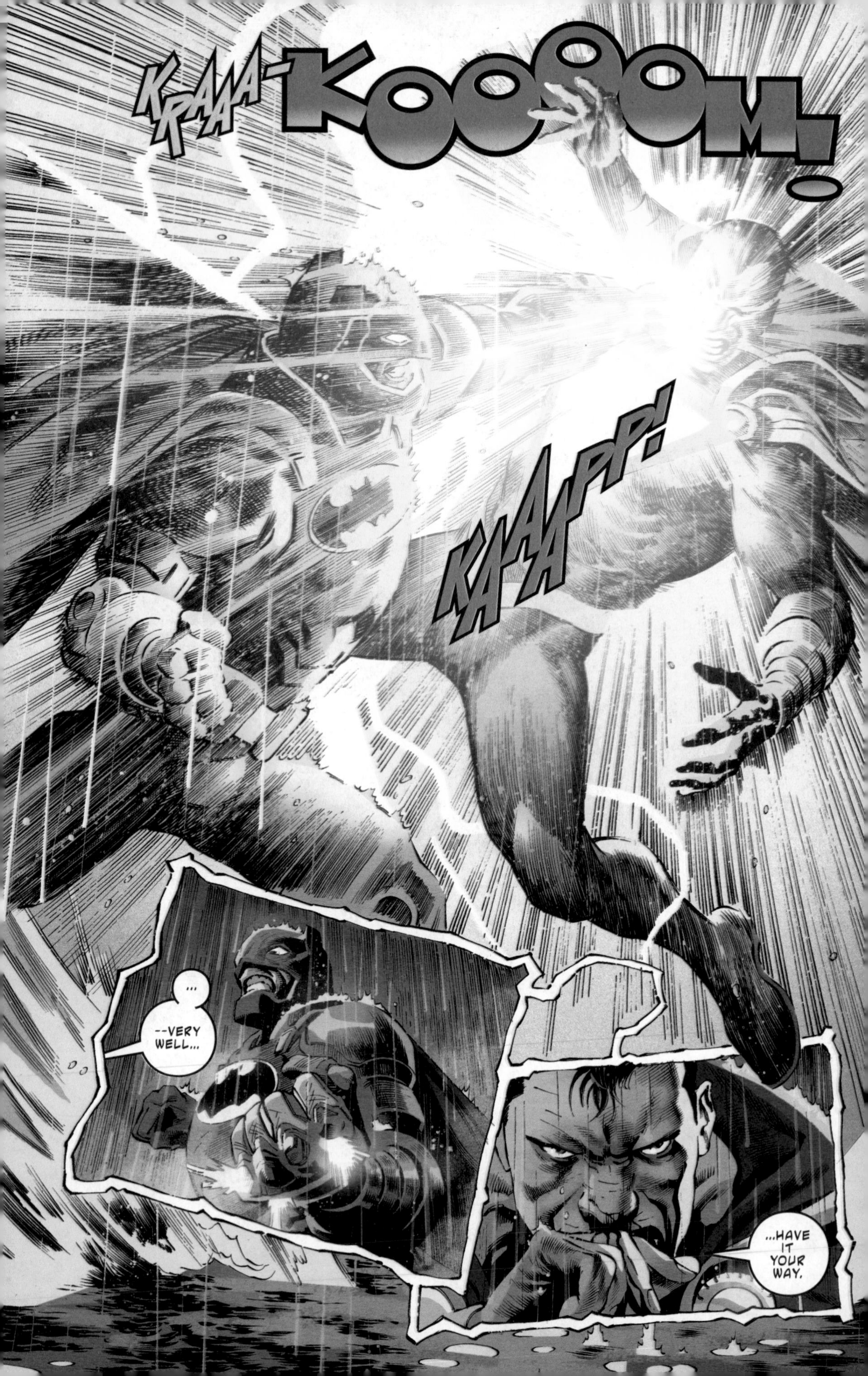
KRAAA-KOOOOOM!
KAAAAPP!
...
--VERY WELL...
...HAVE IT YOUR WAY.

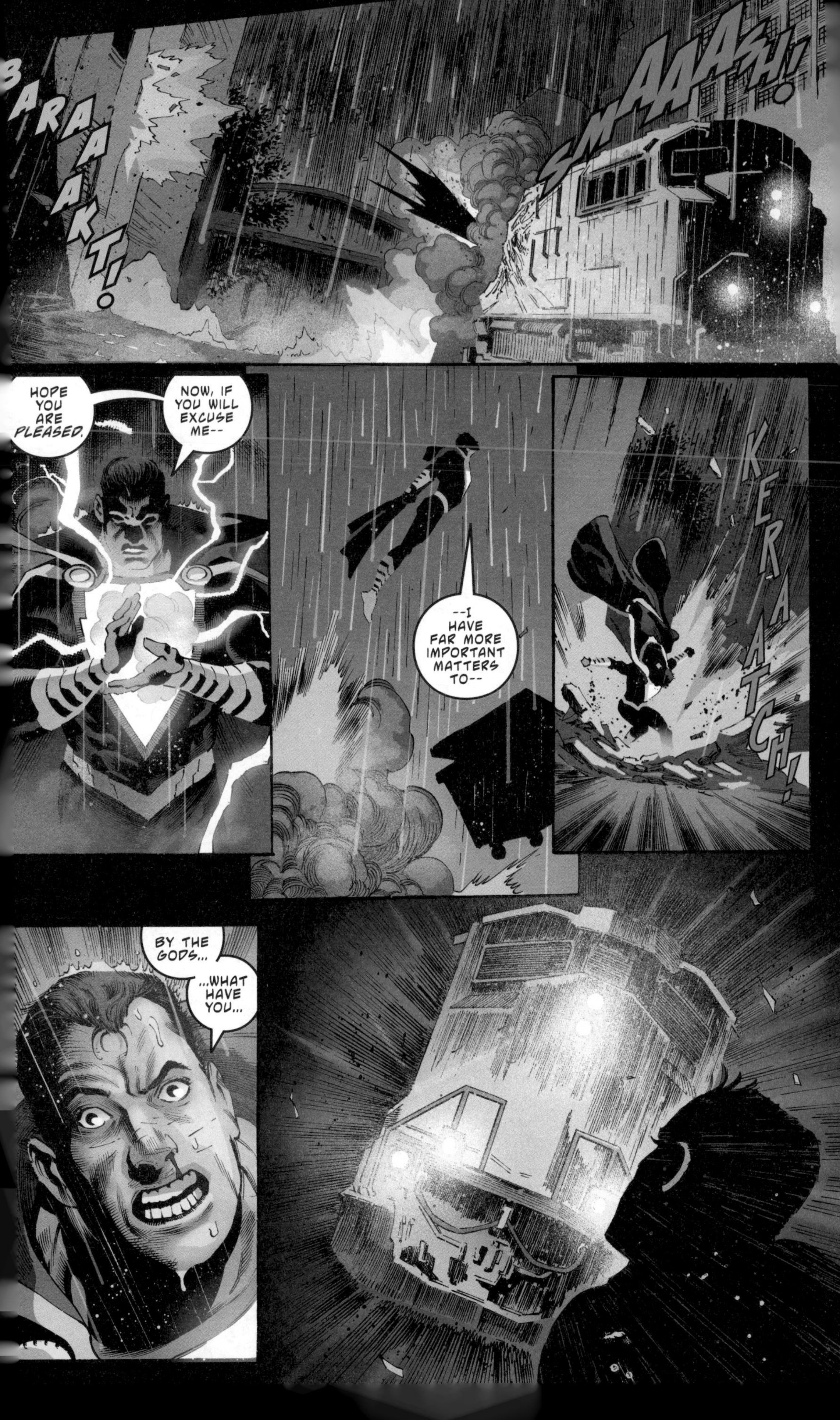
BARAAAKT!
SMAAASH!
HOPE YOU ARE PLEASED.
NOW, IF YOU WILL EXCUSE ME--
--I HAVE FAR MORE IMPORTANT MATTERS TO--
KERAATCH!
BY THE GODS...
...WHAT HAVE YOU...

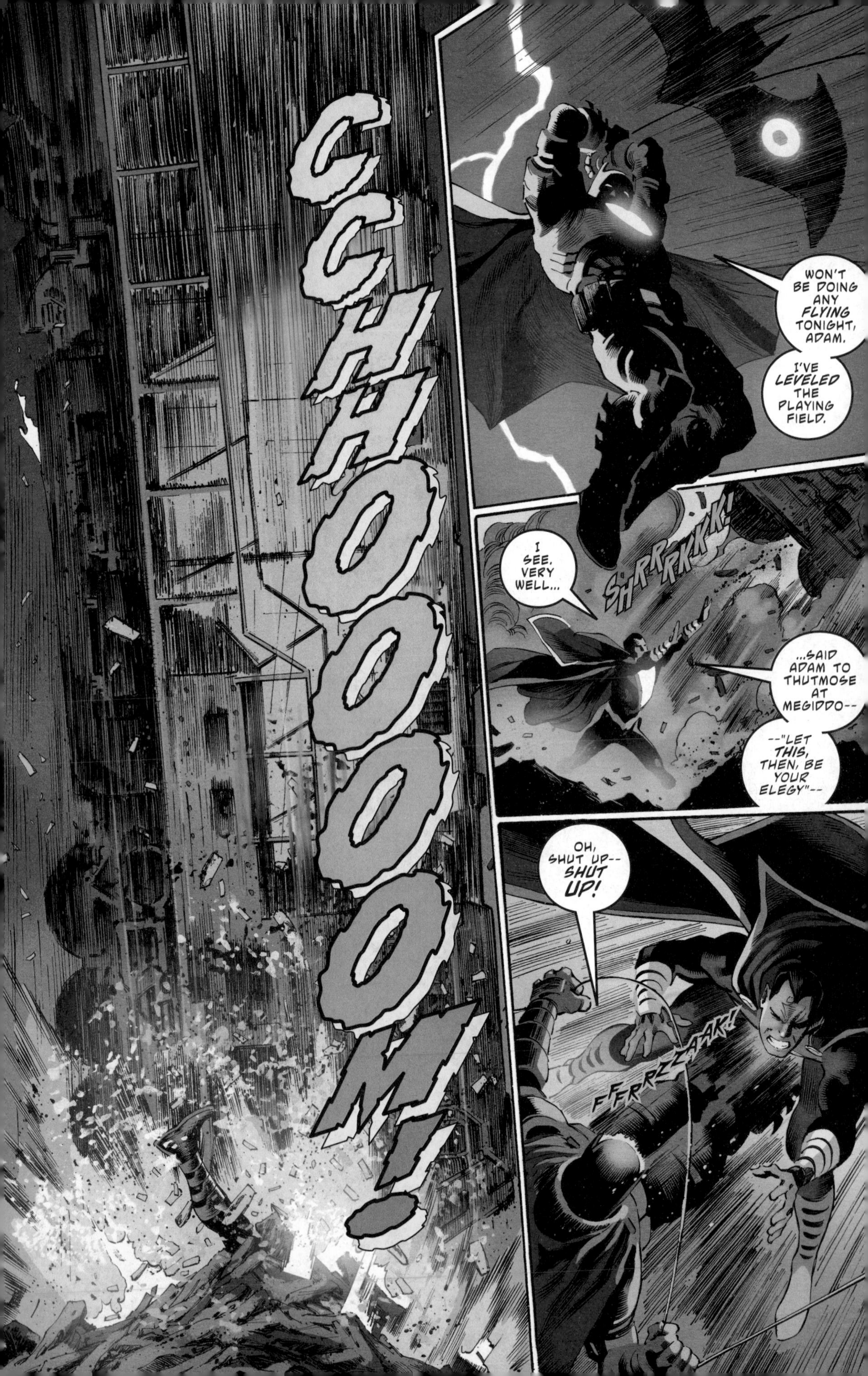

CCHOOOOOM!
WON'T BE DOING ANY FLYING TONIGHT, ADAM.
I'VE LEVELED THE PLAYING FIELD.
SHRRRKKK!
I SEE. VERY WELL...
...SAID ADAM TO THUTMOSE AT MEGIDDO--
--"LET THIS, THEN, BE YOUR ELEGY"--
OH, SHUT UP-- SHUT UP!
FFFRRZZAAAK!

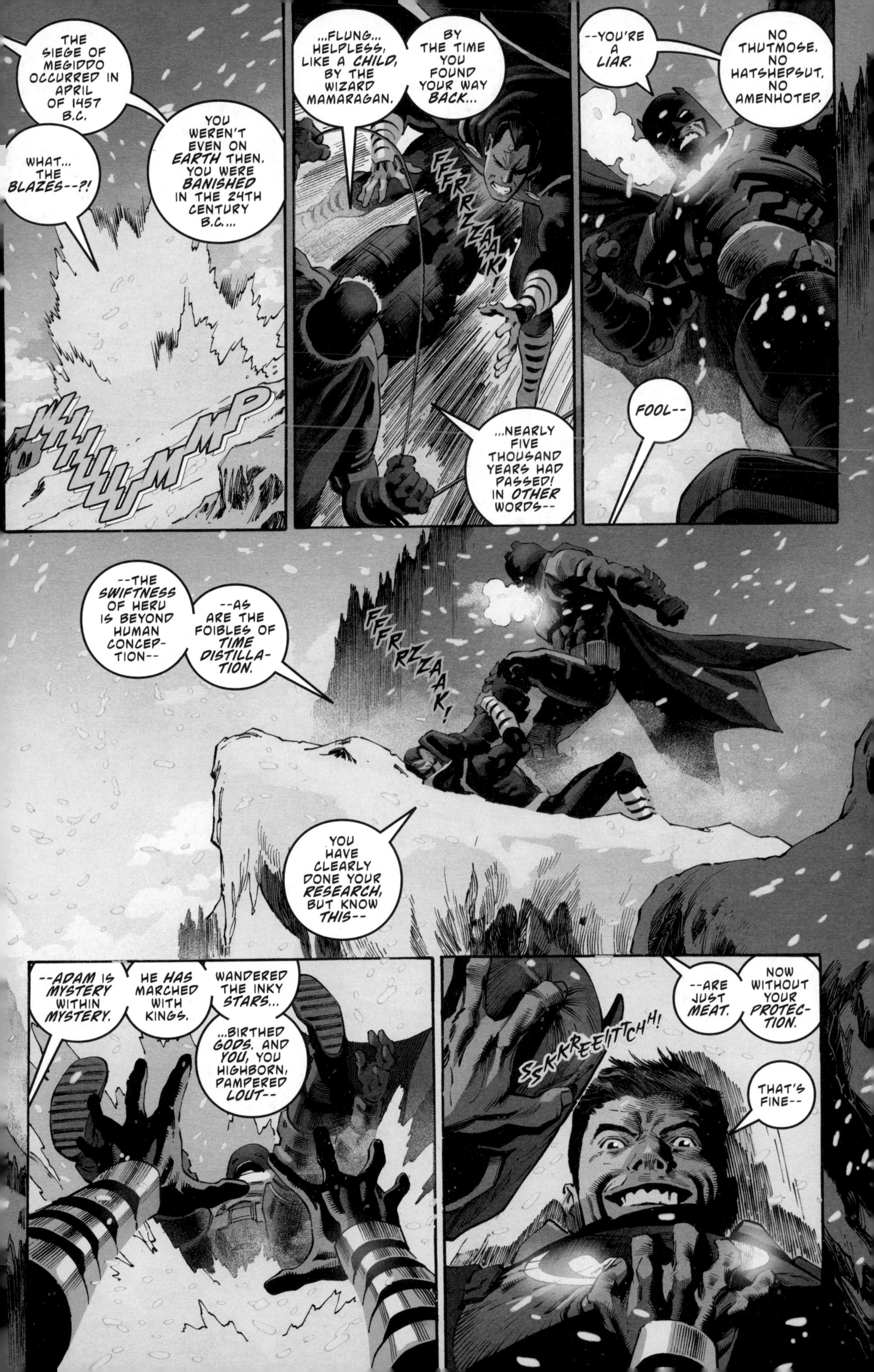
THE SIEGE OF MEGIDDO OCCURRED IN APRIL OF 1457 B.C.
WHAT... THE BLAZES--?!
YOU WEREN'T EVEN ON EARTH THEN. YOU WERE BANISHED IN THE 24TH CENTURY B.C....
WHHUUMMP
...FLUNG... HELPLESS, LIKE A CHILD, BY THE WIZARD MAMARAGAN.
BY THE TIME YOU FOUND YOUR WAY BACK...
FFFRRZZAAK!
...NEARLY FIVE THOUSAND YEARS HAD PASSED! IN OTHER WORDS--
--YOU'RE A LIAR.
NO THUTMOSE. NO HATSHEPSUT. NO AMENHOTEP.
FOOL--
--THE SWIFTNESS OF HERU IS BEYOND HUMAN CONCEPTION--
--AS ARE THE FOIBLES OF TIME DISTILLATION.
FFFRRZZAAK!
YOU HAVE CLEARLY DONE YOUR RESEARCH, BUT KNOW THIS--
--ADAM IS MYSTERY WITHIN MYSTERY.
HE HAS MARCHED WITH KINGS.
WANDERED THE INKY STARS...
...BIRTHED GODS. AND YOU, YOU HIGHBORN, PAMPERED LOUT--
SSKKREEITTCHH!
--ARE JUST MEAT.
NOW WITHOUT YOUR PROTECTION.
THAT'S FINE--

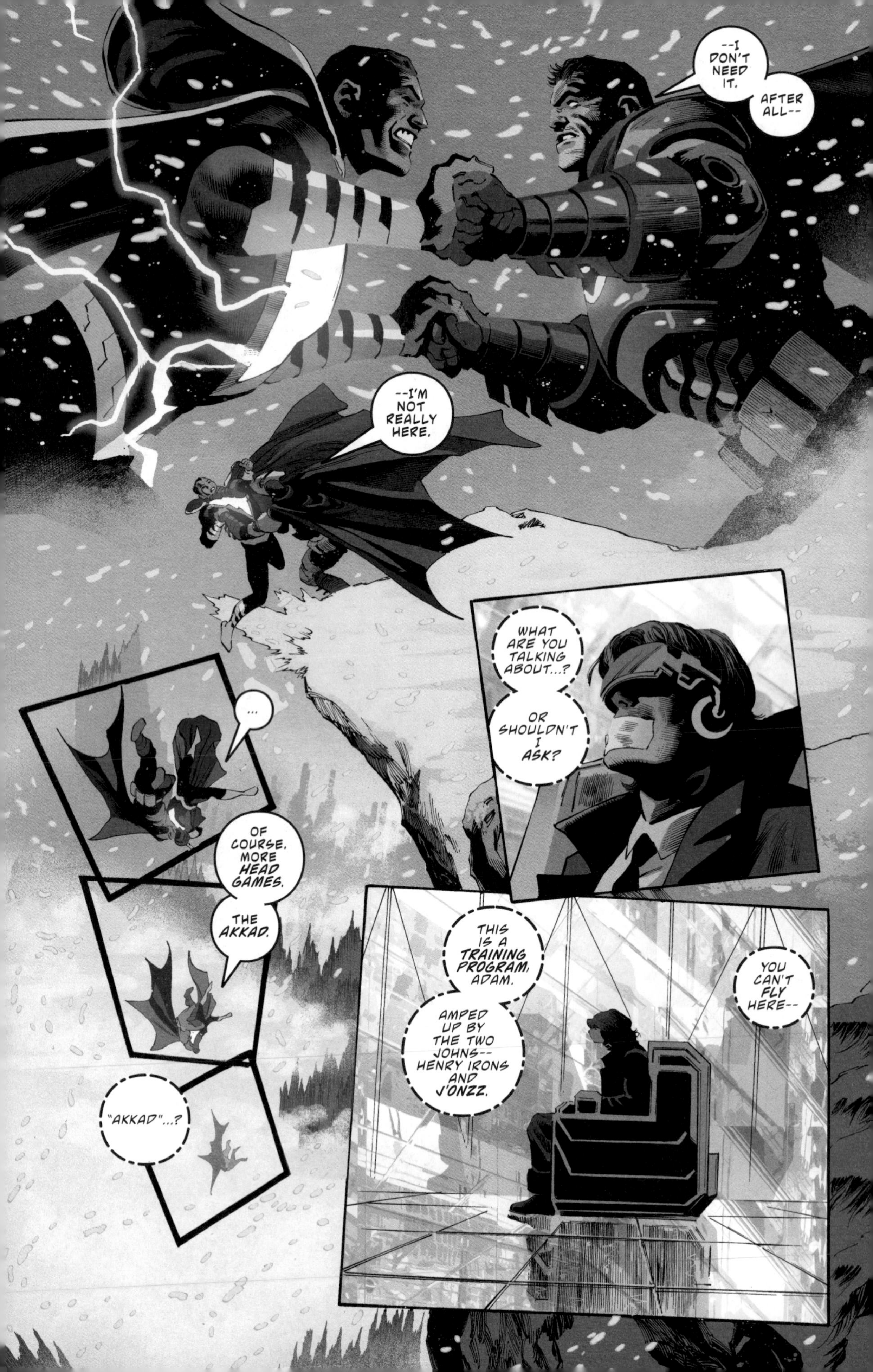

--I DON'T NEED IT.
AFTER ALL--
--I'M NOT REALLY HERE.
WHAT ARE YOU TALKING ABOUT...?
OR SHOULDN'T I ASK?
...
OF COURSE. MORE HEAD GAMES.
THE AKKAD.
"AKKAD"...?
THIS IS A TRAINING PROGRAM, ADAM.
AMPED UP BY THE TWO JOHNS-- HENRY IRONS AND J'ONZZ.
YOU CAN'T FLY HERE--

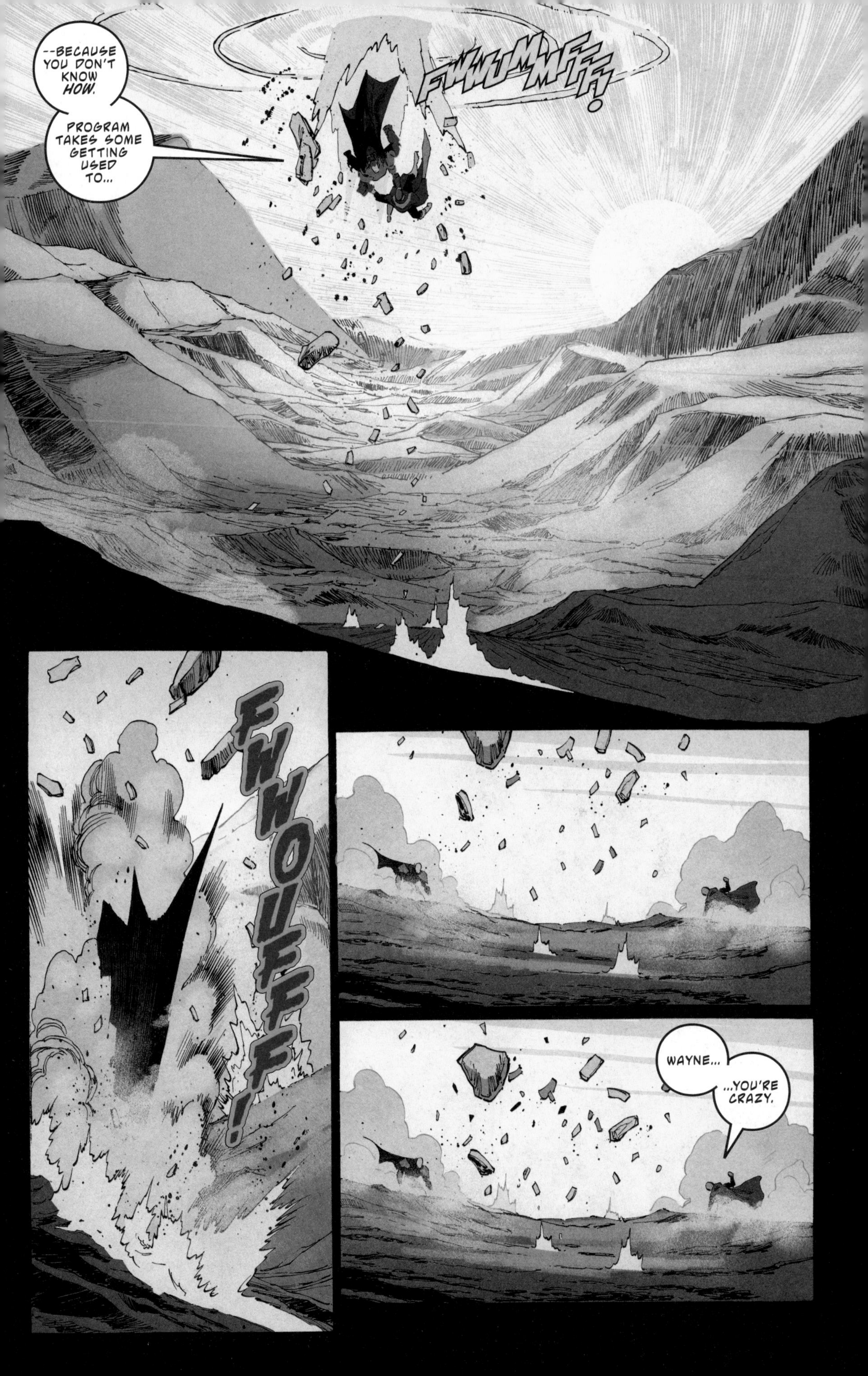
--BECAUSE YOU DON'T KNOW HOW.
PROGRAM TAKES SOME GETTING USED TO...
FWUMMFF!
FWOUFF!
WAYNE...
...YOU'RE CRAZY.

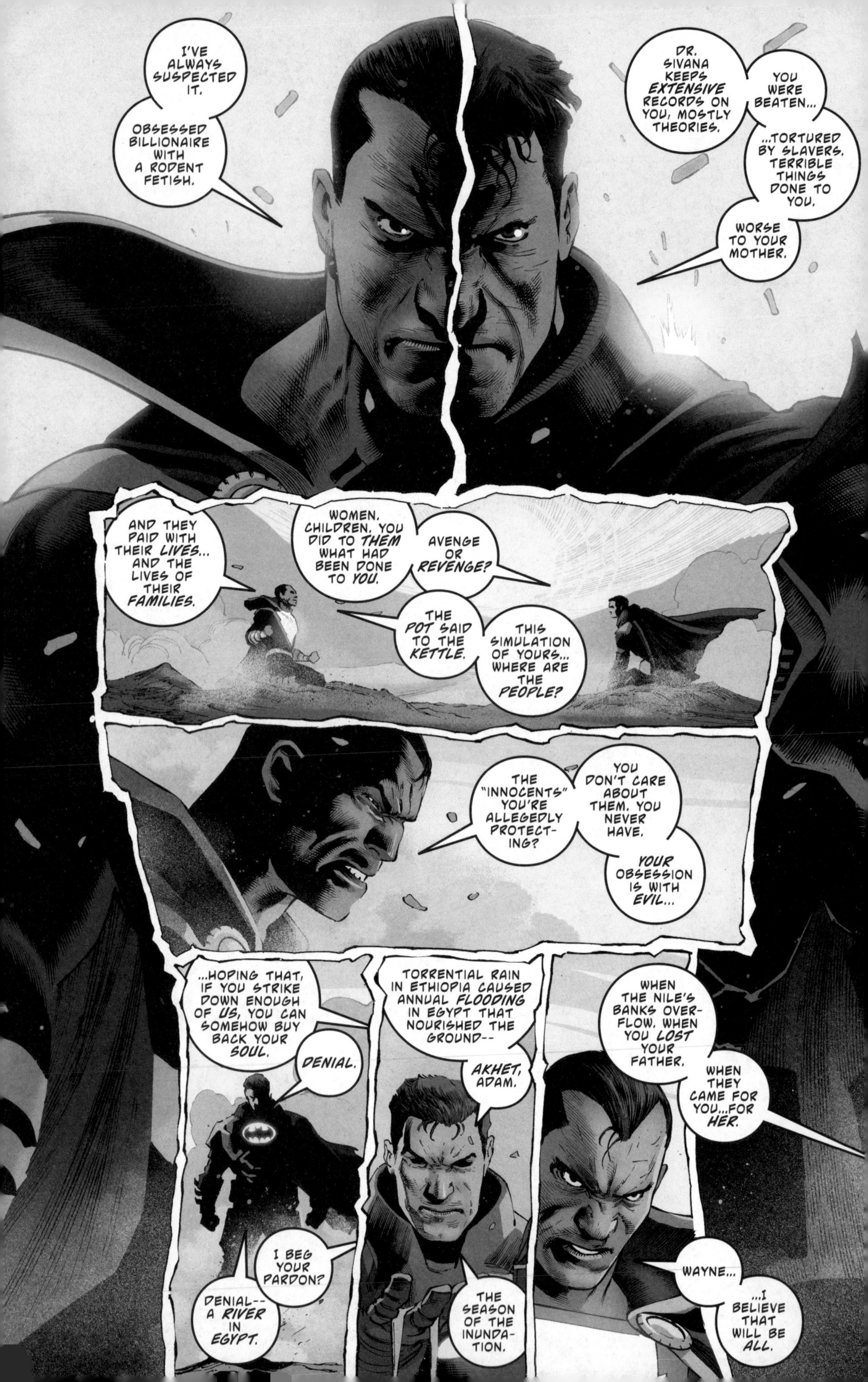
I'VE ALWAYS SUSPECTED IT.
OBSESSED BILLIONAIRE WITH A RODENT FETISH.
DR. SIVANA KEEPS *EXTENSIVE* RECORDS ON YOU, MOSTLY THEORIES.
YOU WERE BEATEN...
...TORTURED BY SLAVERS, TERRIBLE THINGS DONE TO YOU.
WORSE TO YOUR MOTHER.
AND THEY PAID WITH THEIR *LIVES*... AND THE LIVES OF THEIR *FAMILIES*.
WOMEN, CHILDREN. YOU DID TO *THEM* WHAT HAD BEEN DONE TO *YOU*.
AVENGE OR *REVENGE?*
THE *POT* SAID TO THE *KETTLE*.
THIS SIMULATION OF YOURS... WHERE ARE THE *PEOPLE?*
THE "INNOCENTS" YOU'RE ALLEGEDLY PROTECT-ING?
YOU DON'T CARE ABOUT THEM. YOU NEVER HAVE.
YOUR OBSESSION IS WITH *EVIL*...
...HOPING THAT, IF YOU STRIKE DOWN ENOUGH OF *US*, YOU CAN SOMEHOW BUY BACK YOUR *SOUL*.
DENIAL.
I BEG YOUR PARDON?
DENIAL-- A *RIVER* IN *EGYPT*.
TORRENTIAL RAIN IN ETHIOPIA CAUSED ANNUAL *FLOODING* IN EGYPT THAT NOURISHED THE GROUND--
AKHET, ADAM.
THE SEASON OF THE INUNDA-TION.
WHEN THE NILE'S BANKS OVER-FLOW. WHEN YOU *LOST* YOUR FATHER.
WHEN THEY CAME FOR YOU...FOR *HER*.
WAYNE...
...I BELIEVE THAT WILL BE *ALL*.

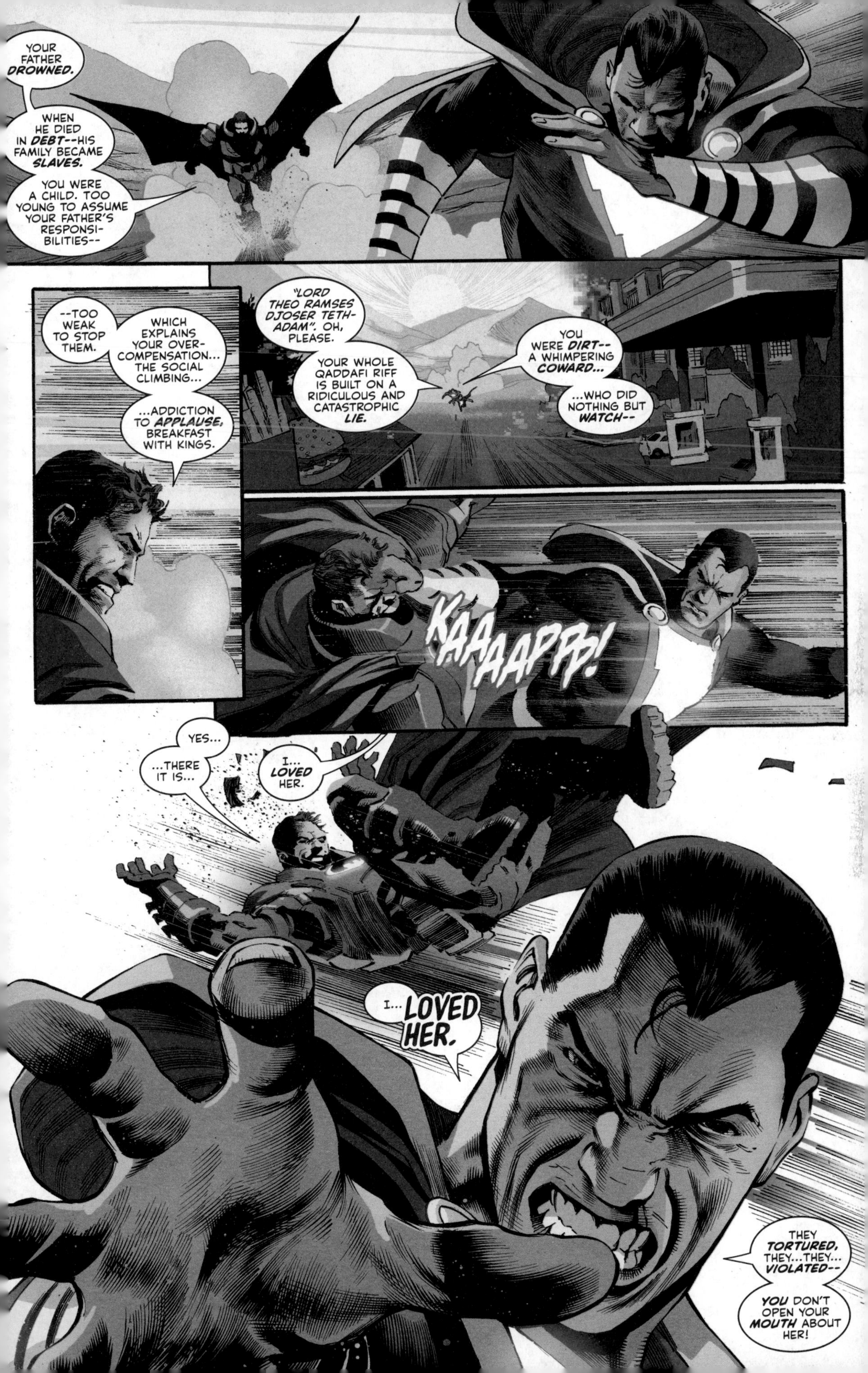
YOUR FATHER DROWNED.
WHEN HE DIED IN DEBT--HIS FAMILY BECAME SLAVES.
YOU WERE A CHILD. TOO YOUNG TO ASSUME YOUR FATHER'S RESPONSI- BILITIES--
--TOO WEAK TO STOP THEM.
WHICH EXPLAINS YOUR OVER- COMPENSATION... THE SOCIAL CLIMBING...
...ADDICTION TO APPLAUSE, BREAKFAST WITH KINGS.
"LORD THEO RAMSES DJOSER TETH- ADAM". OH, PLEASE.
YOUR WHOLE QADDAFI RIFF IS BUILT ON A RIDICULOUS AND CATASTROPHIC LIE.
YOU WERE DIRT-- A WHIMPERING COWARD...
...WHO DID NOTHING BUT WATCH--
KAAAAAPPD!
YES...
...THERE IT IS...
I... LOVED HER.
I... LOVED HER.
THEY TORTURED, THEY...THEY... VIOLATED--
YOU DON'T OPEN YOUR MOUTH ABOUT HER!

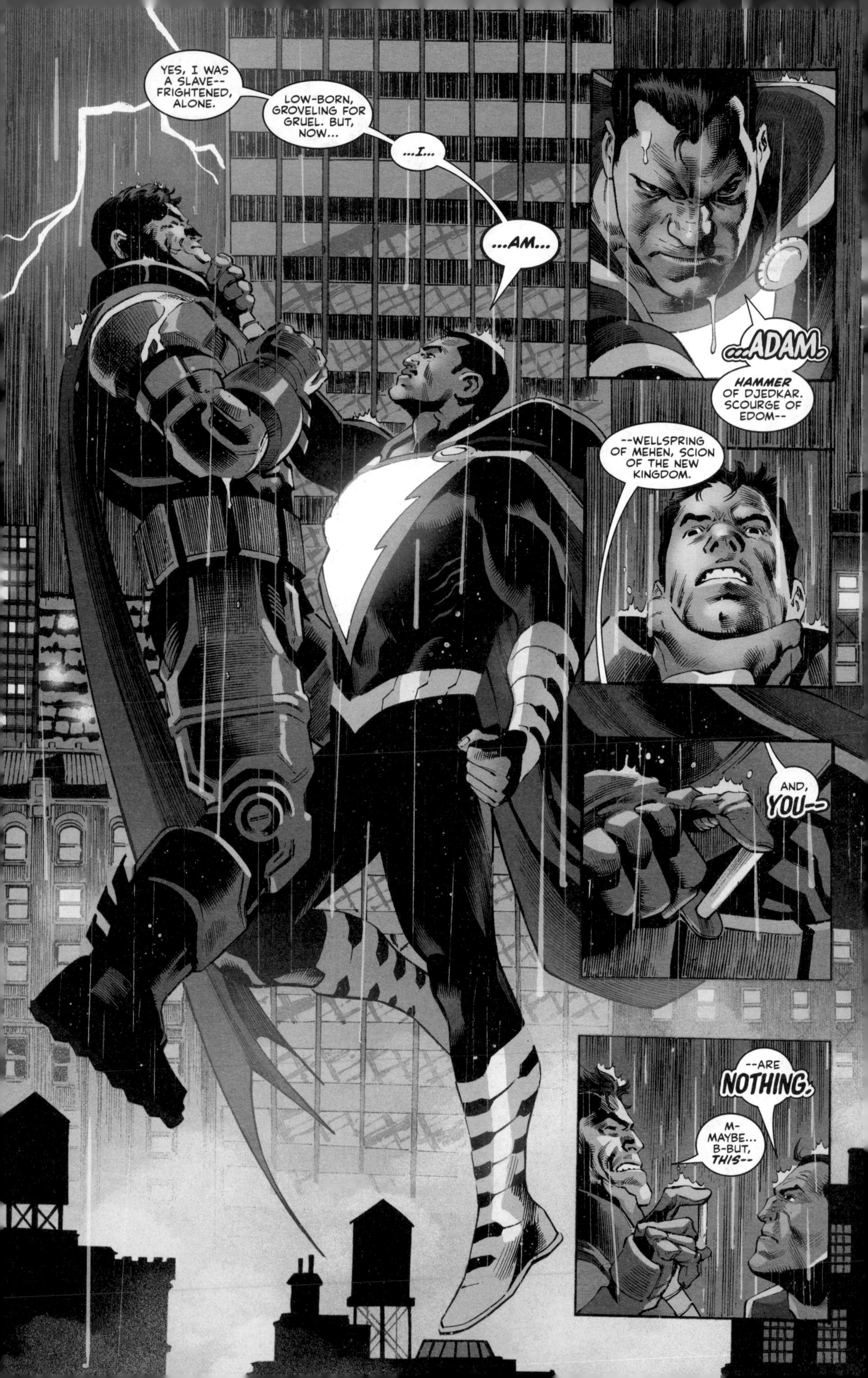
YES, I WAS A SLAVE-- FRIGHTENED, ALONE.
LOW-BORN, GROVELING FOR GRUEL. BUT, NOW...
...I...
...AM...
...ADAM.
HAMMER OF DJEDKAR. SCOURGE OF EDOM--
--WELLSPRING OF MEHEN, SCION OF THE NEW KINGDOM.
AND, YOU--
--ARE NOTHING.
M-MAYBE... B-BUT, THIS--

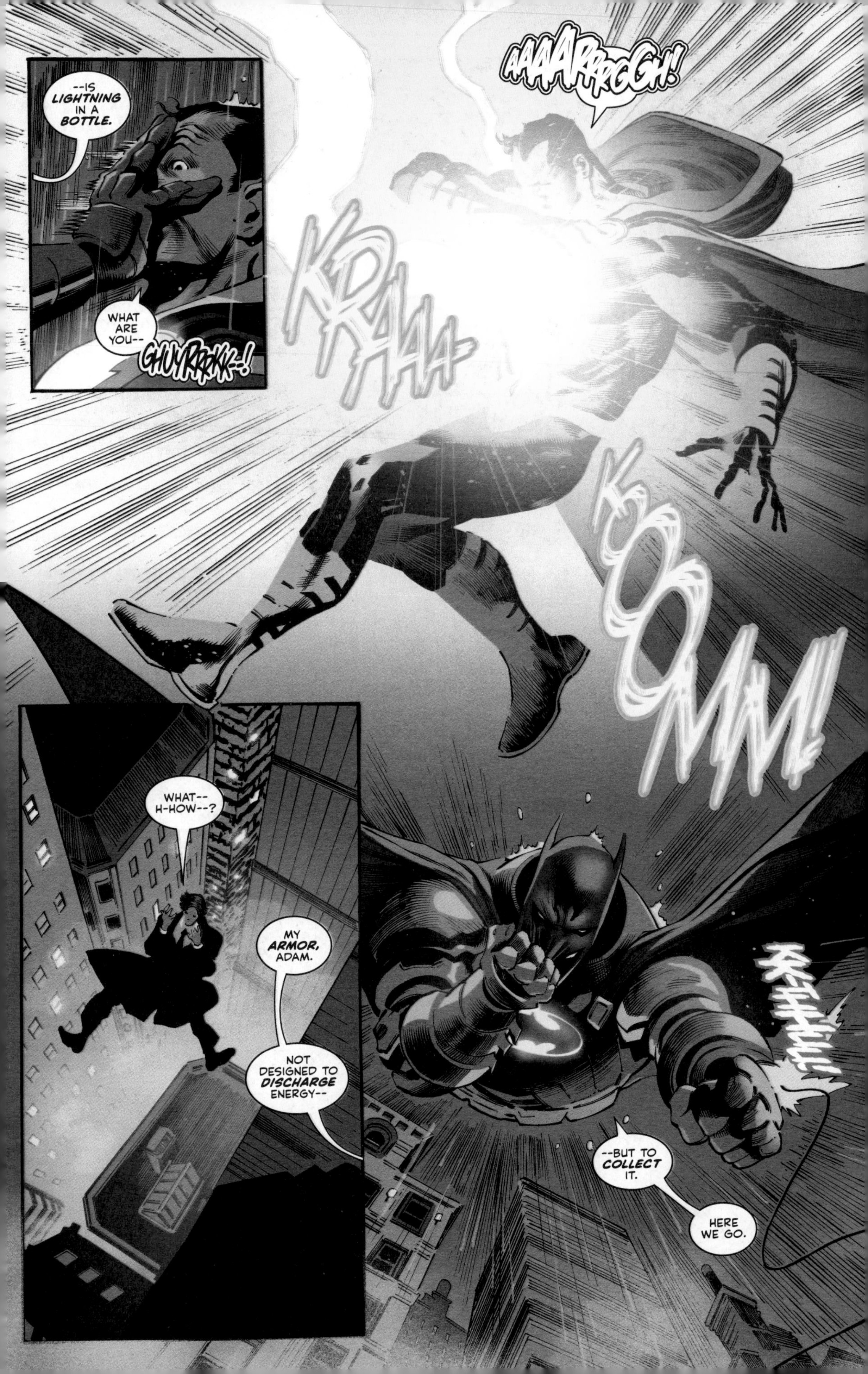
--IS LIGHTNING IN A BOTTLE.
WHAT ARE YOU--
GHUYRRKK--!
AAAAARRRGGH!
KRAAAA
KOOOMM!
WHAT-- H-HOW--?
MY ARMOR, ADAM.
NOT DESIGNED TO DISCHARGE ENERGY--
--BUT TO COLLECT IT.
HERE WE GO.

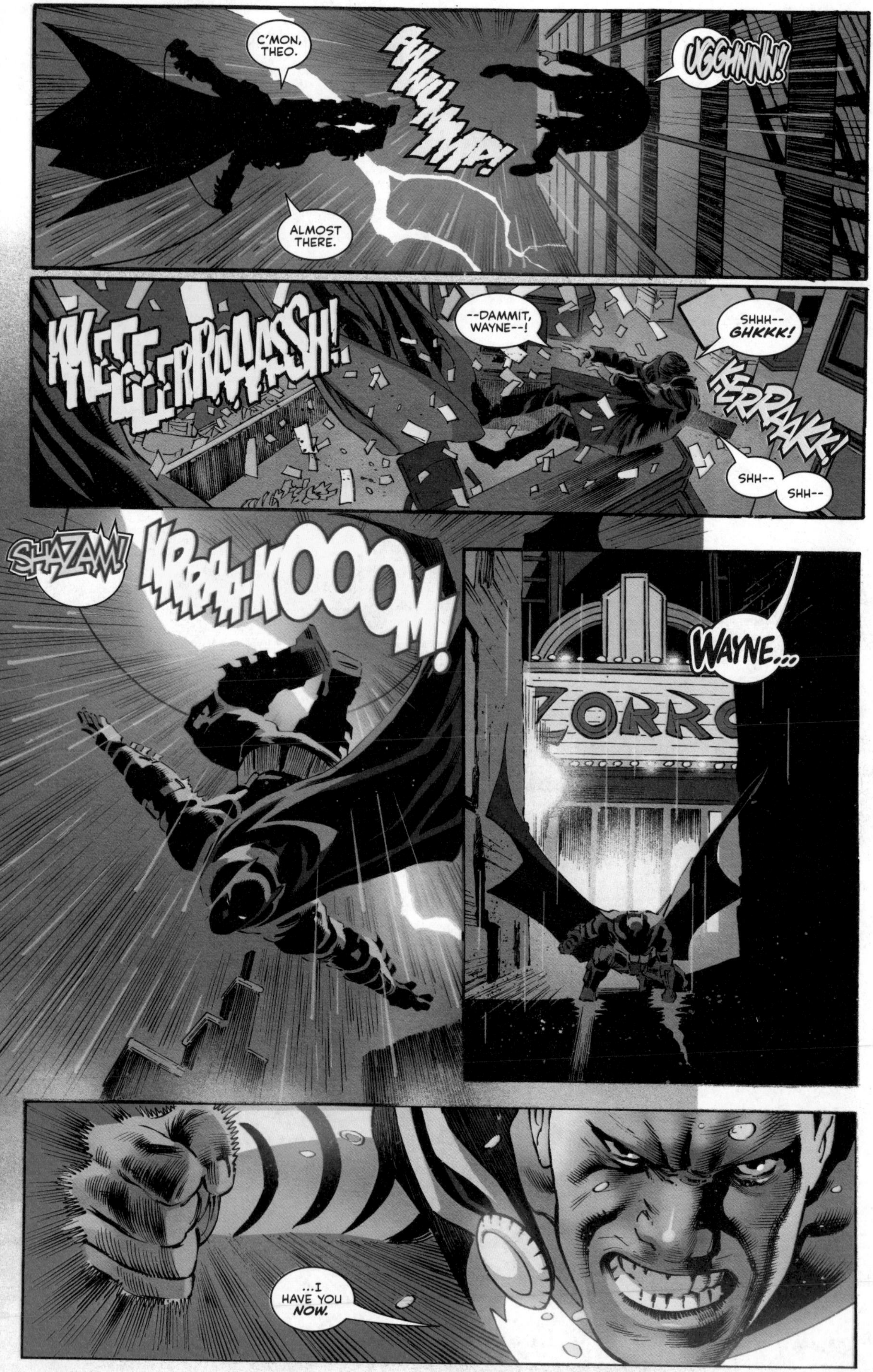

C'MON, THEO.
FWUMMP!
UGGHNNN!
ALMOST THERE.
KKEEERRAAASSH!
--DAMMIT, WAYNE--!
SHHH-- GHKKK!
KERRAKK!
SHH--
SHH--
SHAZAM!
KRRAA-KOOOM!
WAYNE...
ZORRO
...I HAVE YOU NOW.

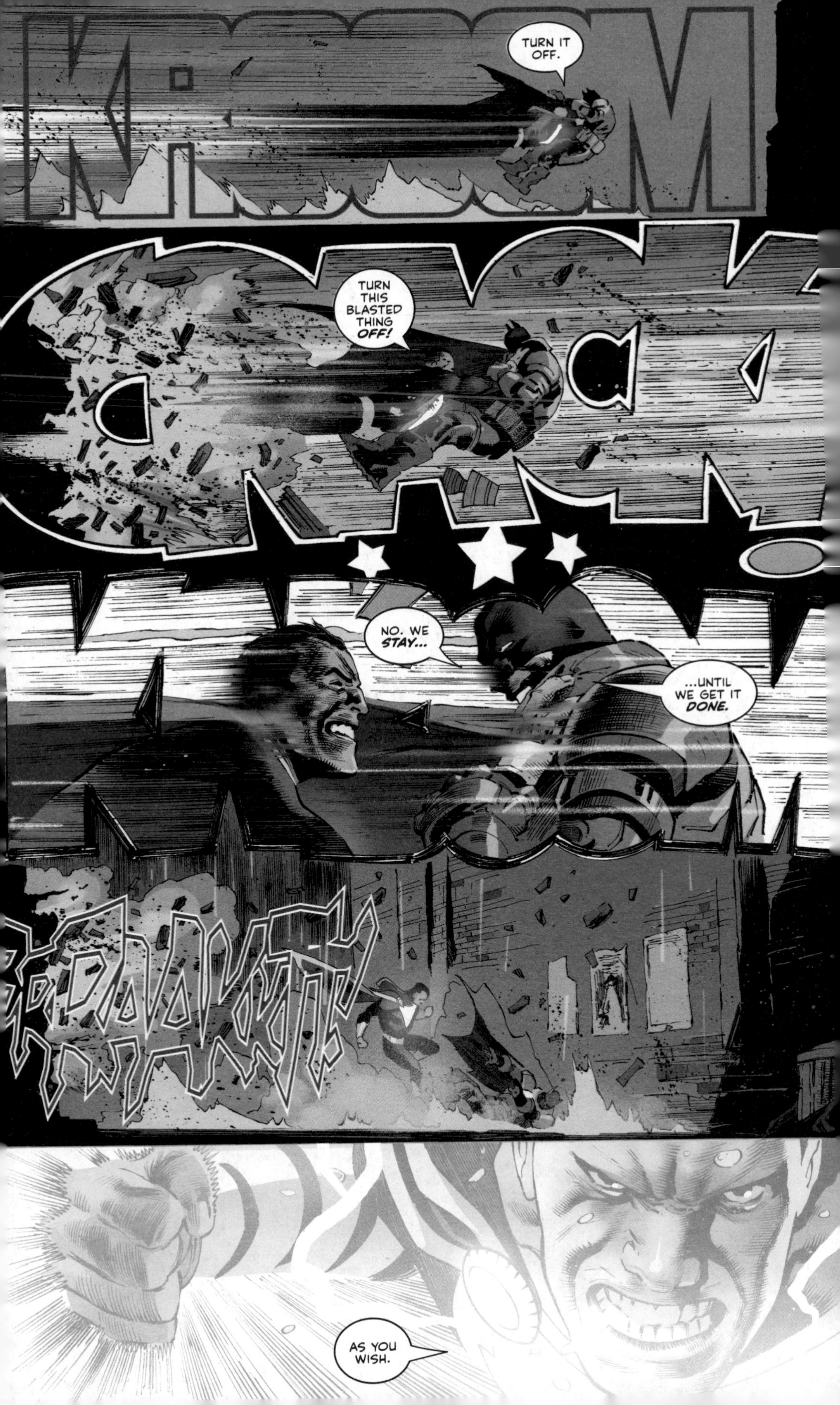
TURN IT OFF.
TURN THIS BLASTED THING *OFF!*
NO. WE *STAY...*
...UNTIL WE GET IT *DONE.*
AS YOU WISH.

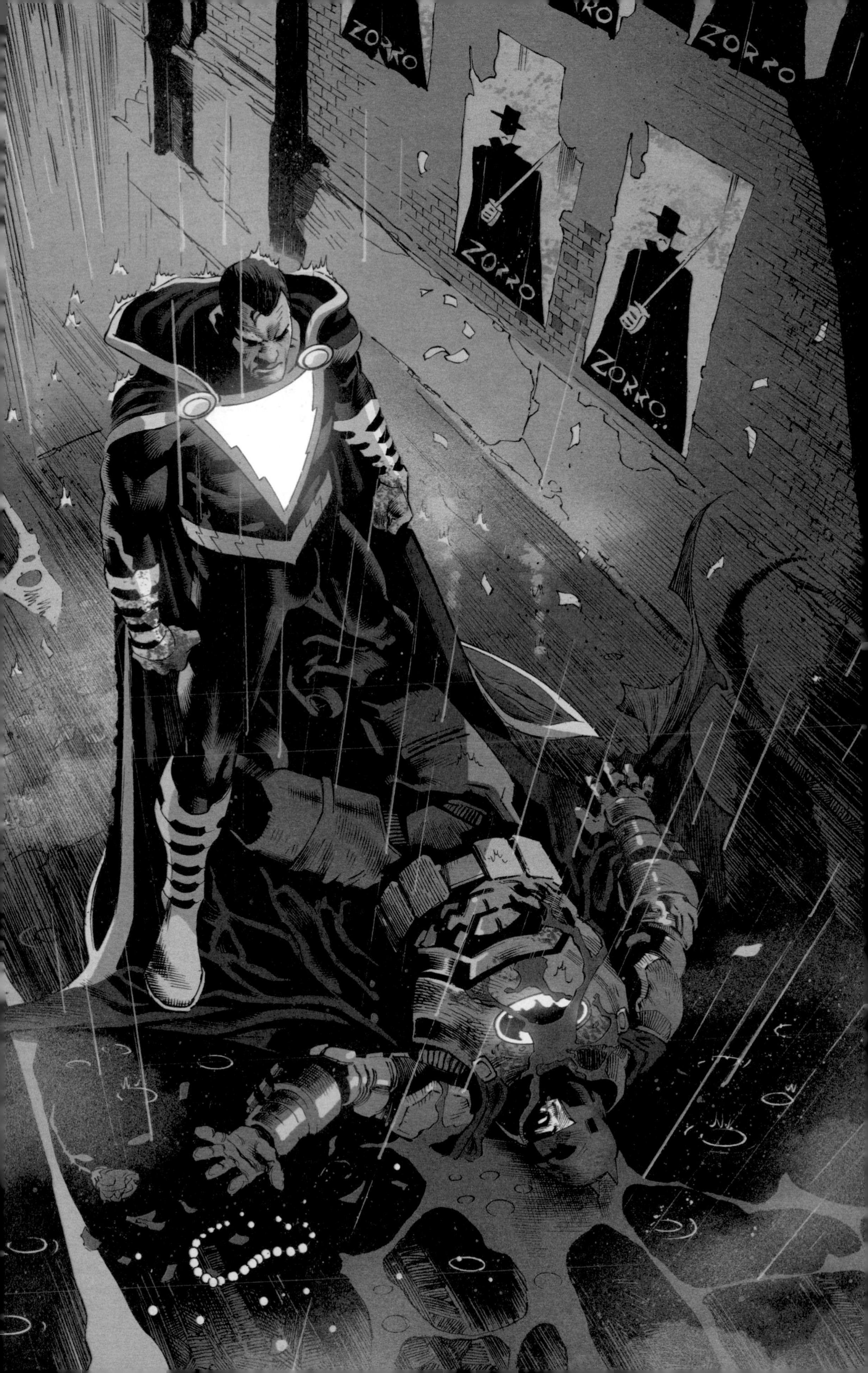
ZORRO
ZORRO
ZORRO
ZORRO

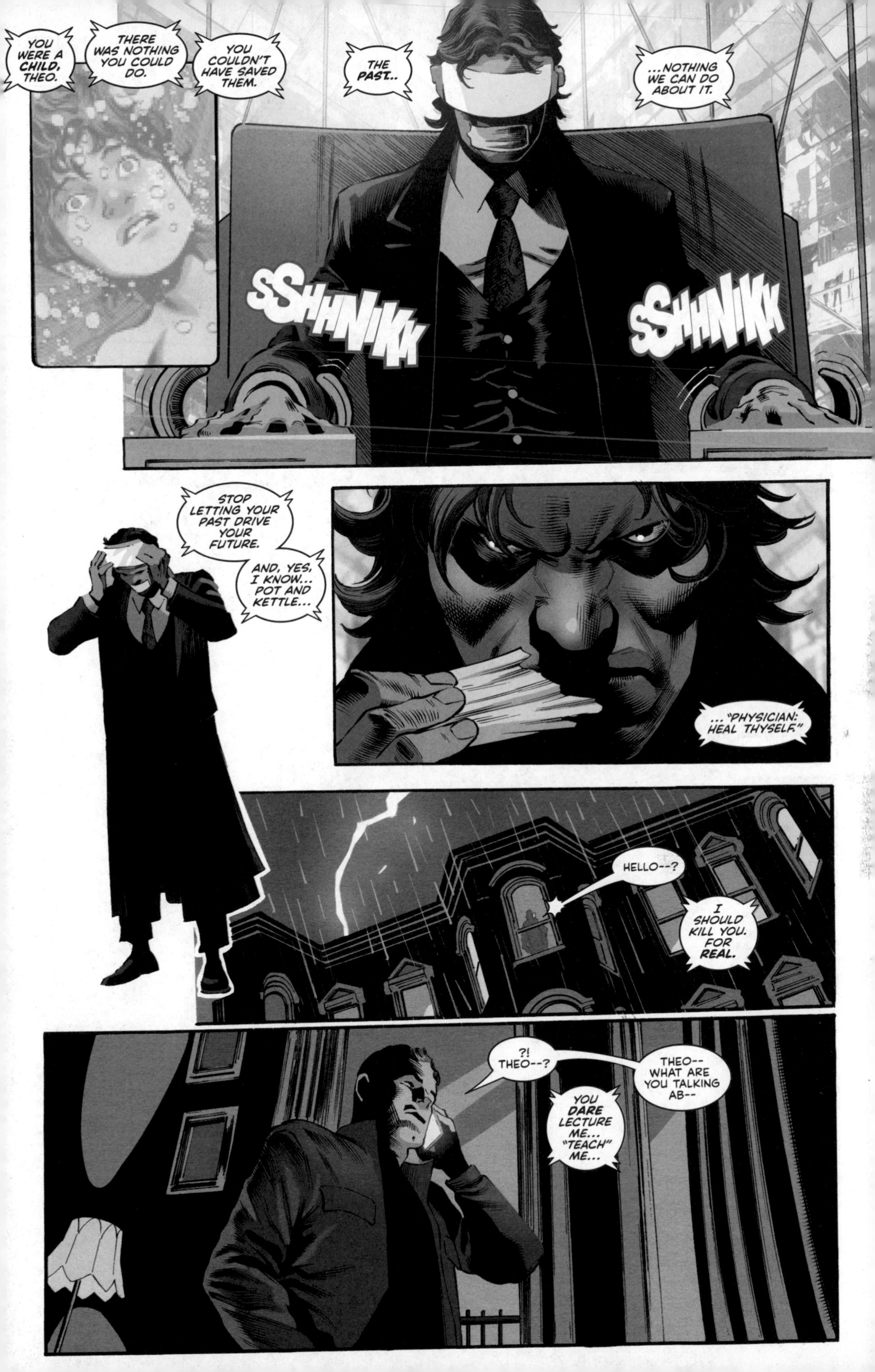
YOU WERE A CHILD, THEO.
THERE WAS NOTHING YOU COULD DO.
YOU COULDN'T HAVE SAVED THEM.
THE PAST...
...NOTHING WE CAN DO ABOUT IT.
SSHHNIKK
SSHHNIKK
STOP LETTING YOUR PAST DRIVE YOUR FUTURE.
AND, YES, I KNOW... POT AND KETTLE...
..."PHYSICIAN: HEAL THYSELF."
HELLO--?
I SHOULD KILL YOU. FOR REAL.
?! THEO--?
THEO-- WHAT ARE YOU TALKING AB--
YOU DARE LECTURE ME... "TEACH" ME...

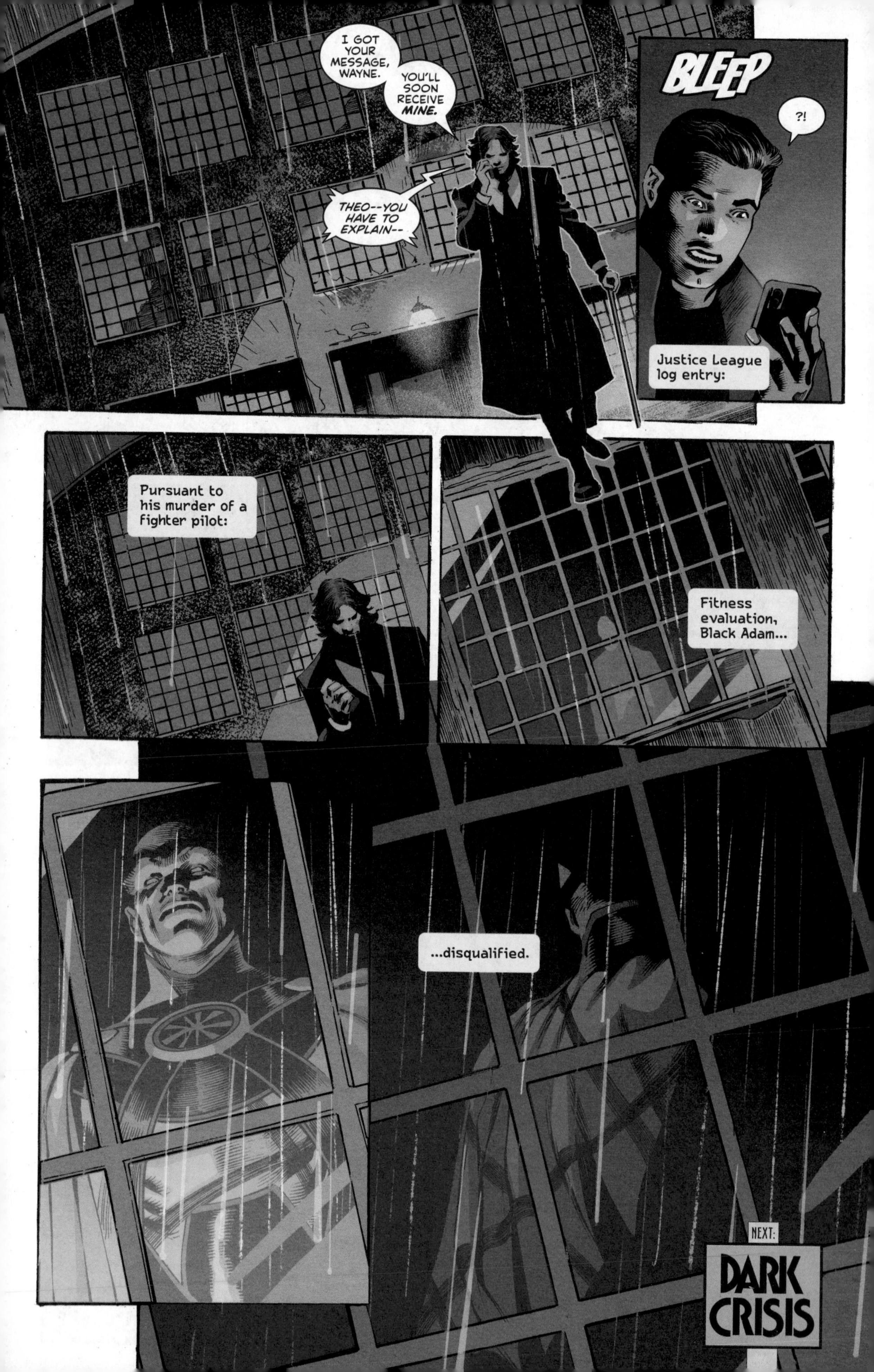
I GOT YOUR MESSAGE, WAYNE.
YOU'LL SOON RECEIVE MINE.
THEO--YOU HAVE TO EXPLAIN--
BLEEP
?!
Justice League log entry:
Pursuant to his murder of a fighter pilot:
Fitness evaluation, Black Adam...
...disqualified.
NEXT:
DARK CRISIS

VARIANT COVER GALLERY

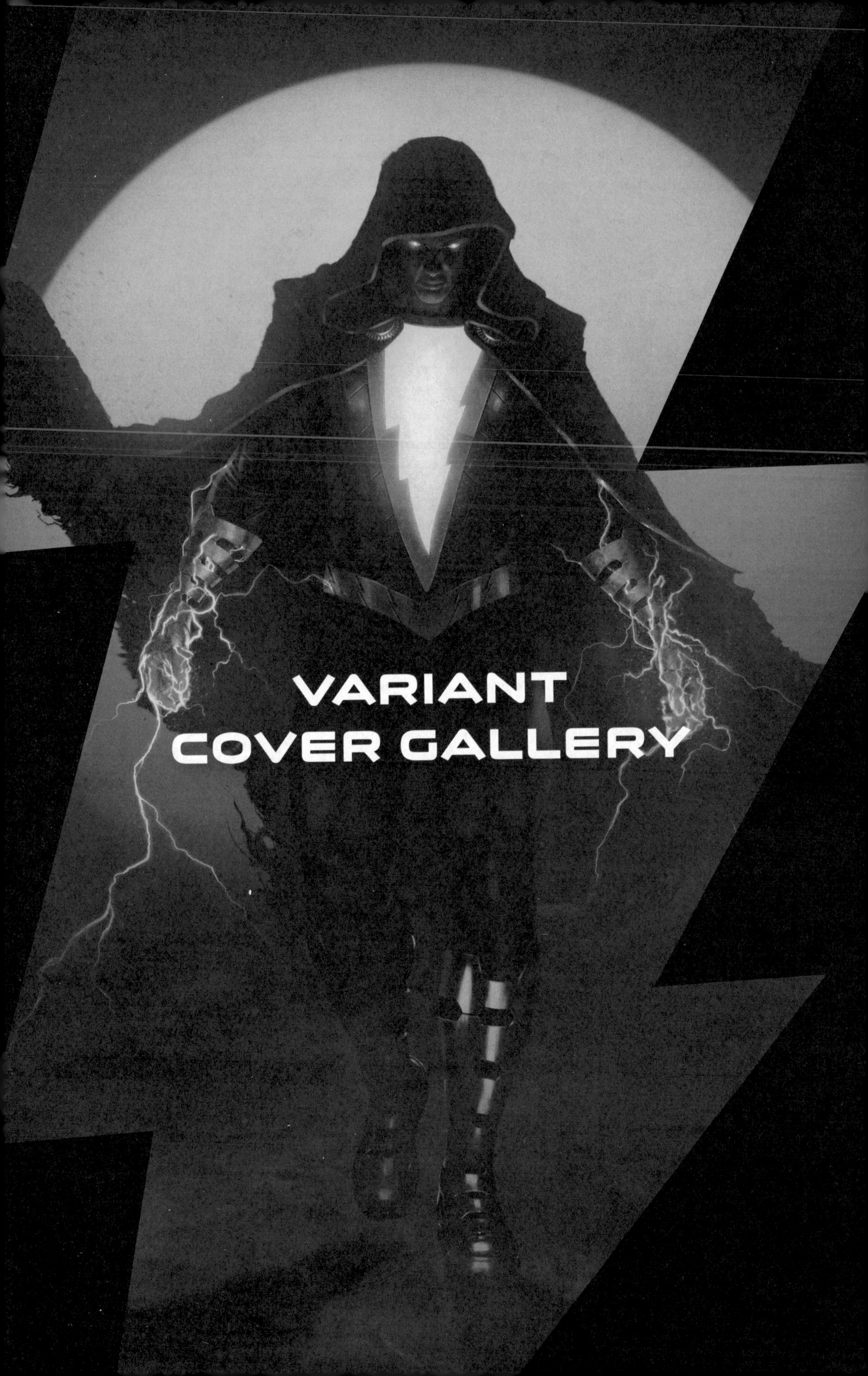

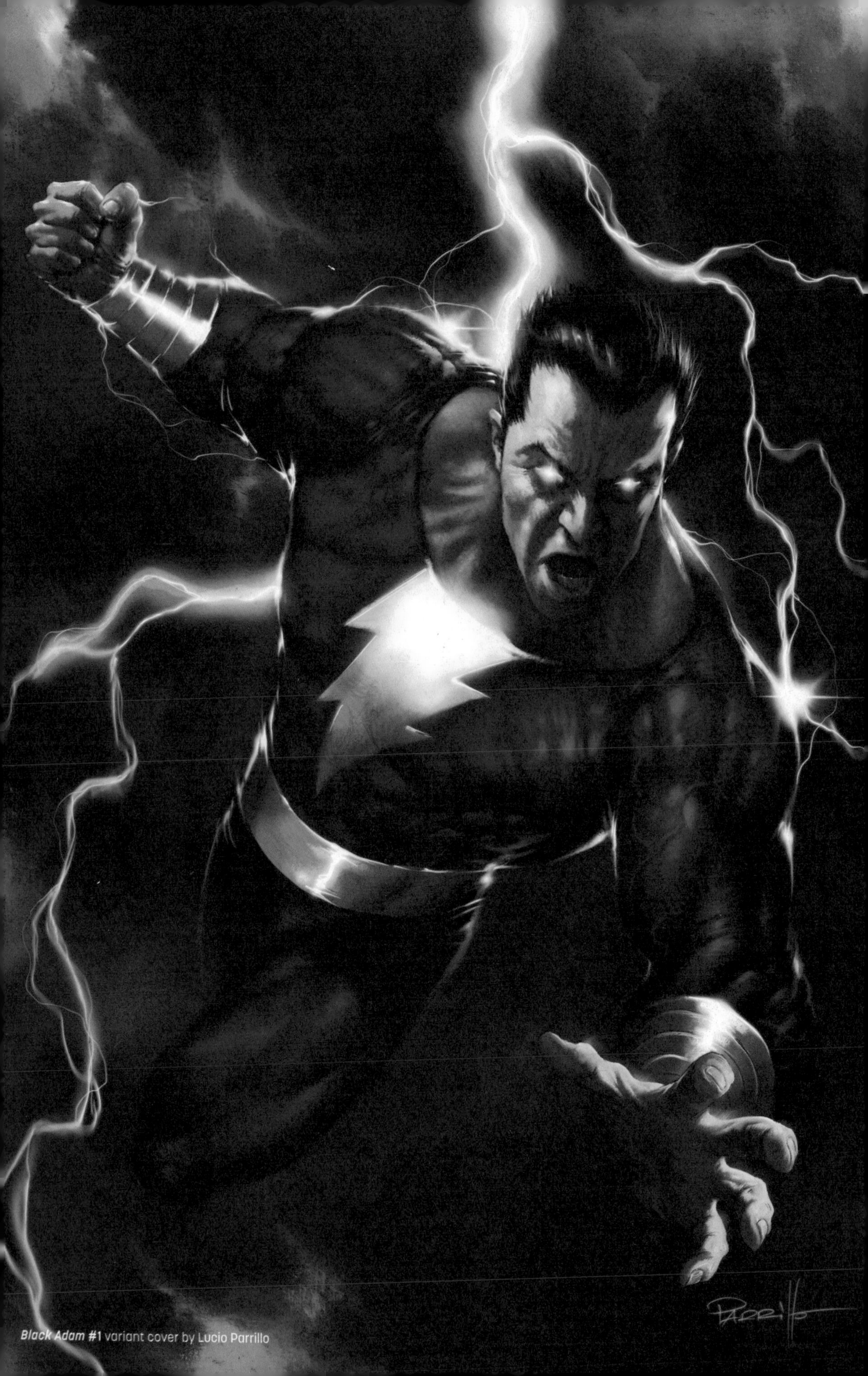

Black Adam #1 variant cover by Lucio Parrillo

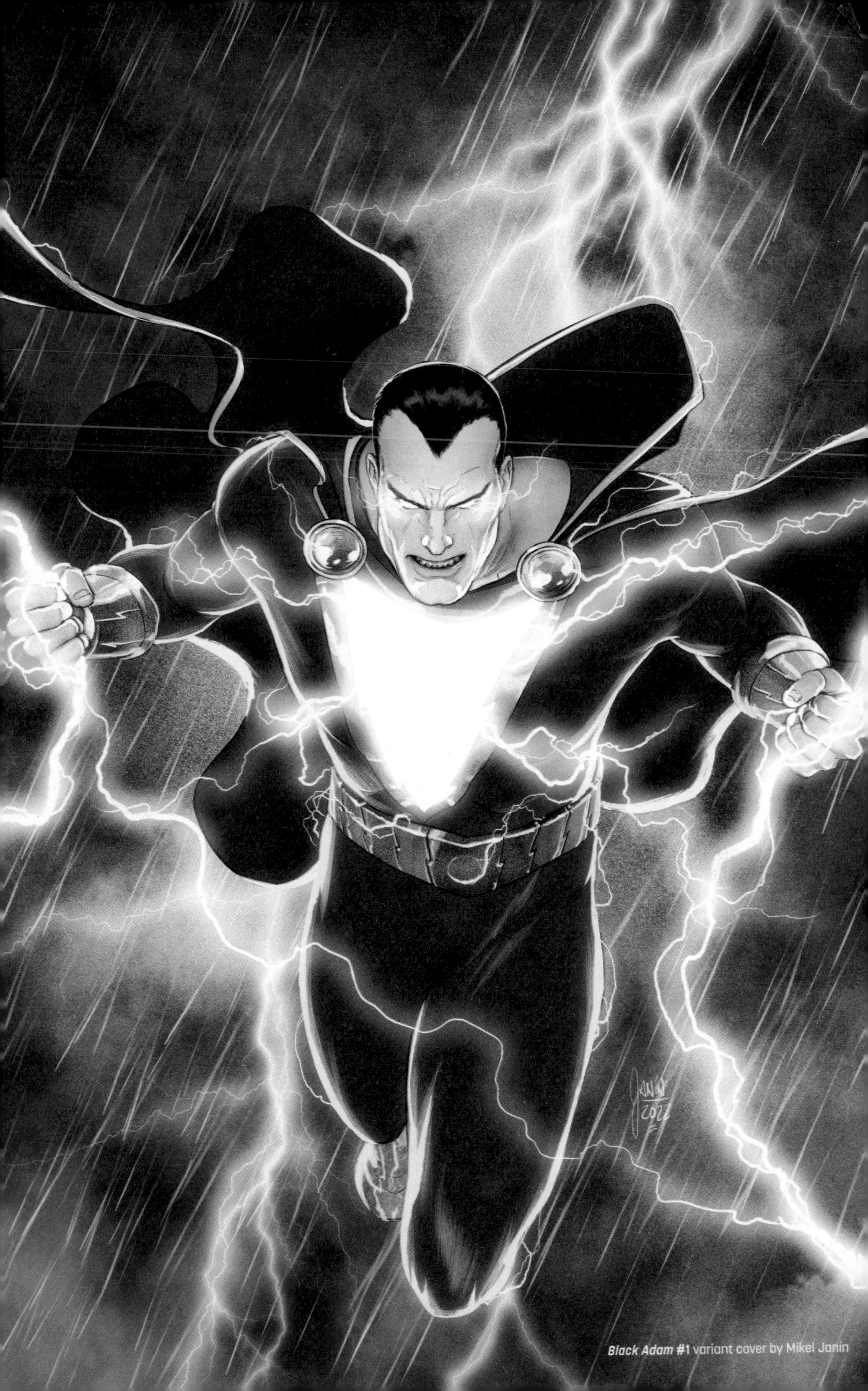

Black Adam #1 variant cover by Mikel Janín

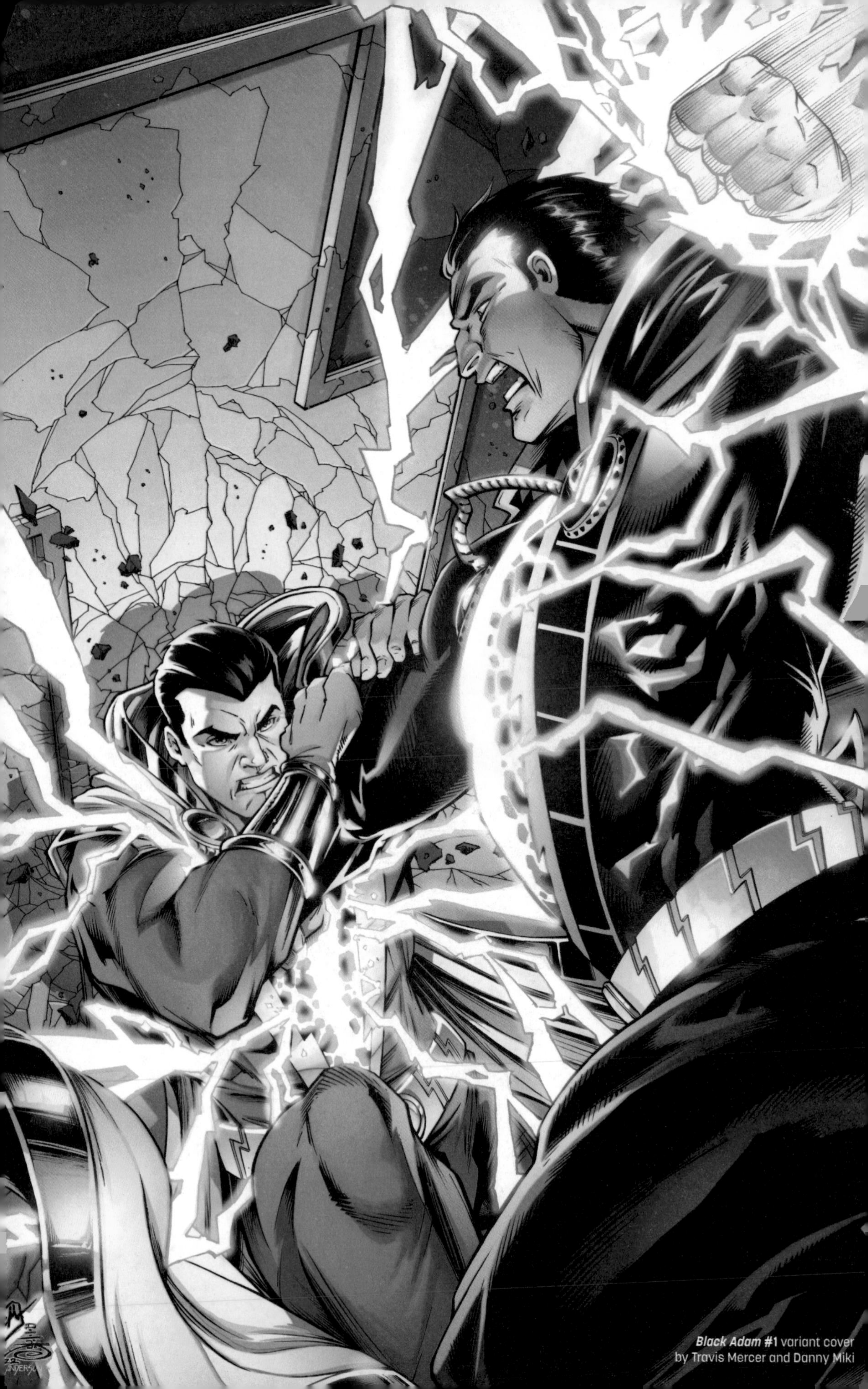

Black Adam **#1** variant cover
by Travis Mercer and Danny Miki

Black Adam #1 variant cover by Crystal Kung

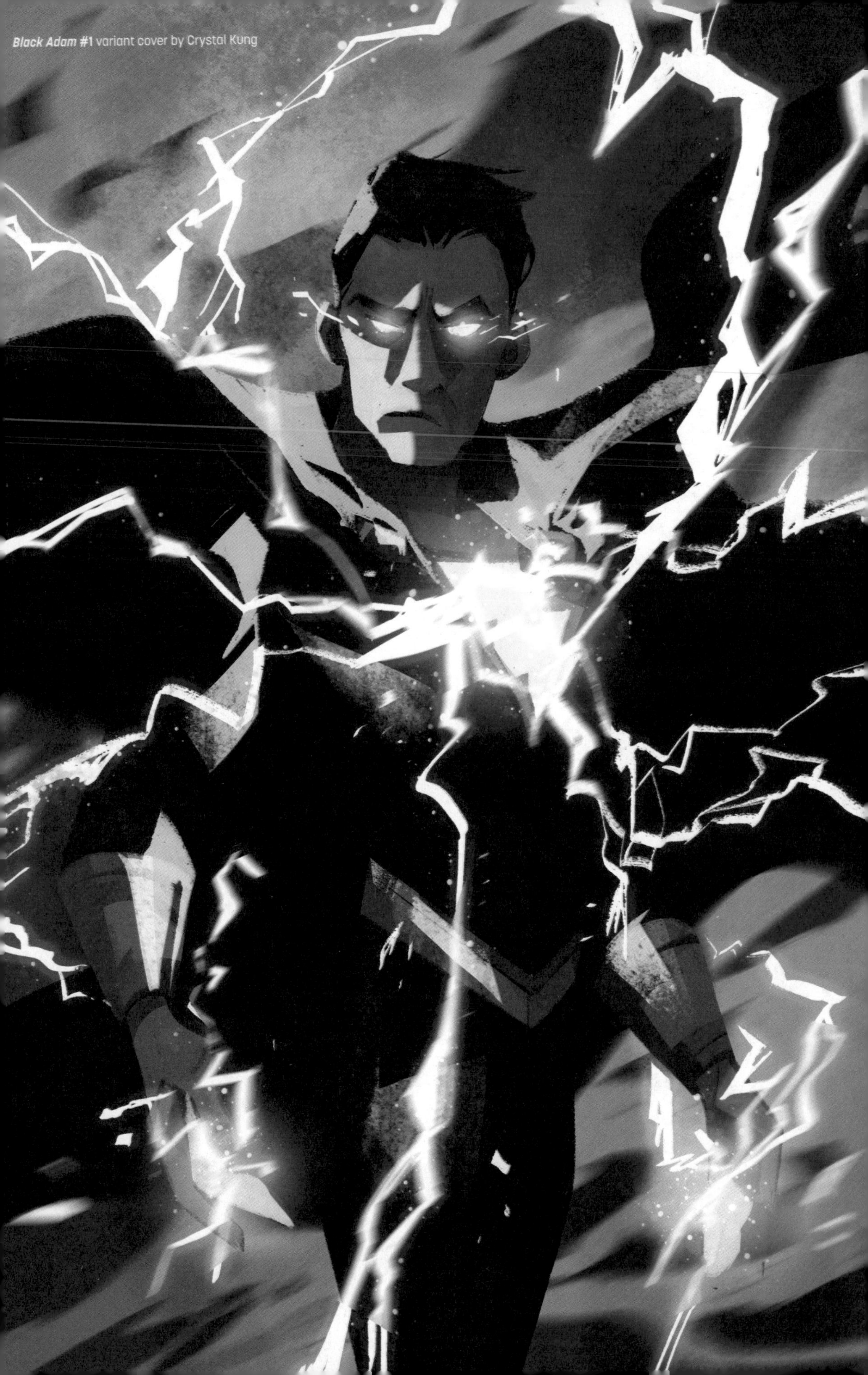

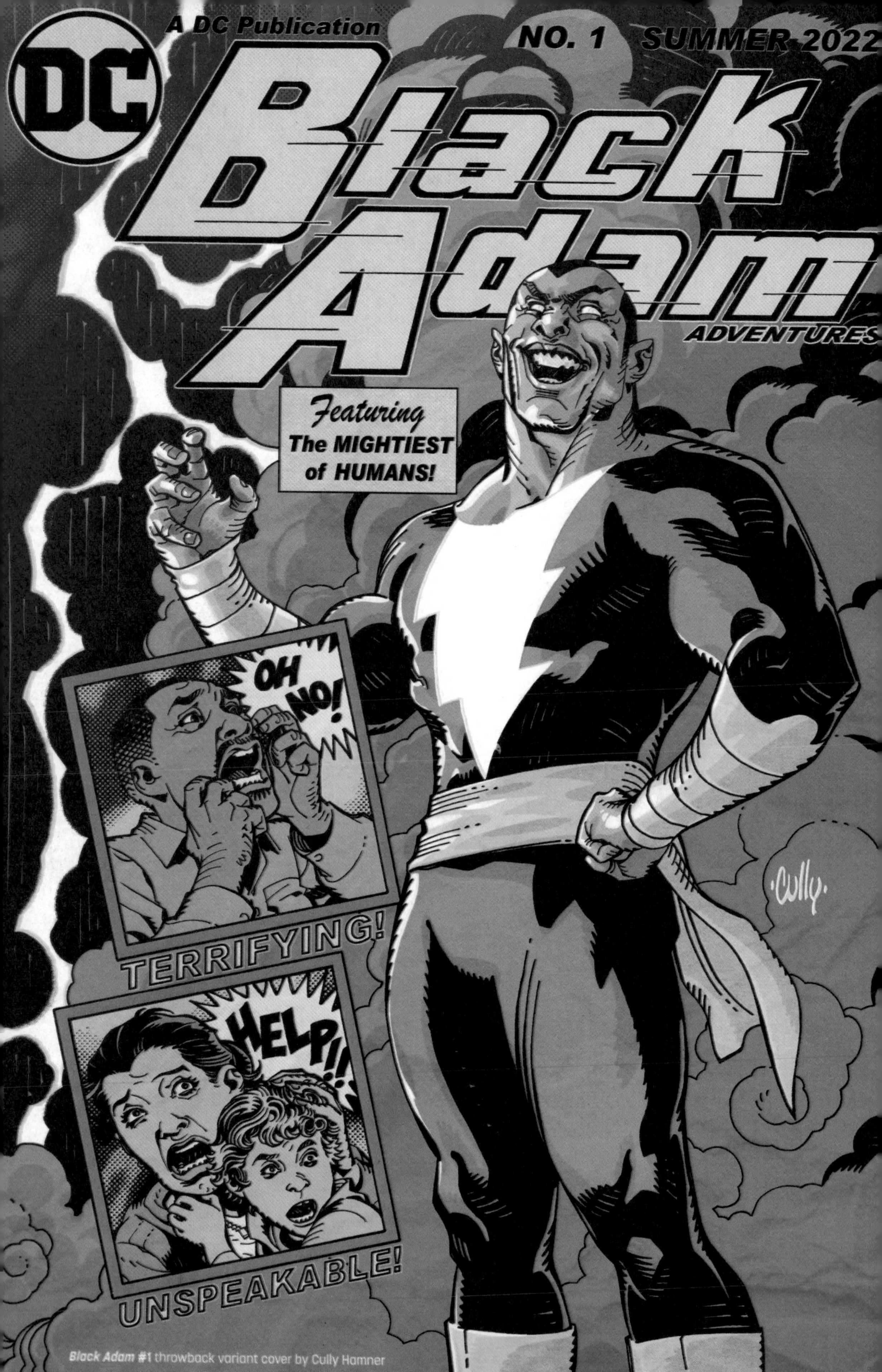
A DC Publication
DC
NO. 1 SUMMER 2022
Black Adam
ADVENTURES
Featuring The MIGHTIEST of HUMANS!
OH NO!
TERRIFYING!
HELP!!
UNSPEAKABLE!
Cully

Black Adam #1 throwback variant cover by Cully Hamner

Black Adam **#2** variant cover
by Brandon Peterson

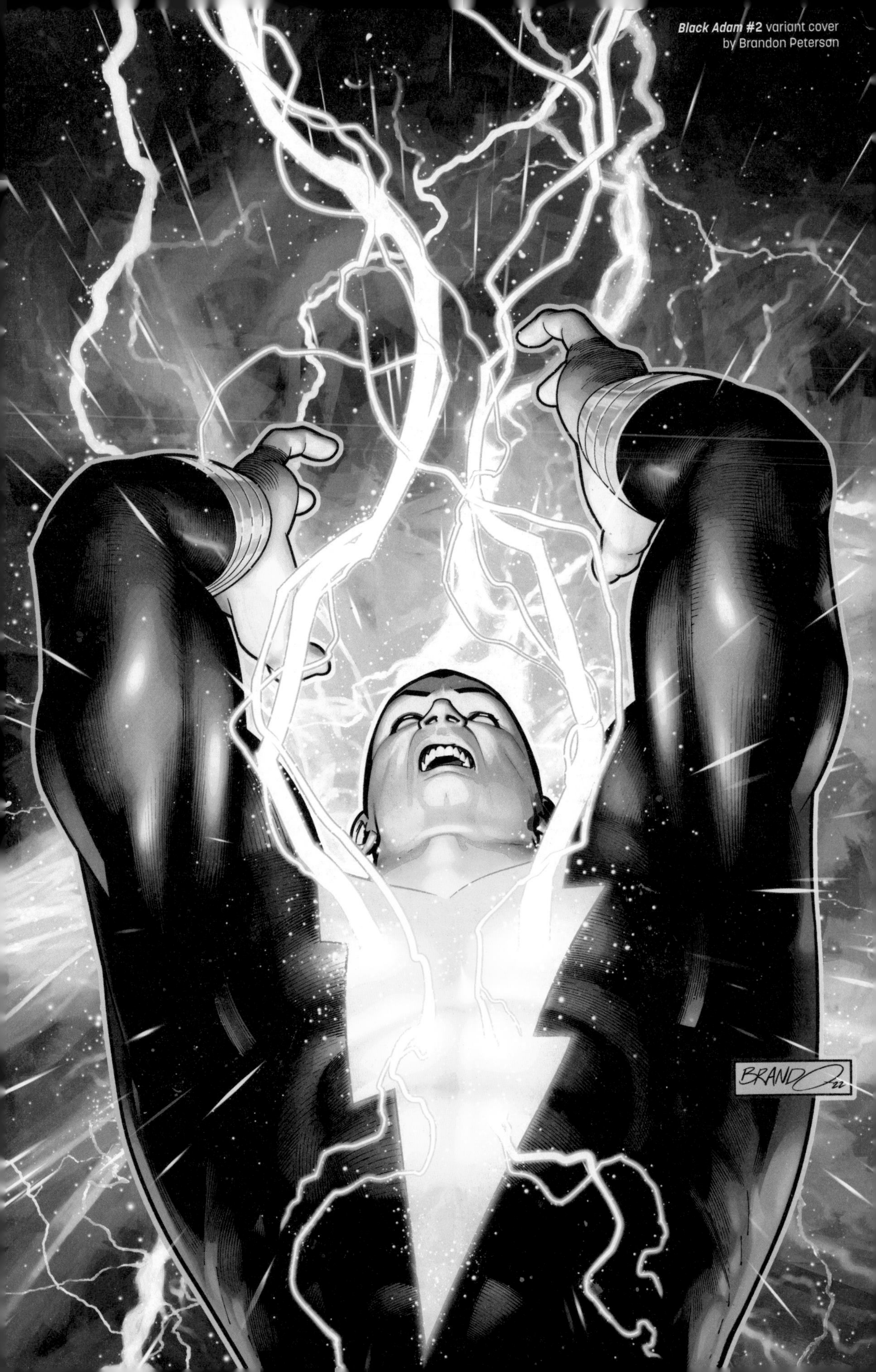

***Black Adam* #2** variant cover by Simone Di Meo

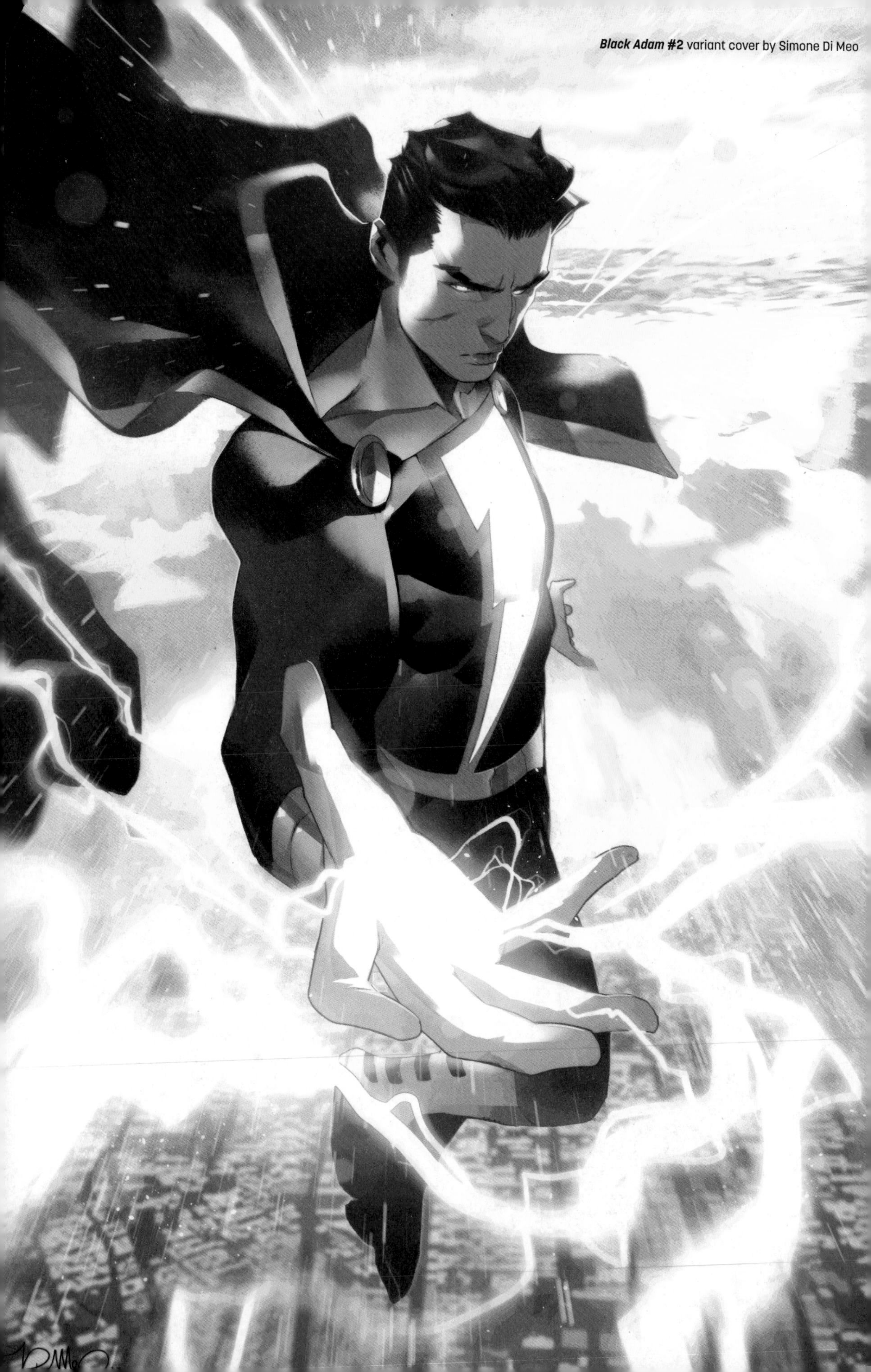

***Black Adam* #2** variant cover by Rafael Sarmento

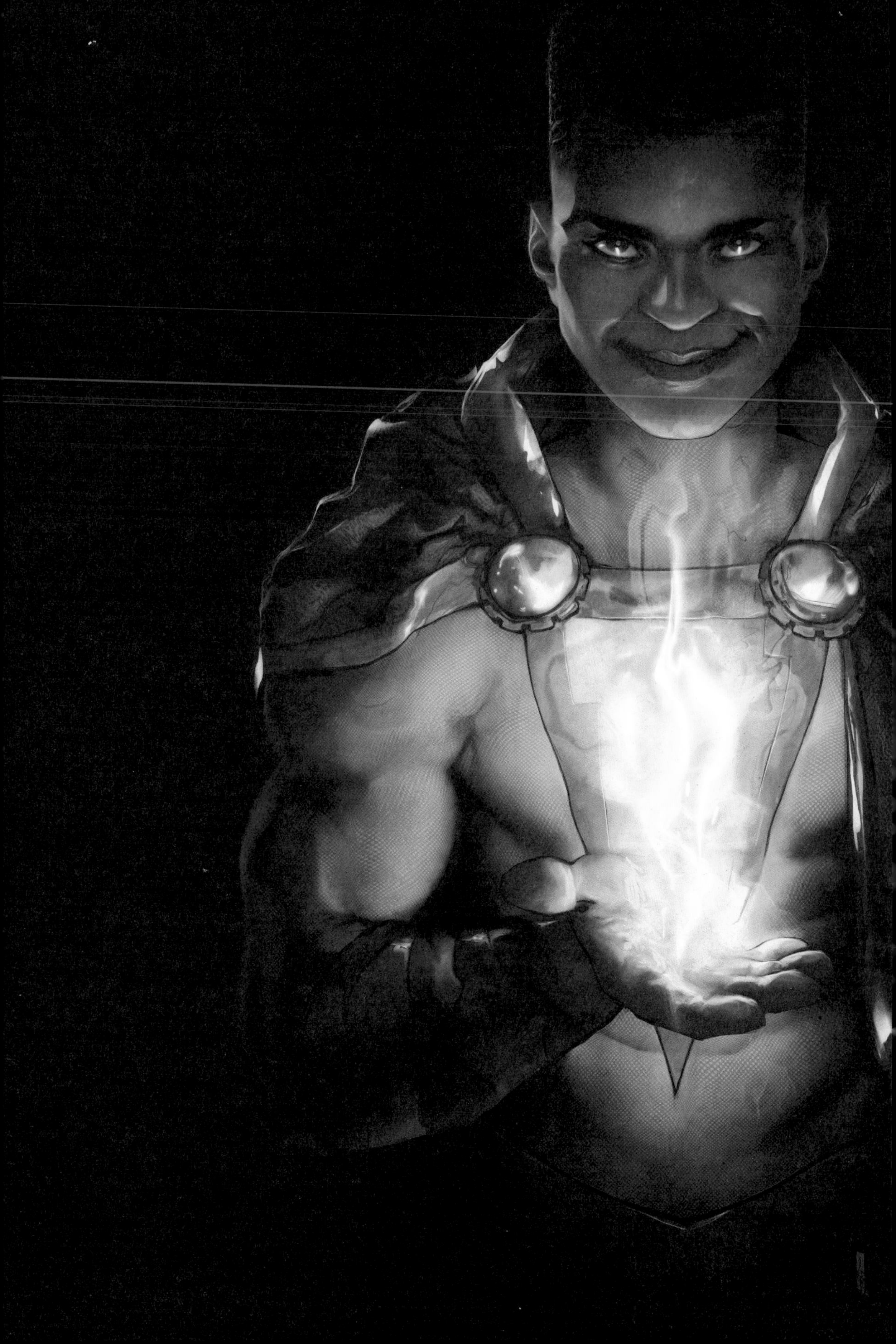

***Black Adam* #3** variant cover by Rahzzah

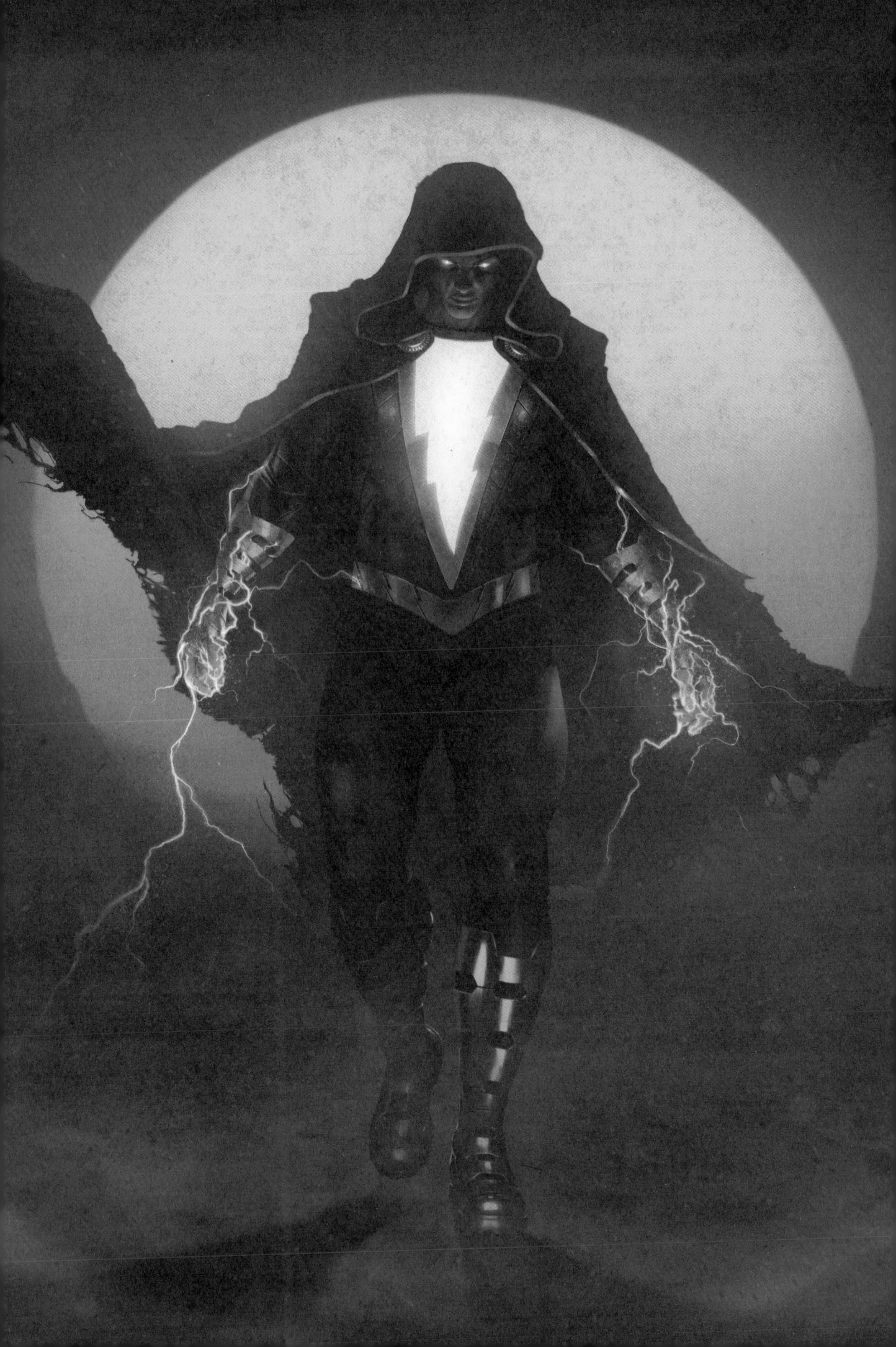

Black Adam **#3** swimsuit variant cover
by Emanuela Lupacchino and Dave McCaig

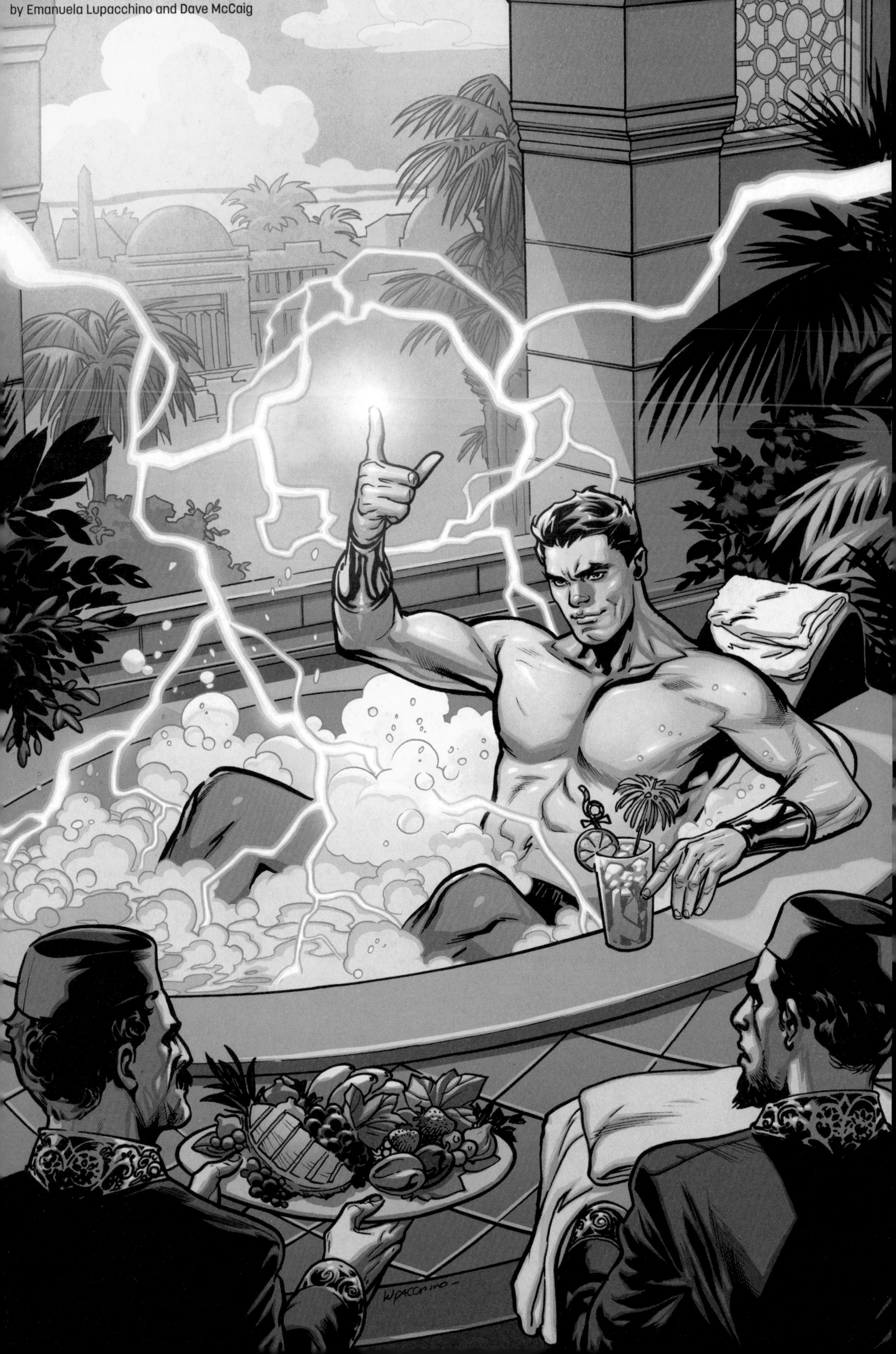

***Black Adam* #3** variant cover by Rafael Sarmento

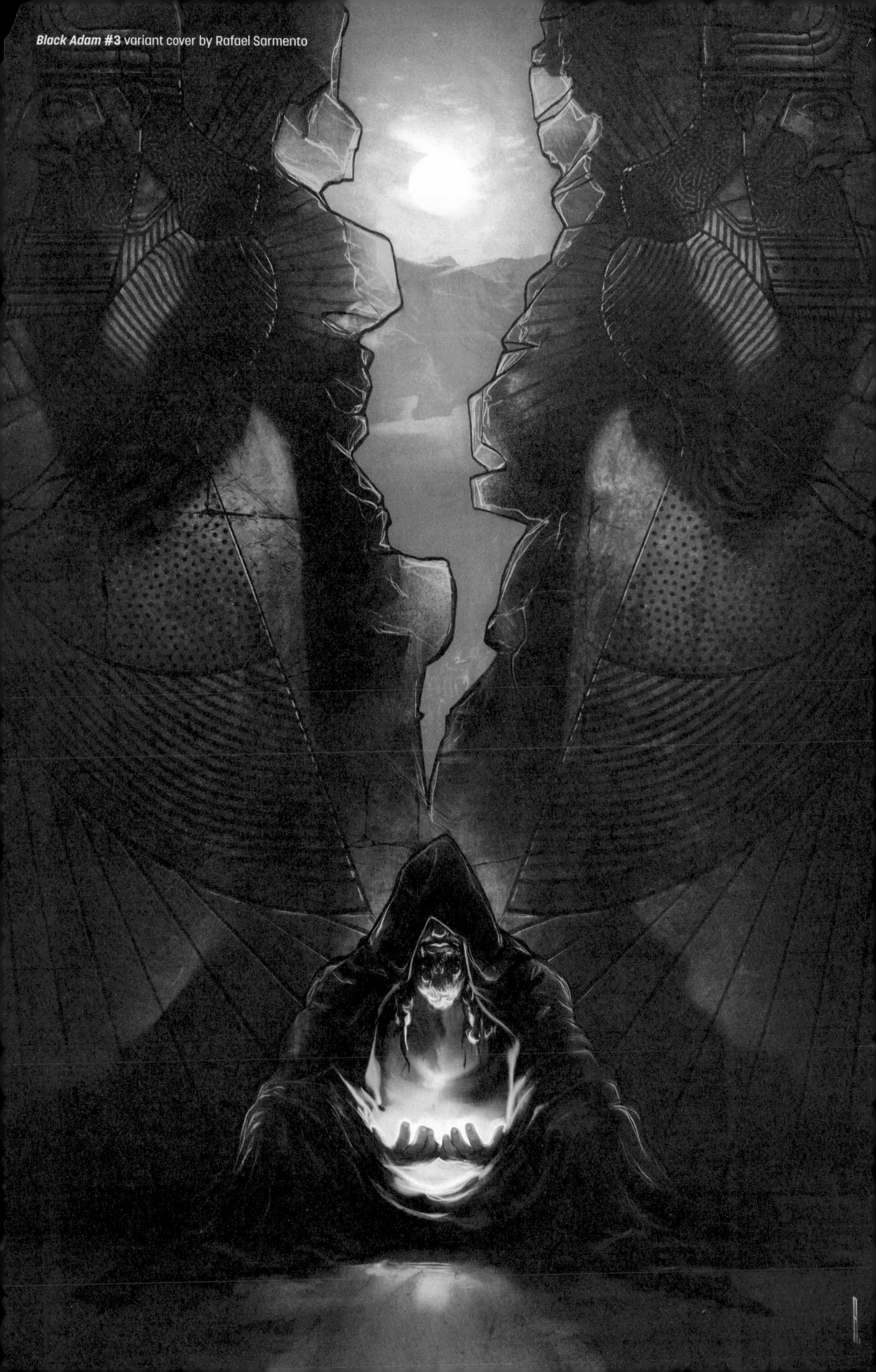

Black Adam #4 variant cover by Taurin Clarke

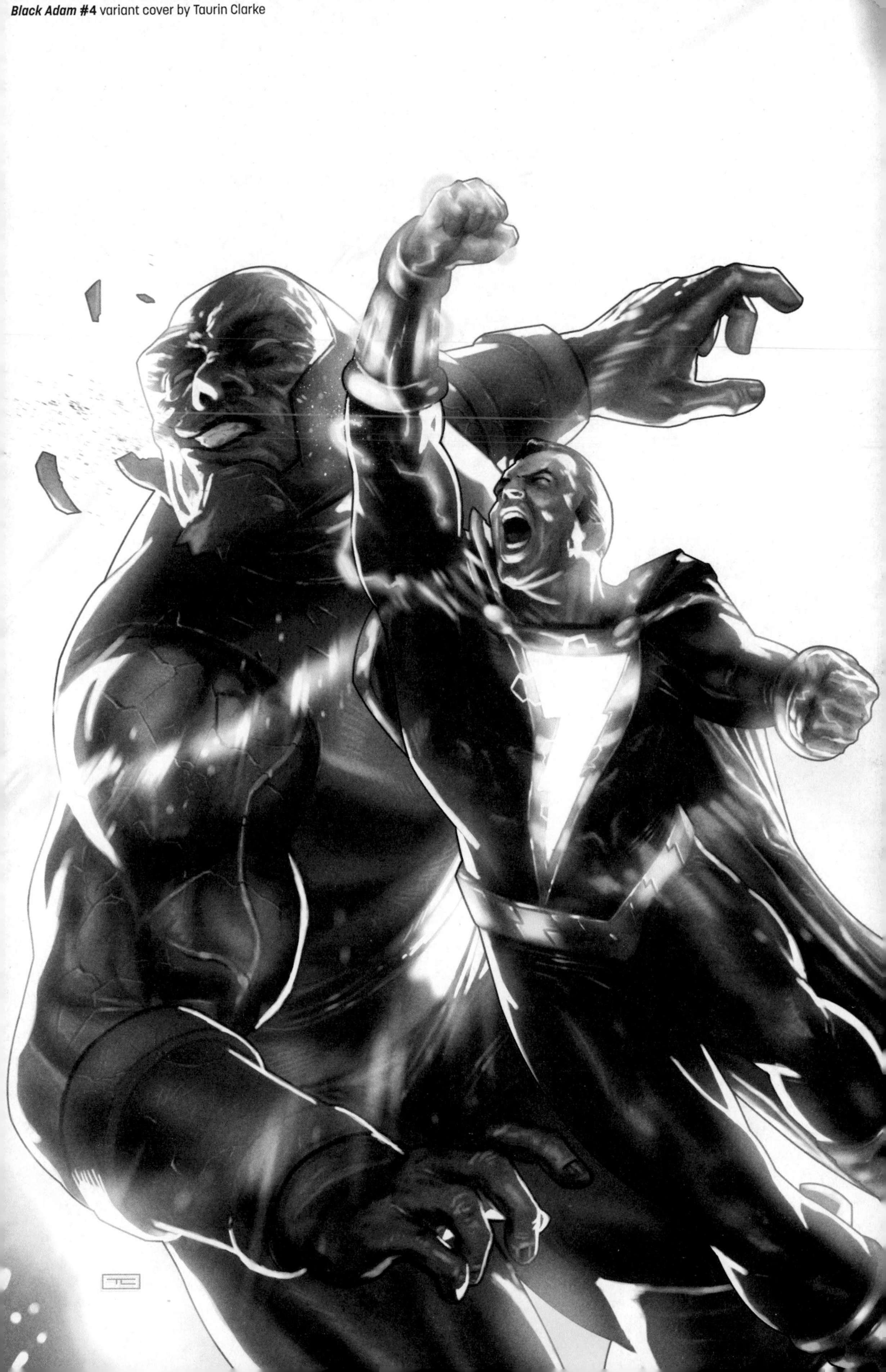

Black Adam **#4** variant cover
by Pamela Hoogeboom

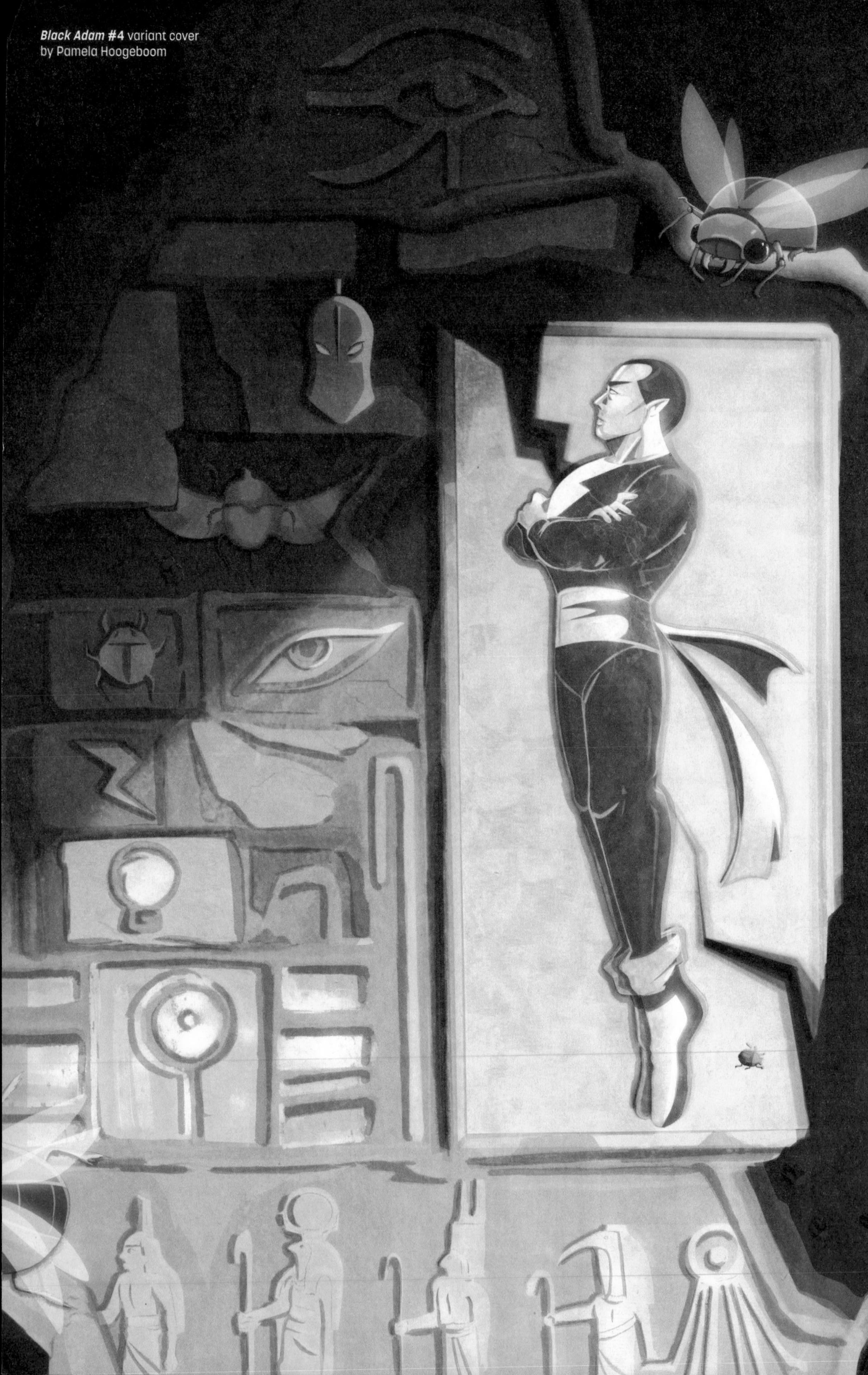

Black Adam **#5** variant cover by Ariel Colón

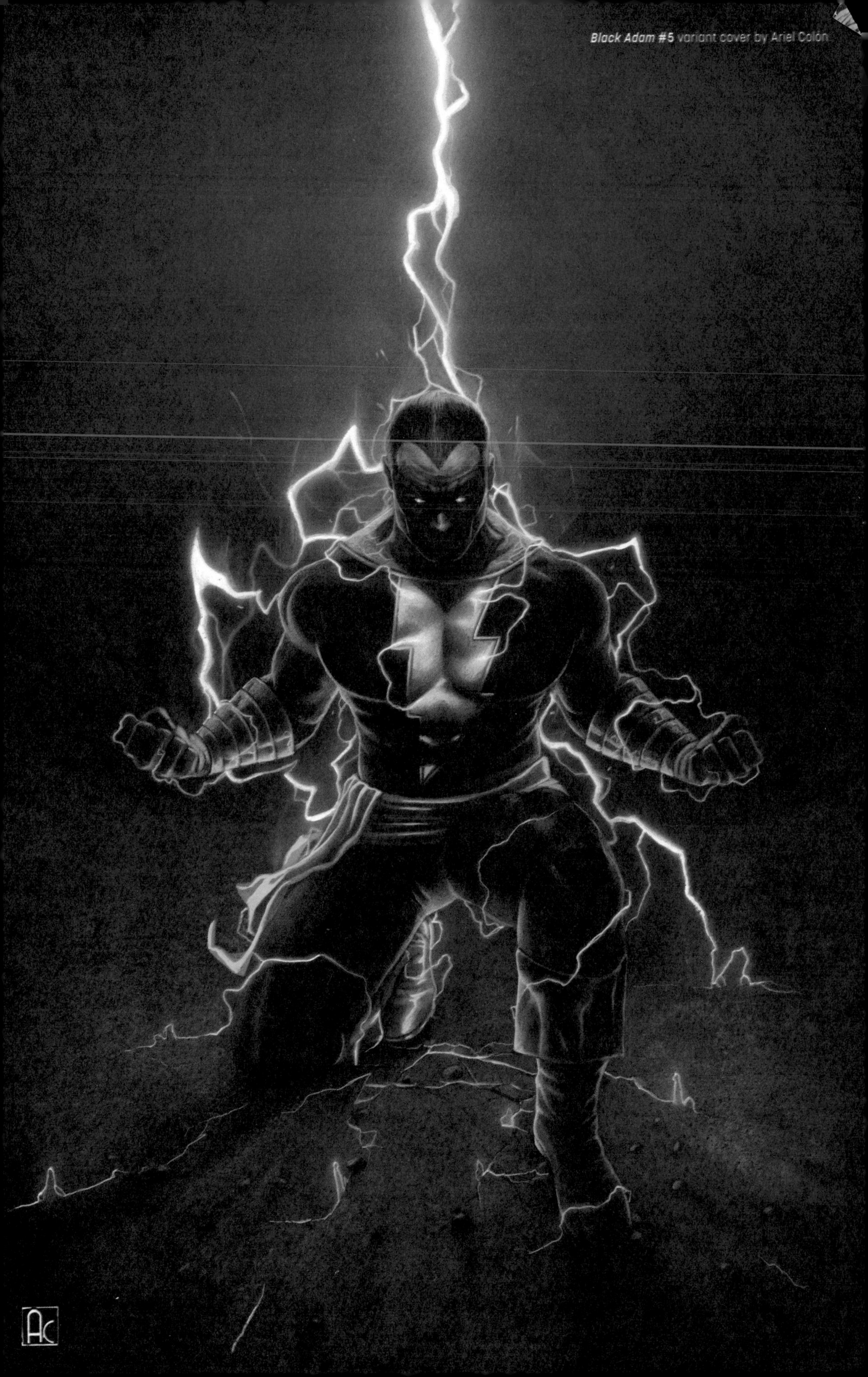

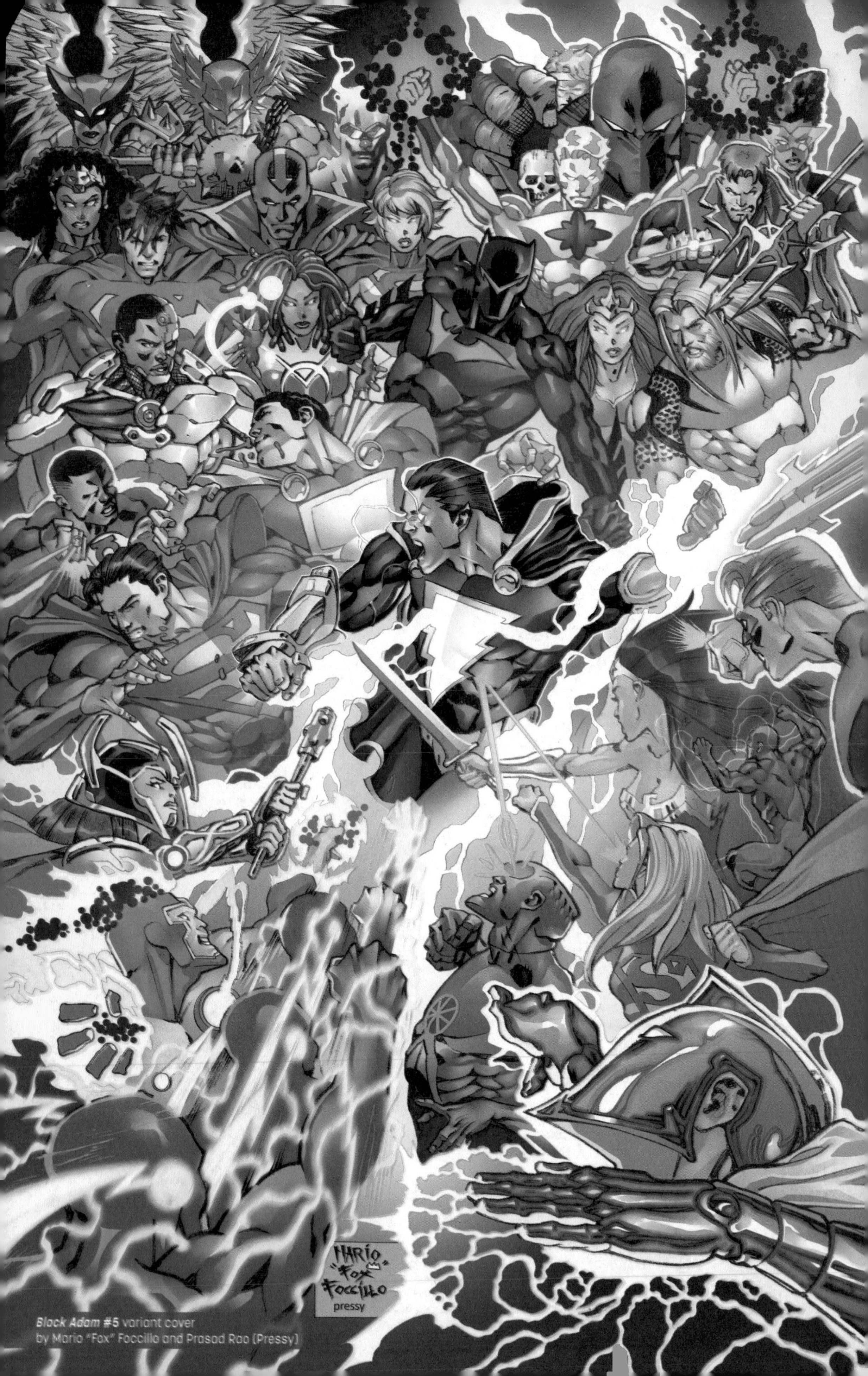
MARIO "FOX" FOCCILLO
pressy

Black Adam #5 variant cover
by Mario "Fox" Foccillo and Prasad Rao (Pressy)

***Black Adam* #5** variant cover
by Rafa Sandoval and Matt Herms

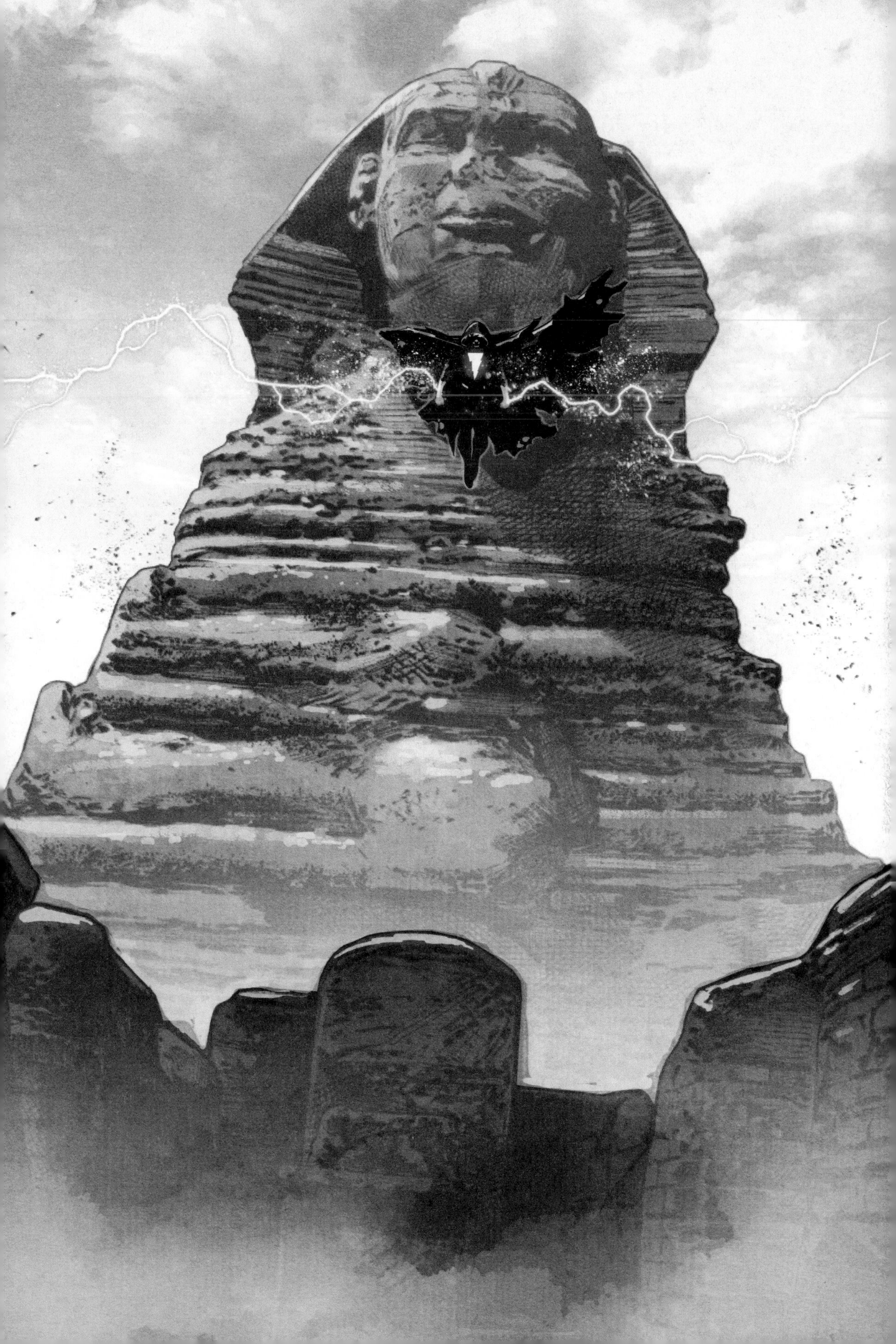

Black Adam #6 variant cover
by David Lapham and Trish Mulvihill

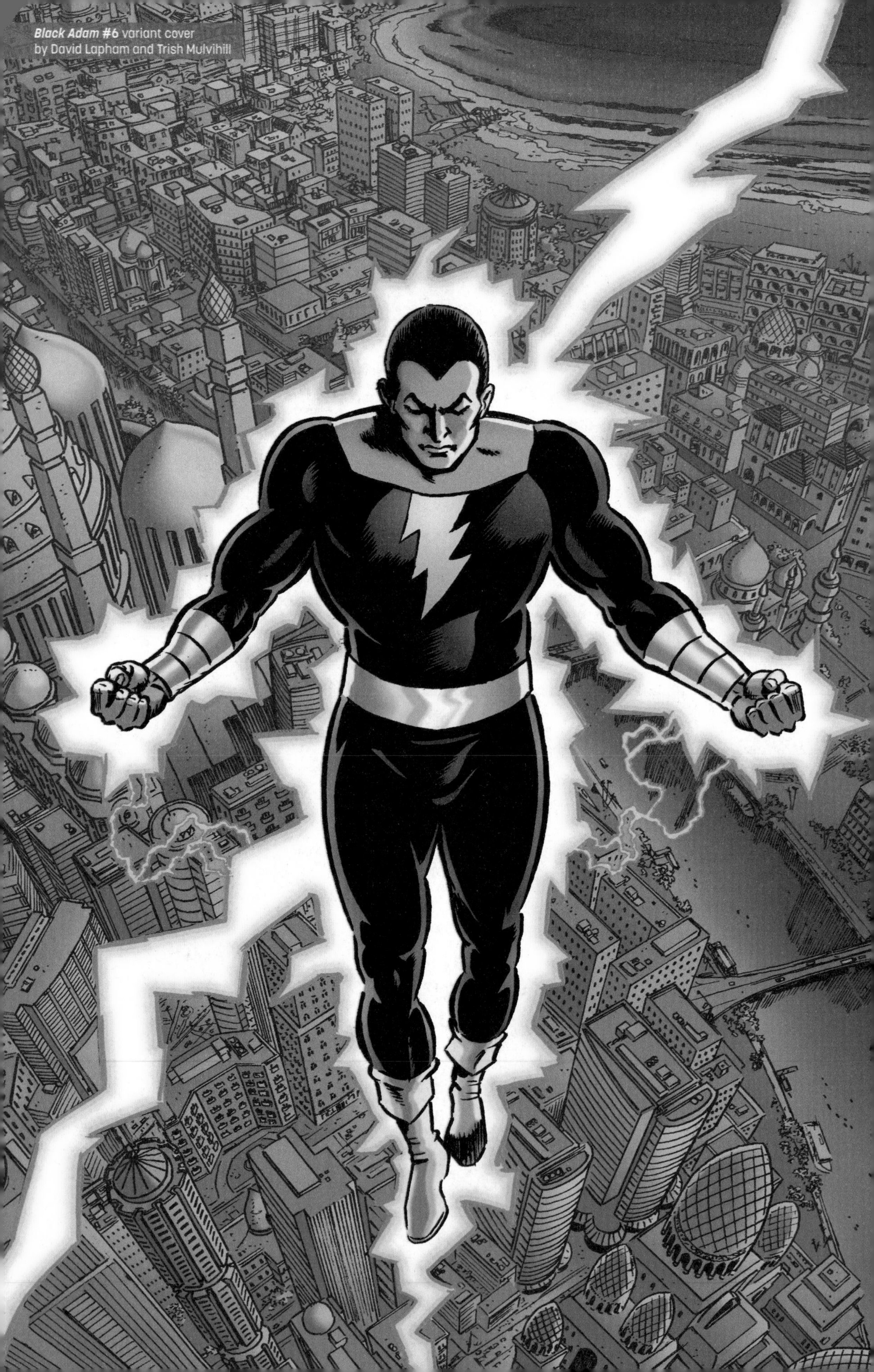

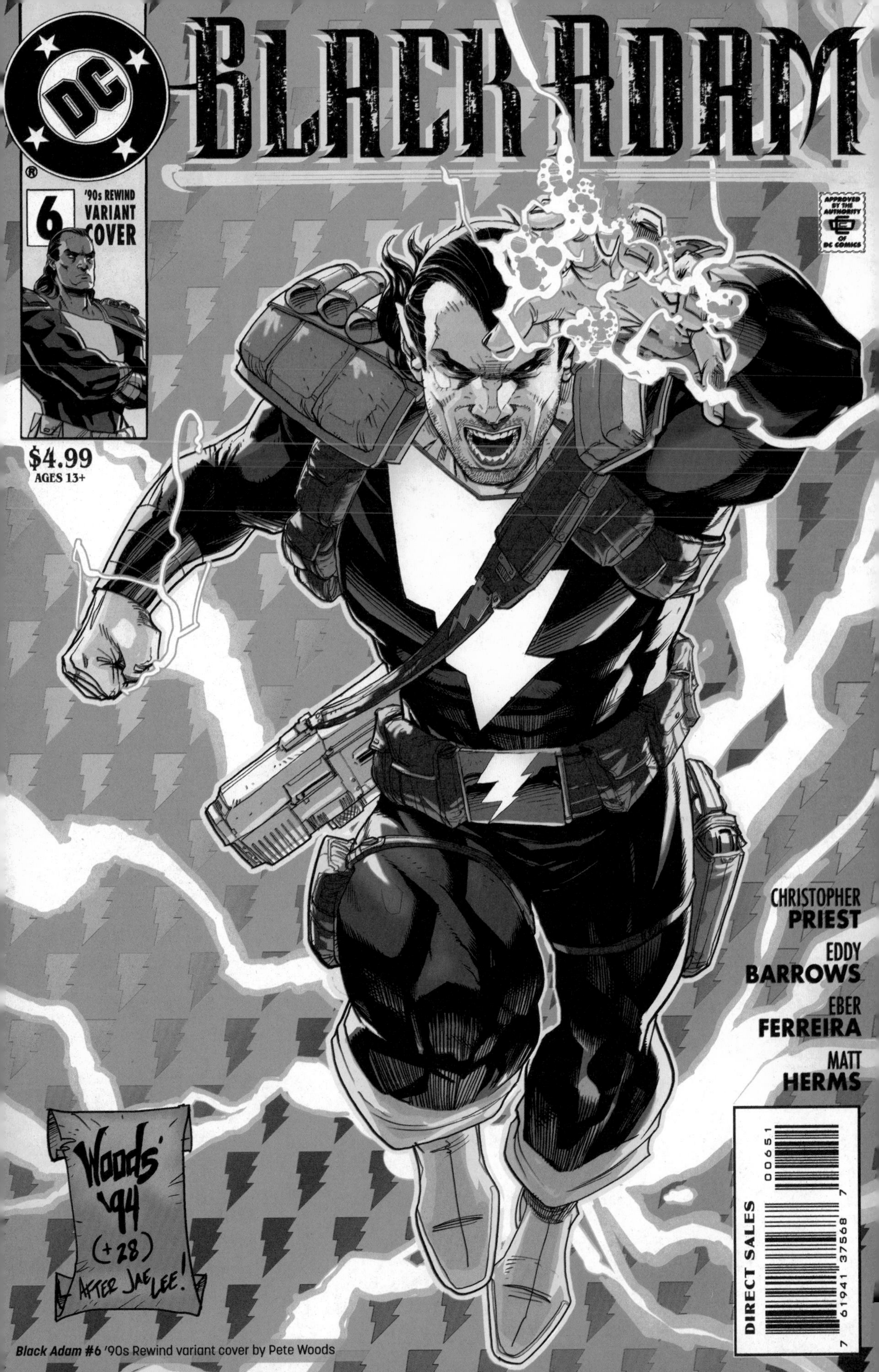
DC
BLACK ADAM
6
'90s REWIND
VARIANT
COVER
$4.99
AGES 13+
APPROVED BY THE AUTHORITY OF DC COMICS
CHRISTOPHER
PRIEST
EDDY
BARROWS
EBER
FERREIRA
MATT
HERMS
Woods '94
(+28)
AFTER JAE LEE!
DIRECT SALES

Black Adam #6 '90s Rewind variant cover by Pete Woods

Black Adam **#6** variant cover
by Brandon Peterson

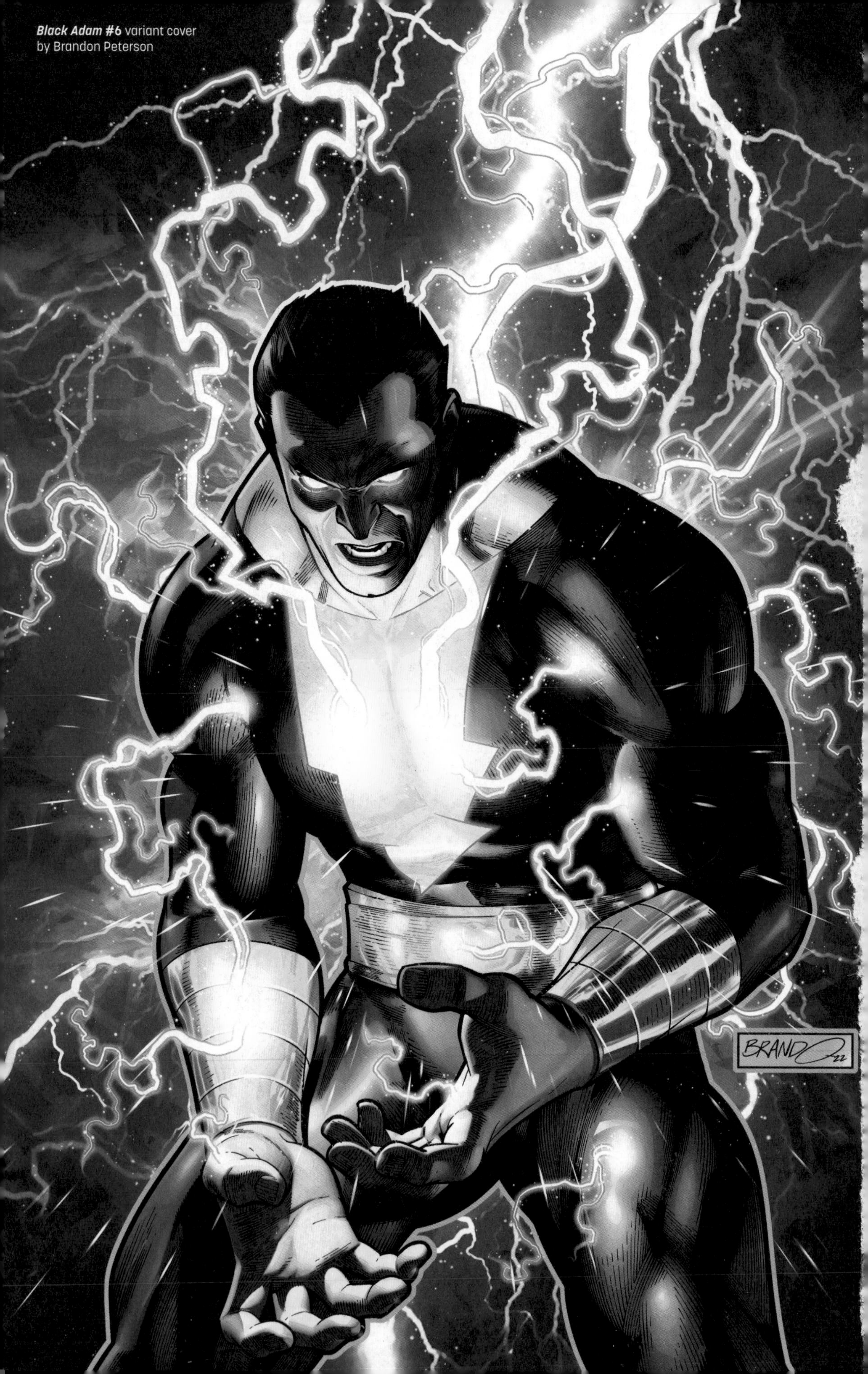
BRANDO 22